Rogov's Guide to Israeli Wines
2008

Daniel Rogov

ROGOV'S GUIDE TO ISRAELI WINES

2008

The Toby Press

First Edition 2008
The Toby Press LLC

POB 8531, New Milford, CT 06776-8531, USA
& POB 2455, London W1A 5WY, England

www.tobypress.com

ISBN 1 159264 171 7, *hardcover*

A CIP catalogue record for this title is
available from the British Library.

Typeset in Chaparral by Jerusalem Typesetting.

Printed in Israel.

TABLE OF CONTENTS

FOREWORD

The young wines from the 2006 vintage are now making their way to market, as are the best Israeli wines from the 2004 and 2005 vintages. Following the pattern of recent years, many of these wines are proving to be of enviably high quality. The wines of Israel are now earning respected ratings at prestigious wine fairs the world over and are receiving highly favorable reviews from influential wine critics in North America and Europe. Although the export of Israeli wines is still limited, wines of Israel's major wineries as well as boutique wineries are now appearing on the shelves in countries as diverse in character as the United States, Russia, Canada, Denmark, France, Japan, Korea, Hungary, Finland and the United Kingdom.

The days when Israel was producing primarily sweet red wines for sacramental purposes are long gone, and today Israel is acknowledged as a serious wine producer. Wines are being made from highly prized grape varieties at more than one hundred and fifty wineries scattered all over the country, from the Upper Galilee and the Golan Heights to the Judean Hills and the Negev Desert. The construction of state-of-the-art wineries, the ongoing import and cultivation of good vine stock from California, France and Australia, and the enthusiasm and knowledge of young, well-trained winemakers who are not afraid to experiment with new wine varieties and blends has yielded an abundance of quality wines that can compete comfortably with many of the fine wines of the New and Old Worlds.

The purpose of this book is to provide readers with extensive knowledge about the wineries and wines of Israel, and to serve as a convenient guide for selecting and storing local wines. The introduction supplies the reader with the necessary historical and geographical background, while the major part of the guide is devoted to the wines, offering tasting notes and scores for wines that are now on the shelves or scheduled to appear within the next six to nine months, as well as wines that are still stored in the cellars of wine lovers.

How to Use the Guide

Wineries are arranged in the book by alphabetical order, and in the few cases where wineries may be known by more than one name, especially outside of Israel, readers will find the alternative names listed in the index. Following a brief description of the location, history and production of each winery are the reviews, ranging from the top-level series to the lower. Each series is arrayed from red wines to whites, followed by sparkling and dessert wines. These are further divided into grape varieties such as Cabernet Sauvignon, Merlot, etc. Each variety is arranged according to vintage years, from the most current release to the most mature available or still likely to be found in a fine wine cellar. Each review concludes with a score and a suggested drinking window.

Key to Symbols and Scores

THE WINERIES

*****	A WORLD-CLASS WINERY, REGULARLY PRODUCING EXCELLENT WINES
****	CONSISTENTLY PRODUCING HIGH-QUALITY WINES
***	SOLID AND RELIABLE PRODUCER WITH AT LEAST SOME GOOD WINES
**	ADEQUATE
*	HARD TO RECOMMEND

SCORES FOR INDIVIDUAL WINES

96–100	Truly great wines
90–95	Exceptional in every way
85–89	Very good to excellent and highly recommended
80–84	Recommended but without enthusiasm
70–79	Average but at least somewhat faulted
Under 70	Not recommended

Special Note about Tentative Scores:
The scores of wines tasted only from the barrel—that is to say, well before release and sometimes even before final blends have been made—are scored within a range and noted as *tentative*. Wines attaining such scores will be re-tasted and updated in future editions.

DRINKING WINDOWS

A drinking window is the suggested period during which the wine is at its very best. The notation "best 2009–2012", for example, indicates that the wine needs further cellaring before it comes to its peak and will then cellar comfortably through 2012. "Drink now–2012" indicates that although the wine is drinking well now it will continue to cellar nicely until 2012. "Drink now" indicates that the wine is drinking well now but can be held for a year or so. "Drink up" suggests that the wine is at or past its peak and should not be cellared any longer. "Drink from release" refers to wines that are not yet on the market. Some will appear within the coming nine months and others may appear only in two to three years. Such wines were tasted either from bottles as advance tastings or from barrels.

KOSHER WINES

There is no contradiction between making fine wine and the laws of kashrut , as is made apparent in the introduction to this guide. Within the guide, the reviews of all wines that have received a kashrut certificate from a recognized rabbinic authority are followed by the symbol K.

Introduction

The History of Wine in Israel

Ancient Times

The history of wine in the land of Israel is as old as the history of the people who have inhabited that land over the centuries. As early as five thousand years ago people cultivated vines and made, stored and shipped wines. The first mention of wine in the Bible is in a reference to Noah, who is said to have planted the first vineyard and to have become intoxicated when he drank the wine (Genesis 9:20–21). Another well known reference concerns the spies sent by Moses to explore the Land of Canaan. They returned after their mission with a cluster of grapes said to have been so large and heavy that it had to be borne on a carrying frame (Numbers 13:23). The vine is also mentioned as one of the blessings of the good land promised to the children of Israel (Deuteronomy 8:8).

Much of the process of winemaking has remained consistent throughout this time. Already in the Bible, we find a list of the necessary steps to care for a vineyard:

> My beloved had a vineyard in a very fruitful hill;
> And he dug it; and cleared it of stones,
> And planted it with the choicest vine,
> And built a tower in the midst of it,
> And also hewed out a vat therein;
> And he looked that it should bring forth grapes.
> He broke the ground, cleared it of stone and planted
>   it with choice vines.
> He built a watchtower inside it,
> He even hewed a wine press inside it.
>
> *(Isaiah 5: 1–2)*

Vintners in ancient times knew as we do today that locating vineyards at higher altitudes, where there are greater temperature changes between night and day, would cause the fruit to ripen more slowly, adding to the sweetness of the fruit and its ability to produce fine wines. Two ways of growing vines were known: in one the vines were allowed to grow along the ground; in the other they were trained upward on trellises (Ezekiel 17:6–8). It was widely accepted then as today that vines cultivated by the second method almost always produce superior grapes.

Remains of ancient wine presses may be found today in all parts of Israel, from the Galilee to Jerusalem and the Negev Desert. In nearly every part of Israel, archaeologists have discovered hundreds of jars for the storage and transportation of wine. Many of these amphorae list in detail where and by whom the wine was made, as well as the year of the vintage, indicating that even in antiquity the source of the grapes and the quality of the harvest were considered important.

It is known today that even during the Bronze Age, Egyptian Pharaohs enjoyed wines that were shipped from Canaan. The growing of grapes and the production of wine was a major agricultural endeavor during the periods of the First and Second Temples, and the kings of Judah and Israel were said to have owned large vineyards as well as vast stores of wine. The vineyards and stores of King David in particular were so numerous that he is said to have appointed two officials, one to be in charge of the vineyards, and the other to be charge of storage (1 Chronicles 27:27).

In biblical times the harvest was a celebratory period as well as a period of courtship. The treading of the grapes was done most often on a *gat* or an *arevah*, the *gat* being a small, generally square, pressing floor that had been cut into bedrock, and the *arevah* a smaller treading surface that could be moved from vineyard to vineyard. From either of these the must (that is to say, the fresh and as yet unfermented grape juice) ran into a *yekev*, which was a vat for collecting the must as it flowed from the treading floor through a hole carved in the stone. When natural bedrock was unavailable, an earthen treading surface lined with mosaics was used. In several areas, caves or large cisterns carved from natural bedrock have been found, which would have served two purposes—first for storing the grapes until they were pressed, and then, because they were cool and dark, for storing the wine while it fermented and then aged in clay jugs.

Once fermentation had been completed, the wines were stored in pottery vessels which were sealed with wood, stone or clay stoppers. For purposes of shipping, the stoppers were wrapped in cloth and coated with clay. Since new clay vessels tend to absorb as much as 20 percent of the wines stored in them, it became common practice to store better wines in older jars. A major development, during the third century BCE, was the discovery that stoppers made from cork were an effective way to seal amphorae.

As much as these wines were prized, it must be understood that they were very different from wines as we know them today. They were often so intense and coarse that they needed a fair amount of "adjustment" before they were considered drinkable. To improve the bouquet, the Romans were known to add spices and scents to their wines. To make the wine sweeter, they added a syrup made by heating grape juice in lead containers for a long period over a low flame. To improve flavors and hide faults it was customary to add honey, pepper, chalk, gypsum, lime, resin, herbs and even sea water.

In the time of the First and Second Temples, wine was widely consumed by the local populace, but the very best wines were set aside for libations in the Temple. The Bible specifies the different types of offerings—a quarter of a *hin* (one *hin* was the equivalent of about 5.7 liters or 1.5 gallons) of wine when offering a sheep; a third of a *hin* for a ram; and half a *hin* for an animal from the herd, such as a cow (Numbers 15:5). In addition, people were required to give tithes of new wine to the Temple (Deuteronomy 12:17). Wines were so central to the culture during that period that those who planted vineyards were exempt from military service, and illustrations of grapes, grape leaves, amphorae and drinking vessels were often used as symbols on seals and coins as well as for decorations on the friezes of buildings.

After the destruction of the Second Temple, wine was integrated into all religious ceremonies including *brit milah* (circumcision), weddings, the Sabbath and high holidays. It is especially central in the Passover *Seder*, where it is customary to drink four glasses of wine.

During the late Roman and Byzantine periods, running from the fourth to sixth century, the wine industry shifted from Judea to the southern part of the land, where the port towns of Ashkelon and Gaza became centers of wine trading. The wines produced in the area were so coveted by the Romans that they shipped them to their legions throughout the Mediterranean and North Africa, and Christian pilgrims brought them back to Europe.

The Moslem conquest of the Holy Land in the seventh century put an end to this prosperous industry. The Moslem rulers banned the drinking of alcohol and as a result the flourishing local wine industry almost ceased to exist. The only wines allowed were the small amounts that Christians and Jews required for sacramental purposes. Throughout the twelfth and thirteenth centuries, the Crusaders made sporadic attempts to revive the wine industry in the Holy Land, but these were short-lived, as it was easier to ship wines from Europe. It was only with the renewal of Jewish settlement in the nineteenth century that the local winemaking industry was reestablished.

Modern Times

The Jewish philanthropist Sir Moses Montefiore, who visited the Holy Land numerous times in the nineteenth century, encouraged the Jews living there to work the land and replant vines. One person who heeded his call was Rabbi Itzhak Schorr, who founded a new winery in Jerusalem in 1848. Rabbi Abraham Teperberg followed suit, founding the Efrat winery in 1870 in the old city of Jerusalem. In addition, he also opened an agricultural school in Mikveh Israel, not far from Jaffa. This school was financed and run by *Alliance Israelite Universelle*, a Jewish organization based in France that aimed at training Jewish settlers in agricultural work. The school was the first to plant European grape varieties, and had a winery as well as large wine cellars. Many of its graduates became vine growers.

An important boost to the local industry came about when Baron Edmond de Rothschild, the owner of the famed Chateau Lafite in Bordeaux, agreed to come to the help of the Jewish colonies, and financed the planting of the first vineyards near Rishon Letzion, on the coastal plain. Rothschild hoped that the Holy Land would serve as the source of kosher wines for Jews the world over, and that the wine industry would provide a solid economic basis for the new Jewish communities. He brought in experts from Europe and imported grape varieties from the south of France including Alicante Bouchet, Clairette, Carignan, Grenache, Muscat and Semillon. He also funded the first wineries of the new Jewish settlements—first the Rishon Letzion Winery in 1882, then the Zichron Ya'akov winery in the Mount Carmel area in 1890—thus marking the beginning of the modern wine industry in the Land of Israel. Unfortunately, not all ran smoothly. The first harvests were lost to heat and in 1890–1891 the land was overrun by phylloxera, a plague of aphid-like insects that destroyed all of the vines. The vineyards were dug up, and replanted with vines grafted onto phylloxera-resistant root stocks.

In 1906 Rothschild helped to set up a cooperative of grape growers that managed the two wineries, and in 1957 his heirs sold their share to the cooperative. It took the name Carmel Mizrachi, and continued to be the dominant factor in the local wine industry until the early 1980s.

However, Rothschild's dream that viticulture would provide a major source of income for the region was shattered with the advent of three major events which virtually eliminated the fledgling industry's three largest potential markets: the Russian Revolution, the enactment of Prohibition in the United States, and the banning of imported wines to Egypt. Many vineyards had to be uprooted. While several new wineries opened in the following decades, including Segal, Eliaz and Stock, for the most part they and Carmel continued to produce wines largely destined for sacramental purposes. 1948 records testifying to the annual consumption of a mere

3.9 liters of wine per person demonstrate that wine had not yet become part of the culture of life in Israel.

The Israeli Wine Revolution

In 1972, Professor Cornelius Ough of the Department of Viticulture and Oenology at the University of California at Davis visited Israel and suggested that the soil and climate of the Golan Heights would prove ideal for the raising of grapes. In 1976 the first vines were planted in the Golan, and in 1983 the then-newly-established Golan Heights Winery released its first wines. Almost overnight it became apparent that Israel was capable of producing wines of world-class quality. During the early 1980s the Israeli wine industry endured an economic crisis, but the revolution had begun and there was no turning back.

Unfettered by outdated winemaking traditions or by a large stagnant corporate structure, the young winery imported excellent vine stock from California, built a state-of-the-art winery, and added to this the enthusiasm and expertise of young American winemakers who had been trained at the University of California at Davis. Equally important, the Golan winery began to encourage vineyard owners to improve the quality of their grapes and, in the American tradition, paid bonuses for grapes with high sugar and acid content, while rejecting substandard grapes. The winery was also the first to realize that wines made from Grenache, Semillon, Petite Sirah and Carignan grapes would not put them on the world wine map, and focused on planting and making wines from Cabernet Sauvignon, Merlot, Sauvignon Blanc, Chardonnay, white Riesling, Gewurztraminer and other noble grape varieties.

The Golan wines were a success from the beginning, not only within Israel but abroad. This success had a great impact on other Israeli wineries, which have made major steps in improving the quality of their wines. There are now five major wineries, twelve medium-sized wineries and a host of small wineries in the country, many of which are producing wines that are of high quality, and several producing wines good enough to interest connoisseurs all over the world.

The Current and Future State of Wine Production in Israel

Accurate data about the local wine industry is difficult to come by due to lack of coordination between the Israeli Wine Institute, the Ministry of Agriculture, the Export Institute and the Grape Grower's Association. When wineries submit their production and export figures, for example, they make no distinction between exports of table wines, sacramental wines, grape juice and even brandy and liqueurs. It is estimated that today Israel produces about thirty-six million bottles of table wine a year, an amount representing continued growth of five to ten percent annually over the past five years. Approximately forty thousand dunams (twenty thousand acres) of land are currently under grape cultivation, an increase of fifty percent in cultivated land area since 1995. Moreover, the development of vineyards is once again on the rise, and several of the medium-sized wineries are planting vineyards that are intended to double or triple their production. Approximately sixty percent of the table wines produced today are dry reds, while as recently as 1995 production was seventy percent whites and only thirty percent reds.

Following an extended period in which the imagination of the wine-drinking public within Israel was captured by boutique wineries and *garagistes*, the years 2003–2007 might be regarded as the years of the larger wineries. In 2003, the Golan Heights Winery released the country's first varietal wines made from Sangiovese, Pinot Noir and Gamay grapes, as well as the country's first single-vineyard organically grown Chardonnay. Under its Yarden label, the winery also produced the country's first Semillon-botrytis wine. During that same year, Carmel released the first wines from its new boutique winery Yatir, and has continued to give us exciting single-vineyard Cabernet Sauvignon, Syrah and Chardonnay wines. Barkan introduced the country's first Pinotage wine. During 2005, Recanati released the country's first wine made from Barbera grapes and several of the medium-sized wineries gave us the country's first Zinfandel wines.

Although the Golan Heights Winery, with its Katzrin, Yarden, Gamla and Golan series, remains the obvious quality leader among the large wineries in the country, a great deal of excitement continues to be generated by Clos de Gat, Tabor, Yatir, Pelter and the upper series of Carmel. Two other large wineries, Binyamina and Teperberg (until recently known as Efrat), have now joined the ranks of those wineries on the way up. Both of these wineries, now with well-trained winemakers aboard, are in the process of modernizing their equipment, gaining better control over their vineyards and producing several series of wines that are successfully capturing the attention of sophisticated wine drinkers.

Despite these positive signs and despite the relative economic prosperity within Israel today, at least some of the larger wineries continue to face potential problems—some structural and economic, others relating to a grape glut resulting from years of overplanting, and the former investment in grapes that hold no hope for producing fine wines.

The Phenomenon of the Boutique Wineries

In recent years, the country has seen a dramatic growth in boutique wineries, *garagistes*, micro-wineries and artisanal producers, each striving to create world-class wines. Such wineries, producing anywhere from under five hundred to one hundred thousand bottles annually, can remain highly personalized affairs, the winemakers having full control over their vineyards, knowing precisely what wine is in what barrel at any given moment and what style they want their wines to reflect. The label of a boutique winery does not, however, guarantee quality. At the top end of the range, a handful of small wineries founded by competent, well-trained professionals are producing some of the very best wines in the country. At the bottom end are numerous wineries founded by hobbyists that produce wines that are barely acceptable.

With well over a hundred small wineries dotting the country, some are struggling to get their wines on the shelves of local outlets. At the same time, more and more boutique wineries open and the prediction for the near future is that this trend will persist. The majority of the boutique wineries continue to grow, but feeling they may have peaked in their local sales, are now seeking to export. To date, however, the various consortiums that have been formed to promote such foreign sales have not shown exciting results.

Grape Growing Regions

The ideal areas for the cultivation of wine grapes lie in the two strips between 30–50 degrees north and south of the equator. Israel, which is located on the southern side of that strip in the Northern Hemisphere, is thus ideally situated. Considering Israel's specific climate, it is important to note that the vine can thrive in many different types of soil, as well as in regions that receive little rainfall.

Although the land area of Israel is a mere 7,992 square miles (which is five percent of the land area of California), like many wine-growing regions that have a long north-south axis (Italy, Chile or California, for example), the country has a large variety of microclimates. In the north, snow falls in winter and conditions are comparable to those of Bordeaux and the Northern Rhone Valley of France, yet within a few hours' drive one arrives at the Negev Desert, where the climate is similar to that of North Africa.

The country is divided into five vine-growing regions, the names of which are generally accepted by the European community and appear on all labels of varietal wines that are designated for sale both locally and abroad. Each region is divided into sub-regions, encompassing specific valleys, mountains or other locales. Although various governmental and quasi-governmental agencies are considering implementing a more stringent *appellation controlee* system, the major regions today remain as follows:

GALILEE: Located in the northern part of the country, this area extends to the Lebanese border and incorporates the Golan Heights. It is the region most suited for viticulture in Israel. The high altitude, cool breezes, marked day and night temperature changes and rich, well-drained soils make the area ideal for the cultivation of a large variety of grapes. The area is divided into four sub-regions: the Upper Galilee, the Lower Galilee, Tabor and the Golan Heights. Some of the wineries located here are the Golan Heights Winery, Galil Mountain, Chateau Golan, Dalton, Saslove and Tabor. Development of new vineyards continues apace in the area, many of these owned by wineries located in other parts of the country.

SHOMRON (SAMARIA): Located near the Mediterranean coast south of Haifa, it including the Carmel Mountain Range and the vineyards surrounding the towns of Zichron Ya'akov and Binyamina. This region remains the largest grape growing area in the country. The area has medium-heavy soils and a Mediterranean climate, with warm summers and humid winters. Wineries in the area include Margalit, Tishbi, Binyamina, and the Zichron Ya'akov branch of Carmel, all relying at least in part on grapes grown in other areas for their better wines.

SHIMSHON (SAMSON): Located between the foothills of the Jerusalem Mountains and the Mediterranean coast, this region encompasses the central plains, including the area around Rishon Letzion and Rehovot. Although the area boasts many vineyards, the limestone, clay and loamy soils and the coastal Mediterranean climate of warm, humid summers and mild winters do not offer ideal conditions for the cultivation of fine varieties, and many of the wineries in the area rely on grapes from other parts of the country. Among the wineries located here are Carmel, Barkan, Karmei Yosef, and Soreq.

JERUSALEM MOUNTAINS: Sometimes referred to as the Judean Hills, this region surrounding the city of Jerusalem offers a variety of soil conditions and a cool Mediterranean climate due to its relatively high altitude. For many years the region served as home primarily to wineries that specialized in sweet sacramental wines, but about a decade ago it became clear that this area could prove excellent for raising noble varieties. The area underwent strenuous revitalization with the major planting of sophisticated vineyards and the opening of several medium-sized and an increasing number of small wineries. More than twenty-five wineries are found in the area, including Castel, Clos de Gat, Sea Horse, Flam, Ella Valley Vineyards, Mony, Tzora and Teperberg. It is clear that a true *route de vins* is developing in this region.

NEGEV: Ten years ago, few would have thought this semi-arid desert region appropriate for growing grapes, but now, sophisticated computerized drip-irrigation systems have made it possible to grow high quality grapes here, including among others Merlot, Cabernet Sauvignon and Chardonnay. The region is divided into two sub-areas: Ramat Arad, which is situated 600–700 meters above sea level and has impressive night-day temperature changes, where results with noble varieties have been excellent; and the Southern Negev, a lower, more arid area where sandy to loamy soils and very hot and dry summers offer a special challenge to grape growers. Carmel was the first to plant extensive vineyards at Ramat Arad. More recently, Barkan has begun wide-ranging development of vineyards at Mitzpe Ramon in the heart of the Negev. Among the wineries found here, some rely entirely on desert-raised grapes. Others that draw as well on grapes from other areas are Yatir and Sde Boker.

Grape Varieties in Israel

The last two decades have seen a major upheaval in the vineyards of Israel. Prior to 1985 the grapes planted were largely Carignan, Petite Sirah and Grenache for red and rosé wines, and Semillon, Emerald Riesling, and Colombard for whites. The wineries focused on light, white and often sweet wines, and only a handful of noble varieties were to be found in the country. The scene shifted dramatically with the development of vineyards planted with noble varieties, first on the Golan Heights, then in the Upper Galilee. Today, from the Negev Desert to the northernmost parts of the country, the focus is on many of those varieties that have proven themselves throughout the world.

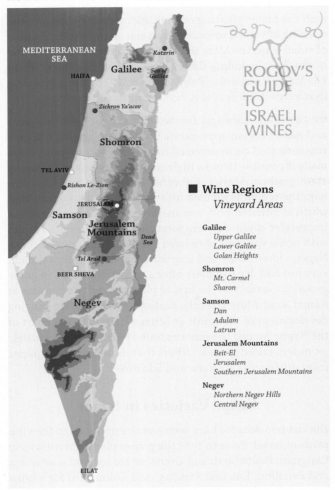

MEDITERRANEAN
SEA

Katzrin

Galilee

Sea of
Galilee

HAIFA

Zichron Ya'acov

Shomron

TEL AVIV

Rishon Le-Zion

JERUSALEM

Samson

Jerusalem
Mountains

Dead
Sea

Tel Arad

BEER SHEVA

Negev

EILAT

ROGOV'S
GUIDE
TO
ISRAELI
WINES

■ **Wine Regions**
Vineyard Areas

Galilee
  Upper Galilee
  Lower Galilee
  Golan Heights

Shomron
  Mt. Carmel
  Sharon

Samson
  Dan
  Adulam
  Latrun

Jerusalem Mountains
  Beit-El
  Jerusalem
  Southern Jerusalem Mountains

Negev
  Northern Negev Hills
  Central Negev

Unlike many of the wine-growing regions, especially in Europe, Israel does not have any indigenous grapes that might be considered appropriate for making wine. The closest the country came to having its own grape was the introduction of the Argaman grape, a cross between Souzao and Carignan grapes. Widely planted in the early 1980s, that experiment proved a fiasco: although the grape yielded wines deep in color, they lacked flavor, depth or body. In the list that follows, those grapes capable of producing quality wines in Israel are noted with an asterisk (*).

White Wine Grapes

CHARDONNAY: The grape that produces the great dry white wines of Burgundy and is indispensable to the production of Champagne. The most popular white wine grape in the world today, producing wines that can be oaked or un-oaked, and range in flavors from flinty-minerals to citrus, pineapple, tropical fruits and grapefruit, and in texture from minerally-crisp to creamy. (*)

CHENIN BLANC: Originating in France's central Loire Valley, this thin-skinned and acidic grape has a high sugar content that can give aromas and flavors of honey and damp straw. Within Israel the grape has largely produced wines best categorized as ordinary, and often semi-dry.

COLOMBARD: Known in Israel as French Colombard and producing mostly thin and acidic wines.

EMERALD RIESLING: A cross between the Muscadelle and Riesling grapes developed in California primarily for growth in warm climates, the grape produces mostly semi-dry wines of little interest.

GEWURZTRAMINER: This grape originated in Germany, came to its glory in Alsace and has now been transplanted to many parts of the world. Capable of producing aromatic dry and sweet wines that are often typified by their softness and spiciness, as well as distinctive aromas and flavors of litchis and rose petals. (*)

MUSCAT: There are many varieties of Muscat, the two most often found in Israel being the Muscat of Alexandria and Muscat Canelli, both of which are capable of producing wines that range from the dry to the sweet and are almost always typified by their perfumed aromas.

RIESLING: Sometimes known in Israel as Johannisberg Riesling, sometimes as White Riesling and sometimes simply as Riesling, this noble German variety has the potential to produce wines, that although light in body and low in alcohol, are highly flavored and capable of long aging. Typified by aromas and flavors of flowers, minerals, lime, and when aged, sometimes taking on a tempting petrol-like aroma. (*)

SAUVIGNON BLANC: At its best in the Loire Valley and Bordeaux for producing dry white wines, this successful transplant to Israel is capable of producing refreshing, sophisticated and distinctively aromatic and grassy wines, often best consumed in their youth. (*)

SEMILLON: Although this native French grape was used for many years in Israel to produce largely uninteresting semi-dry white wines, its susceptibility to noble rot is now being used to advantage to produce sweet dessert wines with the distinctive bouquet and flavors of melon, fig and citrus. (*)

TRAMINETTE: A not overly exciting hybrid, a derivative of the Gewurztraminer grape, developed primarily for use in cold weather New York State and Canadian climates.

VIOGNIER: The most recent white wine transplant to Israel, this grape produces the fascinating Condrieu wines of France's Rhone Valley. Capable of producing aromatic but crisply dry whites and full-bodied whites, some of which have long aging potential. (*)

Red Wine Grapes

ARGAMAN: An Israeli-inspired cross between Souzao and Carignan grapes. Possibly best categorized as the great local wine failure, producing wines of no interest. Many of the vineyards that were planted with Argaman continue to be uprooted to make room for more serious varieties.

BARBERA: From Italy's Piedmont region, this grape has the potential for producing wines that although light and fruity are capable of great charm. (*)

CABERNET FRANC: Less intense and softer than Cabernet Sauvignon, most often destined to be blended with Merlot and Cabernet Sauvignon, but even on its own capable of producing dramatically good, leafy, fruity and aromatic reds. (*)

CABERNET SAUVIGNON: The most noble variety of Bordeaux, capable of producing superb wines, often blended with smaller amounts of Merlot and Cabernet Franc. The best wines from this grape are rich in color and tannins, and have complex aromas and depth of flavors, those often typified by black currants, spices and cedarwood. At their best, intriguing and complex wines that profit from cellaring. (*)

CARIGNAN: An old-timer on the Israeli scene, this originally Spanish grape produces largely dull and charmless wines. Still commonly planted within Israel but increasingly destined for distillation in the making of brandy and liqueurs. Several smaller wineries are, however, demonstrating that old-vine Carignan grapes, especially those in fields that have been unwatered for many years, can produce interesting and high quality wines. (*)

GAMAY: The well-known grape of France's Beaujolais region, this fairly recent introduction to Israel is capable of producing light to medium-bodied wines of fragrance and charm, intended primarily for drinking in their youth. (*)

GRENACHE: Although this grape has done well in France's Rhone Valley and Spain, it has not yielded sophisticated wines in Israel, most being somewhat pale, overripe and sweet in nature. Probably at its best for blending.

MALBEC: Well-known in France's Bordeaux, the Loire and Cahors, this grape is capable of producing dense, rich, tannic and spicy wines that are remarkably dark in color. (*)

MERLOT: Softer, more supple and often less tannic than Cabernet Sauvignon—with which it is often blended—but capable of producing voluptuous, opulent, plummy wines of great interest. A grape that has proven popular on its own as it produces wines that are easier to drink and are approachable earlier than wines made from Cabernet Sauvignon. (*)

NEBBIOLO: The grape from which the Barolo and Barbaresco wines of Italy's Piedmont region are made. Still experimental in Israel but with the potential for producing perfumed, fruity and intense wines that are full-bodied, high in tannins, acidity and color, and have the potential for long-term cellaring. (*)

PETIT VERDOT: Planted only in small quantities and used in Israel as it is in Bordeaux, primarily for blending with other noble varieties to add acidity and balance. Capable on its own of producing a long-lived and tannic wine when ripe. (*)

PETITE SIRAH: Related only peripherally to the great Syrah grape, this grape is, at its best, capable of producing dark, tannic and well-balanced wines of great appeal and sophistication. This potential has been obtained only once or twice in Israel, the grape being used too often to produce mass-market wines that tend to be hot, tannic and without charm. A few small wineries manage to obtain excellent wines from this variety. (*)

PINOT NOIR: A relatively recent transplant to Israel, this grape, which is responsible for the great reds of Burgundy, is making a very good initial showing. At its best the grape is capable of producing smooth, rich and intricate wines of exquisite qualities, with flavors of cherries, wild berries and violets which as they age take on aromas and flavors of chocolate and game meat. Also used in Israel, as in the Champagne region of France, to blend with Chardonnay to make sparkling wines. (*)

PINOTAGE: A South African cross between Pinot Noir and Cinsault, capable of being flavorful and powerful, yet soft and full, with a pleasing sweet finish and a lightly spicy overlay. (*)

SANGIOVESE: Italy's most frequently planted variety, found in the simplest Chianti and most complex Brunello di Montalcino wines, this is another grape recently introduced to Israel, showing fine early results with wines that are lively, fruity and full of charm. (*)

SYRAH: Some believe that this grape originated in ancient Persia and was brought to France by the Romans, while others speculate that it is indigenous to France. Syrah found its first glory in France's northern Rhone Valley, and then in Australia (where it is known as Shiraz). Capable of producing deep royal-purple tannic wines that are full-bodied enough to be thought of as dense and powerful, but with excellent balance and complex aromas and flavors of plums, berries, currants, black pepper and chocolate. First results from this grape have been exciting and plantings are increasing dramatically. (*)

TEMPRANILLO: The staple grape of Spain's Rioja area, with recent plantings in Israel, this is a grape with the potential for producing long-lived complex and sophisticated wines typified by aromas and flavors of black fruits, leather, tobacco and spices. (*)

ZINFANDEL: Zinfandel (the Italian variety of which is known as Primitivo) is not exactly new in Israel, but until recently the vines that had been planted were capable of producing only mediocre semi-dry blush wines. What is new are recently planted high-quality vines from California that offer the potential for producing full-bodied to massive wines, moderately to highly alcoholic, with generous tannins and the kind of warm berry flavors that typify these wines at their best. (*)

Vintage Reports: 1976–2006

The first formal vintage tables appeared in the 1820s and since then wine lovers have relied on them to help make their buying and drinking decisions. As popular as they are, however, it is important to remember that because all vintage tables involve generalizations, there are no firm facts to be found in them. In a sense, these charts are meant to give an overall picture and perhaps to supply clues about which wines to consider buying or drinking. In making one's decisions it is wise to remember that the quality of wines of any vintage year and in any region can vary enormously between wineries. Also worth keeping in mind is that vintage reports and tables such as those that follow are based on what most people consider "quality wines" and not those made for everyday drinking and thus not intended for aging. More than this, estimates of drinkability are based on wines that have been shipped and stored under ideal conditions.

Following are short reports on the last five vintage years, these followed by a listing of the years of interest going back to 1976. Vintage years are rated on a scale of 20–100, and these numerical values can be interpreted as follows:

100	=	Extraordinary
90	=	Exceptional
80	=	Excellent
70	=	Very Good
60	=	Good But Not Exciting
50	=	Average But With Many Faulted Wines
40	=	Mediocre/Not Recommended
30	=	Poor/Not Recommended
20	=	Truly Bad/Not Recommended

The following symbols are used to indicate drinking windows (Predictions of drinking windows are based on ideal storage since the wine was released.):

C	=	Worthy of Cellaring
D/C	=	Drink or Cellar
D	=	Drink Now or in the Next Year or So
D–	=	Past Its Prime but Probably Still Drinkable
SA	=	Well Beyond Its Prime and Probably Undrinkable

The Last Five Years

2006 VINTAGE RATING 86

An especially dry winter, a cold rainy April and then rains during mid-harvest in October (five times the seasonal norm) led to an extended harvest lasting from August to November, yielding a surprisingly small crop. Probably better for reds than whites, this was not an exciting year and many of the top-of-the line series and single-vineyard releases will not be released from this vintage. D/C

2005 VINTAGE RATING 89

One of the most promising years in the last decade, with a prolonged harvest of overall high quality, exceptionally good in many parts of the country for reds and whites alike. Barrel tastings reveal wines of excellent balance, structure and aging potential. C

2004 VINTAGE RATING 88

Colder than average temperatures and heavy rainfall during the winter months followed by an unusually warm and dry period during March and April caused early budbreak in warmer vineyards. Relatively cool temperatures returned in May leading to a relatively short and hectic harvest but with an overall excellent crop. A promising year. D/C

2003 VINTAGE RATING 90

A cold and wet winter with precipitation about one third higher than normal was followed by unusually warm weather in May, leading to strong and rapid shoot growth and a hectic month of shoot positioning. Due to moderate and stable summer temperatures, harvest was stretched out to 17 weeks, concluding on November 18th. Overall, an excellent vintage year for both reds and whites. D/C

2002 VINTAGE RATING 82

In the north of the country the warm weather in February and March followed by a particularly cold spell in April and May stretched out the ripening season and resulted in an extended 15-week harvest. May rains during blooming caused a 15% reduction to yields. In the rest of the country several prolonged hot spells caused some vineyards to lose as much as 80% of their crop. Overall, only few acceptable wines and fewer appropriate for long-term cellaring. D

Somewhat Older Vintages

2001	85	D/C
2000	89	D/C
1999	86	D
1998	85	D
1997	90	D/C
1996	82	D-
1995	90	SA
1994	84	SA
1993	92	D
1992	85	SA
1991	82	SA
1990	91	D
1989	90	SA
1988	85	SA
1987	78	SA
1986	76	SA
1985	90	SA
1984	86	SA
1983	55	SA
1982	55	SA
1979	92	SA
1976	92	SA

Questions of Kashrut

For many years, wines that were kosher had a justifiably bad name, those in the United States being made largely from Concord grapes, which are far from capable of making fine wine, and many of those from Israel following the perceived need for kosher wines to be red, sweet, coarse and without any sign of sophistication. The truth is that those wines were not so much consumed by knowledgeable wine lovers as they were used for sacramental purposes. Such wines are still made but are today perceived largely as oddities. With kosher wines now being made from the most noble grape varieties in state-of-the-art wineries by talented winemakers, there need be no contradiction whatsoever between the laws of kashrut and the production of fine wine.

Some Israeli Wines are Kosher, Others are Not

A look at the current Israeli wine scene indicates that the wines of every large winery and the majority of medium-sized wineries in Israel are kosher, but those of the smaller wineries are often not.

For many years, all of the wines produced in Israel were kosher, with the exception of those made in Christian monasteries. The reasons for this were and still are twofold. The first reason relates to the fact that a large proportion of the Israeli population, even among the non-observant, consume only foods and beverages that are kosher. The second, also with a clear economic basis, is that only kosher products can enter the large supermarket chains in the country. Because the majority of wines produced in the country continue to be purchased in supermarkets, no large winery can give up that considerable sales potential. In addition, kashrut is maintained because many of the wineries continue to target their export sales largely toward Jewish consumers worldwide.

The wines of several medium-sized producers and many of the boutique wineries have a somewhat different goal in mind—that of producing upper-end wines that are targeted toward higher-end and not necessarily kashrut-observant wine consumers both in Israel and abroad. The production of kosher wines, which more than anything adds the need for additional staff (for example, rabbinical supervisors), as well as fees to the rabbinical authorities, can add prohibitively to the costs and the eventual retail price of wines, especially for small wineries.

What Makes an Israeli Wine Kosher?

In order for an Israeli wine to be certified as kosher, several requirements must be met. As can easily be seen, none of these requirements has a negative impact on the quality of the wine being produced and several are widely acknowledged to be sound agricultural practices even by producers of non-kosher wines.

1. According to the practice known as *orla*, the grapes of new vines cannot be used for winemaking until the fourth year after planting.

2. No other fruits or vegetables may be grown in between the rows of vines (*kalai hakerem*).

3. After the first harvest, the fields must lie fallow every seventh year. Each of these sabbatical years is known as *shnat shmita*.

4. From the onset of the harvest only kosher tools and storage facilities may be used in the winemaking process, and all of the winemaking equipment must be cleaned to be certain that no foreign objects remain in the equipment or vats.

5. From the moment the grapes reach the winery, only Sabbath observant Jews are allowed to come in contact with the wine. Because many of the winemakers in the country are not Sabbath observant, this means that they cannot personally handle the equipment or the wine as it is being made and are assisted in several of their more technical tasks by Orthodox assistants and kashrut supervisors (*mashgichim*).

6. All of the materials (e.g. yeasts) used in the production and clarification of the wines must be certified as kosher.

7. A symbolic amount of wine, representing the tithe (*truma vema'aser*) once paid to the Temple in Jerusalem, must be poured away from the tanks or barrels in which the wine is being made.

The Question of Wines that are Mevushal

Some observant Jews demand that their wines be pasteurized (*mevushal*), especially in restaurants and at catered events, where there is the possibility that a non-Jew may handle the wine. This tradition dates to ancient times, when wine was used by pagans for idolatrous worship: the Israelites used to boil their wines, thus changing the chemical composition of the wine so that it was considered unfit for pagan worship. Wines that are *mevushal* have the advantage that they can be opened and poured by non-Jews or Jews who are not Sabbath observant.

Today, *mevushal* wines are no longer boiled. After the

grapes are crushed, the common practice is to rapidly raise the temperature of the liquids to 176–194 degrees Fahrenheit (80–90 Celsius) in special flash pasteurizing units, hold it there for under a minute and then return the temperature, equally rapidly, to 60 degrees Fahrenheit (15 Celsius).

There is no question but that modern technology has reduced the impact of these processes on the quality of the wine, but most winemakers and consumers remain in agreement that, with very few exceptions, wines that have been pasteurized lose many of their essential essences, often being incapable of developing in the bottle and quite often imparting a "cooked" sensation to the nose and palate.

Some wines are produced in both regular and *mevushal* versions, the *mevushal* editions destined for the export market or for the highly observant within Israel. Because it is almost impossible for anyone outside of the wineries to keep track of and taste all of those wines, no attempt is made within this book to report on such "double bottlings".

Simply stated, a wine that is *mevushal* is no more or less kosher than a wine that is not, and none of the better wines of Israel today fall into this category. Those who are concerned with such issues will find the information they require on either the front or rear labels of wines produced in the country.

A Few Lists

Ten Best Wine Producers

1. Golan Heights Winery (Katzrin, Yarden, Gamla)
2. Castel
3. Yatir
4. Margalit
5. Clos de Gat
6. Flam
7. Amphorae
8. Carmel (Limited Edition, Single Vineyard)
9. Chateau Golan
10. Ella Valley

Ten Up-and-Coming Producers

1. Pelter
2. Tabor
3. Assaf
4. Odem Mountain
5. Vitkin
6. Savion
7. Psagot
8. Tulip
9. Avidan
10. Kadita

Ten Best Value Producers

1. Galil Mountain
2. Golan Heights Winery (Gamla, Golan)
3. Tabor
4. Dalton
5. Amphorae
6. Recanati
7. Saslove
8. Barkan
9. Tishbi
10. Teperberg

Ten Best Wines Released in the Last Twelve Months

1. Golan Heights Winery, Katzrin, 2003
2. Golan Heights Winery, Cabernet Sauvignon, Elrom, 2003
3. Carmel, Limited Edition, 2003
4. Margalit, Cabernet Sauvignon, 2004
5. Castel, Grand Vin Castel, 2004
6. Clos de Gat, 2003
7. Yatir, Yatir Forest, 2004
8. Flam, Merlot Reserve, 2004
9. Galil Mountain, Yiron, 2003
10. Château Golan, Eliad, 2003

Drinking Habits

Within Israel

Since the founding of the state in 1948 and until 1997, annual Israeli wine consumption held steady at about 3.9 liters per capita. Although there is some debate about precisely how much wine is being consumed by Israelis, recent years have seen a major increase, and consumption now stands at between 6–8 liters annually. This figure puts Israelis far behind the French and Italians, who consume 56 and 49 liters respectively, or even the Australians who consume 20 liters per year. That does, however, place Israel close to North American consumption of 9–11 liters annually. It is also interesting that recent studies show that in Israel there is no significant correlation between wine consumption and either alcoholism or automobile accidents.

The increase in local consumption reflects of course the increasing quality of local wines. However, it also reflects the fact that more and more Israelis are traveling abroad and dining in fine restaurants where wine is an integral part of the meal. Today, many Israelis are touring the fine wineries of Bordeaux, Tuscany and the Napa Valley, and even though such wine appreciation is still limited to the upwardly mobile segment of the population, more and more people now order wine to accompany their meal in a fine restaurant.

In addition to showing a growing appreciation of wine in general, Israelis are moving in several directions that can be seen in many other countries as well. Consumption is shifting from semi-dry to dry wines, from whites to reds, from light to heavier wines and most importantly, there is a movement toward buying higher quality wines. Twenty-five years ago, more than eighty percent of the wines produced in the country were sweet. Today, nearly eighty percent of the wines produced are dry.

Israelis also continue to increase their consumption of imported wines, and the better wine shops of the country stock wines from every region of France, Italy, Australia, New Zealand, California, Washington State, Spain, Portugal,

Germany, Austria, Chile and Argentina. Some members of the local wine industry perceive this phenomenon as having a negative impact on the local industry. Others, perhaps with a greater sense of foresight, realize that imported wines pose a challenge to the local wine industry to continue to improve the quality of its products.

Sacramental versus "Wine Culture"

Within Israel, as in nearly every country with a Jewish population, some continue to drink wine entirely for sacramental purposes—as, for example, for the *Kiddush* blessing that opens the two main meals of the Sabbath and holidays. An increasing number have realized that any kosher wine is appropriate for such purposes, but others hold to the perceived tradition that such wines should be red, thick and sweet. Although such wines hold no interest for sophisticated wine drinkers, several of the large wineries continue to produce *Kiddush*-wines and there are wineries that focus entirely on these consumers.

Within the "Jewish World"

Nearly all of the better wine stores of the major cities of North America, the United Kingdom and France have at least a small section devoted to kosher wines, and in recent years the wines of Israel have taken a more prominent space on those shelves alongside kosher wines from California, France, Spain, Australia, Chile and Argentina. The reception of Israeli wines, both kosher and non-kosher, is gradually getting warmer: They are now being reviewed more regularly in magazines devoted to wine as well as in the weekly wine columns of many critics, and are appearing on the menus of many prestigious restaurants.

Israel as a Potential Supplier of "Niche Wines"

Wine lovers enjoy few things more than hunting for previously unknown or little-known wines. So it has been in recent years, for example, with the wines of Sicily, and the Penedes region of Spain: When those wines first arrived on the shelves of wine stores in New York, London and Toronto, they filled an empty "niche." The first wines sold out quickly, those that proved to be of high quality were reordered, and those that came to be accepted as truly excellent moved out of the niche category and onto the regular shelves.

Many, including this critic, feel that Israeli wines are on the verge of being accepted as niche wines, especially in North America and the United Kingdom. When this happens, the wines will move off those shelves limited only to kosher holdings and begin to appear in a special Israeli or Mediterranean section. Their appeal to the broader population will come from their unique qualities, reflecting their Mediterranean and specifically Israeli character.

The Wineries and Their Wines

For many years it was possible to group Israeli wine producers into one of two broad categories—large and small wineries. The last five years have seen dramatic changes, for during that time five new medium-sized producers have appeared on the local scene, several of the wineries that could be categorized as boutiques have expanded their production, and a host of small wineries continue to open. Within each category there are wineries that produce excellent and often exciting wines.

The wines reviewed in this guide include only those I have tasted—wines already on the market, wines due to be released within the next several months, or those still in the cellars or homes of wine lovers. Also listed are barrel tastings, some being those of wines scheduled to be released only in another 2–3 years. Not included in the guide are wineries that produce wines primarily for sacramental purposes, as those wines hold no interest for wine consumers at large. Nor, with only a few exceptions, does the guide rate the wines of those wineries producing under 1,500 bottles annually. Ratings for wineries (1–5 stars) are based on current status. For those wineries that have released only one or two vintages, the ratings should be considered as tentative, since they might move up or down in the next edition of this guide.

Agur ***

Set on Moshav Agur in the Judean plains, this small winery, owned by winemaker Shuki Yashuv, has grown from releasing 1,800 bottles in the 2000 vintage to about 14,000 in 2006. The winery has its own vineyards on the *moshav* and also draws on grapes from the Ella Valley, those including Cabernet Sauvignon, Merlot, Cabernet Franc and Petit Verdot. Grapes from each vineyard are fermented separately, some in stainless steel vats, others in new and used *barriques*. The winery has just moved into a new facility.

Special Reserve

SPECIAL RESERVE, CABERNET SAUVIGNON, 2005: Dark royal-purple, full-bodied, with generous spicy oak integrating with chewy tannins and fruits. Concentrated, showing currant and plum fruits along with hints of cedar, green olives and sage, with the tannins rising on the persistent finish. Drink now–2011. Score 87.

SPECIAL RESERVE, CABERNET SAUVIGNON, 2004: Dark garnet, with firm tannins and spicy oak. Showing currant, blackberry and licorice aromas and flavors, all leading to a gripping and moderately long finish. Drink now. Score 86.

SPECIAL RESERVE, CABERNET SAUVIGNON, 2003: With its once firm tannins now integrating nicely, this dark ruby red is showing generous oak and spicy blackberry and currant fruits. Drink now. Score 86.

Agur

AGUR, CABERNET SAUVIGNON, 2006: Dark garnet, full-bodied, with good balance between dusty wood, black currants and blackberries supported by a potpourri of spices and cedar and a hint of minerals on the firm and complex finish. Drink from release–2010. Tentative Score 86–88.

AGUR, CABERNET SAUVIGNON, 2004: Dark ruby towards garnet, medium to full-bodied, with chunky country-style tannins and appealing blackberry, currant, and spicy aromas and flavors. Drink now. Score 86.

AGUR, CABERNET SAUVIGNON, 2003: Deep garnet, medium to full-bodied, with near-sweet tannins, gentle wood and appealing currant, berry, and herbal aromas and flavors. Drink now. Score 86.

AGUR, MERLOT, 2006: Super-dark purple, with gripping tannins that turn supple from mid-palate and reveal cherry cola, black cherry and plum fruits on a background of mocha and spicy oak. The best yet from Agur. Drink from release–2012. Tentative Score 88–90.

AGUR, CABERNET SAUVIGNON-MERLOT, KESSEM, 2005: This blend of 60% Cabernet Sauvignon, 30% Merlot and about 5% each Cabernet Franc and Petit Verdot was developed in *barriques* for 12 months, and is showing gentle overlays of spices and a hint of vanilla, with soft tannins integrating nicely and generous blackberry, red currant and red plums, all leading to a round and lingering finish. Score 89.

AGUR, CABERNET SAUVIGNON-MERLOT, KESSEM, 2004: Garnet-red, medium-bodied, with soft tannins balanced by a gentle wood influence and forward berry, black cherry and cassis fruits. On the finish hints of dried apricots and orange peel. Drink now. Score 86.

AGUR, CABERNET SAUVIGNON-MERLOT, KESSEM, 2003: Medium-bodied, with good balance between country-style tannins, spicy wood and berry, black cherry, and currant fruits. Drink up. Score 85.

AGUR, ROSA, 2006: A rosé wine from Cabernet Sauvignon grapes. Dark pink towards orange, medium-bodied with not much on the nose but tempting flavors of spicy blackberries and raspberries. Drink now. Score 86.

Alexander ★★★★

Located on Moshav Beit Yitzhak in the Sharon region, the winery, founded in 1996 by Yoram Shalom, receives grapes largely from contract vineyards over which it has full control at Kerem Ben Zimra in the Upper Galilee. Primary output to date has been of Cabernet Sauvignon, Merlot, Chardonnay and Sauvignon Blanc and now coming on line are Syrah and Grenache.

Growth has been steady, increasing from about 12,000 bottles in 2002 to 45,000 in 2005 and 2006. With the 2006 vintage the winery switched over to kosher production and planned output for that harvest is 60,000–70,000 bottles. In addition to producing two top-of-the-line series, Alexander the Great and The Wine of Alexander, the winery also releases two blended wines, Sandro and Gaston. In addition, the winery produces private label wines for several restaurants.

Alexander the Great

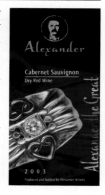

ALEXANDER THE GREAT, CABERNET SAU-VIGNON, 2005: Made from grapes from 26-year-old vines, this medium to full-bodied dark garnet-red wine shows soft tannins, spicy wood and a tempting array of mineral, black fruit, herbal and chocolate aromas. On the long finish, cloves and a hint of iodine. Best 2009–2013. Score 90.

ALEXANDER THE GREAT, CABERNET SAU-VIGNON, GRAND RESERVE, 2004: Reflecting its 48 months in mostly new oak *barriques* with generous but not imposing smoky and vanilla overlays, those in good balance with firm but yielding tannins and fruits. On the nose and palate plums, berries and currants, with overlays of mocha, and herbs. More powerful than elegant at this stage. Best from 2009. Tentative Score 89–91.

ALEXANDER THE GREAT, CABERNET SAUVIGNON, 2004: Full-bodied and reflecting the *barriques* in which it developed with firm, near-sweet tannins and hints of spicy wood. Generous and long with a complex array of currant, herbal and mineral aromas and flavors. Drink now–2011. Score 90.

ALEXANDER THE GREAT, CABERNET SAUVIGNON, 2003: Generous wood and tannins in fine balance with currant, plum and herbal aromas and flavors, those complemented on the long finish by mocha and sweet cedar. Drink now–2011. Score 89.

ALEXANDER THE GREAT, CABERNET SAUVIGNON, 2002: Full-bodied, with firm tannins integrating nicely with generous smoky oak. On the nose and palate black currant, blackberry and light hints of herbs. Generous and mouth-filling. Drink now–2010. Score 90.

ALEXANDER THE GREAT, CABERNET SAUVIGNON, 2001: Fully mature now but still massive in structure and body as in its youth, now showing spicy wood, black fruits and a rising influence of herbs and eucalyptus. Drink up. Score 90.

The Wine of Alexander

THE WINE OF ALEXANDER, CABERNET SAUVIGNON, 2005: Medium to full-bodied, dark ruby in color, with soft tannins; showing vanilla and spices from the casks in which it aged. On the nose and palate, rich black currant and blackberry fruits along with hints of earthiness. Drink now–2010. Score 88.

THE WINE OF ALEXANDER, CABERNET SAUVIGNON, 2004: Medium to full-bodied, with gripping tannins and wood nicely balanced by generous black fruits. Drink now–2009. Score 87.

THE WINE OF ALEXANDER, CABERNET SAUVIGNON, 2003: Not aromatic, but opening to an array of flavors including black fruits, Mediterranean herbs and licorice. Medium to full-bodied, with soft tannins and a moderately long vanilla and mint finish. Drink now. Score 88.

THE WINE OF ALEXANDER, CABERNET SAUVIGNON, 2002: Dark royal-purple, with firm tannins opening to reveal currant, blackberry and earthy-herbal aromas and flavors. Drink up. Score 86.

THE WINE OF ALEXANDER, MERLOT, 2005: Deep royal-purple, with firm but nicely integrating tannins. Hints of spicy wood and tobacco balanced nicely by a generous array of black plum, raspberry, cassis and chocolate aromas and flavors. Drink now–2009. Score 89.

THE WINE OF ALEXANDER, MERLOT, 2004: Dark cherry towards garnet, medium-bodied, with soft tannins integrating nicely. Round and generous, with cassis, blackberry and black cherry fruits accompanied by hints of pepper and nutmeg. Drink now. Score 86.

THE WINE OF ALEXANDER, MERLOT, 2003: Well balanced with ripe plum, black cherry, currant, sweet cedar and hazelnut aromas and flavors. Smooth and supple, with soft tannins and a hint of mocha on the finish. Drink now. Score 88.

THE WINE OF ALEXANDER, MERLOT, 2002: Garnet to adobe brick in color, full-bodied, with plum and currant fruits. The once youthful anise and menthol flavors are now rising. Drink up. Score 88.

THE WINE OF ALEXANDER, SYRAH, 2005: Dark royal-purple, full-bodied, with deep but remarkably soft tannins. Hints of smoky wood, freshly turned earth and spices on a background of black fruits and, on the finish, light smoked meat. Drink now–2010. Score 90.

THE WINE OF ALEXANDER, MERLOT-SYRAH-GRENACHE, 2004: Deep royal-purple, full-bodied, with soft tannins integrating nicely and showing an appealing array of plum, cassis and orange peel fruits, those backed up by Mediterranean herbs. Lingers nicely on the palate. Drink now–2010. Score 90.

THE WINE OF ALEXANDER, ROSÉ, 2005: Made entirely from Grenache grapes, this deep pink towards ruby wine shows light to medium body, crisp acidity and an array of tutti-frutti aromas and flavors, including bananas, raspberries, strawberries and chopped citrus peel. Drink up. Score 85.

THE WINE OF ALEXANDER, CHARDONNAY, LIZA, 2006: With one-dimensional citrus fruits and far too much acidity, the wine seems to have gone wrong somewhere along the way. Score 75. K

THE WINE OF ALEXANDER, CHARDONNAY, LIZA, 2005: Medium-bodied, showing an appealing oak influence. Lively, with citrus, melon, and apple aromas and flavors leading to a long finish which shows hints of figs and pie crust. Drink now. Score 85.

THE WINE OF ALEXANDER, CHARDONNAY, LIZA, 2004: Golden-straw in color, medium to full-bodied, with hints of cream and yeast. Opens with a distinct hint of pineapple that turns to figs, pears and apples, all with a spicy and pleasingly light bitter overtone. Drink up. Score 87.

THE WINE OF ALEXANDER, SAUVIGNON BLANC, LIZA, 2006: Light golden-straw in color, with appealing citrus, green apple and light herbal and floral overtones. Drink now. Score 84.

THE WINE OF ALEXANDER, SAUVIGNON BLANC, 2005: Unoaked and straw colored. Concentrated, with generous lime, citrus peel, green apple and grapefruit aromas and flavors matched by hints of herbs, honeysuckle and sweet peas on a tart and lively finish that lingers nicely. Drink up. Score 85.

Sandro

SANDRO, 2005: A medium-bodied blend of Cabernet Sauvignon and Merlot, with soft tannins and light spicy wood, opening in the glass to reveal traditional blackberry and currant fruits. Soft, round and easy to drink. Drink now–2009. Score 87.

SANDRO, 2004: Dark ruby to garnet, medium-bodied and softly tannic, this round, smooth blend of Cabernet Sauvignon and Merlot shows black and red berries, cassis and a light smoky overtone. Drink now. Score 86.

SANDRO, 2003: Medium-bodied, dark garnet in color, with soft tannins and reflecting a gentle hand with the wood, this blend of Cabernet Sauvignon and Merlot offers up currant, cranberry and red plum fruits. Soft and round. Drink up. Score 86.

Gaston

GASTON, 2004: An oak blend of 76% Merlot and 12% each of Grenache and Syrah. Dark, nearly inky-garnet in color, with intense almost jam-like cherry and berry fruits, those supported by Oriental spices. On the moderately long finish an attractive herbal-earthiness. Drink now. Score 87.

Aligote **

Established by Tsvika Fante and located on Moshav Gan Yoshiya on the central Coastal Plain, the first wines released by this winery were 800 bottles from the 2002 harvest. Production is currently 4,000 bottles annually.

ALIGOTE, CABERNET SAUVIGNON, 2005: Traditional Cabernet aromas and flavors of blackberries and currants, those matched nicely by hints of green olives, spices and espresso coffee. Drink now–2009. Score 85.

ALIGOTE, CABERNET SAUVIGNON, 2004: A blend of 92.5% Cabernet Sauvignon and 7.5% Shiraz. Medium to full-bodied, with generous soft tannins balanced nicely by toasty oak and appealing aromas and flavors of currants, wild berries and tobacco. Drink now. Score 85.

ALIGOTE, CABERNET SAUVIGNON, 2003: Dark garnet, this full-bodied red shows good balance between soft tannins and sweet vanilla from the American oak in which it was aged. Round and mouth-filling, with black currant, plum and orange peel aromas and flavors. Long and comfortable on the palate. Drink up. Score 85.

ALIGOTE, MERLOT, 2005: Dark ruby towards garnet, medium-bodied, with soft tannins. Generous cherry, berry and spice flavors with a hint of sandalwood on the finish. Drink now. Score 84.

ALIGOTE, MERLOT, 2004: Garnet towards purple, this medium-bodied blend of 90% Merlot with 5% each of Cabernet Sauvignon and Shiraz shows chunky country-style tannins balanced nicely by spicy wood and appealing blackberry and black cherry aromas and flavors. Drink now. Score 85.

ALIGOTE, MERLOT, 2003: This deep garnet, medium-bodied, softly tannic wine shows appealing berry, black cherry and orange peel aromas and flavors as well as light overlays of bittersweet chocolate and freshly picked tarragon on the long finish. Drink now. Score 85.

ALIGOTE, SANGIOVESE, 2005: Ruby towards purple, medium-bodied, with appealing black cherry, blackberry and spicy aromas and flavors. Not complex but a good quaffer. Drink now. Score 84.

ALIGOTE, SANGIOVESE, 2004: An almost watery ruby in color and equally watery on the palate, with only a few simple berry, cherry and tutti-frutti flavors. Drink up. Score 78.

Alon **

Located on Moshav Alonei Aba, north of Haifa, this small winery recently changed hands. Under former owner Gal Segev the winery produced 3,000 bottles from the 2003 vintage from Cabernet Sauvignon and Merlot grapes. No wines were released from the 2004 vintage but new owner-winemaker  Chaim Cachala released about 4,000 bottles from the 2005 vintage and 5,000 from the 2006 vintage, primarily from Tempranillo, Cabernet Franc, Carignan, Petit Verdot and Petite Sirah grapes, grown mostly in the Galilee and Jezreel Valley.

ALON, CABERNET SAUVIGNON, 2006: Dark garnet towards purple, medium to full-bodied, with spices and vanilla from the wood in which it aged. Opens on the palate to reveal blackberry and blueberry fruits and on the finish hints of Oriental spices. Drink from release. Tentative Score 85–87.

ALON, CABERNET SAUVIGNON, 2005: Deep royal-purple, medium to full-bodied, with soft, near-sweet tannins and spicy wood integrating nicely to show appealing black fruits on a background of Mediterranean herbs. Mouth-filling and moderately long. Drink now. Score 85.

ALON, CABERNET SAUVIGNON, 2003: Dark ruby, medium-bodied, with a somewhat woody influence but also showing cassis and berry fruits along with hints of vanilla. Firmly tannic on the finish. Drink up. Score 83.

ALON, MERLOT, 2003: Dark ruby in color, a somewhat oaky and tannic country-style wine with a few black fruits and a hint of spiciness. Drink up. Score 83.

ALON, MERLOT, 2002: Ruby towards garnet in color, this simple medium-bodied, oak-aged wine has well-integrated soft tannins and pleasant currant and berry fruits. Drink up. Score 82.

ALON, CARIGNAN, 2005: Dark garnet and aromatic, this blend of 86% Carignan and 7% each of Tempranillo and Cabernet Sauvignon shows chunky tannins that are nonetheless settling in nicely with berry, cherry and currant fruits. Somewhat musky aroma on the finish. Drink now. Score 84.

ALON, CABERNET FRANC, 2006: Deep ruby towards garnet, medium to full-bodied, with silky smooth tannins and gentle spicy wood opening to show raspberry, cassis and light herbal aromas and flavors. Best 2009–2011. Tentative Score 86–88.

ALON, PETIT VERDOT, 2005: Royal-purple, medium-bodied, with soft tannins and somewhat generous smoke as it first opens, that yields to reveal berry and cherry fruits together with a hint of licorice. Drink now. Score 84.

ALON, TEMPRANILLO, 2005: Blended with 15% Petite Sirah, this ruby-towards-garnet, medium-bodied red shows soft tannins, gentle spiciness and appealing plum and herbal notes. Drink now–2009. Score 85.

ALON, PETITE SIRAH, 2005: A pleasant little country-style wine, coarse and tannic but opening to reveal generous red plum and blueberry fruits. Drink now–2009. Score 84.

Alona ***

Founded in 2001 by the Azoulay and Rabau families on Givat Nili, not far from the city of Zichron Ya'akov, the vineyards of this small winery spread on the slopes above Nachal Taninim and contain Cabernet Sauvignon and Merlot grapes. Current production is about 8,000 bottles annually.

ALONA, CABERNET SAUVIGNON, 2005: Dark garnet, full-bodied, with caressing soft tannins and spicy oak, those in good balance with fresh blackberry and currant aromas and flavors. On the finish a touch of cedar. Drink now–2010. Score 88.

ALONA, CABERNET SAUVIGNON, 2004: Dark, almost impenetrable garnet, full-bodied, with red plum, currant and citrus peel in fine harmony with spicy wood, soft tannins and hints of sweet licorice and milk chocolate. Long and generous. Drink now–2009. Score 89.

ALONA, MERLOT, 2005: Deep garnet towards royal-purple, medium to full-bodied, with appealing aromas and flavors of spicy plums and currants. Graceful and elegant. Drink now–2010. Score 90.

ALONA, MERLOT, 2004: Dark royal-purple in color, medium to full-bodied, with good concentration and density. Showing black currant, berry, vanilla and creamy notes. Lingers nicely with hints of mocha and cream on the finish. Drink now–2010. Score 90.

Amphorae ✴✴✴✴

Set in the green and luxuriant mouth of a long dormant volcano on the western slopes of Mount Carmel, the winery is situated on the Makura Ranch. It draws on grapes from some of the best vineyards of the Golan Heights and the Upper Galilee.

Production from the 2000 vintage was 23,000 bottles, from the 2003 vintage about 55,000 and in 2004 and 2005, 70,000 bottles. In 2005 the winery moved into a new state-of-the-art winery and target production is 80,000–100,000 bottles annually. Because the harvest of 2006 was particularly low in yield, the winery released only 40,000 bottles from that year.

Top-of-the-line series is Amphorae with a Reserve wine issued in selected years; second wines are under the Rhyton label. Both of these series are age-worthy. Wines in the Med.Red and Med.Blend series are meant for relatively early drinking.

Amphorae is the Greek term for tall, double-handled jugs with narrow necks and bases, often made of clay, that were used by the Greeks and later by the Romans for storing and shipping wine. The original rhyton was an ancient Greek cup, most often shaped like a drinking horn.

Amphorae Reserve

Cabernet Sauvignon 2001 **Amphorae**vineyard

AMPHORAE, CABERNET SAUVIGNON, RESERVE, 2005: Still in embryonic form but already revealing comfortably yielding firm tannins and, on the nose and palate, generous black fruits. Shows the potential for true elegance and great length. Best 2009–2012. Tentative Score 92–94.

AMPHORAE, CABERNET SAUVIGNON, RESERVE, 2000: Deep garnet-red, remarkably rich, complex and aromatic. Excellent balance, with tiers of currant, plum, Mediterranean herbs and sweet oak coming to a long finish. A wine worthy of cellaring. Drink now–2014. Score 93.

AMPHORAE, RESERVE, 2003: A blend of Cabernet Sauvignon, Merlot and Cabernet Franc (70%, 15% and 15% respectively). Dark royal-purple, deeply aromatic and full-bodied, with caressing tannins. On the nose and palate a complex array of currant, blackberry, blueberry, cedar and herbs with hints of cola on the long, generous finish. Best 2009–2014. Score 93.

Amphorae

AMPHORAE, CABERNET SAUVIGNON, 2006: Medium to full-bodied, with soft tannins and gentle wood, a supple and velvety wine offering black currant, blackberry and raspberry fruits, those supported nicely by hints of tobacco and anise. Tightly wound now but with time will show complexity and elegance. Best 2009–2013. Tentative Score 92–94.

AMPHORAE, CABERNET SAUVIGNON, 2005: Deep garnet, full-bodied, with mouth-coating near-sweet tannins well balanced by cedary oak. Concentrated and intense but elegant and balanced, showing generous aromas and flavors of spicy plums, currants and mocha. A long, rich mineral and sage finish. Drink now–2010. Score 90.

AMPHORAE, CABERNET SAUVIGNON, 2004: Deeply aromatic, full-bodied with firm tannins, showing fine balance and structure. On the nose and palate blackberries, currants, and black cherries, those off-set by mocha, vanilla and spicy oak. Drink now–2010. Score 91.

AMPHORAE, CABERNET SAUVIGNON, 2003: Garnet to adobe-brick red, this full-bodied, firmly tannic but harmonious wine shows fine balance and structure. On the nose and palate currant, black cherry, spices, with hints of mint chocolate on the long finish. Drink now–2011. Score 91.

AMPHORAE, CABERNET SAUVIGNON, 2002: An appealing medium to full-bodied wine with generous fruits well balanced by oak and moderate tannins; lacks the concentration or structure for long-term cellaring. Drink up. Score 88.

AMPHORAE, CABERNET SAUVIGNON, 2001: Delicious Cabernet with a small amount of Syrah blended in. This full-bodied, deep garnet toward royal-purple wine shows a tempting array of black currant and plum fruits, those backed up nicely by generous hints of spices and mocha, wood and fruits, with a long and luxurious finish. Drink now. Score 90.

AMPHORAE, CABERNET SAUVIGNON, 2000: Full-bodied, intense and powerful, with its firm tannins nicely integrated, this dark and deep wine is showing currant, blackberry and plum aromas and flavors, all with generous overlays of pepper and chocolate. Drink now. Score 91.

AMPHORAE, MERLOT, ORGANIC, 2006: From the organic vineyard at Makura Ranch, this dark ruby-red and deeply aromatic wine is made entirely according to organic principles, Medium to full-bodied, showing still gripping tannins and a fine balance and structure that bode well for the future. On the nose and palate near-sweet black cherries, blackberries and currant fruits, those showing appealing hints of spices and spring flowers. Plush, open-textured and long. Best 2009–2012. Tentative Score 91–93.

AMPHORAE, MERLOT, 2006: Dark ruby towards garnet, medium to full-bodied, with firm tannins and a gentle hand with the wood. Seductive, showing ripe blackberry, currant and wild berries, those with overlays of dark chocolate and freshly ground coffee. Complex and concentrated but showing elegance and length. Best 2009–2013. Tentative Score 90–92.

AMPHORAE, MERLOT, ORGANIC, 2005: Made from organically raised Merlot grapes, aged in French oak for 12 months and bottled unfiltered, this deep, almost inky garnet wine shows full-body and generous but soft tannins. Blueberries on the nose, then opening in the glass to reveal aromas and flavors of blackberries, blueberries and ripe plums, those on a spicy and lightly earthy-herbal background. Drink now–2011. Score 90.

AMPHORAE, MERLOT, 2005: Firm, with chewy tannins matched by spicy wood, both of those integrating nicely and revealing currant, black cherry, vanilla bean and near-sweet cedarwood. Tight, focused, rich and long. Best 2009–2013. Score 92.

AMPHORAE, MERLOT, 2004: Dark royal-purple and dense, with firm and chewy tannins; generous wood well balanced by ripe black cherry, plum, raspberry and briar flavors, all lingering nicely on the palate. Drink now–2012. Score 90.

AMPHORAE, MERLOT, 2003: Dark garnet towards royal-purple, medium to full-bodied, this outstanding 100% Merlot-based wine offers up aromas and flavors of black and red cherries, cassis and cedarwood, all with long-lingering spicy overtones. Drink now–2010. Score 91.

AMPHORAE, MERLOT, 2002: Supple and fruity, with soft tannins well balanced by gentle oak and appealing berry, cassis and plum fruits. Not complex and not for further cellaring. Drink up. Score 86.

AMPHORAE, MERLOT, 2001: Medium to full-bodied, with firm tannins integrating nicely, and with tempting berries, plums, herbs and light spices. Aromatic, rich and with a long ripe finish, clearly reflecting its Mediterranean *terroir*. Drink now. Score 90.

AMPHORAE, SYRAH, 2006: Dark cherry-red, medium to full-bodied, with rich, ripe tannins and generous peppery and leathery overlays highlighting blackberry, boysenberry and red plum fruits. Destined for length, breadth and elegance. Best 2009–2013. Tentative Score 91-93.

AMPHORAE, SYRAH, 2005: Developing in American and French oak barrels, this wine is full-bodied, with softly caressing tannins. Round, ripe and generous, with red plums, raspberries, cherry and exotic spices supported nicely by hints of black pepper, vanilla and citrus peel. Best 2009–2015. Tentative Score 92–94.

AMPHORAE, SYRAH, 2004: Full-bodied, with firm and well-structured tannins integrating nicely and showing a core of leather, spicy wood and earthiness that highlight rich currant, wild berry, anise and lightly beefy flavors. On the long finish generous hints of espresso coffee, violets and toffee. Destined for elegance. Drink now–2012. Score 91.

AMPHORAE, SYRAH, 2003: Medium to full-bodied, a deep almost inky-purple in color, with tempting plums and violets from the first sip, those yielding to smoke, chocolate and earthy-herbal aromas and flavors. Long and intriguing. Drink now–2009. Score 91.

AMPHORAE, CABERNET FRANC, 2004: Deep garnet with bright raspberry and plum flavors, this dark, rich and plush wine shows thick, earthy tannins and gamy currant and cedarwood aromas and flavors. Perhaps not elegant but certainly powerful and complex. Drink now–2012. Score 90.

AMPHORAE, CABERNET SAUVIGNON-MERLOT, 2002: Ripe and complex, with layers of black cherry, plum, berry and spices, and with hints of herbs and black olives that come in near the finish, this medium to full-bodied wine offers well-integrated tannins, a smooth texture and a moderately long fruity finish. Drink up. Score 90.

AMPHORAE, ROSÉ, ORGANIC, 2006: Made entirely from organically raised Merlot grapes, with six hours of skin contact and a minimal addition of sulfites. Pink towards light ruby in color, medium-bodied, with an appealing array of raspberry, blueberry and cassis fruits, those on a crisply dry, mineral rich background. Round, generous and refreshing with just the right hints of complexity. Drink now. Score 88.

AMPHORAE, ROSÉ DE MERLOT, 2005: Light to medium-bodied, with the color of the first reddish-orange blush that a ripe peach attains, this rosé shows as dry, crisp and fresh as one could wish. Pleasant and understated, with hints of black cherries, licorice and spices. Hardly a typical rosé. Drink up. Score 88.

AMPHORAE, CHARDONNAY, 2006: Golden-straw in color, medium to full-bodied, reflecting its eight months in used *barriques* with a light touch of spicy oak and plenty of natural acidity to keep it lively. On the nose and palate tempting guava, passion fruit and citrus and behind those, hints of minerals. A wine that is simultaneously complex and 'easy'. Drink now–2009. Score 90.

AMPHORAE, CHARDONNAY, 2005: Golden-straw in color, with harmony and elegance rather than power, this gently oaked white shows good acidity and gentle minerality along with aromas and flavors of pear, apple and kiwi fruits, all leading to a long, fresh finish. Drink now. Score 90.

AMPHORAE, CHARDONNAY, 2003: Deep gold in color with orange reflections, this medium to full-bodied white reflects its 12 months in *barriques* with complex, rich and concentrated aromas and flavors of figs, mandarin oranges, nectarines and spicy nuts. Light buttery-oak shadings on the finish add understated elegance. Drink now. Score 91.

AMPHORAE, VIOGNIER, 2006: Light golden-straw in color, medium-bodied, with peach, nectarine, pear and mineral aromas and flavors balanced by flinty minerals and hints of almonds that run through to the long and vibrant finish. Drink now–2010. Score 90.

AMPHORAE, VIOGNIER, 2005: Unoaked and with no malolactic fermentation, this medium-bodied lively wine offers crisp tropical fruits, peaches, melons and a floral accent. Lightly spicy, aromatic, generous and delicious. Drink now. Score 89.

Rhyton

Rhyton Red 2001 Amphorae$\vee$ineyard

RHYTON, 2005: Garnet-red, a medium to full-bodied blend of Cabernet, Merlot and Syrah showing soft tannins integrating nicely and offering blackberry, black cherry and currant fruits. Look for hints of chocolate and spices on the generous finish. Drink from release–2009. Tentative Score 87–89.

RHYTON, 2004: Dark garnet, medium to full-bodied, with distinctly Provencal aromas and flavors of wild berries and cassis matched by hints of fresh mushrooms and spices. A few sharp edges to this blend of Cabernet, Merlot and Syrah, but those adding to the wine's country-style charm. Drink now–2009. Score 88.

RHYTON, 2003: This medium to full-bodied blend of 81% Cabernet Sauvignon, 10% Merlot and 9% Syrah shows firm tannins integrating well with generous but gentle oak; revealing raspberries, cherry and cassis fruits along with white chocolate, a hint of spices and, on the moderately long finish, a tantalizing hint of freshly turned earth. Drink now. Score 89.

RHYTON, 2002: Developed in *barriques* for 18 months, this well-balanced, round and generous blend of Cabernet Sauvignon, Merlot and Petit Sirah shows soft tannins, gentle wood and near-sweet currant and berry aromas and flavors, those with an appealing hint of spiciness. Drink up. Score 88.

Med.Blend

MED.BLEND, 2004: A first release and not to be confused with the Red.Med blend. This blend of 56% Cabernet Sauvignon and 22% each of Syrah and Merlot, was aged in French oak for 14 months and is showing medium to full-bodied, with soft, gently mouth-coating tannins and a well-measured hand with spicy oak. On first attack red currants and wild strawberries, those leading to bitter cherries, tobacco and appealing herbal overtones. On the long finish tantalizing hints of bay and anise. A wine that demands a fine T-bone, Porterhouse or sirloin steak. Drink now–2010. Score 90.

Med.Red

MED.RED, 2005: Deep ruby towards garnet, medium-bodied, this blend of Cabernet Sauvignon and Shiraz shows soft tannins and a judicious hand with spicy wood; opens in the glass to reveal appealing berry, currant and black cherry fruits. Drink now–2009. Score 88.

MED.RED, 2004: Dark garnet towards royal-purple and medium-bodied, this blend of Cabernet Sauvignon, Merlot and Syrah shows silky, well-integrating tannins, in fine balance with gentle spicy wood and black fruits. Soft, round and delicious. Drink now. Score 88.

MED.RED, 2003: An oak-aged blend of 97% Cabernet Sauvignon and 3% Shiraz. Deep garnet-red, medium-bodied, with spicy oak and soft tannins backed up nicely by black currant and black cherry fruits. Drink now. Score 88.

Amram's *

Founded in 2001 on Moshav Ramot Naftali in the Upper Galilee
by grape grower Amram Azulai
and his son Ehud, the team has
vineyards of Cabernet, Merlot,
Shiraz and Sangiovese grapes in
Emek Kadesh. Production from
2004 was 2,800 bottles and projected release from the 2006 vintage is about 8,000 bottles. The
winery releases two series—the
oak-aged Bresheit (literally 'Genesis') and the unoaked Amram's.

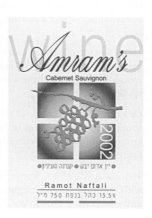

Bresheit

BRESHEIT, CABERNET SAUVIGNON, 2005: Dark but not completely
clear garnet in color, partly oak-aged, this soft and round but quite
simple wine reveals a not-fully-wanted hint of sweetness on the berry
and currant fruits. Drink now. Score 79.

BRESHEIT, CABERNET SAUVIGNON, 2004: With medicinal and
iodine aromas, almost searing tannins and with a distinctly alcoholic
sting, it is difficult to find any fruit in this wine. Score 55.

BRESHEIT, MERLOT, 2005: Dark garnet towards purple in color,
medium-bodied, with soft tannins and primarily berry and black
cherry fruits. Lacks complexity but an acceptable entry-level wine.
Drink now. Score 80.

BRESHEIT, CABERNET SAUVIGNON-SHIRAZ, 2005: Dark purple,
medium-bodied, with chunky tannins and a generous hand with spicy
wood, this blend of 75% Cabernet and 25% Shiraz shows plum and berry
fruits. Drink now. Score 80.

Amram's

AMRAM'S, CABERNET SAUVIGNON, 2005: Dark garnet in color but lacking clarity, this medium to full-bodied wine shows skimpy black fruits hidden under a far too generous layer of sweetness. Drink up. Score 75.

AMRAM'S, CABERNET SAUVIGNON, 2004: Ruby towards garnet, medium-bodied, with near-sweet tannins and hints of wood, soft and round, showing straightforward berry, cherry and currant fruits. Drink up. Score 83.

AMRAM'S, CABERNET SAUVIGNON, 2003: Medium-dark garnet towards purple, medium to full-bodied, with soft tannins; showing aromas and flavors of currants and spices. Past its peak. Drink up. Score 78.

AMRAM'S, MERLOT, 2005: Garnet towards purple, medium-bodied, with soft tannins and raspberry and red currant fruits, a too simple entry-level wine. Drink now. Score 79.

AMRAM'S, MERLOT, 2004: Light to medium-bodied, with soft, almost unfelt tannins and basic berry, cherry aromas and flavors. Drink up. Score 80.

AMRAM'S, CABERNET SAUVIGNON-MERLOT, 2005: A dark purple blend of 60% Cabernet Sauvignon and 40% Merlot. Medium-bodied, with soft tannins and primarily blueberry aromas and flavors. An acceptable entry-level wine. Drink up. Score 80.

AMRAM'S, CABERNET SAUVIGNON-SHIRAZ, 2005: Medium-dark garnet, medium-bodied, with soft tannins. Shows simple berry, cherry fruits on a somewhat overly acidic background. Drink up. Score 78.

AMRAM'S, CABERNET SAUVIGNON-SHIRAZ, 2004: Dark and somewhat cloudy garnet towards brick red in color, medium-bodied, with chunky tannins. A country-style wine with basic black fruits. Drink up. Score 78.

AMRAM'S, CABERNET SAUVIGNON-SHIRAZ, 2003: Dark, somewhat dusty garnet, medium-bodied, with more of an herbal, vegetal character than a fruity one. Drink up. Score 70.

AMRAM'S, CABERNET SAUVIGNON-SANGIOVESE, 2003: Dark brick-red, showing clearing at the rim and hinting of premature aging, with primarily berry fruits now somewhat buried under rising earthy aromas and flavors. Drink up. Score 77.

Anatot **

Founded in 1998 by Aharon Helfgot and Arnon Erez, the winery is located in Anatot, a community north of Jerusalem, and draws on grapes primarily from vineyards in the Lachish and Shiloh regions. Current annual production is 17,500 oak-aged bottles from Cabernet Sauvignon and Merlot grapes. Wines are produced in two series, Anatot and Notera.

Anatot

ANATOT, CABERNET SAUVIGNON, 2005: Medium to full-bodied, the wine has soft tannins, smoky oak and gripping acidity. Opens slowly, showing black fruits, spices, and on the finish, ripe plums. Drink from release. Score 85.

ANATOT, CABERNET SAUVIGNON, 2004: Dark ruby towards purple, medium-bodied, with generous oak and chunky tannins. Opens in the glass to reveal berry, black cherry and currant fruits. Drink now. Score 84.

ANATOT, CABERNET SAUVIGNON, 2003: Dark garnet, medium to full-bodied, with chunky, country-style tannins and generous smoky oak yielding in the glass to reveal currant and plum fruits. Drink up. Score 84.

ANATOT, MERLOT, 2004: Medium-bodied, dark garnet towards purple in color, with firm tannins, spicy oak and aromas and flavors of plums and berries. An entry-level wine. Drink now. Score 80.

ANATOT, MERLOT, 2003: Dark royal-purple in color, with firm tannins, dusty oak and an underlying earthiness. Shows an appealing hint of black fruits on the nose and palate. Drink up. Score 76.

ANATOT, SHIRAZ, 2005: Deep royal-purple in color, medium-bodied, with soft tannins and spicy wood integrating nicely. Aromas and flavors of plums, berries and hints of tar and licorice. Drink now. Score 84.

Notera

NOTERA, 2004: As always, a blend of 60% Merlot and 40% Cabernet Sauvignon. Medium-bodied with generous spicy oak and somewhat chunky tannins. Showing a few blackberry and currant fruits. Drink now. Score 80.

NOTERA, 2003: A medium to full-bodied blend of 60% Merlot and 40% Cabernet Sauvignon. Reflects its 24 months in oak with very generous smoky wood and coarse tannins that tend to hide the berry-cherry fruits. Drink up. Score 80.

Assaf ★★★★

Founded in 2004 by Assaf Kedem, who was formerly a partner in the Bazelet Hagolan Winery, the winery is located in the village of Kidmat Tzvi on the Golan Heights. Draws on its own vineyards, those containing Cabernet Sauvignon, Cabernet Franc, Shiraz, Zinfandel, Pinotage and Sauvignon Blanc grapes. Production from the 2004 vintage was 11,000 bottles and from 2006, 22,000 bottles. The same wines, bottled under the Lili label, are meant entirely for export.

ASSAF, CABERNET SAUVIGNON, 2006: Oak-aged for 8 months, dark purple in color, with still firm tannins, and showing fine balance and structure that bode well for the future. On the nose and palate currants, blackberries, vanilla, dusky herbs and a generously meaty overlay that rises on the long finish. Best 2009–2013. Score 90.

ASSAF, CABERNET SAUVIGNON, 2005: Blended with 7% of Cabernet Franc, this medium to full-bodied, softly tannic, dark garnet-towards-royal-purple wine shows fine balance and structure. Seductive, rich and supple, with lush raspberry, blackberry and currant fruits supported nicely by vanilla and, on the long finish, the tannins rising again. Drink now–2011. Score 90.

ASSAF, CABERNET SAUVIGNON, RESERVE, 2004: Garnet towards deep purple, medium to full-bodied, this blend of 85% Cabernet Sauvignon and 15% Cabernet Franc was aged in partly French, partly American *barriques* for 12 months. Good balance between mouth-coating tannins, vanilla-tinged spicy oak, and acidity. On the palate wild berries, red currants and a light but appealing mineral hint, all lingering nicely. Drink now–2009. Score 90.

ASSAF, SHIRAZ, 2006: Thoroughly modern, this dark garnet-towards-royal-purple wine has fine balance between spicy wood, acidity and plum and blackberry fruits. Concentrated and intense but settling down to an elegant roundness and a long, mouth-filling finish. Drink from release–2011. Tentative Score 90–92.

ASSAF, CABERNET FRANC, ROSÉ, 2005: Made entirely from Cabernet Franc grapes, with skin contact limited to seven hours, this medium-bodied, rose-petal pink wine offers up generous raspberry, strawberry and black cherry fruits, those on a rich mineral background, all with just enough acidity to keep it lively. Drink now. Score 88.

ASSAF, SAUVIGNON BLANC, 2005: Light golden-straw in color, medium-bodied, with lively citrus and grassy aromas and flavors. Somewhat one dimensional but an appealing quaffer. Drink up. Score 86.

Avidan ✦✦✦

Founded in 2000 by Shlomo and Tsina Avidan, this boutique winery is located on Kibbutz Eyal in the Sharon region and relies on Chardonnay, Shiraz, Cabernet Sauvignon, Petite Sirah and Merlot grapes selected from various vineyards in the Upper Galilee, and is currently producing about 15,000 bottles annually. Wines are released in three series—the age-worthy Reserves, the varietal Avidan, and the Blend des Noirs, meant for earlier consumption.

Reserve

RESERVE, CABERNET SAUVIGNON, 2006: Deep royal-purple, medium to full-bodied, with soft, mouth-coating tannins and generous black fruits supported by earthy minerals. In time it will develop intriguing tobacco and chocolate aromas and flavors. Generous fruits rise on the long finish. Drink from release–2011. Tentative Score 88–90.

RESERVE, CABERNET SAUVIGNON, 2005: Oak-aged for 16 months, and blended with 15% of Merlot, this full-bodied red shows traditional blackberry and black currant aromas and flavors, but is bold for its firm tannins and distinctive peppery and anise overtones which lead to a long and mouth-filling finish. Drink now–2012. Score 91.

RESERVE, CABERNET SAUVIGNON, 2004: Dark garnet, medium to full-bodied, with soft tannins, this blend of 85% Cabernet Sauvignon and 15% Merlot spent 16 months in oak. Wild berry and black currant fruits on the nose and palate, with a hint of spiciness on a moderately long finish. Drink now–2009. Score 89.

RESERVE, SHIRAZ, 2006: Almost impenetrably deep garnet in color, and so dense and full-bodied that it brings to mind a syrupy consistency, this wine nonetheless unfolds on the palate to reveal soft tannins, rich blackberries, dark plums and peppery spices, along with overall fine balance. Long and generous. Drink from release–2011. Tentative Score 88–90.

RESERVE, SHIRAZ, 2005: Made from an Australian clone but with a distinctly Rhome nose and palate. Developed for 16 months in French oak, it shows a generous mouthful of blackberry, blueberry, plum and cherry fruits, those overlaid nicely by hints of leather, earth and Oriental spices that go on to a long finish. Drink now–2011. Score 90.

Avidan

AVIDAN, CABERNET SAUVIGNON, 2005: Still in embryonic form but already showing firm tannins well balanced by spicy wood, herbaceousness and currant and plum fruits. Firm but near-elegant. Drink now–2009. Score 87.

AVIDAN, CABERNET SAUVIGNON, 2004: Aged in oak for ten months, this medium-bodied, softly tannic, dark garnet blend of 85% Cabernet Sauvignon, 10% Merlot and 5% Shiraz offers up jammy plum and red and black berry flavors and aromas. Drink now. Score 85.

AVIDAN, CABERNET SAUVIGNON, 2003: Dark ruby towards garnet, this medium-bodied blend of Cabernet Sauvignon and Merlot shows generous oak and firm tannins, those matched nicely by currant, berry and black cherry fruits. Drink now. Score 86.

AVIDAN, CABERNET SAUVIGNON, 2002: Deep garnet in color, this blend of 85% Cabernet Sauvignon and 15% Merlot spent 18 months in oak. Ripe and plummy, with fleshy tannins and medium body backed up by supple cherry, berry and spice notes and a nice fruity finish. Drink up. Score 86.

AVIDAN, MERLOT, 2005: Soft and round, with silky tannins that allow berry, black cherry and currant notes to make themselves felt on a background of spicy cedar. Drink now. Score 86.

AVIDAN, SHIRAZ, 2005: Full-bodied but not dense, a rich, polished and thoroughly modern wine, with generous plum and blackberry fruits backed up nicely by dark chocolate, pepper and hints of licorice. Drink from release. Tentative Score 89–91.

AVIDAN, SHIRAZ, LIMITED EDITION, 2004: Dark garnet and medium-bodied, this oaked, unfiltered wine shows good balance between soft tannins, spicy oak, and berry, currant and cassis aromas and flavors. Moderately long. Drink now. Score 86.

AVIDAN, SHIRAZ, 2003: Medium-dark ruby, medium to full-bodied, with good balance between soft tannins, wood, and plum, cherry and earthy aromas and flavors. On the moderately long finish look for a hint of leather. Drink now. Score 86.

AVIDAN, PETITE SIRAH, 2006: Deep garnet, full-bodied, with ripe and supple tannins. Opens with a mint-like nose, going on to plums, blueberries and huckleberry fruits, all backed up by light hints of spices and grilled meat. Drink from release–2011. Tentative Score 88–90.

AVIDAN, PETITE SIRAH, 2005: Blended with a small amount of Shiraz, this deep garnet, full-bodied wine shows firm tannins, those in fine balance with spicy wood and plum, currant and berry fruits. Drink now. Score 87.

AVIDAN, CHARDONNAY, PETITE SOLEIL, 2006: Made from late-harvested Chardonnay grapes, with a nice hint of wood from six months of aging in Burgundy-style barrels; showing citrus, tropical and crème brulee aromas and flavors. Intentionally off-dry but lively, and with just enough complexity. Drink now–2009. Score 87.

AVIDAN, CHARDONNAY, PETITE SOLEIL, 2004: Deep gold in color, reflecting six months in Burgundy style oak barrels. With gentle smoky wood and spices, those overlaying tropical fruits, citrus peel and a light herbal essence. Full-bodied, with a near crème-fraiche finish. Drink now. Score 88.

AVIDAN, RUBY, N.V.: A brandy-reinforced red wine, one of the few worthwhile red dessert wines made in Israel today. Dark ruby in color, rich and complex, loaded with spices, walnut, nutmeg and espresso coffee on raspberry and cassis fruits. Smooth, well balanced, with no syrupy sensation . Drink from release. Tentative Score 88–90.

AVIDAN, GOLD, N.V.: A white dessert wine based on Chardonnay grapes, and reinforced with brandy to a 17% alcohol level. Generous maple syrup sweetness set off nicely by spices, orange peel and an appealing floral hint that lingers nicely. Not complex but enjoyable. Drink from release. Tentative Score 86–88.

Blend des Noirs

BLEND DES NOIRS, MERLOT-CABERNET-SHIRAZ, 2005: Oak-aged for ten months, dark garnet towards royal-purple in color, this blend

(50%, 35% and 15% respectively as listed on the label) shows medium to full-bodied, with firm, almost gripping tannins, those opening to reveal aromas and flavors of blackberries, currants and espresso coffee, all leading to a medium-long near-sweet finish. Drink now. Score 86.

BLEND DES NOIRS, GRENACHE-PETITE SIRAH-MERLOT, 2005: A blend of equal amounts of Grenache, Petit Sirah and Merlot, each oak-aged separately for ten months. Medium to full-bodied, dark garnet, with tannins now integrating nicely and showing spicy wood, an appealing array of currant, plum and berry fruits, those supported by hints of tobacco and saddle leather. Drink now. Score 87.

BLEND DES NOIRS, 2004: Dark cherry-red, this medium-bodied blend of 70% Shiraz and 30% Merlot spent ten months in oak. Fresh, fruity and aromatic, with plum and spicy wood aromas and flavors. Drink now. Score 85.

Bar **

Established in 2002 by Ilan Bar in the town of Binyamina in the Sharon area and drawing largely on grapes from the surrounding vineyards, this family-owned winery produces Cabernet Sauvignon, Merlot, Carignan, Sauvignon Blanc and Chardonnay wines as well as Jonathan Red, a blend of Merlot and Cabernet. The winery is currently producing about 4,500 bottles annually.

BAR, CABERNET SAUVIGNON, 2005: Ruby towards garnet, medium-bodied, with gripping tannins and spicy wood opening to reveal not-overly-generous red and black berry fruits, this wine is somewhat one dimensional. Drink now. Score 82.

BAR, CABERNET SAUVIGNON, 2004: Dark ruby, medium-bodied, with generous smoky wood and firm tannins hiding the black fruits that struggle to make themselves felt. Drink now. Score 83.

BAR, CABERNET SAUVIGNON, 2003: Medium-bodied, dark garnet in color, with soft tannins integrating nicely with aromas and flavors of spicy wood, black currant, plum and oriental spices. Drink now. Score 85.

BAR, CABERNET SAUVIGNON, 2002: Soft and round, medium-bodied, with soft, well-integrated tannins, the wine offers appealing currant and berry flavors. Drink now. Score 85.

BAR, MERLOT, 2002: Soft and round with forward black cherry, raspberry and herbal aromas and flavors. Soft tannins and an earthy-tobacco and smoky wood finish to add charm. Drink up. Score 86.

BAR, JONATHAN RED, 2005: Medium-bodied, garnet in color, with chunky, country-style tannins. On the nose and palate berries, black cherries and hints of spices. A good quaffer. Drink now. Score 84.

BAR, JONATHAN RED, 2004: A country-style, medium-bodied blend of Merlot and Cabernet Sauvignon with chunky tannins and spicy cedar. Aromas and flavors of wild berries, cassis liqueur and herbaceousness. Drink up. Score 83.

BAR, JONATHAN RED, 2002: Aged in used oak barrels for nine months, this blend of 70% Merlot and 30% Cabernet Sauvignon shows good balance between blackberries, earthiness and spices. Medium-bodied, with chunky tannins, a pleasing country-style wine. Drink up. Score 85.

Baram **

Located on Kibbutz Baram in the Upper Galilee, this small winery released its first wines from the 2004 vintage. Winery-owned vineyards contain Cabernet Sauvignon and Merlot grapes. First release was of 1,800 bottles growing to 2,500 bottles from the 2005 and 2006 vintages.

BARAM, CABERNET SAUVIGNON, 2005: Garnet towards purple, medium-bodied, with gripping tannins and spicy wood opening to reveal berry, black cherry and fresh herbal aromas and flavors. Drink now. Score 84.

BARAM, CABERNET SAUVIGNON, 2004: Dark ruby towards garnet, medium-bodied, with generous tannins integrating nicely with appealing spicy wood and black fruits. Drink now. Score 85.

BARAM, MERLOT, 2004: Medium to full-bodied, with firm tannins, spicy wood, and straightforward wild berry and plum fruits. Drink now. Score 84.

BARAM, MERLOT, 2004: Medium-bodied, with soft tannins and smoky oak influences. Showing simple but appealing berry, red plum and spices on the nose and palate. Drink now. Score 84.

Barkai ✷✷

Headed by winemaker Itai Barkai, the winery is located on Moshav Roglit in the Ella Valley at the foothills of the Jerusalem Mountains, and relies on Cabernet Sauvignon, Merlot and Shiraz grapes from its own vineyards. Production for 2002 and 2003 was under 1,000 bottles annually and 2004 production was 2,400 bottles. A new winery is currently being constructed with a capacity for 10,000 bottles annually.

BARKAI, CABERNET SAUVIGNON-MERLOT, 2005: Garnet towards royal-purple, medium-bodied, with soft tannins. On the nose and palate berries, cherries and sweet cedarwood. Drink now. Score 84.

BARKAI, CABERNET SAUVIGNON-MERLOT, 2004: Deep ruby towards garnet, medium-bodied with generous near-sweet tannins and flavors and aromas of sur-ripe berries, cherries, and cassis. Drink now. Score 84.

BARKAI, CABERNET SAUVIGNON-MERLOT, 2003: Medium-bodied, with soft, near-sweet tannins and hyper-ripe, almost jammy berry and plum aromas and flavors. Drink up. Score 83.

BARKAI, CABERNET SAUVIGNON-MERLOT, 2002: Dark garnet-red, medium-bodied, with chunky, country-style tannins and appealing blackberry and cassis fruits. A bit earthy and alcoholic and starting to show age. Drink up. Score 83.

Barkan ***

Founded in 1990 by Shmuel Boxer and Yair Lerner with the buyout of the former wine and liqueur producer, Stock, the winery was first located in the industrial area of Barkan, not far from Kfar Saba on the Trans-Samaria Highway. In 1999 Barkan began planting extensive vineyards in Kibbutz Hulda, on the central plain near the town of Rehovot, where it now has a state-of-the-art winery. Under the supervision of winemakers Ed Salzberg, Yotam Sharon and Itay Lahat, the first of whom studied in California, the second in France, and the third in Australia, this is now the second-largest winery in Israel, with current production at 7.5–9 million bottles annually and projected growth to 10 million by 2010.

Barkan's current investment exceeds $20 million, and includes the winery, the adjoining vineyards (1500 dunams owned jointly by the winery and the *kibbutz*, making this the largest single vineyard in the country), a visitors' center currently under construction, and an underground barrel room. In addition, Barkan is now also the parent company of Segal Wines.

The winery releases varietal wines in four series: Superieur, Reserve (of which the Altitude wines may be considered a sub-label), Classic, and Domaine, the last an upgrade on what was formerly the Lachish series. In addition, the winery is currently developing a vineyard of 150 dunams (75 acres) at Mitzpe Ramon in the Negev Desert, and will release wines from there under the label Negev Project.

Superieur

SUPERIEUR, CABERNET SAUVIGNON, 2003: Dark, almost impenetrable royal-purple in color, firm and concentrated, this is one of the best ever from Barkan. Full-bodied, with gently mouth-coating tannins and a judicious hand with spicy oak, shows intense aromas and flavors of black currants, blackberries and black cherries, those complemented by hints of dates, sage and near-sweet cedarwood. A long finish bursting with minerals and black fruits. Drink now–2010. Score 91. K

SUPERIEUR, CABERNET SAUVIGNON, 2002: Full-bodied, with generous spicy oak and lively acidity. Features a core of ripe blueberry, cassis and black currant fruits, those matched nicely by overlays of spices and cocoa and, on the long finish, appealing hints of minerals and licorice. Drink now. Score 89. K

SUPERIEUR, CABERNET SAUVIGNON, 2000: Aged first in new oak and transferred later to used oak, this full-bodied and concentrated, deep garnet-towards-royal-purple wine offers up generous black currant, blackberry and chocolate aromas, all with an overlay of Mediterranean herbaceousness. Drink up. Score 87. K

SUPERIEUR, MERLOT, 2004: Medium to full-bodied, with soft tannins integrating nicely; showing smoky blackberry, berry, black cherry and cassis fruits, those on a light background of red peppers and vanilla, all leading to a long, smooth, mouth-filling finish. Drink now–2010. Score 89. K

SUPERIEUR, PINOTAGE, 2002: Full-bodied, with sur-ripe blackberry, black cherry and currant fruits, those backed up nicely by moderately firm tannins and generous spicy, meaty and herbal aromas and flavors. Deep, round and long. Drink up. Score 90. K

Reserve

RESERVE, CABERNET SAUVIGNON, 2004: Dark royal-purple in color, dense and intense, with layers of black currants, plums, raspberries and spices, those in fine tune with firm tannins. Drink now–2009. Score 89. K

RESERVE, CABERNET SAUVIGNON, 2003: Medium-bodied but with super-soft tannins and generous acidity that make the wine feel somewhat light on the palate. Black currant, plums, pepper and smoky aromas and flavors backed up by a nice mineral hint. Appealing but without great complexity. Drink now. Score 86. K

RESERVE, CABERNET SAUVIGNON, 2002: Dark garnet to royal-purple, medium to full-bodied, with good balance between wood, tannins and black currant and blackberry fruits. Look as well for light hints of spices, vanilla and earthiness, those lingering nicely. Drink now. Score 88. K

RESERVE, MERLOT, 2005: Dark garnet, medium to full-bodied, with gripping tannins on first attack which yield in the glass to reveal good balance between gentle wood and cassis, red plum and wild berry fruits complemented by hints of pepper, vanilla and chocolate. Lingers nicely on the palate. Drink now. Score 87. K

RESERVE, MERLOT, 2004: Medium-dark ruby towards garnet, full-bodied, with firm tannins. On the nose and palate, ripe, near-sweet berries, chocolate and eucalyptus coming nicely to the surface of what has the potential to be an elegant wine. Drink now–2009. Score 88. K

RESERVE, MERLOT, 2003: Medium-dark garnet, full bodied, with soft tannins and spicy oak integrating well with aromas and flavors of blackberries, currants, plums and appealing hints of mint and minerals all of which linger nicely. Drink now. Score 89. K

RESERVE, SHIRAZ, 2005: Dark purple, firm, and faithful to the Shiraz variety, this red shows oak-accented berry, cherry and licorice flavors backed up by light hints of leather and mint. Lingers nicely. Drink now. Score 87. K

RESERVE, PINOT NOIR, NEGEV PROJECT, 2003: Subdued ruby, medium-bodied, with soft, well-integrated tannins and appealing berry and black cherry fruits backed up by light herbal and earthy sensations. Drink up. Score 88. K

RESERVE, PINOT NOIR, 2002: This medium-bodied red spent ten months in small oak barrels and reflects dusty plum and berry fruits together with an appealing earthy finish. Look as well for a pleasing lightly bitter herbal sensation on the finish. Drink up. Score 88. K

RESERVE, PINOTAGE, 2004: Deep garnet, medium to full-bodied, with generous but not exaggerated wood and tannins, those yielding in the glass to reveal blackberry, black cherry and plum flavors. Good balancing acidity and a moderately long finish. Drink now. Score 88. K

RESERVE, PINOTAGE, 2003: Dark and deep, this full-bodied red shows fine balance between generous tannins, not-exaggerated wood, and tempting plum, black cherry, blueberry and chocolate aromas and flavors all lingering nicely. Drink now. Score 89. K

RESERVE, PINOTAGE, 2002: Garnet to royal-purple, this medium to full-bodied red is packed with lush raspberry, blackberry, black cherry and currant fruits, those matched nicely by sweet spices and dark chocolate. A tantalizing hint of smoked bacon on the moderately long finish. Drink up. Score 90. K

RESERVE, TEMPRANILLO, 2005: Still in its infancy but already showing deep color, a near-muscular structure and mouth-coating tannins. A generous array of ripe plum, red cherry, licorice, tobacco and prune aromas and flavors, all ending with a hint of sweet cedarwood. Drink from release. Tentative Score 90–92. K

RESERVE, CHARDONNAY, 2006: Light gold in color, one-third of this medium-bodied white was aged in oak. Shows appealing peach, melon and citrus fruits, those complemented by gentle hints of wood. Crisp, fruity and mouth-filling. Drink now. Score 87. K

RESERVE, CHARDONNAY, 2003: Golden-straw in color, medium to full-bodied and satisfyingly mouth-filling, with citrus, apple and melon fruits that blend nicely with toasty oak and vanilla. Look for a hint of cinnamon on the moderately long finish. Drink up. Score 88. K

RESERVE, CHARDONNAY, NEGEV PROJECT, 2003: Medium-bodied, this unoaked white shows a stony dryness together with white peaches, green apples and citrus fruits on an herbaceous background. Unusual and delicious. Drink up. Score 89. K

RESERVE, SAUVIGNON BLANC, 2006: With 20% of the wine aged *sur lie* in new wood for three months and the remainder developed in stainless steel, this light golden-straw, medium-bodied white shows deeply aromatic with good balancing acidity. On the nose and palate tropical fruits, citrus peel and hints of Mediterranean herbs. Drink now. Score 88. K

RESERVE, SAUVIGNON BLANC, 2005: Light-straw colored, light to medium-bodied, with crisp clean aromas and flavors of citrus and tropical fruits, all of which linger nicely on the palate. Drink up. Score 86. K

RESERVE, EMERALD RIESLING, 2006: Light to medium-bodied, with mild sweetness set off by balancing acidity and fresh aromas and flavors of pineapple, citrus fruits and dried apricots. Drink up. Score 84. K

Altitude

ALTITUDE, CABERNET SAUVIGNON, +720, 2005: Deep royal-purple, ripe, and spicy. Shows fine balance between soft tannins, wood and generous plum, blackberry and currant fruits, those with appealing hints of allspice, cloves and anise. A tantalizing hint of earthy bitterness comes in on the long finish. Best 2009–2013. Score 90. K

ALTITUDE, CABERNET SAUVIGNON, +624, 2005: Made from grapes from the vineyards at Moshav Alma in the Upper Galilee and aged in oak for 14 months, this medium to full-bodied wine is intensely deep royal-purple in color and is showing appealing but not overpowering spicy cedarwood and generous blackberry, currant and wild berry fruits on a background of spices, minerals, and a hint of Mediterranean herbs that comes in on the long finish. Best 2009–2012. Score 90. K

RESERVE, CABERNET SAUVIGNON, ALTITUDE +412, 2005: Medium-dark garnet in color, medium to full-bodied, with soft tannins and reflecting its 14 months in oak with spicy wood. On the nose and palate berries, currants and blueberries, those with nice hints of chocolate and tobacco on the finish. Drink now. Score 88. K

ALTITUDE, CABERNET SAUVIGNON, +720, 2003: Made from grapes from the Har Godrim vineyard near the Lebanese border and aged for 12 months in primarily French oak casks, this full-bodied, concentrated wine is dark garnet towards royal-purple in color, with firm tannins that are integrating nicely. Showing generous red currants and plums on a tantalizing earthy-herbal and lightly minty background. Drink now–2012. Score 90. K

RESERVE, CABERNET SAUVIGNON, ALTITUDE +624, 2003: Deep, almost impenetrable garnet in color, this medium to full-bodied wine shows on first attack firm, drying tannins and spicy oak but those receding in the glass to add a near-sweetness to the black and red fruits, oriental spices and hints of freshly picked mushrooms and green olives. Long and generous. Drink now–2010. Score 90. K

RESERVE, CABERNET SAUVIGNON, ALTITUDE +412, 2003: Made from grapes from two vineyards—85% harvested at Avnei Eitan on the Southern Golan Heights and 15% at Kerem Dishon in the Upper Galilee—this deep garnet, full-bodied wine was aged in primarily French *barriques* for 14 months. Near-sweet tannins and a gentle influence of the wood reveal generous cassis, blackberry and raspberry fruits, those backed up by spices and a light mineral overlay. Drink now–2011. Score 89. K

Classic

CLASSIC, CABERNET SAUVIGNON, 2006: Simple but pleasant. Medium-bodied, soft and round, with appealing berry and black cherry fruits. Drink now. 85. K

CLASSIC, CABERNET SAUVIGNON, 2005: Dark ruby-red, medium-bodied, with soft tannins and forward currant, berry and peppery notes. A good quaffer. Drink now. Score 85. K

CLASSIC, CABERNET SAU-VIGNON, 2004: Medium-bodied, with tannins integrating nicely and showing simple but appealing traditional Cabernet aromas and flavors of peppery currant and black cherry fruits. Drink up. Score 85. K

CLASSIC, MERLOT, 2006: Soft and round, with a bare hint of spicy wood and straightforward berry, cherry and cassis fruits. Drink now. Score 85. K

CLASSIC, MERLOT, 2005: Garnet-red, medium-bodied, with chunky country-style tannins and straightforward black cherry and currant fruits. Drink now. Score 84. K

CLASSIC, MERLOT, 2004: Medium-bodied, with soft, well-integrated tannins, this lightly oak-aged red shows just hints of smoky wood and vanilla, and on the nose and palate appealing blackberry, plum and berry fruits with a pleasant hint of herbaceousness. Drink up. Score 85. K

CLASSIC, SYRAH, 2004: Light garnet-red, light to medium-bodied, with soft tannins and some appealing plum and berry aromas and flavors backed up by a hint of spiciness. Drink up. Score 84. K

CLASSIC, SYRAH, 2003: Medium-bodied, with appealing black fruits and spices, a not-at-all complex but simple and appealing little wine. Drink now. Score 84. K

CLASSIC, PINOT NOIR, 2004: After ten months in oak this medium-dark garnet, medium-bodied, and softly tannic wine shows clean and fresh, but is somewhat skimpy on its fruits and has an unwelcome bitter-herb finish. Drink up. Score 83. K

CLASSIC, PINOTAGE, 2004: Dark ruby, medium-bodied, with soft tannins, gentle hints of spicy wood and cherry and wild berry fruits. Nothing complex here and precious little to remind us of Pinotage but an easy-to-drink wine. Drink up. Score 84. K

CLASSIC, PETITE SIRAH, 2004: Dark in color, with brooding tannins and somewhat skimpy black fruits. Somewhat flat and one dimensional. Drink up. Score 82. K

CLASSIC, SHIRAZ ROSÉ, 2006: Rose-petal pink, medium-bodied, crisply dry, with generous red berry, strawberry and citrus peel aromas and flavors, all lingering nicely on the palate. Drink now. Score 86. K

CLASSIC, CHARDONNAY, 2006: Light to medium-bodied, crisply dry, with tropical, citrus and green apple fruits on a lightly spicy and mineral background. Drink now. Score 85. K

CLASSIC, CHARDONNAY, 2005: Light straw colored, light to medium-bodied, with pineapple, green apple and tropical fruits. A simple quaffer. Drink up. Score 84. K

CLASSIC, SAUVIGNON BLANC, 2006: Without complexities but light, lively and appealing, with citrus, melon and tropical fruits. Drink now. Score 85. K

CLASSIC, SAUVIGNON BLANC, 2005: Bright and lively, this unoaked white shows lime, grapefruit and passion fruits, those opening on the finish to reveal hints of herbs and pears. Drink up. Score 85. K

CLASSIC, EMERALD RIESLING, 2006: Light golden-straw in color, off-dry and floral, with citrus and citrus peel aromas and flavors. Drink up. Score 80. K

CLASSIC, EMERALD RIESLING, 2005: Semi-dry, with not quite enough acidity to add liveliness. Floral and with tropical and citrus fruits. Drink up. Score 82. K

Domaine

DOMAINE, CABERNET SAUVIGNON, 2006: Light in body, soft and round, with light tannins and berry, black cherry and currant fruits. An entry-level quaffer. Drink now. Score 80. K

DOMAINE, CABERNET SAUVIGNON, 2005: Light and acidic and show-ing none of the true Cabernet Sauvignon traits, this light to medium-bodied wine has scarcely any tannins. Drink up. Score 79. K

DOMAINE, MERLOT, 2006: Light to medium-bodied, garnet towards purple in color, with spicy black fruits. An easy-to-drink entry-level wine. Drink now. Score 81. K

DOMAINE, MERLOT, 2005: Medium-bodied, soft and round, without complexity or depth but with appealing spicy berry and black cherry fruits. For those just switching from semi-dry whites to reds. Drink up. Score 82. K

DOMAINE, SHIRAZ, 2006: Garnet to royal-purple, medium-bodied, with tannins integrating nicely and showing berry and plum fruits on a lightly spicy background. Drink now. Score 84. K

DOMAINE, SHIRAZ, 2005: Medium-dark royal-purple in color, me-dium-bodied and with soft tannins. Plum, cassis and berry flavors on a soft and round background make this an easy-to-drink entry-level wine. Drink up. Score 84. K

DOMAINE, PETITE SIRAH, 2006: Deep royal-purple, medium-bodied, with soft but chunky tannins and appealing wild berry and spicy aromas and flavors. Drink now. Score 84. K

DOMAINE, EMERALD RIESLING, 2006: Categorized as semi-dry yet quite sweet on the palate and lacking balancing acidity. Floral and fruity but dull on the palate. Drink up. Score 78. K

Bashan ✶✶✶

Founded by Uri Rapp and Emmanuel Dassa, the winery is located on the southern Golan Heights and produces kosher wines that are fully organic from grapes raised in its own vineyards. The first releases were from the 2004 vintage, and to date are based entirely on Cabernet Sauvignon and Merlot grapes. Current releases are 10,000–15,000 bottles annually, and tentative plans are to grow to production of 50,000–100,000 bottles. Wines are released in two series, Eitan and Nave.

BASHAN, CABERNET SAUVIGNON, EITAN, 2006: The best yet from this small winery. Dark royal-purple and firmly tannic but showing fine balance and structure that bode well for the future. Well focused, with currant and plum fruits highlighted by mineral and herbal notes and, on the moderately long finish, a hint of toasty oak. Drink from release. Tentative Score 87–89. K

BASHAN, CABERNET SAUVIGNON, EITAN, 2005: Living up to its barrel-tasting promise. Medium to full-bodied, this organic wine shows good balance between sweet oak, generous yeasts and on the nose and palate appealing ripe and spicy black fruits. Drink now–2009. Score 88. K

BASHAN, CABERNET SAUVIGNON, EITAN, 2004: Oak-aged for 16 months, with vanilla and spice-laded smoky wood backed up by soft, nicely integrating tannins and forward currant and blackberry fruits. A moderately long finish with hints of chocolate and Mediterranean herbs. Drink now. Score 86. K

BASHAN, CABERNET SAUVIGNON, 2006: Dark garnet, with silky tannins integrating nicely, and showing intense plum, berry and herbal aromas and flavors. Not complex but appealing. Drink from release–2009. Tentative Score 86–88. K

BASHAN, CABERNET SAUVIGNON, 2004: Dark garnet, reflects its 16 months in oak with pepper, vanilla and soft, mouth-coating tannins. On the nose and palate generous black currant and blackberry fruits, those finishing moderately long with hints of chocolate and Mediterranean herbs. Drink now. Score 86. K

BASHAN, MERLOT, EITAN, 2006: A lovely wine. Garnet towards royal-purple, medium-bodied, with soft tannins. Showing generous berry, black cherry and milk chocolate aromas and flavors. A caressing if not long finish. Drink from release. Tentative Score 86–88. K

BASHAN, MERLOT, EITAN, 2005: Dark ruby towards garnet, reflecting its 16 months in oak with firm tannins and spicy wood, those yielding in the glass to show black fruits, eucalyptus and black olives all coming to a medium-long finish. Drink now. Score 86. K

BASHAN, MERLOT, EITAN, 2004: A dark garnet blend of 85% Merlot and 15% Cabernet Sauvignon, developed in oak for 14 months. Opens with a strong medicinal aroma, and although that fades somewhat in the glass, it remains difficult to get to the black fruits that are struggling to get through. Drink now. Score 83. K

BASHAN, CABERNET SAUVIGNON-MERLOT, NAVE, 2005: A dark garnet, medium to full-bodied blend of 70% Cabernet Sauvignon and 30% Merlot that spent 14 months in oak. Opens with a light bottle stink, but that passes quickly to reveal a clean, well-balanced wine with soft tannins and appealing currant, berry and eucalyptus aromas and flavors. Not complex but quite appealing. Drink now–2009. Score 86. K

Bazelet Hagolan ***

Founded in 1998 by Yo'av Levy and Assaf Kedem on Moshav Kidmat Tsvi in the Golan Heights, the first facility of this winery was located in a cow shed and initial production from that vintage year was 1,800 bottles. Today, entirely under the auspices of Levy, the winery is producing about 25,000 bottles annually, all from grapes grown in its own vineyards on the Golan Heights. Until 2005 the winery released only Cabernet Sauvignon wines, but will be releasing its first Merlot from the 2006 vintage.

The wines are in two series: Reserve and Bazelet Hagolan, the first aged in oak for about 20 months, the second for 8–10 months. Production has been kosher since the 2004 vintage.

Reserve

RESERVE, CABERNET SAUVIGNON, 2006: Dark garnet towards royal-purple, full-bodied and deeply aromatic, with firm tannins in fine balance with wood and fruits. On the nose and palate spicy blackberry, currant and citrus peel, and, on the long finish, a generous hint of espresso coffee. Drink from release–2010. Tentative Score 87–89. K

RESERVE, CABERNET SAUVIGNON, 2005: Rich, ripe, smooth, generous and well balanced with currant, berry and plum flavors coming together with near-sweet tannins and tempting smoky oak. Best 2009–2012. Tentative Score 87–89. K

RESERVE, CABERNET SAUVIGNON, 2004: Dark garnet towards royal-purple, full-bodied, with firm tannins in fine balance with acidity, spicy wood and fruits. On first attack, black currants and black licorice, those followed by wild berries, earthy minerals and Mediterranean herbs. Long and generous. Drink now–2011. Score 90. K

RESERVE, CABERNET SAUVIGNON, 2003: Full-bodied, with tannins on the ascendant and holding the wine back somewhat. Opens slowly to reveal currants, berries, orange peel, Oriental spices and pepper, all leading to a near-sweet and lightly oaky finish. Drink now. Score 89.

RESERVE, CABERNET SAUVIGNON, 2002: Inky-dark purple, with firm tannins and generous wood, those integrating nicely to reveal complex aromas and flavors of black currant and black cherry fruits and Mediterranean herbs. Drink up. Score 87.

RESERVE, CABERNET SAUVIGNON, 2000: Dark garnet with a bit of browning, medium to full-bodied, with tannins and wood now almost fully integrated. Still showing currant, berry and mineral aromas and flavors but with earthy and meaty flavors rising. Fully mature and somewhat past its peak. Drink up. Score 85.

Bazelet Hagolan

BAZELET HAGOLAN, CABERNET SAUVIGNON, 2006: Medium to full-bodied, with chunky country-style tannins and a hint of sweet cedarwood that runs throughout. Opens to show traditional Cabernet currant and blackberry fruits, those matched by hints of light earthiness and sweet herbs. Drink from release. Tentative Score 86–88. K

BAZELET HAGOLAN, CABERNET SAUVIGNON, 2005: Youthful garnet towards royal-purple, medium to full-bodied, with soft tannins integrating nicely and showing a pleasing array of currant, blackberry, vanilla and, on the long finish, minerals and a layer of toasty oak. Spoiled somewhat by a rising musky aroma that comes in from mid-palate. Drink now. Score 85. K

BAZELET HAGOLAN, CABERNET SAUVIGNON, 2004: Dark ruby towards garnet, medium-bodied, and reflecting its ten months in French and American *barriques* with smoky oak and soft tannins. Good balance and an appealing array of cherry, raspberry and currant fruits, those with a light spicy overlay that lingers nicely. Drink now. Score 88. K

BAZELET HAGOLAN, CABERNET SAUVIGNON, 2003: Deep garnet, medium to full-bodied with aromas and flavors of spicy cherries, currants, Mediterranean herbs and chocolate leading to a medium-long lightly spicy finish. Mouth-filling and generous. Drink now–2010. Score 89.

BAZELET HAGOLAN, CABERNET SAUVIGNON, 2002: Deep cherry-red towards garnet, medium to full-bodied, with concentrated currant, blackberry, spice and peppery notes. Good balance between wood and soft tannins and a moderately long finish. Drink now. Score 87.

BAZELET HAGOLAN, CABERNET SAUVIGNON, 2001: Dark garnet toward inky black, this full-bodied, firmly tannic wine shows rich aromas and flavors of black currants and blackberries, generous spiciness and nice earthy-olive hints, as well as a long finish. Drink up. Score 88.

BAZELET HAGOLAN, MERLOT, 2006: Youthful royal-purple, medium to full-bodied, with near-sweet tannins and delicately spicy oak highlighting plum and currant fruits. In the background light toasty bread and smoked meat that linger nicely. Drink from release. Tentative Score 85–87. K

Beit-El ✶

Established by California-trained winemaker Hillel Manne in 2001 and located in the settlement of Beit-El, north of Jerusalem, this small winery has been producing Cabernet Sauvignon and Merlot wines from its own vineyards. The winery is currently producing about 8,000 bottles annually, nearly all of those destined for export to the United States.

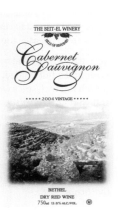

BEIT-EL, CABERNET SAUVIGNON, 2006: Full-bodied enough to be thought thick, with searing tannins and spices hiding stewed plum fruits. Tentative Score 65–67. K

BEIT-EL, CABERNET SAUVIGNON, 2005: Medium-bodied, with chunky country-style tannins and aromas and flavors of cooked fruits on a sweet, alcoholic and coarse background. Score 65. K

BEIT-EL, CABERNET SAUVIGNON, 2004: Medium to full-bodied, with coarse tannins and an unwanted touch of sweetness. Aromas and flavors of stewed plums, a foxy sensation on the palate and an alcoholic finish. Score 72. K

BEIT-EL, MERLOT, 2005: Medium-bodied, showing signs of oxidation despite its youth, and with stewed, sweet fruits on the palate. Score 70. K

BEIT-EL, MERLOT, 2004: Medium-bodied, with chunky tannins, too-generous wood influence and forward aromas and flavors of ripe black fruits. Drink up. Score 77. K

Ben Barak **

Located on Moshav Ramot Naftali in the Upper Galilee, this small winery draws on grapes from its own vineyards and is temporarily sharing facilities with Ramot Naftali winery, in which its founder Yossi Ben Barak was a former partner. Current releases are about 3,000 bottles annually.

BEN BARAK, CABERNET SAUVIGNON, 2006: Deep royal-purple, medium to full-bodied, showing still-firm tannins and dusty cedar but those yielding well to currant, blackberry and spices, all lingering nicely. Drink from release–2009. Tentative Score 86–88.

BEN BARAK, CABERNET SAUVIGNON, 2005: Dark royal-purple, medium to full-bodied, with soft, mouth-coating tannins and a judicious hand with spicy wood. Flavors and aromas of currant, blackberry and wild cherry fruits, those supported nicely by hints of herbs and vanilla. On the medium-long finish a hint of green olives. Drink from release–2009. Tentative Score 84–86.

BEN BARAK, MERLOT, 2006: Dark garnet, medium to full-bodied, with soft tannins integrating nicely and showing spicy red plum, raspberry and currant aromas and flavors. Drink from release–2009. Tentative Score 85–87.

Benhaim ✦✦✦

Founded in 1997 by the Benhaim family on Moshav Kfar Azar in the Sharon region, the winery is currently producing about 35,000 bottles annually from Cabernet Sauvignon, Merlot, Cabernet Franc, Petite Sirah, Chardonnay and Muscat grapes largely from its own vineyards. Under development are vineyards with Shiraz and Traminette and the winery also produces a Port-style wine.

With vineyards now planted on the eastern slopes of Mount Meron in the Upper Galilee, the winery is planning to expand its production to 50,000 bottles. Wines are released in three series—Grande Reserve, Reserve and Tradition—and have been kosher since the 2001 vintage.

Grande Reserve

GRANDE RESERVE, CABERNET SAUVIGNON, 2003: Reflecting more than two years in new oak with full-body, generous spicy and dusty wood, and firm tannins that tend to overpower the fruits. Given time in the glass, the wine opens to reveal currant, purple plum and chocolate, the wood rising again on the finish. Drink now. Score 86. K

GRANDE RESERVE, CABERNET SAUVIGNON, 2001: Dark garnet with distinct clearing at the rim, fully mature but still drinking nicely. The once-generous oak and firm tannins are now integrating somewhat, but still hold back the black fruits that rise only on the medium-long finish. Drink up. Score 85. K

GRANDE RESERVE, CABERNET SAUVIGNON, 2000: As in its youth, very generous spicy and smoky oak and firm tannins, those opening slowly in the glass to reveal a generous earthy, herbal and mineral personality. Drink up. Score 85.

GRANDE RESERVE, CABERNET SAUVIGNON, 1999: Some may disagree with me, but even after this seventh tasting of the wine, I still find it reflecting its 26 months in oak as a wood and tannin bomb. Now beyond its peak, those open to reveal super-ripe plum fruits. A hint of barnyard flavor sneaking in. Drink up. Score 80.

Reserve

RESERVE, CABERNET SAUVIGNON, 2006: Still in embryonic form Showing dark royal-purple towards garnet, medium to full-bodied with generous soft tannins and the onset of spicy and dusty oak. On the nose and palate black currants, berries and plums, with light herbal and green olive overtones. Round and well balanced. Drink from release–2011. Tentative Score 88–90. K

RESERVE, CABERNET SAUVIGNON, 2005: This medium to full-bodied blend of Cabernet Sauvignon, Merlot and Petite Sirah (90%, 7% and 3% respectively), with soft, mouth-coating tannins is showing generous dusty and spicy oak from its 24 months in *barriques*. Opens slowly to reveal currant and blackberry fruits, those matched nicely by generous hints of Oriental spices and leather. Drink from release–2010. Tentative Score 88–90. K

RESERVE, CABERNET SAUVIGNON, 2003: Deep ruby towards garnet in color, this blend of Cabernet Sauvignon, Merlot and Petite Sirah (88%, 7% and 5% respectively) opens with generous oak and tannins, but those integrating nicely to reveal currant, berry and purple plum fruits with appealing overlays of chocolate and vanilla. Drink now. Score 88. K

Tradition

TRADITION, CABERNET SAUVIGNON, 2004: Dark royal-purple medium to full-bodied, with firm tannins and generous wood, opening slowly to reveal skimpy currant, blackberry fruits and light herbal and spicy aromas and flavors. Drink now. Score 85. K

TRADITION, CABERNET SAUVIGNON, 2003: A blend of 88% Cabernet Sauvignon, 7% Merlot and 5% Petite Sirah, this dark garnet, medium to full-bodied wine reflects its 14 months in *barriques* with generous spicy oak and tannins settling in nicely and showing good balance with currant, blackberry, chocolate and notes of espresso coffee on the long finish. Drink now–2009. Score 89. K

TRADITION, CABERNET SAUVIGNON, 2002: A blend of 85% Cabernet Sauvignon rounded out by the addition of Merlot and Petite Sirah. Medium to full-bodied, with soft tannins and generous spicy oak matched by wild berry, cassis and on the moderate finish a hint of minty-chocolate. Drink now. Score 85. K

TRADITION, MERLOT, 2006: Medium-bodied, with soft, mouth coating tannins and spicy wood. Youthful royal-purple in color, opens on the palate to show generous wild berries, spices and a hint of choco-late. Drink from release. Tentative Score 86–88. K

TRADITION, MERLOT, 2005: Gar-net towards ruby, medium-bodied, and reflecting its 18 months in oak with firm tannins and generous sweet and spicy cedarwood. Blended with about 10% of Cabernet Franc, opens to reveal blackberry and black cherry fruits, those complemented by a hint of chocolate that lingers nicely on the medium-long finish. Drink from release–2009. Tentative Score 86–88. K

TRADITION, MERLOT, 2004: Dark garnet, medium-bodied with soft tannins integrating nicely and showing a judicious hand with spicy oak. On the nose and palate blueberries, currants and chocolate, those with a light herbal overlay. Smooth, soft and moderately long. Drink now. Score 88. K

TRADITION, MERLOT, 2003: Medium-dark garnet, medium-bodied, with generous soft tannins and wood, those in good balance with fruits and acidity. On first attack, plums and spices, those opening to reveal black cherries and cassis fruits together with hints of smoke, all leading to a pleasing hint of bitterness on the finish. Drink now. Score 87. K

TRADITION, PINOT NOIR, 2003: Cherry-red towards light garnet, medium-bodied, with soft tannins, blended with 15% of Merlot and oak-aged for 14 months. On the nose and palate berry, cherry and plum fruits. Lacking complexity. Drink up. Score 84. K

TRADITION, PETITE SIRAH-MERLOT, 2004: Oak-aged for 14 months, this blend of 60% Petite Sirah and 40% Merlot shows generous oak and firm tannins, those coming together in the glass to reveal spicy currant and berry flavors and aromas. Drink now. Score 84. K

TRADITION, CHARDONNAY, 2005: Light gold in color, reflecting its 12 months in new oak with generous spicy and vanilla-rich wood that dominates on the first attack but then opens to reveal appealing citrus, pineapple and tropical fruits. Drink up. Score 85. K

TRADITION, CHARDONNAY, 2004: Medium-bodied, light gold in color, reflecting 12 months in oak with just enough spicy wood to set off aromas and flavors of green apples and pears. Crisp and generous. Drink up. Score 85. K

Benhaim

BENHAIM, LA PETITE SIRA, 2004: Not a typographical error, the *sira* in question being a small boat, reflecting the family's love of sailing. A blend of 60% Petite Sirah and 40% Merlot, aged in oak for 12 months. Super-dark garnet, medium-bodied, showing silky tannins and generous black fruit. Drink up. Score 85. K

BENHAIM, LA PETITE SIRA, 2003: Oak-aged for 12 months, this garnet-red blend of 60% Petite Sirah and 40% Merlot offers up soft tannins that allow the currant and black cherry fruits to make themselves nicely felt. Drink up. Score 85. K

BENHAIM, MUSCAT, 2004: Treating wine made from Muscat grapes to oak-aging is an unusual practice, but this one had 12 months in large oak casks. Generous sweetness here but that balanced by acidity and showing smoky, spicy aromas and flavors of peaches, apricots and mango. An appealing dessert wine. Drink now. Score 87. K

BENHAIM, MARINA, 2004: Made from Petite Sirah grapes from the 2004 harvest, those blended with some of the same wine from the 2003 vintage, and given additional alcohol by adding grape juice which then continues the fermentation process. Bright garnet, medium-bodied, with super-soft tannins and generous but not cloying sweetness. Said to be in the style of Port but with its primarily cherry, raspberry and currant fruits, a pleasant enough and easy-to-drink red dessert wine. Drink now. Score 85. K

Ben Hanna ✳✳✳

Located on Moshav Gefen, on the plains between Beit Shemesh and Kiryat Malachi, and receiving Cabernet Sauvignon, Merlot, Grenache, Petit Verdot, Cabernet Franc,
Viognier and Argaman grapes from the Judean Mountains,
this winery is the venture of Shlomi Zadok, who is also the
winemaker at Nachshon Winery. The winery's first release
was of 2,500 bottles and production for 2006 was 3,600
bottles.

BEN HANNA, CABERNET SAUVIGNON, 2006: Aging entirely in
French oak, this medium to full-bodied wine opens with surprisingly
soft tannins but those build nicely together with spicy oak as the wine
sits on the palate. Traditional Cabernet blackberry and currant fruits
unfolding to reveal hints of mocha that linger pleasantly on the long,
fruity finish. Drink from release–2012. Tentative Score 87–89.

BEN HANNA, CABERNET SAUVIGNON, 2005: Dark royal-purple, full-
bodied, with soft tannins integrating nicely and showing fine balance
between spicy wood, acidity and fruits. On the nose and palate black
currants, blackberries, a hint of green olives and, on the long finish,
fine spices. Drink now–2011. Score 89.

BEN HANNA, CABERNET SAUVIGNON, 2003: Aged in barrels originally used for Chardonnay, this dark cherry-red, medium to full-bodied
and still firmly tannic wine shows currant, blueberry and mineral

aromas and flavors all well balanced by lightly spicy oak. Drink now. Score 85.

BEN HANNA, CABERNET SAUVIGNON, ORCA SELECTION, 2003: Aged in *barriques* for 24 months, with firm tannins and generous wood. Opening in the glass to reveal fine balance and ripe blueberry, plum and currant fruits, all lingering nicely on the palate. Drink now. Score 91.

BEN HANNA, MERLOT, 2006: Garnet-red with purple reflections and, in accordance with the winemaker's philosophy, soft and round. On the nose and palate black cherries and wild berries. Easy to drink but with just the right touch of complexity. Drink from release. Tentative Score 86–88.

BEN HANNA, MERLOT, SHALEM, 2004: Dark garnet, medium-bodied, reflecting its 19 months in oak with generous spices and medium-firm tannins, but opening nicely in the glass to reveal cherry, blackberry, vanilla and toasty oak. Drink now–2009. Score 86.

BEN HANNA, MERLOT, SINGLE HUMPED, 2004: The 'Humped' refers to the picture of a camel on the label. Based largely on grapes from the Negev, this is a soft, round and generous wine showing blueberry, blackberry and currant notes along with hints of mint and sweet herbs, all coming together harmoniously. Drink now–2009. Score 90.

BEN HANNA, MERLOT, BAMIDBAR, SDE BOKER, 2003: Made from grapes from both the Negev and the Jerusalem Hills and aged in oak for 14 months, an appealing medium-bodied red, with soft tannins and aromas of plums and currants on a mineral-rich background. Drink up. Score 87.

BEN HANNA, CABERNET FRANC, 2006: Garnet towards royal-purple, medium to full-bodied, with soft, round tannins and layers of plum, blueberry and currant fruits along with notes of vanilla and spices. Rich and well balanced. Drink from release–2011. Tentative Score 88–90.

BEN HANNA, CABERNET FRANC, 2005: Developed in French oak, this medium to full-bodied wine shows soft, near-sweet tannins integrating nicely and black currant, berry and hints of citrus. On the long finish, hints of what seems one moment to be mint and another black licorice. Drink now–2009. Score 88.

BEN HANNA, PETIT VERDOT, 2006: Medium to full-bodied with soft but mouth-coating tannins, this dark garnet wine is showing rich aromas and flavors of plums, raspberries and currant fruits, those matched nicely by a lightly spicy oak nature. Round, generous and long. Drink from release–2011. Tentative Score 87–89.

BEN HANNA, PETIT VERDOT, SINGLE HUMPED, 2005: Medium to full-bodied with silky smooth tannins, this round and well-balanced wine is showing plum and raspberry fruits, those highlighted nicely by generous acidity and a light gamy touch on the long generous finish. Drink now–2010. Score 90.

BEN HANNA, PETIT VERDOT, 2005: Bright garnet-red in color, with silky tannins, medium-body and generous black fruits, this wine promises to be round, generous and elegant. Drink from release–2009. Tentative Score 87–89.

BEN HANNA, MEDITERRANEAN BLEND, 2005: An oak-aged blend of 50% Grenache, 33% Petit Verdot, 12% Syrah and 5% Cabernet Franc. Soft, round, with tantalizing hints of spicy oak and sweet cedar and showing an appealing array of blackberry, currant and wild berry aromas and flavors. Long and elegant. Drink from release–2010. Tentative Score 88–90.

BEN HANNA, CABERNET SAUVIGNON-MERLOT, SHALEM, 2003: Dark ruby towards royal-purple, medium to full-bodied, with firm tannins nicely balanced by spicy wood and tempting berry, currant and black cherry fruits, those showing light hints of earthiness and herbaceousness. Drink now. Score 87.

BEN HANNA, VIOGNIER, 2006: The winery's first white wine and a rousing success. Unoaked and unfiltered, bright light golden-straw in color, with fine balancing acidity and an appealing array of peach, nectarine, pineapple and lime fruits, those backed up nicely by spicy and floral components. Well balanced and long. Drink now. Score 88.

Ben-Shoshan **

Established by agronomist Yuval Ben-Shoshan on Kibbutz Bror Hail in the northern Negev Desert, this winery released its first wine from the vintage of 1998. Desert-raised grapes include Cabernet Sauvignon and Merlot, and other grapes are drawn from the area of Kerem Ben Zimra in the Galilee. The winery's production is currently about 10,000 bottles annually.

YUVAL BEN-SHOSHAN, CABERNET SAU-VIGNON, HAR'EL, 2005: Dark royal-purple, medium to full-bodied, with chunky country-style tannins and appealing currant, berry and black cherry fruits. Drink from release. Tentative Score 82–84.

YUVAL BEN-SHOSHAN, CABERNET SAU-VIGNON, HAR'EL, 2004: Dark royal-purple, medium to full-bodied, with chunky country-style tannins and aromas and flavors of plum compote. Drink up. Score 76.

YUVAL BEN-SHOSHAN, CABERNET SAUVIGNON, AVDAT, 2002: Deep garnet-red, medium to full-bodied, with generous tannins, spicy oak, and black currant and anise aromas and flavors. Drink up. Score 84.

YUVAL BEN-SHOSHAN, MERLOT, AVDAT, 2005: Ruby towards garnet, medium-bodied, with soft tannins and a hint of sweetness that overlays the black fruits. Drink from release. Tentative Score 76–78.

YUVAL BEN-SHUSHAN, MERLOT, AVDAT, 2004: Garnet towards royal-purple, medium- to full-bodied, with chunky, country-style tannins and generous spicy oak. Opens in the glass to reveal black and red berries and a pleasing earthy overtone. Drink now–2009. Score 85.

YUVAL BEN-SHOSHAN, MERLOT, AVDAT, 2003: Dark garnet, medium-bodied, with tannins now integrating nicely. Shows soft and round with tempting plum, black cherry and smoky-vanilla flavors from the oak. Well balanced and drinking nicely. Drink up. Score 85.

YUVAL BEN-SHUSHAN, CABERNET SAUVIGNON-MERLOT, KFAR SHAMAI, 2005: A blend of equal parts of Cabernet Sauvignon and Merlot, oak-aged for 14 months. Dark garnet, medium to full-bodied, with soft, near-sweet tannins and showing sur-ripe raspberry and red plum fruits on a background of freshly turned earth and tobacco. Drink now. Score 87.

Ben-Zimra **

Founded by vintner Yossi Ashkenazi on Moshav Ben Zimra in the Upper Galilee, with Assaf Kedem serving as the winemaker, this boutique winery has been producing two wines, a reserve and a regular edition of Cabernet Sauvignon since 2003. The winery vineyards, near the moshav, at 870 meters above sea level, are among the best in Israel.

BEN-ZIMRA, CABERNET SAUVIGNON, RESERVE, 2005: Dark garnet towards royal-purple, full-bodied, with firm tannins just starting to settle down, and reflecting its 14 months in *barriques* with spicy wood. The wine shows an appealing array of currant, blackberry and eucalyptus, all leading to a long and generous finish. Best 2008–2011. Score 87.

BEN-ZIMRA, CABERNET SAUVIGNON, 2005: Dark garnet, medium to full-bodied, with soft, mouth-coating tannins. Reflecting its ten months in oak with gentle spices and a hint of smoke. Slow to open but when it does shows appealing berry, currant and black cherry fruits. Moderately long. Drink now–2010. Score 86.

Binyamina ✦✦✦

First established in 1952 as Eliaz Wineries, the winery is located in the town of Binyamina at the foothills of the Carmel Mountains. In 1994 a group of investors bought out and renamed the outdated winery, replacing the existing management. They continued to introduce modern technology and equipment, and in recent years, thanks to increasing quality control in the vineyards and fine winemaking practices, the wines have improved dramatically.

Under the supervision of senior winemaker Sasson Ben-Aharon and winemaker Assaf Paz, the winery is now the fourth largest in the country and produces nearly 2.8 million bottles annually from a large variety of grapes, those from vineyards in nearly every part of the country. To the winery's credit, they were the first in the country to introduce Viognier and Tempranillo varietals.

The winery releases several series: Special Reserve, Avnei Hachoshen, Yogev and Tiltan. The basic series, Binyamina, is now marketed under a new label, Teva. In Hebrew, *Avnei Hachoshen* refers to the precious stones that adorned the vest of the high priest in the days of the Temple; *Tiltan* is the Hebrew name for clover, a plant that has three distinct leaves on every branch (the logic being that these wines are blends of three different vintage years); *Yogev* is the Biblical term for a farmer, in this case a clear bow to the grape-growers; and *Teva* means nature.

Special Reserve

SPECIAL RESERVE, CABERNET SAUVIGNON, 2005: Full-bodied, with firm tannins integrating nicely with spicy and lightly smoky wood, those yielding to generous red berries, cassis and spices. Concentrated and intense but promising elegance. Drink from release–2012. Tentative Score 89–91. K

SPECIAL RESERVE, CABERNET SAUVIGNON, 2004: Medium to full-bodied, with soft tannins integrating nicely and reflecting a generous but well-balanced wood influence from its 18 months in oak. On the nose and palate currant and blackberry fruits supported by generous hints of Mediterranean herbs and, on the medium-long finish, a note of tobacco. Drink now. Score 87. K

SPECIAL RESERVE, CABERNET SAUVIGNON, 2003: Medium to full-bodied, dark garnet in color, with firm tannins and showing ripe plum, blackberry and cherry fruits, a gentle overlay of spicy oak and an appealing herbal overtone on the finish. Drink now. Score 87. K

SPECIAL RESERVE, CABERNET SAUVIGNON, 2002: This medium to full-bodied wine continues to show firm tannins that seem to not want to integrate and a hint of sweetness that runs through. There are some dark, minty fruits here but those are a bit stingy. Drink up. Score 85. K

SPECIAL RESERVE, MERLOT, 2005: Dark garnet, medium to full-bodied, reflecting its development in French oak barrels with hints of spicy wood and generous near-sweet tannins. On the nose and palate raspberry, strawberry and vanilla, those supported nicely by herbal and spicy notes. Drink from release–2010. Tentative Score 87–89. K

SPECIAL RESERVE, MERLOT, 2004: With its youthful acidity now integrated, this garnet-red medium to full-bodied wine now shows near-sweet tannins and spicy oak in good balance with wild berry, plum and currant notes. Drink now. Score 88. K

SPECIAL RESERVE, MERLOT, 2003: This dark cherry-red medium-bodied wine is not overly complex but has soft tannins and good balance between those, wood and fruits. Look for hints of licorice and chocolate on the berry-cherry fruits. Drink now. Score 87. K

SPECIAL RESERVE, SHIRAZ, 2005: This dark garnet wine's once firm tannins are now settling down nicely and showing a gentle hand with spicy oak. Fine balance between those and plum, black cherry and cassis and, on the background, appealing hints of leather and chocolate all leading to a long, mouth-filling finish. Drink now–2010. Score 90. K

SPECIAL RESERVE, SHIRAZ, 2004: Dark garnet towards royal-purple, reflecting its 14 months in oak with firm tannins and generous smoky wood and vanilla. Blended with 2% of Viognier grapes, medium to full-bodied and showing clean blueberry, blackberry and plum fruits along with hints of spices, smoked meat and earthiness. Drink now. Score 89. K

SPECIAL RESERVE, SHIRAZ, 2003: Royal-purple, medium to full-bodied, with soft tannins, sweet cedarwood, black cherries, plums and a lightly earthy background. Well balanced, long and generous. Drink up. Score 87. K

SPECIAL RESERVE, CABERNET SAUVIGNON-MERLOT-SHIRAZ, 2003: Dark garnet-red, full-bodied and deeply tannic at this stage, but showing good balance between tannins, wood and fruits, already opening to show currant, berry and plum fruits, those intertwining nicely with hints of tobacco and chocolate. Drink up. Score 88. K

SPECIAL RESERVE, CHARDONNAY, 2006: Developed partly in oak, partly in stainless steel, this bright golden, medium-bodied white shows appealing apricot and citrus aromas and flavors, those leading to an appealing buttery note on the long finish. Drink now. Score 88. K

SPECIAL RESERVE, CHARDONNAY, 2005: Light gold, medium to full-bodied, with fine balancing acidity and a hint of spices from the oak in which it aged. On the nose and palate citrus, peach and tropical fruits matched by an appealing hint of cream on the finish. Drink now. Score 88. K

SPECIAL RESERVE, SAUVIGNON BLANC, 2006: Light straw, medium-bodied, this unoaked white shows bright and lively aromas and flavors that shift nicely on the palate, at one moment orange blossoms and nectarines, at another a hint of gooseberries, and at yet another green apples and light grassy hints rising. Drink now. Score 88. K

SPECIAL RESERVE, SAUVIGNON BLANC, 2005: Medium-bodied and light golden-straw in color, this crisp and lively unoaked white shows appealing apple and pineapple aromas and flavors. Not complex but very pleasant. Drink up. Score 87. K

SPECIAL RESERVE, VIOGNIER, 2005: Medium-bodied, light golden in color, with appealing aromas and flavors of citrus and apricot as well as hints of cinnamon and minerals, all with good balancing acidity and a warm earthy finish. Drink now. Score 86. K

SPECIAL RESERVE, VIOGNIER, 2004: Aged *sur lie*, with gentle acidity that yields to buttery-mineral nuances and with lemon and apple aromas and flavors, as well as a lightly earthy note on the finish. Drink up. Score 86. K

SPECIAL RESERVE, GEWURZTRAMINER, 2006: Lively golden-straw in color, medium-bodied, this off-dry and aromatic white opens with litchis and a hint of spices and then goes on to a lemon, pear, almond and dried apricot character. Drink now. Score 86. K

SPECIAL RESERVE, GEWURZTRAMINER, 2005: As during its youth, an aromatic wine with grassy, pear and apple aromas and flavors, but lacking any of the spicy or litchi notes that would give this a Gewurztraminer personality. Drink up. Score 84. K

SPECIAL RESERVE, GEWURZTRAMINER, 2004: Golden-straw in color, medium-bodied, barely off-dry and with good balancing acidity to keep it lively. Appealing spicy aromas and flavors of citrus, litchis and summer fruits. Drink up. Score 86. K

SPECIAL RESERVE, GEWURZTRAMINER, DESSERT WINE, 2003: Medium-bodied, with tropical fruits, citrus peel and floral aromas. Lacking the spiciness that should typify the variety and the acidity that might have made the wine more lively. Drink now. Score 83. K

SPECIAL RESERVE, GEWURZTRAMINER, LATE HARVEST, N.V.: This light gold, medium-bodied dessert wine shows generous sweetness balanced nicely by acidity. On the nose and palate good Gewurztraminer spiciness, together with litchis, hints of dried apricots and a tempting peppery note on the finish. Drink now–2009. Score 88. K

Avnei Hachoshen

AVNEI HACHOSHEN, CABERNET SAUVIGNON, TARSHISH, 2004: Full-bodied, with spicy, vanilla-rich wood and near-sweet tannins in good balance with black currant, wild berries and minerals, all leading to a long and appealing spicy finish. Drink now. Score 88. K

AVNEI HACHOSHEN, CABERNET SAUVIGNON, TARSHISH, 2003:
Deep garnet towards purple, full-bodied, with
mouth-coating tannins that are opening to show
harmony, and in addition to traditional black currants, sweet berries and spices, generous mineral,
toasty and vanilla notes. Drink now–2011.
Score 91. K

AVNEI HACHOSHEN, SYRAH, ODEM, 2006: Dark,
dense and concentrated, with fine balance and structure. Firm tannins need time to integrate with spicy
wood and to show the black and red berries, cherries
and licorice flavors that are here, lingering comfortably on a long fruity finish. One of the best wines
to date from Binyamina. Best 2009–2013. Tentative
Score 91–93. K

AVNEI HACHOSHEN, SYRAH, ODEM, 2005:
Blended with 2–3% of Viognier, medium to full-
bodied, softly tannic, and showing smooth, ripe,
bright and lively. True to the Syrah traits, with berry,
cherry and plum aromas and flavors all lingering
nicely on a well-balanced finish. Drink now–2010. Score 89. K

AVNEI HACHOSHEN, SYRAH, ODEM, 2004: With 15 months in oak,
showing medium to full-bodied, soft well-integrated tannins and light
herbal-earthy aromas and flavors complemented nicely by plum, berry
and cassis fruits. Hints of tobacco and chocolate on the finish. Drink
now. Score 87. K

AVNEI HACHOSHEN, SYRAH, ODEM, 2003: Blended with 2% of Viognier, full-bodied, firm and concentrated, dark garnet in color, with firm
and mouth-coating tannins opening in the glass to reveal near-sweet
berry, plum, meaty and earthy aromas and flavors, all leading to a long
finish. Drink now–2012. Score 91. K

**AVNEI HACHOSHEN, CABERNET SAUVIGNON-SHIRAZ-MERLOT,
SAPIR, 2004:** This blend of 40% Cabernet Sauvignon, 35% Shiraz and
25% Merlot spent 15 months in French oak. Dark garnet, medium-
bodied, with soft tannins and ripe currant and plum fruits backed up
by Oriental spices and pepper. Easy drinking but lacking complexity.
Drink now–2009. Score 87. K

**AVNEI HACHOSHEN, CABERNET SAUVIGNON-SHIRAZ-MERLOT,
SAPIR, 2003:** A full-bodied, firmly tannic blend of 40% each of Cabernet and Shiraz and 20% Merlot. Oak-aged for 15 months, showing

good balance between wood, tannins and a tempting array of aromas and flavors, those including chocolate, tobacco, dusty-oak and minerals, all on a warm background of black currants, blackberries and spices. Drink now. Score 90. K

AVNEI HACHOSHEN, CHARDONNAY, SHOHAM, 2005: Developed for 16 months in oak, deep golden-straw in color, with generous smoky oak balanced by appealing citrus, melon and tropical fruits. Luxurious. Drink now. Score 90. K

AVNEI HACHOSHEN, CHARDONNAY, SHOHAM, 2004: This deep golden-straw wine reflects its 16 months in *barriques* with smoky oak on the ascendant but with appealing citrus, tropical and melon fruits. Drink now. Score 87. K

AVNEI HACHOSHEN, SAUVIGNON BLANC FUMÉ, LESHEM, 2005: Light golden-straw in color, medium-bodied, with citrus, sweet pea, herbal and grassy aromas and flavors that come together nicely along with a light creamy finish. Drink now. Score 86. K

AVNEI HACHOSHEN, SAUVIGNON BLANC FUMÉ, LESHEM, 2004: Light gold in color, medium-bodied, lively, vibrant and focused, reflecting six months in oak with hints of spices and vanilla along with aromas and flavors of pears, melon, honeysuckle and fresh cut hay. Drink up. Score 88. K

AVNEI HACHOSHEN, CHARDONNAY-SAUVIGNON BLANC-VIOGNIER, YASHFEH, 2005: Developed in French oak for six months, golden-straw in color, medium-bodied and showing good balance between fruits and acidity. Opens with citrus flowers, those yielding nicely to ripe peach, melon and lime fruits, all on an appealing mineral-rich background. Drink now. Score 86. K

Yogev

YOGEV, CABERNET SAUVIGNON, 2005: Medium to full-bodied, with soft tannins and sur-ripe plums, berry fruits and generous alcohol that give the wine a near-sweet finish. Drink now. Score 85. K

YOGEV, CABERNET SAUVIGNON-MERLOT, 2005: A medium-bodied blend of 50% each of Cabernet and Merlot, aged in oak for eight months. Generous currant, raspberry, red plum and cedar aromas and flavors yield a smooth-textured appealing wine with a moderately long, lightly herbal finish. Drink now. Score 86. K

YOGEV, CABERNET SAUVIGNON-MERLOT, 2004: Medium-bodied, with soft, almost unfelt tannins, this lightly oaked blend of 50% each of Cabernet Sauvignon and Merlot shows straightforward berry, cassis and plum fruits. A good quaffer. Drink now. Score 85. K

YOGEV, CABERNET SAUVIGNON-SHI-RAZ, 2005: Medium-bodied, with light, spicy oak and bright cherry, and red and black berry aromas and flavors that linger nicely. Ripe and open and, on the moderately long finish, appealing hints of licorice. Drink now–2009. Score 88. K

YOGEV, CABERNET SAUVIGNON-SHI-RAZ, 2004: A blend of 50% each of Cabernet Sauvignon and Shiraz, oak-aged for eight months. Medium-bodied, with soft tannins and tempting hints of vanilla and smoky oak and appealing spicy currants, berries, and light earthiness. Drink now. Score 88. K

YOGEV, ROSÉ, 2005: A blend of 50% each Cabernet Sauvignon and Zinfandel, this light to medium-bodied peach-towards-pale-pink colored rosé shows clean and refreshing berry, cherry and strawberry aromas and flavors. Simple but pleasant. Drink up. Score 85. K

YOGEV, SAUVIGNON BLANC-CHARDONNAY, 2005: Light golden-straw colored, this aromatic, medium-bodied, unoaked blend of 70% Sauvignon Blanc and 30% Chardonnay shows appealing pineapple, peach and apple aromas and flavors. A well-done quaffer. Drink now. Score 86. K

Tiltan

TITLAN, N.V.: Made from Cabernet Sauvignon grapes harvested in the 2003, 2004 and 2005 harvests, each developed in wood for a different period of time. Full-bodied, with soft, caressing tannins and a moderate hand with peppery wood, the wine opens on the palate to reveal currants, black cherries and herbal aromas and flavors, all of which are concentrated but not heavy. Finishes with generous tannins and an appealing hint of sage. Drink now–2012. Score 90. K

TILTAN, N.V.: Made from Cabernet Sauvignon grapes from the 2002, 2003 and 2004 vintages, this medium to full-bodied blend shows generous wood and tannins, those in good balance with spicy and lightly earthy black fruits. On the finish, nice hints of herbs and vanilla. Drink now. Score 88. K

Teva

TEVA, CABERNET SAUVIGNON, 2006: Dark cherry-red towards garnet in color, medium-bodied, with light hints of spicy oak and an appealing cherry, blackberry personality. On the short, fruity finish an appealing hint of tobacco. Drink now. Score 85. K

TEVA, MERLOT, 2006: Ruby towards garnet, medium-bodied with soft tannins. Not at all complex but with pleasant blackberry and black cherry fruits on a light spicy background. Drink now. Score 84. K

TEVA, SHIRAZ, 2006: Dark garnet in color, medium-bodied, with caressing tannins, this is a soft, round and easy-to-drink red with blackberry and spicy aromas and flavors that sit comfortably on the palate. Drink now. Score 85. K

TEVA, PINOTAGE, 2006: Bright royal-purple in color, medium-bodied, with soft tannins balanced by lively acidity and just a hint of spicy wood. On the nose and palate cherries and an intimation of cassis, those matched by a light touch of white pepper. Nothing complex but a round, easy to drink quaffer. Drink now. Score 84. K

TEVA, TEMPRANILLO, 2006: Blended with 15% of Cabernet Sauvignon, treated lightly to American oak *barriques*, this medium-bodied and softly tannic wine shows appealing black cherries, purple plums and hints of cigar tobacco leading to a round and moderately long finish. Drink now–2009. Score 85. K

TEVA, CABERNET BLUSH, 2006: Attractive light pink with an orange hint, light in body, with red berry and cherry fruits. Barely off-dry but lacking the acidity that might have made it a bit more lively. Drink up. Score 80. K

TEVA CHARDONNAY, 2006: Light golden-straw in color, medium-bodied and unoaked, this crisp, lively and refreshing white shows grapefruit, nectarine and flinty minerals that add charm. Drink now. Score 85. K

TEVA, EMERALD RIESLING, 2006: Half-dry, light, floral and with citrus, peach, tropical and green apple fruits. Moderately but not overly sweet and with a pleasant citrus finish. Drink up. Score 82. K

TEVA, MUSCAT OF ALEXANDRIA, 2006: Golden-straw in color, this light to medium-bodied semi-dry white shows generous floral aromas, opening on the palate to reveal fig and apricot flavors. A bit more natural acidity would have made this a more interesting wine. Drink up. Score 83. K

Birya **

Porat Wine
יין פורת

ד"ר פ"שה פורת – מייסד יקב בירה
Cabernet Souvignon
קברנה סובניון
יין אדום יבש
Superb

Founded by Moshe Porat in the community of Birya near the town of Safed in the Galilee, the winery draws on grapes from Ramot Naftali in the Upper Galilee, and released its first wines from the 2003 vintage. Production for the 2005 vintage was 4,000 bottles Because of damage during the Israel-Hezbollah war during the summer of 2006, no wines were produced from that vintage.

BIRYA, CABERNET SAUVIGNON, 2005: Dark ruby towards garnet this medium to full-bodied wine shows soft tannins and generous currant, blackberry and mint on the nose and palate. On the moderately long finish a hint of fresh herbs. Drink now–2009. Score 85. K

BIRYA, CABERNET SAUVIGNON, 2004: Deep garnet towards royal-purple in color, medium to full-bodied, with soft tannins integrating nicely with wood and fruits. Aromas and flavors of black currants and berries on a light herbal background. Drink now. Score 84. K

BIRYA, CABERNET SAUVIGNON, PORAT WINE, 2003: Medium to full-bodied with firm but well-integrating tannins and traditional Cabernet fruits of black currants and berries with hints of herbs and spices on the finish. Drink up. Score 85. K

BIRYA, MERLOT, 2005: Generous blackberry, purple plum and black cherry fruits on a medium-bodied, softly tannic frame. A generous quaffer. Drink now. Score 85. K

BIRYA, MERLOT, 2004: Medium-bodied, soft and round, with forward berry, black cherry and currant fruits. Drink now. Score 85. K

Bnei Baruch *

Founded in 2002 by Emmanuel Goldstein and the members of the Bnai Baruch Yeshiva, a school devoted to study of the Talmud and Kabbalah, grapes are received and undergo initial fermentation at the Nachshon winery before being transferred to the yeshiva for further development. The winery is currently producing about 6,000 bottles of Cabernet Sauvignon, Merlot and Chardonnay annually.

Special Edition

SPECIAL EDITION, CABERNET SAUVIGNON, 2003: Oak-aged for one year, this medium-bodied, 100% Cabernet Sauvignon shows chunky tannins, high acidity and some hyper-ripe berry-cherry aromas and flavors. Drink now. Score 80. K

Bnei Baruch

BNEI BARUCH, CABERNET SAUVIGNON, 2005: Cloudy in color, already throwing sediment, and with black fruit aromas and flavors buried under an odd barnyard aroma. Score 70. K

BNEI BARUCH, CABERNET SAUVIGNON, 2004: Garnet-red, medium-bodied, with chunky tannins and smoky oak muting the black fruits that try to make themselves felt. Drink now. Score 78. K

BNEI BARUCH, CABERNET SAUVIGNON, 2003: Developed with oak chips, this medium-bodied dark garnet and somewhat coarsely tannic wine offers up a few currant and plum flavors. One dimensional and short. Drink up. Score 78. K

BNEI BARUCH, MERLOT, 2005: Medium-bodied, with coarse tannins, a hot alcoholic sensation and only skimpy black fruits. Drink up. Score 75. K

BNEI BARUCH, MERLOT, 2004: Medium to full-bodied, royal-purple in color, with too generous spicy and dusty oak and only a few blackberry fruits. Drink up. Score 75. K

BNEI BARUCH, MERLOT, 2003: With dusty oak from the oak chips, a somewhat coarse and simple wine with a few black fruits. Drink up. Score 76. K

BNEI BARUCH, CHARDONNAY, 2004: Dark golden, going to bronze, with a hint of unwanted sweetness running through and with a few citrus and pineapple fruits. Drink up. Score 72. K

Bustan ★★★★

Founded in 1994 by Ya'akov Fogler, this small winery situated on Moshav Sharai Tikva near Tel Aviv draws Cabernet Sauvignon and Merlot grapes from the Jerusalem and Judean Mountains, and produces about 2,000 bottles annually. The winery has earned a good name for its distinctly French-style wines, which have had a formal kashrut certificate since 1999.

BUSTAN, CABERNET SAUVIGNON, 2004: Dark garnet, full-bodied, with soft, mouth-coating tannins; showing aromas and flavors of blackberries, currants, chocolate and spicy cedar. Long and generous. Drink from release–2012. Score 90. K

BUSTAN, CABERNET SAUVIGNON, 2003: Dark ruby to garnet, medium-bodied, with soft tannins integrating well and with generous but not overwhelming spicy oak. Spicy currant and berry fruits along with chocolate and tobacco on the powerful but elegant finish. Drink now–2011. Score 90. K

BUSTAN, CABERNET SAUVIGNON, 2002: Medium to full-bodied, deep garnet towards royal-purple, with firm tannins now integrating nicely to reveal sweet cedarwood, currants, wild berries and hints of chocolate, espresso and anise. Drink now. Score 89. K

BUSTAN, CABERNET SAUVIGNON, 2000: Medium-bodied, lacking balance between too soft tannins, heavy acidity and black fruits that seem too sweet on the palate, this is the first disappointing wine from an otherwise excellent winery. Drink now. Score 84. K

BUSTAN, CABERNET SAUVIGNON, 1999: An intense wine with rich and vibrant currant, black cherry and mocha aromas and flavors, these unfolding on the palate to reveal complexity and depth. After losing the rough edges of youth, the wine is now long and elegant and is starting to reveal delicious chocolate, tobacco and anise notes. Drink now. Score 90. K

BUSTAN, CABERNET SAUVIGNON, 1998: Full-bodied and rich, the wine shows aromas and flavors of black cherries, currants and oak as well as spicy overtones, all sitting comfortably on the palate. Deep, long and complex, the wine opens in the glass to reveal its elegance. Drink now. Score 91.

BUSTAN, CABERNET SAUVIGNON, 1997: With 21 months in small oak casks, this ripe and generous wine has distinctive mouth-filling aromas and flavors of black currants and black cherries as well as minty and spicy overtones that linger on and on. Well structured, stylish and graceful, and with soft, now well-integrated tannins. Drink now. Score 90.

BUSTAN, CABERNET SAUVIGNON, 1996: During its youth this wine was searingly tannic but even then showed balance that boded well for its future. Now full-bodied and deep, with the tannins soft and round and aromas of black and red currants, wild berries, tobacco, coffee and oak, the wine is drinking beautifully. Drink up. Score 92.

BUSTAN, CABERNET SAUVIGNON, 1995: Oak-aged for 20 months, now fully mature and showing tempting black currant, plum and berry fruits, those matched nicely by aromas and flavors of toasty oak, espresso coffee and black olives on the finish. Drink up. Score 92.

BUSTAN, CABERNET SAUVIGNON, 1994: Oak-aged for 19 months, with its tannins and wood now fully integrated, this well-balanced wine from a problematic vintage still shows complex aromas and flavors of currants, berries and black cherries, those matched nicely by minerals, while the finish yields spices and a hint of mint. Drink up. Score 89.

BUSTAN, MERLOT, 2003: Deep, dark, rich and aromatic. Full-bodied, with soft tannins, this smooth and round wine opens to reveal generous blueberry, cherry and currant fruits on a spicy floral background, all lingering nicely on the generous finish. Drink now–2012. Score 91. K

BUSTAN, MERLOT, 2002: Aged in oak for 22 months, this dark garnet, full-bodied, firmly tannic and concentrated wine shows generous black fruits, spices and sweet cedar, all coming to a long licorice and chocolate finish. Drink now–2010. Score 92. K

BUSTAN, MERLOT, 2000: Dark royal-purple, this medium to full-bodied red shows good balance between soft tannins, sweet cedar, plum and blackberry aromas and flavors. Softening nicely on the palate, this is a round and flavorful wine. Drink now. Score 89. K

BUSTAN, MERLOT, 1999: Deep, dark, rich and full-bodied, with spicy currant, mocha, nut, herbal and coffee aromas and flavors, this well-balanced wine has firm but well-integrated tannins and a long complex finish. The best Merlot from Bustan to date. Drink now. Score 93. K

BUSTAN, MERLOT, 1998: Round and soft, and with deep layers of wild berries, black cherries, mint and spices that open nicely in the glass, the wine has generous but well-integrated tannins, a good hand with the oak and a long, mouth-filling finish. Drink now. Score 91.

BUSTAN, MERLOT, 1997: Bold, ripe and delicious, with layers of rich plums, currants and black cherries along with a bare herbal accent. The wine has deep flavors that linger comfortably on the palate, good balance between fruits, acids and tannins, and a long finish. Drink up. Score 90.

BUSTAN, SYRAH, 2003: Aromatic enough to be thought of as per-fumed, this full-bodied, chewy and richly tannic wine offers up flavors of blackberries, currants, and boysenberry jam, those with tempting overlays of pepper, wet earth, and just a hint of grilled meat. Deep and intense, with a long, complex finish. Drink now–2012. Score 92. K

Bustan Hameshusheem *

Located on Moshav Had Ness on the Golan Heights, wine-maker-owner Benny Josef released his first wines to the market from the 2001 vintage. Production of 8,000 bottles annually is primarily of Cabernet Sauvignon, Merlot, Barbera and Sangiovese, and the grapes are drawn from the Upper Galilee and nearby vineyards.

BUSTAN HAMESHUSHEEM, CABERNET SAUVIGNON, 2005: Full-bodied, with chunky, country-style tannins and smoky oak holding back the black fruits and spices. Drink now. Score 80.

BUSTAN HAMESHUSHEEM, CABERNET SAUVIGNON, 2004: Dark in color, with generous firm tannins, those balanced nicely by spicy oak, currant and wild berry aromas and flavors. Drink up. Score 80.

BUSTAN HAMESHUSHEEM, CABERNET SAUVIGNON, 2003: Deep royal-purple, medium-bodied, with country-style chunky tannins matched nicely by smoky oak, plum and blackberry aromas and flavors. Drink up. Score 80.

BUSTAN HAMESHUSHEEM, SANGIOVESE-CABERNET SAUVIGNON, 2005: Light in body, color and tannins, with a stewed fruit nose and overly sweet on the palate. Drink up. Score 75.

BUSTAN HAMESHUSHEEM, BARBERA-SANGIOVESE-CABERNET SAUVIGNON, BANIAS, 2004: As light in color as in body, reflecting its eight months in oak with only the barest hint of spiciness and stingy and overripe black fruits. Drink up. Score 75.

Carmel ✶✶✶✶

Carmel was founded as a cooperative of vintners in 1882 with funding provided by the Baron Edmond de Rothschild. Its first winery was constructed that same year in Rishon Letzion, in the central coastal region of the country, followed in 1890 by a winery in Zichron Ya'akov, in the Mount Carmel area. Carmel receives grapes from about 300 vineyards throughout the country, some owned by the winery, others by individual vintners and by *kibbutzim* and *moshavim*. Even though their share of the local wine market has dropped from over 90% in the early 1980s to somewhat under 50% today, Carmel remains the largest wine producer in the country, currently producing over 13 million bottles annually.

For many years, Carmel was in a moribund state, producing wines that while acceptable, rarely attained excellence and failed to capture the attention of more sophisticated consumers. In the last four years, Carmel took dramatic steps to improve the level of its wines. Senior winemaker Lior Laxer is now overseeing a staff of talented winemakers, most of whom have trained and worked outside of Israel; the winery is developing new vineyards in choice areas of the country and gaining fuller control over contract vineyards; in the 1990s Carmel was the first winery to plant major vineyards in the Negev Desert, and a new state-of-the-art winery has been partly completed at Ramat Dalton in the Upper Galilee. More recently Carmel has established an in-house boutique arm in Zichron Ya'akov, and is also the owner of the Yatir winery. Despite all of this, it is no secret that Carmel is undergoing serious economic difficulties and, with nearly all new faces at the helm of the company, many are now waiting to see precisely what the future holds in store.

Current releases include the top-of-the-line varietal Limited Edition, the Single Vineyard series, the Regional series (sometimes referred to as the Appellation Series), and the Private Collection series. Other wines are in the Reches series, Zichron Ya'akov series, and the Selected series (sometimes known as Vineyards or Vineyards Selected Series outside of Israel). The vineyards mentioned in the tasting notes of the Single Vineyard Wines—Zarit, Ben Zimra and Kayoumi—are located in the Upper Galilee, and Sha'al is on the Golan Heights.

Limited Edition

CARMEL WINERY

Limited Edition
2003

No. 13,422

LIMITED EDITION, 2004: This blend of 65% Cabernet Sauvignon, 20% Petit Verdot and 15% Merlot shows soft tannins and generous but gentle wood, those in fine balance with currant, blackberry and black cherry fruits, all melding together with light hints of pepper, anise and cigar box aromas and flavors. Round and caressing, elegant and long. Best 2009–2013. Score 93. K

LIMITED EDITION, 2003: A full-bodied blend of 50% Cabernet Sauvignon, 32% Petit Verdot, 17% Merlot and 1% Cabernet Franc. Deeply aromatic, with soft tannins and generous wood in fine balance with fruits and well-tuned acidity. On the nose and palate black currants, blackberries, spices and sweet cedar, all leading to a remarkably long and elegant finish. Drink now–2015. Score 93. K

LIMITED EDITION, 2002: Deep royal-purple in color, with orange reflections, a Bordeaux blend of 60% Cabernet Sauvignon, 30% Merlot and 10% Cabernet Franc, each variety vinified separately and developed for 14 months in French oak. Medium to full-bodied, with soft tannins and good balance between sweet and smoky wood, aromas and flavors of black currants, berries and dark chocolate, all leading to a long finish. Drink now–2012. Score 92. K

Single Vineyard

SINGLE VINEYARD, CABERNET SAUVIGNON, ZARIT, 2004: Deep garnet towards royal-purple, reflecting its 15 months in *barriques* with judicious oak integrating nicely with solid tannins. Opens with currants and dusty wood, moving on to spices and blackberries, and from first sip to last, hints of vanilla, freshly hung tobacco leaves and an intimation of mint. Long and generous. Drink now–2011. Score 91. K

SINGLE VINEYARD, CABERNET SAUVIGNON, ZARIT, 2003: Dark garnet, with firm, near-sweet tannins that yield nicely in the glass to reveal an appealing touch of rustic earthiness that adds dimension to rich, ripe black fruits. Complex, concentrated and elegant. Drink now–2011. Score 90. K

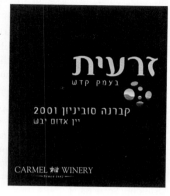

SINGLE VINEYARD, CABERNET SAUVIGNON, ZARIT, 2002: Dark cherry-red, this medium to full-bodied wine shows soft tannins and generous vanilla and smoky overtones. First impressions are of berries and eucalyptus, those yielding to currants, vanilla, black tea, green peppers and a light spiciness that lingers nicely on the moderately long finish. Warm, round and well balanced. Drink now–2009. Score 90. K

SINGLE VINEYARD, CABERNET SAUVIGNON, ZARIT, 2001: Made entirely from Cabernet Sauvignon grapes and aged in French oak *barriques* for 12 months, the wine has a lively cherry-ruby color. The opening impression on the nose is of eucalyptus and black fruits, and on the palate, of sweet berries. Medium-bodied and with soft tannins, the wine opens nicely in the glass and has a medium-long finish. Drink now–2009. Score 87. K

SINGLE VINEYARD, CABERNET SAUVIGNON, KAYOUMI, 2004: Aged in oak for 15 months, the wine is dark, almost impenetrable purple in color. Firm tannins and smoky wood come together with currant, blackberry, plum and mineral aromas and flavors, those showing hints of Mediterranean herbs and light Oriental spices. Long and generous. Drink now–2012. Score 91. K

SINGLE VINEYARD, CABERNET SAUVIGNON, KAYOUMI, 2003: Luscious and elegant, deep garnet, full-bodied and softly tannic. The nose and palate are still showing the black currant, berry and spicy wood that were here but now these are complemented by hints of smoked meat, together with oriental spices and tobacco. Long and complex. Drink now–2014. Score 92. K

SINGLE VINEYARD, CABERNET SAUVIGNON, BEN ZIMRA, 2002: Deep garnet-purple towards black, full-bodied, reflecting its 14 months in oak with generous tannins and spicy oak well balanced by berry, plum and currant fruits, set off nicely by notes of vanilla and eucalyptus. On the long, round finish look for hints of tobacco and green olives. Drink now–2009. Score 91. K

SINGLE VINEYARD, CABERNET SAUVIGNON, RAMAT ARAD, 2002: Dark garnet-red, full-bodied, with abundant but soft, near-sweet and well-integrating tannins. Opens with black fruits and sweet cedarwood, those yielding to currants, berries and vanilla and finally to a tempting herbal-earthy sensation. Long and complex. Drink now. Score 92. K

SINGLE VINEYARD, CABERNET SAUVIGNON, RAMAT ARAD, 2000: Aged in French *barriques* for 14 months, this deep red-toward-garnet, full-bodied and now fully mature wine boasts excellent balance between fully integrated and almost unfelt tannins, just the right hints of vanilla and smoke from the wood, and tempting aromas and flavors that start off with stewed black fruits and then lead to a long earthy-spicy finish. Drink up. Score 88. K

SINGLE VINEYARD, CABERNET SAUVIGNON, SCHECH, 2004: From a not-yet-well-known vineyard on the Golan Heights, this red lives up nicely to the stereotypes of what makes a wine 'feminine'. Soft, round and caressing, elegant without being intense, full-bodied without being muscular, with tempting aromas and flavors of black cherries, currants and anise. Drink now–2012. Score 90. K

SINGLE VINEYARD, MERLOT, BEN ZIMRA, 2004: Garnet towards royal-purple in color, ripe, round and polished, and showing fine balance and focus to highlight its dark plum, blueberry and dusky spice flavors. Finishes with hints of oak and red bell peppers. Long and generous. Drink now–2010. Score 91. K

SINGLE VINEYARD, SHIRAZ, KAYOUMI, 2004: Full-bodied, intense and concentrated, with soft tannins integrating nicely and showing layer after layer of spicy oak, smoked meat and tar, those highlighting red berries, black cherries and licorice. Drink now–2015. Score 91. K

SINGLE VINEYARD, SHIRAZ, KAYOUMI, 2003: Firm and well structured, a soft, caressing and elegant wine. Generous soft tannins highlight a tempting array of currant, plum, blackberry and anise flavors and aromas, all of which culminate in a long, mouth-filling finish. Drink now–2012. Score 91. K

SINGLE VINEYARD, SYRAH, RAMAT ARAD, 2003: Oak-aged for about nine months, this dark cherry-red towards purple, medium to full-bodied wine shows excellent balance between soft tannins, smoke, spices, and aromas and flavors of currants, plums and chocolate. Long, smooth and generous. Drink now. Score 90. K

SINGLE VINEYARD, SYRAH, RAMAT ARAD, 2002: Made from the grapes of young vines, this fresh and lively medium-bodied wine was wisely placed in oak for only four months and now shows soft tannins, generous plum, currant and berry fruits as well as a nice layer of spiciness, and the barest hint of freshly turned earth. Drink up. Score 89. K

SINGLE VINEYARD, CHARDONNAY, KAYOUMI, 2006: With 75% developing in stainless steel and 25% in 300 liter Burgundy oak, this white is showing an aromatic Chablis-like personality, with minerals and light spices backing up hazelnuts, pears, figs and citrus. On the long finish a hint of toasted brioche. Drink from release–2009. Tentative Score 90–92. K

SINGLE VINEYARD, CHARDONNAY, KAYOUMI, UPPER GALILEE, 2005: Gentle pressing and cold fermentation, aged partly in new and partly in one-year-old 300 liter French barrels. Showing elegance and focus. Crisp and fresh, and on the nose and palate rich apple, pear, fig and light toasty notes coming together very nicely indeed. Drink now. Score 89. K

SINGLE VINEYARD, CHARDONNAY, KAYOUMI, UPPER GALILEE, 2004: Maturing gracefully, this medium-bodied white shows aromas and flavors of citrus peel, vanilla pastry cream and brioche, all lingering nicely. Drink up. Score 88. K

SINGLE VINEYARD, SAUVIGNON BLANC, RAMAT ARAD, 2006: Shining light straw in color, light to medium-bodied, this aromatic wine opens to reveal apple and citrus fruits. Not complex but lively and refreshing. Drink now. Score 86. K

SINGLE VINEYARD, SAUVIGNON BLANC, RAMAT ARAD, 2005: Developed partly in two-year-old French oak and partly in stainless steel tanks, this crisp, lively and well-focused white offers up a generous mouthful of pear, orange, grapefruit, spice and herbal aromas and flavors that go on to a nicely balanced finish. Drink now. Score 88. K

SINGLE VINEYARD, SAUVIGNON BLANC, RAMAT ARAD, 2004: Light golden-straw in color with a surprising tinge of pink, medium-bodied, unoaked and remarkably light on the palate. Bright, clean and crisp, with fresh citrus, tropical fruits and appealing herbal overtones leading to a moderately long finish. Drink up. Score 88. K

SINGLE VINEYARD, JOHANNISBERG RIESLING, KAYOUMI, 2006: Bright and juicy, more off-dry than sweet, with tangy acidity highlighting green apple, grapefruit and mineral aromas and flavors. Good concentration in a medium-bodied wine that seems to float gently on the palate. Drink now–2009. Score 89. K

SINGLE VINEYARD, JOHANNISBERG RIESLING, KAYOUMI, UPPER GALILEE, 2005: Off-dry but bright and lively, with fine focus and balancing acidity. Unoaked, with tempting peach and apple flavors set off nicely by floral and mineral edges. Elegant and satisfying. Drink now. Score 90. K

SINGLE VINEYARD, GEWURZTRAMINER, LATE HARVEST, SHA'AL, 2006: Made from grapes harvested in the upper Golan Heights, some affected by botrytis. Moderately sweet, with rose petal and orange peel overtones and honeyed pear, apricot and litchi fruits. Succulent, with a long-lingering finish. Drink now–2010. Score 90. K

SINGLE VINEYARD, GEWURZTRAMINER, LATE HARVEST, SHA'AL, 2005: This medium to full-bodied white shows generous sweetness and fine balancing acidity along with traditional Gewurztraminer litchis and spiciness, those matched by peach and nectarine fruits and, on the long finish, hints of rosewater and honey. Drink now–2010. Score 91. K

SINGLE VINEYARD, GEWURZTRAMINER, LATE HARVEST, SHA'AL, 2004: Medium-bodied, with generous sweetness set off by good balancing acidity, and on the nose and palate apricot, cinnamon, rose petal and honeyed flavors. Rich, spicy and elegant, with a long silky finish. Drink now–2009. Score 92. K

Regional (Appelation)

REGIONAL, CABERNET SAUVIGNON, UPPER GALILEE, 2005: Blended with 7% Cabernet Franc, this firm, concentrated red shows bright, juicy currant and raspberry fruits, those with overlays of near-sweet cedarwood and sage and, on the long finish, a hint of licorice. Drink now–2010. Score 89. K

REGIONAL, CABERNET SAUVIGNON, UPPER GALILEE, 2004: Deep garnet, medium to full-bodied, with soft tannins and gentle wood highlighting aromas and flavors of currants, wild berries and, on the medium-long finish, a hint of sweet cedar. Drink now. Score 87. K

REGIONAL, CABERNET SAUVIGNON, UPPER GALILEE, 2003: Dark garnet, medium to full-bodied, with firm tannins integrating nicely, and appealing blackberry and currant fruits matched well by hints of minerals and mint. Moderately long. Drink now. Score 88. K

REGIONAL, CABERNET SAUVIGNON, UPPER GALILEE AND RAMAT ARAD, 2002: Deep garnet towards purple, medium to full-bodied and reflecting generous but well-integrated tannins after aging in new French oak for 14 months. Compact and well focused, showing aromas and flavors of cedary oak, red currants, violets and dark chocolate. On the medium-long finish look for appealing hints of spices and tobacco. Drink now. Score 87. K

REGIONAL, MERLOT, UPPER GALILEE, 2005: Made from old vine Merlot blended with 7–10% of Cabernet Franc, this medium to full-bodied wine shows soft, near-sweet tannins integrating nicely and tempting aromas and flavors of ripe berries, plums, chocolate and licorice. Rich, round and delicious. Drink now–2010. Score 90. K

REGIONAL, MERLOT, UPPER GALILEE, 2004: Blended with 15% of Cabernet Sauvignon, this red reflects its aging in French oak for 12 months with spicy, near-sweet tannins and on the nose and palate shows plums and cassis fruits. On the moderately long finish appealing hints of sweet chewing tobacco and eucalyptus. Drink now. Score 87. K

REGIONAL, MERLOT, UPPER GALILEE, 2003: Garnet towards brick-red in color, with somewhat chunky tannins and perhaps too-generous oak. A bit skimpy with its berry, cherry and cassis aromas and flavors. Lacking complexity but pleasant. Drink now. Score 86. K

REGIONAL, CARIGNAN, ZICHRON YA'AKOV, 2005: Made from old vines and blended with 10% Petit Verdot, this dark purple wine is deeply aromatic. Showing firm tannins and generous toasty wood but with fine balance. On the nose and palate purple plums, blackberries, hints of pepper and near-sweet cocoa, all leading to a generous finish. Drink from release–2011. Tentative Score 89–91. K

REGIONAL, CARIGNAN, ZICHRON YA'AKOV, 2004: Made from old vine Carignan grapes (30–40 years old), blended with 10% of Petit Verdot and aged in French oak for 12 months. Still firm tannins here but those showing signs of integrating nicely and already revealing raspberry, cherry and cassis fruits, highlighted by hints of dark chocolate and espresso coffee. Drink now–2010. Score 89. K

REGIONAL, CABERNET FRANC, JERUSALEM MOUNTAINS, 2003: Medium-bodied, with generous fresh herbal and tobacco notes set off nicely by blackberry and black cherry fruits. Soft tannins and a hint of sweetness throughout make this a supple wine. Drink now. Score 87. K

REGIONAL, PETITE SIRAH, JUDEAN HILLS, 2005: Made from grapes from 35-year-old vines, this almost impenetrably dark purple, still firmly tannic wine opens in the glass to reveal a rich array of dark plum, wild berry, peppery, herbal and spicy cedar notes. Dense enough to be thought of as chewable but opens to show harmony and grace. Best 2009–2012. Tentative Score 90–92. K

REGIONAL, PETITE SIRAH, JUDEAN HILLS, 2004: Garnet towards royal-purple, medium to full-bodied, with chunky tannins that give the wine an appealing country-style. Look for aromas and flavors of wild berries, citrus peel and spring flowers leading to a moderately long finish. Drink now. Score 86. K

REGIONAL, CABERNET SAUVIGNON-SHIRAZ, UPPER GALILEE, 2005: A blend of 70% Cabernet and 30% Merlot, this medium to full-bodied, softly tannic wine fills the palate beautifully. On first attack, light earthy-meaty aromas and flavors, those yielding to blackberries, currants and black cherries and finally, on the long finish, returning to appealing earthy overtones. Drink now–2010. Score 89. K

REGIONAL, CABERNET SAUVIGNON-SHIRAZ, UPPER GALILEE, 2004: Full-bodied, with soft tannins and spicy wood coming together nicely with wild berry, black cherry and plum fruits on a licorice and vanilla-rich background. Drink now. Score 87. K

REGIONAL, ROSÉ, UPPER GALILEE, 2006: A medium-bodied, pale strawberry-colored blend of Shiraz, Cabernet Sauvignon and Merlot. Not much aroma but appealing flavors of berries and sour cherries. Pleasant quaffing. Drink up. Score 86. K

REGIONAL, CHARDONNAY, UPPER GALILEE, 2006: Developed *sur lie* in *barriques* for 6 months, light golden in color, medium-bodied, with appealing tropical fruits, roasted nuts and flinty minerals. Drink now. Score 88. K

REGIONAL, CHARDONNAY, UPPER GALILEE, 2004: Simple and austere, medium-bodied, with earthy and woody flavors that dominate the pear and melon fruit flavors. Could use more fruit and more acidity to make it livelier. Drink up. Score 84. K

REGIONAL, CHARDONNAY, GALILEE, 2003: Oak fermented and then developed *sur lie* for nine months, this light gold, medium-bodied white offers up a generous mouthful of summer and tropical fruits, those matched nicely by crisp minerals and just the right feel of oak. Drink up. Score 88. K

REGIONAL, JOHANNISBERG RIESLING, UPPER GALILEE, 2006: Floral on the nose, with appealing summer fruits, sweet apple and lightly honeyed overtones. On the long finish a hint of citrus peel. Generous sweetness but a bit overly generous acidity. Drink now. Score 85. K

REGIONAL, JOHANNISBERG RIESLING, UPPER GALILEE, 2005: Generously aromatic, with peach, apple and floral aromas and flavors. Good acidity to keep it lively and interesting. Drink up. Score 86. K

REGIONAL, CARMEL VINTAGE, FORTIFIED PETITE SIRAH, JUDEAN HILLS, 2004: With Tawny-Port-style chocolate, raisins and spice box aromas, this rich dessert wine opens to reveal coffee and a hint of bitter almonds to balance the sweetness. Drink now–2010. Score 89. K

Private Collection

Note: The Private Collection wines made for distribution in the U.S.A. and U.K. are *mevushal* while those distributed in Israel are kosher but not *mevushal*. It is my strong opinion that in the six–nine months following release, the

wines will show only minimal differences, but that *mevushal* wines cellared beyond that will show increasingly "cooked" flavors and aromas over time. The tasting notes that follow are for the non-*mevushal* wines.

PRIVATE COLLECTION, CABERNET SAUVIGNON, 2005: Garnet towards royal-purple, medium to full-bodied, with soft tannins integrated nicely. Opens with blackberries and currants, those yielding to blueberries and spices and on the moderately long finish hints of black licorice. Drink now. Score 87. K

PRIVATE COLLECTION, CABERNET SAUVIGNON, 2004: Aged partly in French and American oak, partly in stainless steel, this dark garnet, medium-bodied red shows near-sweet tannins and generous currant and blueberry aromas and flavors. Not complex but lithe and easy to drink. Drink now. Score 86. K

PRIVATE COLLECTION, CABERNET SAUVIGNON, 2003: Dark royal-purple, medium to full-bodied, with tannins integrating nicely and appealing aromas and flavors of currants, wild berries and spicy oak. Drink up. Score 85. K

PRIVATE COLLECTION, MERLOT, 2005: Dark royal-purple, medium-bodied, with chunky tannins that open in the glass to reveal berry, cherry and currant fruits. A country-style wine but easy to drink. Drink now. Score 84. K

PRIVATE COLLECTION, MERLOT, 2004: Deep garnet towards royal-purple in color and medium-bodied, with soft tannins and appealing ripe cherry-berry flavors as well as a hint of root beer. Drink now. Score 86. K

PRIVATE COLLECTION, MERLOT, 2003: Deep garnet, medium-bodied, reflecting its ten months in oak with hints of vanilla and spices along with firm tannins that may yield in time but now hold back the plum and berry fruits. Drink up. Score 85. K

PRIVATE COLLECTION, SHIRAZ, 2005: Medium to full-bodied, dark garnet-red, with soft tannins well balanced by vanilla and spicy wood. Look for plum and raspberry fruits, those with light vegetal and leathery aromas and flavors. Drink now. Score 87. K

PRIVATE COLLECTION, CABERNET SAUVIGNON-MERLOT, 2005: An oak-aged blend of 55% Cabernet Sauvignon and 45% Merlot. Garnet towards purple, medium to full-bodied, tannins now settled down and opening on the palate to reveal lightly spicy blackberry, currant and plum fruits. Not overly complex but a good quaffer. Drink now. Score 85. K

PRIVATE COLLECTION, CABERNET SAUVIGNON-MERLOT, 2004: Dark garnet-red, medium-bodied, with chunky, country-style tannins but those opening to reveal moderate levels of black cherry, tar and spicy notes. Drink up. Score 85. K

PRIVATE COLLECTION, CABERNET SAUVIGNON-MERLOT, 2003: Medium to full-bodied, with soft tannins and appealing currant and plum fruits backed up by hints of spices and sweet herbs. Drink up. Score 85. K

PRIVATE COLLECTION, CABERNET SAUVIGNON-SHIRAZ, 2003: Dark garnet in color, medium-bodied, with wood, soft tannins and acidity in fine balance with appealing berry, black cherry and cassis fruits. Drink up. Score 84. ᴋ

PRIVATE COLLECTION, GIVAT ZAMARIN, RED, 2004: An uno-aked blend of Cabernet Sauvignon, Merlot, Carignan and Petite Sirah. Medium-bodied, with soft tannins and some blackberry, currant and spicy aromas and flavors. Lacking complexity but an acceptable quaffer. Drink up. Score 84. ᴋ

PRIVATE COLLECTION, CHARDONNAY, 2006: Lightly oaked, this pale golden-straw, medium-bodied white shows nectarine and citrus fruits backed up nicely by a hint of spiciness that runs throughout. Easy to drink. Drink now. Score 87. ᴋ

PRIVATE COLLECTION, CHARDONNAY, 2004: Light golden-straw in color, medium-bodied, with a core of green apple and pineapple flavors. Crisp and clean with some appealing mineral overtones. Drink up. Score 84. ᴋ

PRIVATE COLLECTION, SAUVIGNON BLANC, 2006: This golden-straw-colored, medium-bodied white shows appealing tropical, citrus and melon fruits, those backed up nicely by just the right hint of freshly cut herbs. Crisp, clean and with another burst of fruits on the moderately long finish. Drink now. Score 87. ᴋ

PRIVATE COLLECTION, SAUVIGNON BLANC, 2005: Light straw-colored, medium-bodied, fresh and fruity with appealing green apple, peach and light grassy aromas and flavors. Drink up. Score 85. ᴋ

PRIVATE COLLECTION, EMERALD RIESLING, 2006: Unoaked, light to medium-bodied, this semi-sweet white has good acidity to keep it going and is showing traditional Emerald Riesling floweriness with pineapple and green apple aromas and flavors. Drink up. Score 82. ᴋ

PRIVATE COLLECTION, EMERALD RIESLING, 2005: Clear light straw in color, light in body, with sweetness that lacks acidity to keep it lively. Floral and pineapple aromas and flavors. Drink up. Score 79. ᴋ

PRIVATE COLLECTION, MUSCAT, 2006: Medium-bodied, sweet but not cloying, with herbal, floral and spicy accents to peach, nectarine, melon and bitter orange flavors. Well balanced, fresh and generous. Drink now. Score 86. ᴋ

PRIVATE COLLECTION, CHARDONNAY-SAUVIGNON BLANC, 2006: A blend of about 55% Chardonnay and 45% Sauvignon Blanc. Light golden-straw in color, medium-bodied, reticent when first poured but opening to show aromas and flavors of white peaches, melon, apricots and, towards the finish, hints of citrus peel and spices. Drink now. Score 85. ᴋ

PRIVATE COLLECTION, CHARDONNAY-SAUVIGNON BLANC, 2005: Light straw in color, light to medium-bodied, with sweet apple and spicy spring flower aromas. Not complex but an acceptable quaffer. Drink up. Score 84. K

Reches

RECHES, RED, ZICHRON YA'AKOV, 2006: An unoaked pot pourri of Petite Sirah, Cabernet Sauvignon, Merlot, Shiraz and Carignan. Soft, round and simple with primarily black fruits on the nose and palate. Drink now. Score 82. K

RECHES, ROSÉ, GALILEE, 2006: Made from Zinfandel and Carignan grapes, light to medium-bodied, with fresh tutti-fruitti aromas and flavors. A simple off-dry quaffer. Drink up. Score 83. K

RECHES, WHITE, ZICHRON YA'AKOV, 2006: A blend of Sauvignon Blanc and Chardonnay grapes, those revealing flowery, citrus, melon and tropical fruits. Some will object to the hint of sweetness here. Drink up. Score 84. K

Selected (Vineyard)

SELECTED, CABERNET SAUVIGNON, 2006: Garnet to purple, showing a light hint of spicy oak and currant, berry and black cherry fruits. A good quaffer. Drink now. Score 84. K

SELECTED, CABERNET SAUVIGNON, 2005: Developed with oak staves, this garnet-red, medium-bodied wine has soft tannins and appealing black cherry, blackberry and currant fruits. Drink now. Score 84. K

SELECTED, MERLOT, 2006: Medium-bodied, soft, and round. Look for aromas and flavors of cherries and red and black berries. An entry-level quaffer. Drink now. Score 84. K

SELECTED, MERLOT, 2005: Medium-bodied, with soft tannins and hints of vanilla reflecting the oak staves which were used. Cherry and plum fruits with just a hint of spices make this an uncomplicated but easy-to-drink wine. Drink up. Score 83. K

SELECTED, ZINFANDEL, 2005: As always a semi-dry blush or "white" Zin. Light to medium-bodied, with more of a resemblance to cherry-berry juice than to wine. Drink up. Score 74. K

SELECTED, PETITE SIRAH, 2006: A simple country-style wine with pleasant enough berry, cherry and cassis fruits. Drink now. Score 83. K

SELECTED, PETITE SIRAH, 2005: Soft and round, with forward black-berry, cassis and earthy aromas and flavors. Drink now. Score 80. K

SELECTED, ZINFANDEL BLUSH, 2006: A nice little white Zin. Rose-petal pink, light to medium-bodied, off-dry but with fine balancing acidity to keep it lively, and showing appealing berry and cherry aromas and flavors. Drink now. Score 85. K

SELECTED, CHARDONNAY, 2006: A simple little white wine with pine-apple, citrus and tropical fruits. An entry-level quaffer. Score 83. K

SELECTED, CHARDONNAY, 2005: Nothing complex here but a pleas-ant little white with pineapple and citrus fruits. An entry-level quaffer. Drink up. Score 82. K

SELECTED, SAUVIGNON BLANC, 2006: Light gold in color, light to medium-bodied, with crisp acidity and an appealing array of pineapple, green apple and tropical fruits. An easy-to-drink wine. Drink now. Score 86. K

SELECTED, SAUVIGNON BLANC, 2005: Light, simple, fresh and fruity with green apple, pineapple and peach fruits on a lightly floral background. Drink up. Score 84. K

SELECTED, EMERALD RIESLING, 2006: Light straw in color, light in body, semi-dry but with well proportioned sweetness. On the nose and palate, spring flowers together with citrus and green apple fruits. Best as an aperitif. Drink now. Score 84. K

SELECTED, EMERALD RIESLING, 2005: As light in color as in body and a bit too sweet, with floral and citrus aromas dominating. Drink up. Score 78. K

SELECTED, MOSCATO, 2005: Half-sweet, light, with primarily citrus and pineapple aromas and flavors and not quite lively enough to make it truly *frizzante*. Drink up. Score 78. K

Carmey Avdat **

Founded by Eyal Izrael, after he had spent several years working together with Yuval Ben Shushan, this small winery is based on a private farm on the heights of the Negev Desert not far from Kibbutz Sde Boker. The winery's vineyards of Cabernet Sauvignon and Merlot grapes are planted in a wadi and rely on water from 1,500-year-old water terraces built by the Nabbateans. The winery's first releases were 4,500 bottles from the 2005 vintage, which rose to 6,000 bottles from the 2006 vintage.

CARMEY AVDAT, CABERNET SAUVIGNON, 2006: Deep garnet towards purple, medium-bodied, with soft tannins and a generous but gentle wood influence. On the nose and palate berries, black cherries and currants, those with light earthy-herbal overlays. Drink from release–2009. Tentative Score 85–87.

CARMEY AVDAT, CABERNET SAUVIGNON, 2005: Dark royal-purple, medium to full-bodied with soft tannins and generous spicy wood, those integrating nicely to show currant, berry and herbal aromas and flavors. Drink now–2009. Score 86.

CARMEY AVDAT, MERLOT, 2006: Dark, youthful purple, medium to full-bodied, with still-gripping tannins and generous wood influences but those in good balance with fruits and acidity. On the nose and palate berries, cherries, cassis and appealing chocolate and peppery overlays that linger nicely. Drink from release–2009. Tentative Score 86–88.

CARMEY AVDAT, MERLOT, 2005: Medium-bodied, with silky smooth tannins, this deep ruby-towards-garnet colored wine is showing appealing berry and black cherry fruits on a spicy and lightly oaky background. Lingers nicely on the palate. Drink now–2009. Score 87.

Castel ✶✶✶✶✶

Starting as a micro-winery, the Domaine du Castel grew gradually and now produces approximately 100,000 bottles annually. That change in output, however, has not affected the quality of the wines, and since the release of a mere 600 bottles of his first wine in 1992, owner-winemaker Eli Ben Zaken—who now works with his son Ariel—has consistently made some of the very best wines in the country. The winery, with its exquisitely designed barrel room holding more than 500 *barriques*, is located on Moshav Ramat Raziel in the Jerusalem Mountains. The winery relies entirely on grapes grown in the area, mostly in its own vineyards, some in vineyards under its full supervision. Grape varieties include Cabernet Sauvignon, Merlot, Petit Verdot, Cabernet Franc, Malbec and Chardonnay.

The winery produces three wines annually. The first, Grand Vin Castel, is a superb Bordeaux-style blend with distinct Italian overtones; the fine second label, Petit Castel, is meant for earlier drinking; and "C" is consistently one of the most exciting Chardonnay wines produced in Israel. The winery produced a first kosher version of its Grand Vin in 2002, and from the 2003 vintage all of Castel's wines have been kosher.

Grand Vin Castel

GRAND VIN CASTEL, 2006: A tentative blend of 50% Cabernet Sauvignon, 30% Merlot and the balance of Petit Verdot and Malbec. Firm, solid and concentrated, this dark ruby, full-bodied wine opens to show intense, caressing and generous aromas and flavors of berries, black cherries, currants and bitter chocolate, and, on the long finish, a hint of crystallized fruits. Dense, near-sweet and remarkably rich, with a gripping and mouth-filling long finish. Muscular but gentle, intense but elegant. Best from 2010. Tentative Score 92–94. K

GRAND VIN CASTEL, 2005: Medium-dark garnet, full-bodied, with once searing tannins now settling down and showing admirable structure and balance. On the nose and palate concentrated currants, blackberries and, plums those supported by spicy wood, Mediterranean herbs and, on the long finish, light hints of anise and citrus peel. Best 2009–2013. Tentative Score 92–94. K

GRAND VIN CASTEL, 2004: Cabernet Sauvignon, Merlot, Petit Verdot and Cabernet Franc come together as a remarkably satisfying whole. Dark garnet towards inky black, full-bodied, with deep and still-firm tannins integrating nicely with smoky and spicy wood and fruits. Opens with blackberries and chocolate, those yielding to currants and raspberries and finally to an array of licorice and tobacco that play on the palate. Long, generous and elegant. Drink now–2012. Score 94. K

GRAND VIN CASTEL, 2003: Deep garnet, full-bodied, with tannins integrated nicely and showing a fine range of currant, blackberry and plum fruits, those with overlays of near-sweet cigar tobacco, spices and, on the long finish, an appealing earthy-herbal note. Drink now–2011. Score 94. K

GRAND VIN CASTEL, 2002: Remaining rich and round, continuing to show black fruits, anise and hints of olives and cedarwood, but at its peak now and not for further cellaring. Drink now. Score 90.

GRAND VIN CASTEL, 2002 (KOSHER EDITION): Maturing very nicely, its once exuberant currant, cherry and plum fruits now more subdued though still pronounced, and yielding to the minerals and cedar that were once in the background. Full-bodied, with wood, tannins and fruits nicely balanced and taking on a more earthy-herbal note. Drink now. Score 90. K

GRAND VIN CASTEL, 2001: Maturing and now showing earthy currant, black cherry, sage and cedarwood aromas and flavors. Full-bodied and concentrated, the wine possesses great elegance and features long lingering flavors rich in hints of coffee and chocolate. Drink now. Score 91.

GRAND VIN CASTEL, 2000: With once-firm tannins now wellintegrated, this medium to full-bodied wine is showing excellent balance between spicy black currant, plum and blackberry fruits, those matched nicely by hints of Mediterranean herbs and clean earthy aromas and flavors. Muscular, with firm tannins as well as a long, spicy finish. Perhaps a bit past its peak. Drink up. Score 90.

GRAND VIN CASTEL, 1999: This full-bodied, deep ruby-toward-dark purple wine reveals good balance between generous, well-integrated tannins and elegant black fruits including currants, plums and blackberries. Look also for aromas and flavors of mint and red licorice, all coming together in a just-spicy-enough finish with tobacco aromas and flavors. Maturing rapidly. Drink up. Score 90.

GRAND VIN CASTEL, 1998: A near-elegant wine, slow to open during its youth and now aging somewhat more quickly than anticipated. With now softened tannins, some spicy-smoky wood and plum and currant fruits, all leading to a moderately long vanilla-flavored finish. Drink up. Score 90.

GRAND VIN CASTEL, 1997: Perhaps Castel's most luxurious wine in its youth, with remarkably intense black currant and black cherry fruits, Mediterranean herbs, an abundant but very well-balanced oak and a long finish with pepper and anise. Supple and harmonious but now starting to fade. Drink up. Score 89.

Petit Castel

PETIT CASTEL, 2005: A blend primarily of Merlot, supplemented by Cabernet Sauvignon. Aged in oak for 16 months, this appealing dark red-ruby aromatic wine opens with red berries and spices going on to black cherries, licorice and chocolate. Generous and with a tantalizing hint of sweetness on the long finish. Drink now–2011. Score 91. K

PETIT CASTEL, 2004: Medium to full-bodied and with soft tannins, this caressing red opens with a chocolate and berry-rich nose, joined by cassis, black cherries, dark plums and black pepper, all lingering on a long, polished and round finish. Elegant and supple. Drink now–2010. Score 92. K

PETIT CASTEL, 2003: Softer, smoother and more approachable than the Grand Vin of this vintage. Medium to full-bodied, with forward black fruits, soft tannins already integrating nicely and a pleasing array of currant, wild berry and earthy-herbaceous aromas and flavors. Mouth-filling and moderately long. Drink now. Score 90. K

PETIT CASTEL, 2002: Dark ruby toward garnet, this medium-bodied red shows soft, well-integrated tannins and generous currant and wild berry fruits together with generous touches of sweet cedar, spices and herbs on the moderately long finish. Drink up. Score 89.

PETIT CASTEL, 2001: Medium to full-bodied, with soft and well-integrated tannins and excellent balance between wood and fruit, this wine is living up to its earlier promise. Black currant and blackberry fruits come together very nicely with lightly smoky cedar and an appealing underlying hint of earthiness. Drink up. Score 90.

"C" Chardonnay

"C", CHARDONNAY, 2006: Bright gold in color, with yeasty and nutty aromas complementing tropical fruits, ripe apple and a crème brulee sensation, all reflecting the wine's 12 months in French oak. A rich, full, lightly buttery white, with tantalizing spicy notes and fine balance and length. Drink now–2011. Score 92. K

"C", CHARDONNAY, 2005: Bright gold, full-bodied and concentrated, with light but not imposing buttery and spicy sensations. Rich, complex and opulent, with multiple layers of citrus, figs, pears, summer fruits and toasty oak. Shows finesse and elegance. Drink now–2010. Score 93. K

"C", CHARDONNAY, 2004: Light gold in color, medium to full-bodied, with generous but intentionally subdued oak influences. Deeply aromatic, with tempting citrus, melon, pear and tropical fruit aromas and flavors, those coming to a creamy and long finish. Drink now. Score 92. K

The Cave ✳✳✳

Founded in 1997 as the boutique
arm of Binyamina Wineries, this
small winery has its barrel storage
facilities in a cave at the foothills
of Mount Carmel, not far from the
town of Zichron Ya'akov. The arti-
ficial cave, built in the sixteenth
century, is nine meters high and
maintains a constant natural temperature and humidity. The winery
is releasing 6,000 bottles annually
of a Cabernet Sauvignon-Merlot
blend made by the winemakers of
Binyamina. The grapes come from
a single vineyard in Kerem Ben
Zimra in the Upper Galilee.

THE CAVE, CABERNET SAUVIGNON-
MERLOT, 2003: Full-bodied, with still-
firm tannins and generous spicy oak integrating nicely, this dark garnet
wine is showing fine balance and opening on the nose and palate to
reveal currant, blackberry and plum fruits, those supported nicely by
hints of tobacco and Mediterranean herbs. Drink now. Score 89. K

THE CAVE, CABERNET SAUVIGNON-MERLOT, 2002: This blend of
65% Cabernet Sauvignon and 35% Merlot was oak-aged for 20 months.
Medium to full-bodied, with solid tannins that yield in the glass to
reveal a generously fruity and elegant wine. On the nose and palate
black currants, blackberries and vanilla matched nicely by hints of
Mediterranean herbs. Drink now. Score 89. K

THE CAVE, CABERNET SAUVIGNON-MERLOT, 2001: This moderately
deep garnet, well-balanced, medium to full-bodied red was oak-aged for
18 months. Continuing to show tempting aromas and flavors of currants, plums and berries, those with overlays of coffee, Mediterranean
herbs and spicy oak. Drink up. Score 88. K

Chateau Golan ★★★★★

A fully modern winery located on Moshav Eliad on the Golan Heights, Chateau Golan released their first wines from the 2000 vintage under the hand of Oregon and California-trained winemaker Uri Hetz. Vineyards owned by the winery currently yield Cabernet Sauvignon, Merlot, Cabernet Franc, Petite Sirah, Petit Verdot, Grenache, Sauvignon Blanc, Mouvredre and Viognier grapes. Other grapes being planted include Rousanne and Grenache Blanc. Production is currently between 70,000–75,000 bottles and future production is estimated at somewhat over 100,000 bottles annually. To date the winery has released wines in one series, Royal Reserve, that including the proprietary blend known as Eliad.

Royal Reserve

ROYAL RESERVE, CABERNET SAUVIGNON, 2006: Medium-dark garnet, with a hint of sweetness on the nose, turning firm on the palate with mouth-coating tannins and hints of wood. Although high in alcohol, there is no sign of heat. Opens to light oak and mocha, which support currants, blackberries and a hint of vanilla bean that adds a nice touch; tannins and fruits rising on the finish. Best 2009–2012. Tentative Score 88–90.

ROYAL RESERVE, CABERNET SAUVIGNON, 2005: Almost impenetrably dark garnet in color, this wine is both concentrated and elegant. A blend of 89% Cabernet Sauvignon and 11% Cabernet Franc, opening with spicy, mocha-tinged black currants, those yielding to blackberries, herbs and light oak. Hints of light sea salt and leather on the super-long finish make the wine intriguing. Perhaps the best yet from the winery. Best 2009–2015. Score 94.

ROYAL RESERVE, CABERNET SAUVIGNON, 2004: Blended with 15% Cabernet Franc, and aged in French and American oak for 12 months, this medium to full-bodied wine's tannins and lightly smoky wood are integrating nicely to highlight blackberry, currant and purple plum fruits, those opening to hints of strawberries and spices. Drink now–2012. Score 91.

ROYAL RESERVE, CABERNET SAUVIGNON, 2003: Deep, young and tight, but showing excellent focus and concentration. Full-bodied and packed with nicely integrating tannins, the wine shows aromas and flavors of currants, black cherries and anise, along with attractive earthy-herbal overtones and hints of green olives. Drink now–2011. Score 90.

ROYAL RESERVE, CABERNET SAUVIGNON, 2002: Medium to full-bodied, well-balanced, concentrated and long, this blend of Cabernet Sauvignon with 9% Cabernet Franc offers an appealing array of ripe cherry, currant, red plum, jammy strawberry and spicy flavors overlaid by light-toasty oak, and a near-sweet finish with a hint of tobacco. Drink now. Score 89.

ROYAL RESERVE, CABERNET SAUVIGNON, 2001: Oak-aged for ten months, this deep garnet-toward-purple, medium-bodied wine shows smooth tannins, just the right hints of earth and spices and appealing blackberry and black currant fruits leading to a clean and medium-long finish. Drink now. Score 88.

ROYAL RESERVE, CABERNET SAUVIGNON, 2000: Intense and deep with cherry, currant and mocha aromas and flavors, and with good balance between tannins and fruits, this medium to full-bodied 100% Cabernet fills the mouth nicely and with near-elegance. Drink up. Score 88.

ROYAL RESERVE, CABERNET SAUVIGNON, 1999: Medium to full-bodied, with an appealing royal-purple color, this Cabernet Sauvignon was blended with 4% Merlot to give it some softness. Reflecting ten months in new French oak barrels, the wine is rich and well balanced, with smooth tannins and with currant, mineral, pepper and smoky oak aromas and flavors. Drink up. Score 89.

ROYAL RESERVE, MERLOT, 2006: Medium-bodied with soft tannins, this medium-dark purple wine opens with a green, veggie nature but changes quickly in the glass to currants and damson plums, all with an exotic spicy note that creeps in from mid-palate and lingers through the finish. Vibrant and just complex enough to grab attention. Drink from release–2011. Tentative Score 88–90.

ROYAL RESERVE, MERLOT, 2005: A thoroughly modern but still 'Old-World' wine, with good acidity, gentle wood and fruits in fine balance. Showing a bit green now, but opening to currant and blueberry fruits, those complemented nicely by mocha, chocolate and vanilla. Look for a long, lightly spicy finish. Balance, harmony and finesse here. Drink now–2010. Score 90.

ROYAL RESERVE, MERLOT, 2004: A blend of Merlot, Syrah and Cabernet Franc (89%, 6% and 5% respectively) aged in oak for 13 months, this medium-dark garnet wine shows near-sweet tannins and a light earthy minerality, those supporting generous red currant, berry and cherry aromas and flavors. On the long finish tantalizing hints of sage and anise. Drink now–2012. Score 92.

ROYAL RESERVE, MERLOT, 2003: Aged in oak for 12 months, this deep garnet-towards-royal-purple, medium to full-bodied blend of Merlot, Syrah and Cabernet Sauvignon (86%, 13% and 1% respectively) shows fine balance between generous tannins, spicy wood and currants, berry fruits and herbaceousness. On the long finish hints of licorice and green olives. Concentrated and well focused. Drink now–2010. Score 90.

ROYAL RESERVE, MERLOT, 2002: This deep royal-purple oak-aged blend of 85% Merlot and 15% Cabernet Sauvignon shows firm, well-integrated tannins and appealing currant, wild berry and plum aromas and flavors, together with gentle overlays of spicy chocolate and vanilla. Drink now. Score 88.

ROYAL RESERVE, MERLOT, 2001: Medium to full-bodied, this elegant and intense Merlot, blended with 15% of Cabernet Sauvignon, was aged in French oak casks for one year. Dark in color, the wine has deep, still-firm tannins, well balanced by raspberry, plum and currant fruits, those on a complex background of dark chocolate and vanilla, and a long, sweet finish. Drink now. Score 91.

ROYAL RESERVE, SYRAH, 2006: Ripe, fruity and floral. Medium-dark garnet, medium to full-bodied, with a generous but softly tannic structure and spicy wood in fine balance and showing blackberry, spices, a light vegetal overtone and a hint of lime peel. Best 2009–2012. Tentative Score 89–91.

ROYAL RESERVE, SYRAH, 2005: Blended with 3% Cabernet Sauvignon and aged in large French barrels for 11 months. Dark, rich and plush from first attack, opening to show a tempting array of spicy blackberry, raspberry, red currants and pomegranate fruits, those matched nicely by hints of citrus peel. Bold, with distinctly Old-World charm, showing a light greenness, minerality and tantalizing meaty notes. Long and generous. Drink from release–2012. Score 92.

ROYAL RESERVE, SYRAH, 2004: Aged in large oak barrels for 14 months, this medium to full-bodied and firmly tannic wine opens beautifully in the glass to reveal ripe blackberry, currant and raspberry fruits, all with a delicate hint of near-sweetness and spring flowers. On the long and generous finish hints of spices, licorice and smoked meat. Drink now–2011. Score 90.

ROYAL RESERVE, SYRAH, 2003: Blended with 15% Grenache, this is a classic and elegant Syrah with distinct Mediterranean overtones. Fine balance between wood and soft tannins, a generously gamy wine that offers up smoke and black pepper along with deep raspberry and floral aromas and flavors. Drink now. Score 90.

ROYAL RESERVE, SYRAH, 2002: Big, rich, dense and tannic, and already showing roundness and richness, this wine is a deep garnet-to-purple color and has generous plum, herbal and earthy aromas and flavors. Somewhat astringent in its youth but integrating very nicely now. Drink now. Score 90.

ROYAL RESERVE, SYRAH, 2001: Dark royal-purple, this medium to full-bodied blend of 85% Syrah and 15% Cabernet has inherent good balance and structure. Still young but already showing soft tannins and tempting plum and berry fruits with generous hints of earthiness and herbaceousness. In time it will show olive and mushroom aromas as well. Drink now. Score 91.

ROYAL RESERVE, SYRAH, CUVEE NATUREL, 2001: Intense, tannic and concentrated, medium to full-bodied. Deep purple in color, re-flecting its 14 months in French oak with spices and a generous dash of vanilla, those complemented nicely by jammy black fruits. Drink up. Score 90.

ROYAL RESERVE, CABERNET FRANC, 2005: Subtle and seductive, with generous tannins integrating nicely. On the nose and palate fresh currant, dark berry and black cherry fruits matched nicely by bell peppers, cigar box and lead pencil notes. Promising length, depth and elegance. Drink from release–2011. Tentative Score 90–92.

ROYAL RESERVE, CABERNET FRANC, LIMITED EDITION, 2003: Full-bodied, earthy and aromatic with an appealing array of currant, plum and wild berry fruits, those backed up nicely by vanilla and spices from the oak as well as an appealing hint of earthiness on the moderately long finish. Rich and concentrated. Drink now–2010. Score 90.

ROYAL RESERVE, GRENACHE, 2005: Ripe, rich and with generous oak-accented blackberry, black cherry, spicy and black pepper flavors. True to its variety, with an attractive hint of greenness. Drink from release–2010. Tentative Score 89–91.

ROYAL RESERVE, GRENACHE, 2003: Loyal to its varietal traits, this attractive, pale ruby wine is medium-bodied, with soft tannins and tempting blackberry, black cherry and red currant fruits as well as spicy oak. Drink now. Score 89.

ROYAL RESERVE, MERLOT-CABERNET, 2000: Dark purple toward black, this medium to full-bodied blend of 65% Cabernet and 35% Merlot was aged in French and American oak barrels for 12 months. Well balanced and with tempting black cherry, currant, plum and hazelnut aromas and flavors, this smooth wine has just a hint of coffee on the finish. Drink up. Score 89.

ROYAL RESERVE, GESHEM, 2006: A blend of Grenache and Syrah developed separately. Medium-dark garnet towards royal-purple, showing moderately soft but mouth-coating tannins and tantalizing dusty oak, those yielding to blueberry, plum, vanilla and bittersweet chocolate. Plush, with flavors that linger long and gently on the palate. Drink from release–2012. Tentative Score 90–92.

ROYAL RESERVE, GESHEM, 2005: Medium-dark garnet, a blend of 70% Grenache and 30% Syrah, reflecting its aging in French oak for 12 months with a light, pleasingly musky overtone. Opens with a near-raspberry liquor nose, that settling down to reveal oak-accented aromas and flavors of blackberries, cherries and black pepper. Deep and long. Drink now–2013. Score 93.

ROYAL RESERVE, GESHEM, 2004: The first blend of Syrah and Grenache from the winery (62% and 38% respectively). Dark ruby towards garnet, medium to full-bodied, with soft, ripe tannins integrating well and showing currant and berry fruits, those matched nicely by spices, freshly crushed herbs and, as the wine sits on the palate, hints of orange peel and black tea. Long, super-fruity finish. Drink now–2010. Score 91.

ROYAL RESERVE, ROSÉ, 2006: One of the few rosé wines that actually has a rose-petal reddish-pink color. Made from Cabernet Franc grapes, this medium-bodied wine shows strawberry, raspberry, nectarine and wild berry fruits. Crisply dry and refreshing with just enough complexity to enchant. Drink now. Score 87.

ROYAL RESERVE, ROSÉ, 2005: Made entirely from Cabernet Franc grapes. Crisply dry, with the color of peaches in their first bloom, this medium-bodied wine is far more complex than one usually anticipates in a rosé. On the nose and palate peaches, strawberries, rosewater and wild berries. Picking up a somewhat too-metallic finish. Drink up. Score 86.

ROYAL RESERVE, SAUVIGNON BLANC, 2006: Light gold in color, aromatic, bright and lithe but showing fine concentration and balance. On the nose and palate good balance between ripe fruit, smart acidity and a silky texture echoing lime, passion fruit and the barest hint of spicy oak that goes on to the long finish. Drink now. Score 90.

ROYAL RESERVE, SAUVIGNON BLANC, 2005: Developed partly in oak and partly in stainless steel, this is a medium-bodied wine, delightfully aromatic, with a tempting array of spices and a peppery character, showing pear, apple, melon and mineral flavors that linger very nicely. Impeccably balanced and long. Drink now. Score 90.

Eliad

ELIAD, 2006: Deep garnet towards royal-purple with orange reflections in color, full-bodied, intense and concentrated, opening with a core of raspberry and red currant fruits, going on to black cherries. With ripe tannins, a tantalizing hint of saltiness, this is a ripe and complex wine in which the oak plays only a minor role. Best 2009–2012. Tentative Score 91-93.

ELIAD, 2005: Aged in French oak for 13 months, this blend of 94% Cabernet Sauvignon and 6% Syrah opens with rich, almost syrup-like fruits on the nose, and goes on to show depth and grace. Soft tannins, light smoky wood, fine-grained tannins in good balance with berry, black cherry, currants and licorice. Drink from release–2012. Score 93.

ELIAD, 2004: A blend of Cabernet Sauvignon, Merlot, Cabernet Franc and Petit Verdot (70%, 21%, 3% and 6% respectively), this may be the most intense wine released to date by the winery. Dark garnet in color, ripe and complex, showing deep plum, berry, floral, coffee, peppery and earthy aromas and flavors all coming together beautifully in a long and graceful finish. Drink now–2012. Score 92.

ELIAD, 2003: Oak-aged, this deep garnet blend of 66% Cabernet Sauvignon, 20% Merlot and 14% Cabernet Franc is already showing rich, intense and complex. Concentrated plum, berry, currant and spicy oak aromas and flavors matched nicely by spices and a hint of tobacco. Drink now–2012. Score 92.

ELIAD, 2002: Opening nicely now, this blend of 91% Cabernet Sauvignon and 9% Merlot has crisp tannins and generous currant, black cherry and cedar as well as leathery-earthy aromas and flavors, with a long finish in which the tannins and wood meld beautifully. Drink now–2010. Score 90.

ELIAD, 2001: A blend of Cabernet Sauvignon, Merlot and Syrah (85%, 10% and 5% respectively), each aged separately, some in French and some in American oak. This dark, almost inky royal-purple medium-bodied wine shows soft tannins that are nicely balanced by jammy plum and blackberry fruits, and appealing layers of chocolate and smoky toasty aromas and flavors. Drink now. Score 90.

Chillag ★★★★

After studying oenology in Piacenza, Italy, and working at the Antinori wineries in Tuscany, Orna Chillag released her first wines in Israel in 1998. Now located in a new facility in the industrial area of the town of Yahud, on the central plain, the winery relies on Merlot and Cabernet Sauvignon grapes from the Upper Galilee and recently planted its own Syrah, Petit Verdot and Petite Sirah. Production has grown from 4,000 bottles in 2002 to 20,000 bottles in 2005 and 2006.

In addition to regular releases in two series, Primo Riserva and Giovane, and a first rosé wine from the 2006 vintage, Chillag also produces a line of kosher wines under the label Orna, of which 15,000 bottles of Cabernet Sauvignon were released in the United States from the 2003, 2004 and 2005 vintages.

Primo Riserva

PRIMO RISERVA, CABERNET SAUVIGNON, 2005: Full-bodied, deeply tannic and even now with generous but judicious wood in fine balance with tempting blackberry, red currant and oriental spices, all leading to a rich, long and blueberry-laden finish. Drink from release–2012. Tentative Score 89–91.

PRIMO RISERVA, CABERNET SAUVIGNON, 2004: Deep garnet towards purple in color, with firm tannins well balanced with smoky wood and fruits. Rich blackberry, cherry and licorice flavors with overlays of spicy oak and licorice. Long and elegant. Drink now–2010. Score 90.

PRIMO RISERVA, CABERNET SAUVIGNON, 2003: Blended with a small amount of Merlot and aged in French oak for 18 months, this full-bodied red shows appealing aromas and flavors of black currant and ripe berry fruits, those matched nicely by spicy oak and, on the long finish, tantalizing hints of freshly turned earth and mushrooms. Needs a bit of time to let the tannins settle in. Best 2009–2011. Score 90.

PRIMO RISERVA, CABERNET SAUVIGNON, CASTELLANA, 2002: Dark royal-purple, this full-bodied wine was made by blending 70% Cabernet Sauvignon and 30% Merlot together in the same oak barrels.

Aromas and flavors of spicy currants, anise and cedary oak come together in a complex, mouth-filling, supple wine. Drink up. Score 89.

PRIMO RISERVA, CABERNET SAUVIGNON, 2001: Full-bodied, with real weight and grip and with plenty of tannins, this concentrated blend of 90% Cabernet Sauvignon and 10% Merlot shows a deep purple color. Now opening to reveal fine balance between tannins, wood and fruit, yielding currants, plums and blackberries with meaty and toasty accents. Drink up. Score 89.

PRIMO RISERVA, MERLOT, 2004: Medium to full-bodied, with now soft, round tannins, minerals and toasty oak coming together nicely to show appealing blueberries, blackberries and mineral aromas and flavors that linger comfortably. Drink now–2009. Score 88.

PRIMO RISERVA, MERLOT, 2002: Medium to full-bodied, with velvety tannins, this elegant and harmonious red shows tempting fresh black currant, berry and plum flavors, those with hints of cedary, spicy notes. Look for a long vanilla-and-berry rich aftertaste. Drink up. Score 88.

Giovane

GIOVANE, CABERNET SAUVIGNON, 2005: Showing a distinct Tuscan flair this deep, dark and round medium to full-bodied wine shows soft tannins and a tempting array of cherries, raspberries and cassis all on a warmly spicy background. Drink now–2009. Score 90.

GIOVANE, CABERNET SAUVIGNON, 2004: Deep garnet towards royal-purple, medium-bodied, with firm but well-integrating tannins and tempting black fruits, spices and a long lightly herbal finish. Generous and elegant. Drink now–2009. Score 89.

GIOVANE, MERLOT, 2005: As deep in its rich garnet-red color as it is in tannins, and reflecting the oak casks in which it is developing with a gentle hand, this medium to full-bodied wine shows berry, black cherry and cassis fruits, those matched with gentle hints of bitter herbs and, on the long finish, a hint of peppermint. Drink now–2009. Score 88.

GIOVANE, MERLOT, 2004: Dark royal-purple, full-bodied and with firm but caressing near-sweet tannins opening to reveal lush blackberry, currant, plum, vanilla and mocha aromas and flavors, those leading to a fruit-loaded long herbal finish. Soft, round, and long. Drink now. Score 89.

GIOVANE, MERLOT, 2003: Dark royal-purple with orange and violet reflections, needing some time for the still-firm tannins to integrate but already showing an elegant array of currants, cherries and spices along with a gentle modicum of oak. On the finish, hints of coffee and herbs. Drink now. Score 90.

Orna

CHILLAG, CABERNET SAUVIGNON, ORNA, 2005: Oak-aged for 13 months, this dark garnet, full-bodied red shows soft, mouth-coating tannins in fine balance with plum, berry and currant fruits. Drink now. Score 87. K

CHILLAG, CABERNET SAUVIGNON, ORNA, 2004: Dark royal-purple, full-bodied, with near-sweet tannins integrating nicely. Look for aromas and flavors of black currants, plums and berries, those with a nice, spicy overlay. Drink now. Score 88. K

CHILLAG, CABERNET SAUVIGNON, ORNA, 2003: Aged in French oak for 14 months, this ripe and chewy wine shows soft tannins and plum and black currant fruits. Somewhat past its peak. Drink up. Score 87. K

CHILLAG, ROSÉ, 2006: Made from Cabernet Sauvignon grapes. Rose-petal pink towards orange, this medium-bodied rosé is interesting at first because of light, meaty and herbal overtones on the cherry flavors, but turns flat and earthy on the finish. Drink up. Score 83.

Clos de Gat *****

2003

CLOS de GAT

HAR'EL

Cabernet Sauvignon

Grown, Produced & Estate Bottled by Clos de Gat Winery

14% vol.   PRODUCE OF ISRAEL   750 mL.

Located on Kibbutz Har'el in the Jerusalem Mountains, this joint project of the *kibbutz* and Australian-trained winemaker Eyal Rotem released its first wines from the 2001 vintage. The name "Clos de Gat" is a play on words— the French *clos* is an enclosed vineyard surrounded by stone walls or wind-breaks, while the Hebrew *gat* is an antique wine press. With the exception of the Chardonnay grapes in the 2002 wine, all the grapes have come from the winery's own vineyards, which now include Cabernet, Merlot, Petit Verdot, Syrah and most recently the winery's own Chardonnay. Production in 2002 was 22,000 bottles, in 2004 approximately 60,000 bottles and in 2005, due to reduced yields, about 45,000 bottles. With the 2006 vintage production rose to about 70,000 bottles.

Until recently the winery released wines in two series, the Bordeaux blend Clos de Gat, and a second label, Har'el. This year the winery released its new top-of-the-line series, Sycra (Aramaic for 'bright red'), of wines to be produced only in selected years. From the 2003 vintage on, all the wines have been made with wild-yeasts.

Sycra

SYCRA, MERLOT, 2003: With 24 months in wood and a generous 15% alcohol content, this super-dark garnet-colored wine is full-bodied enough to be chewy and shows tannins that, although gripping, seem soft and comforting. On the nose and palate touches of spice and freshly-turned earth supporting currant, blackberry and floral notes, all leading to a finish that goes on and on. Best 2009–2013. Score 93.

SYCRA, SYRAH, 2004: The flavors and aromas in this firm, dense wine seem to shift and change every few moments. Opens with cherries and currants, goes to grapes and pepper, sage and anise, and then on to freshly ground Arabica coffee. On the superbly long and tannic finish, the cherries and currants rise again. Well focused and intense. Drink now–2012. Score 94.

Clos de Gat

CLOS DE GAT, 2005: A blend of Cabernet Sauvignon, Merlot and Petit Verdot (65%, 30% and 5% respectively), oak-aged for 20 months. Dark garnet, with purple and orange reflections, full-bodied, with soft, mouth-coating tannins integrating gently with spicy oak. Opens with blackberries, slate and cedary oak, those yielding to currant, raspberry and mocha, all culminating in a very long finish. Best 2009–2013. Tentative Score 92–94.

CLOS DE GAT, 2004: Dark, full-bodied, firmly tannic, with generous spicy wood, this blend of 65% Cabernet Sauvignon, 30% Merlot and 5% Petit Verdot shows fine harmony but still needs time to integrate. The wine opens to reveal currant, blackberry, spicy oak and hints of licorice and light earthiness. Best 2009–2012. Score 93.

CLOS DE GAT, 2003: Predominantly Cabernet Sauvignon, fleshed out with Merlot and Petit Verdot. Dark garnet, medium to full-bodied, with firm tannins integrating nicely, this elegant wine shows black currant, black cherry and berry fruits, those supported well by hints of vanilla and licorice, all leading to a long spicy finish. Drink now–2012. Score 92.

CLOS DE GAT, 2002: Full-bodied, with generous but soft tannins, this dark red-towards-black, medium to full-bodied blend of 70% Cabernet Sauvignon and 30% Merlot reflects its 18 months in oak with spicy but not exaggerated wood. On the nose and palate ripe currants and plums matched nicely by hints of coffee, sweet cedar, vanilla and Mediterranean herbs. Drink now–2009. Score 90.

CLOS DE GAT, 2001: A deep ruby-garnet full-bodied unfiltered blend of 70% Cabernet Sauvignon and 30% Merlot, with generous, soft tannins that integrate beautifully, this is a wine that can honestly be said to reflect its *terroir*. Overlaying traditional Cabernet black currants are generous hints of green olives, basil, tarragon and other Mediterranean herbs. The wine shows good balance and structure, with chocolate and leather coming in on the long finish. Drink now. Score 90.

CLOS DE GAT, ROSÉ, 2006: A medium-bodied blend of 67% Syrah and 33% Cabernet Sauvignon, all with very short skin contact, this complex but easy-to-drink rosé is a delightful rose-petal pink towards ruby in color and on the nose and palate shows blackberry, plum and black cherry fruits, those matched by a dash of spicy oak on the finish. Drink now. Score 90.

CLOS DE GAT, ROSÉ, 2005: This medium-bodied, barely-sweet deep pink blend of one-third Syrah and two-thirds Cabernet Sauvignon offers up black currant and blackberry fruits, those with light earthy and spicy hints and far more complexity than one usually expects in a rosé. Drink up. Score 89.

CLOS DE GAT, CHARDONNAY, 2005: Dark gold, full-bodied, but so well balanced that it floats on the palate. Reflects its year in oak with generous spicy wood that turns creamy on the palate and with citrus and green apple notes that develop into peaches, apricots, ginger and lightly chalky-mineral notes that linger comfortably through the long finish. Drink now–2012. Score 92.

CLOS DE GAT, CHARDONNAY, 2004: Deep but lively gold, full-bodied, simultaneously floral and creamy, with fine balancing acidity to show off citrus, pear, green apples and, on the long finish, hints of figs and ginger. Long, generous and mouth-filling. Drink now. Score 92.

CLOS DE GAT, CHARDONNAY, 2003: Delicious medium to full-bodied Chardonnay with ripe pineapple, citrus, apple and spicy notes. Enough mineral crispness here to make one think of fine Chablis, with a good touch of toasty oak but with balancing acidity that carries the wine very well indeed. Drink now. Score 91.

CLOS DE GAT, CHARDONNAY, 2002: Full-bodied with ripe pear and pineapple aromas and flavors on the first attack, these yielding beautifully to citrus flowers, apple, and ripe apricots, all on a spicy background. Fermented and aged *sur lie* in French oak barrels, the wine has very good balance between lively acidity, intentionally underplayed oak and minerals, and a creamy, mouth-filling sensation. Drink up. Score 89.

CLOS DE GAT, CHANSON, 2006: A blend of 70% Chardonnay, 15% Semillon, and 6-8% each of Viognier and Chenin Blanc that comes together in ways that delight. Light gold, medium-bodied, with fine balancing acidity and showing an array of lemon, quince, green apple, stony minerals and floral aromas and flavors that go on to a long and lively finish. Easy to drink but surprisingly complex. Drink now. Score 92.

Har'el

HAR'EL, CABERNET SAUVIGNON, 2005: Blended with 8% of Merlot and 3% of Petit Verdot and aged in oak for 12 months, this deep garnet-towards-royal-purple, full-bodied red shows generous fine-grained tannins that highlight lightly spicy wood and generous red currant and black cherry fruits. On the moderately long finish an appealing mineral streak. Drink from release–2012. Tentative Score 90–92.

HAR'EL, CABERNET SAUVIGNON, 2004: Full-bodied and firmly tannic, reflecting its 12 months in oak with spicy wood which yields in the glass to reveal currants, black cherries and purple plums, those supported nicely by hints of chocolate and cigar tobacco. Fine balance and structure. Drink now–2012. Score 90.

HAR'EL, CABERNET SAUVIGNON, 2003: Medium to full-bodied, an oak-aged blend of 93% Cabernet Sauvignon, 4% Merlot and 3% Petit Verdot, with soft tannins that highlight generous raspberry, ripe cherry and black currant fruits, those matched nicely by moderate oak and a hint of anise. Drink now. Score 90.

HAR'EL, MERLOT, 2005: Deep, dark and intense but with balance and structure that bode very well for the future. Impenetrable royal-purple, full-bodied, with tannins that need taming, but even now reflecting its 15 months in oak with spicy wood that opens to show berries, plums and chocolate. Rich, long and delicious. Best 2009–2012. Tentative Score 91–93.

HAR'EL, MERLOT, 2004: Deep and dark, with near-sweet oak-accented tannins and generous currant, plum and berry aromas and flavors, those coming to a well-focused, lightly smoky and mouth-filling finish. Deeply aromatic from first attack through the long finish. Drink now–2012. Score 90.

HAR'EL, MERLOT, 2003: A dense, muscular wine that needs time to settle down but promising to be deep, dark and absolutely beautiful. Complex oak-accented blackberry, currant and black cherry aromas and flavors on a background of chewy tannins, sweet cedar, and hints of pepper and vanilla, all of which linger beautifully. Drink now–2012. Score 92.

HAR'EL, SYRAH, 2005: Blended with 7% Cabernet Sauvignon, this dark royal-purple, deeply aromatic, mouth-filling, and lush red shows medium to full-bodied, and boasts tannins that are soft but comfortably gripping. A generous array of plum, cherry and berry fruits, those backed up by juniper and white pepper. On the long finish hints of leather and citrus peel. Drink from release–2012. Tentative Score 91–93.

HAR'EL, SYRAH, 2004: Dark garnet, this medium to full-bodied blend

of 85% Syrah and 15% Cabernet Sauvignon shows soft, round tannins and a fruit-forward style on which you will find a fine array of plum, blueberry and blackberry, those complemented by spices and appealing hints of fresh herbs and toffee. Drink now. Score 92.

HAR'EL, SYRAH, 2003: Deep ruby colored, this blend of 85% Syrah and 15% Cabernet Sauvignon shows generous peppery overtones. Medium to full-bodied, with firm but nicely integrating tannins and complex plum, red berry and earthy aromas and flavors, all with a hint of leather on the finish. Drink now–2009. Score 91.

Dalton ✳✳✳✳

Founded by Mat Haruni in 1993, this fully modern winery located in the industrial park of Dalton in the Upper Galilee has vineyards in Kerem Ben Zimra and several high altitude sites along the Lebanese border. Australian and Californian-trained winemaker Na'ama Mualem is currently producing wines in six series, Single Vineyard, Reserve, Dalton Estate, Alma, Dalton and Canaan, the first two of age-worthy varietal wines, the second of similar varieties intended for earlier drinking, and the last of popularly priced series meant for youthful drinking. Grapes include Cabernet Sauvignon, Merlot, Shiraz, Barbera, Zinfandel, Chardonnay, Sauvignon Blanc and Muscat. First production was 50,000 bottles, current production is about 800,000 and the target for 2007 is one million bottles. Dalton has earned a consistently good name for high quality wines, providing excellent value for money.

Single Vineyard

SINGLE VINEYARD, CABERNET SAUVIGNON, MERON, 2004: Perhaps the best wine to date from Dalton. Deep youthful cherry towards garnet, medium to full-bodied, this well-balanced wine was aged in French oak for eight months and then

bottled without filtration. Generous soft tannins and ample wood, those already integrating nicely to reveal a very appealing array of red currant, raspberry and citrus peel on a peppery, lightly herbal, minty background. Round, long and mouth-filling. Drink now–2010. Score 92. K

SINGLE VINEYARD, MERLOT, MERON, 2005: Supple, rich and generous. Aged in oak for 16 months, with soft, near-sweet, mouth-coating tannins and fine balancing acidity to add liveliness to the blueberry and currant fruits. Hints of spices and mint run through to the long finish. Ripe, round and polished. Drink now–2011. Score 91. K

Reserve

RESERVE, CABERNET SAUVIGNON, 2005: In its infancy and tasted from components but already showing medium to full-body, firm tannins, and hints of spicy-smoky wood balanced nicely by currant, plum and berry fruits. Drink from release. Tentative Score 88–90. K

RESERVE, CABERNET SAUVIGNON, 2004: Medium to full-bodied, with a layer of spicy and toasty wood to show for its 18 months in oak, this dark garnet towards royal-purple wine shows moderately soft tannins and acidity coming together nicely. On the nose and palate blackberries, currants and an intimation of purple plums, those complemented by hints of spices and minty chocolate on the long finish. Drink now–2012. Score 91. K

RESERVE, CABERNET SAUVIGNON, 2003: Darker garnet than in its youth, this medium to full-bodied wine is still firmly tannic, with generous oak well balanced by fruits and natural acidity. On the nose and palate black currant, black cherry and herbal-spicy aromas and flavors. Drink now–2009. Score 89. K

RESERVE, CABERNET SAUVIGNON, 2002: As during its youth, medium-bodied, ripe and harmonious. Now showing sweet cedar and herbaceousness that open to reveal currant, ripe plum and black cherry fruits. Drink now. Score 87. K

RESERVE, MERLOT, 2004: Medium to full-bodied, with soft tannins and spicy oak in fine balance with acidity and fruits. On the nose and palate, generous red and black berries and ripe red plums on a light tobacco and herbal background. Look as well for an appealing hint of vanilla that creeps in on the finish. Drink now–2009. Score 89. K

RESERVE, MERLOT, 2003: Aged in oak for 14 months, dark garnet in color, with currant, plum, cherry and herbal aromas and flavors all with a light overlay of vanilla. Showing complexity and finesse. Drink now. Score 89. K

138

RESERVE, MERLOT, 2002: Smooth and elegant, with a core of ripe plum and black cherry fruits, those on a background of toasty oak, spices and very appealing hints of sage and tea. As the wine continues to develop, look for a leathery note on the long finish. Drink now. Score 89. K

RESERVE, SYRAH, 2005: Nearly black in color, but a wine of remarkable elegance. Aromatic, with spicy and floral scents on first attack, those yielding to aromas and flavors of berries and plums, all backed up by hints of white pepper, and on the long finish, surprising notes of peaches and apricots. Drink now–2010. Score 91. K

RESERVE, SHIRAZ, 2004: Full-bodied and concentrated with soft tannins and generous but not overpowering sweet cedar and spices from the *barriques* in which it aged. Aromas and flavors open with raspberries, go on to cherries, berries, red plums, pepper and an attractive earthiness. Generous and long. Drink now–2010. Score 90. K

RESERVE, SHIRAZ, 2003: Medium to full-bodied and solidly tannic, this red reflects its ten months in new American oak with generous hints of smoke and vanilla, those on tempting black fruits, mint and earthiness. Needs time to open and show its elegance. Drink now–2009. Score 89. K

RESERVE, CABERNET SAUVIGNON-MERLOT, 10TH ANNIVERSARY EDITION, 2003: Dark cherry towards garnet, medium-bodied, this gently oaked wine shows an appealing array of aromas and flavors. On first attack blackberries and a hint of mint, those yielding to strawberries, cherries, licorice and earthy minerals. Nicely balanced and moderately long. Drink now–2010. Score 89. K

RESERVE, CHARDONNAY, 2006: Light golden-straw in color, showing tantalizing hints of light but spicy oak, and opening to show grapefruit, orange and apricot fruits, those backed up by good natural acidity to keep the wine both sophisticated and lively. Drink now. Score 89. K

RESERVE, CHARDONNAY, 2005: Developed in new oak barrels for six to eight months, this white shows generous spicy oak, but given time to settle, the oak will integrate nicely with citrus, summer fruits, green apples, yeasty white bread and, on the moderately long finish, a nice hint of tropical fruits. Drink now. Score 88. K

RESERVE, CHARDONNAY, 2003: After eight months *sur lie* in new French oak *barriques*, this medium-bodied white shows appealing earthy, buttery vanilla aromas backed up nicely by flavors of melons and pears. Drink now. Score 88. K

RESERVE, SAUVIGNON BLANC, 2005: Medium-bodied, unoaked, and with aromas and flavors of grapefruit peel, green apples and hints of grassiness, coming together in a vigorous, fresh and lively but just complex enough wine. Drink now. Score 88. K

RESERVE, SAUVIGNON BLANC, 2004: Unoaked, fresh, crisp and aromatic, with light herbal hints. On first sip dominated by grapefruit flavors but those yielding to aromas and flavors of apples, melons, spices and minerals. Drink up. Score 87. K

RESERVE, VIOGNIER, 2006: Light gold in color, having spent only four months in oak to maintain fresh aromas and flavors, this medium-bodied white is showing aromatic on the nose, with an appealing array of white peaches, apricots and a distinct floral character, those backed up by hints of caramel and, on the long finish, a note of cinnamon. Drink now. Score 88. K

Dalton Estate

DALTON ESTATE, CABERNET SAUVIGNON, 2005: Developed for 12 months in French and American *barriques*. Dark garnet, medium-bodied, with somewhat chunky country-style tannins that yield in the glass to reveal plum, blackberry and currant fruits, those with a somewhat heavy mineral-earthy overlay. Drink now. Score 85. K

DALTON ESTATE, CABERNET SAUVIGNON, 2004: Dark garnet, medium-bodied, with moderately firm tannins, spicy oak and appealing currant and plum fruits. Not complex but pleasant. Drink up. Score 85. K

DALTON ESTATE, MERLOT, 2005: Dark royal-purple, medium-bodied, with firm tannins matched nicely by vanilla and cloves from the French oak *barrqiues* in which it developed. A vibrant and lively young red with currant, raspberry and plum aromas and flavors matched nicely by a hint of exotic spices that runs throughout. Long and generous. Drink now. Score 88. K

DALTON ESTATE, MERLOT, 2004: Medium-bodied, with soft tannins and a hint of toasty oak that highlights black cherry, raspberry and plum fruits. Lingers nicely with toasty and floral notes. Drink now. Score 87. K

DALTON ESTATE, MERLOT, 2003: Moderate levels of complexity, soft tannins, medium-body and a band of berry and black cherry fruits with a tempting hint of spices. Good backbone here. Drink now. Score 87. K

DALTON ESTATE, SHIRAZ, 2005: Dark, almost inky garnet, medium-bodied, with soft mouth-coating tannins balanced nicely by hints of vanilla and spices from the American oak in which it aged for ten months. On the nose and palate, appealing cherry, plum and berry fruits, those matched nicely by undertones of earthiness, cardamom and white pepper. Ripe, round and generous. Drink now–2009. Score 88. K

DALTON ESTATE, SHIRAZ, 2003: Deep, almost impenetrable purple, medium to full-bodied, with generous but yielding tannins, this lightly oak-aged wine shows a generous array of earthiness, tobacco and milk chocolate on a background of wild berries and plums. Drink now. Score 88. K

DALTON ESTATE, SHIRAZ, SAFSUFA, 2003: Medium to full-bodied, with firm tannins integrating nicely and with generous smoky oak, those well balanced with plum, blackberry, mint and earthy aromas and flavors leading to a long vanilla and currant finish. *Mevushal* and made only for export. Drink now. Score 88. K

DALTON ESTATE, BARBERA, 2005: Lightly oak-aged, royal-purple in color, with generous acidity, soft tannins and moderate wood influences, those well in balance with fruits. Opens with wild berries and spring flowers, opening to cassis, blackberries and a nice hint of licorice. Round, soft and satisfying. Drink now. Score 88. K

DALTON ESTATE, BARBERA, 2004: A very nice first Barbera release. Developed in oak casks for nine months, dark cherry-red, medium-bodied, soft and round, with good balancing acidity and tempting aromas and flavors of ripe berries, cherries and minerals, ending on a lightly spicy finish. Drink now. Score 87. K

DALTON ESTATE, CHARDONNAY, 2005: Unoaked, medium-bodied and lovely, with crisp dryness highlighting citrus, apple and tropical fruits. Drink up. Score 86. K

DALTON ESTATE, CHARDONNAY, 2004: Unoaked, medium-bodied, with tempting tropical fruits, citrus and minerals, a crisply dry, lightly floral and delicious wine meant for early consumption. Drink up. Score 86. K

DALTON ESTATE, FUMÉ BLANC, 2006: Golden-straw in color, light to medium-bodied, with appealing hints of spicy wood and white bread. On the nose and palate citrus, melon and papaya. Refreshing and generous. Drink now. Score 87. K

DALTON ESTATE, SAUVIGNON BLANC FUMÉ, 2004: Light-straw colored, medium-bodied, with hints of toasted white bread revealing its three months in oak. Appealing aromas and flavors of grapefruit, melon and tropical fruits. Lively and refreshing. Drink up. Score 86. K

DALTON ESTATE, SAUVIGNON BLANC FUMÉ, 2003: Light in color but packed with fresh tropical fruit and citrus flavors, those with a lightly smoky overlay and hints of roasted nuts. Meant for youthful drinking. Drink up. Score 86. K

DALTON ESTATE, SAUVIGNON BLANC FUMÉ, 2002: Toasty-smoky aromas and flavors along with appealing peach and apricot fruits on a clean, just-lively-enough background. Somewhat past its peak. Drink up. Score 84. K

Alma

ALMA, 2005: Garnet towards purple, medium to full-bodied, this blend of 65% Cabernet Sauvignon and 35% Merlot spent 16 months in French oak. Firm tannins integrating nicely with spicy oak. On the nose and palate blackberries, purple plums and a teasing hint of bitter oranges, the fruits backed up nicely by Oriental spices. Still firm tannins, spicy oak and acidity in fine balance. Drink now–2011. Score 88. K

Dalton

DALTON, ZINFANDEL, 2005: This dark royal-purple wine spent 12 months in new American oak. Full-bodied, with generous near-sweet tannins and smoky and vanilla oak, it opens on the palate to reveal black cherry, raspberry and plum fruits, those backed up by hints of chocolate, vanilla and espresso coffee. A generous and mouth-filling finish. Drink now–2009. Score 89. K

DALTON, ROSÉ, 2006: A rich, fruity and aromatic rosé made from a blend of 95% Cabernet Sauvignon and 5% Merlot. In color somewhere between rose-petal pink and cherry-red and showing strawberry, raspberry and dried cherry flavors. With bare sweetness well balanced by acidity, a refreshing wine for sipping on its own or with food. Drink now. Score 87. K

DALTON, ROSÉ, 2005: Semi-dry, light to medium-bodied, with skimpy berry and strawberry aromas and flavors. A bit flat on the palate. Drink up. Score 83. K

DALTON, MOSCATO, 2006: Light, with a moderate 5% alcohol content and lightly frizzante, this unabashedly sweet wine offers up appealing peach and melon fruits but the acidity is a bit on the low side. Best poured over an ice cube or two and served as an aperitif. Drink up. Score 84. K

Canaan

CANAAN, RED, 2006: This blend of Cabernet Sauvignon, Shiraz and Merlot (70%, 10% and 20% respectively) is soft and round, medium-bodied, with gentle tannins and forward berry, plum and raspberry fruits matched by a spicy note that runs throughout. Not complex but quite pleasant. Drink now. Score 85. K

CANAAN, RED, 2005: Medium-bodied, softly tannic, developed in stainless steel with the addition of oak chips that add a hint of spicy wood matched nicely by black cherry and cassis fruits. Not complex but fresh and generous. Drink up. Score 86. K

CANAAN, WHITE, 2006: Light golden-straw in color, this light to medium-bodied semi-dry blend of 70% Sauvignon Blanc and 30% Chardonnay shows citrus and tropical fruits, the sweetness matched by lively acidity. Drink now. Score 84. K

CANAAN, SAUVIGNON BLANC-CHARDONNAY, 2005: Light straw in color, light to medium-bodied, with fresh acidity and citrus, tropical fruits and a nice hint of grassy-herbaceousness here. Drink up. Score 85. K

Dico's *

Founded by David Ben-Arieh in 2001 on Moshav Ginaton on the central plains, this winery relies on Cabernet Sauvignon grapes from Kerem Ben Zimra and Merlot from the Gedera area. Current production is about 2,500 bottles annually.

DICO'S, CABERNET-MERLOT, 2005: Dark royal-purple, medium-bodied, with chunky, country-style tannins and smoky oak yielding slowly in the glass to reveal dried berry and currant notes. Drink now. Score 82.

DICO'S, CABERNET-MERLOT, 2004: Dark but not clear garnet, with firm tannins and overly generous spicy wood that hide the berry, cherry and currant flavors that fail to make themselves adequately felt. Drink up. Score 78.

DICO'S, CABERNET-MERLOT, 2003: A country-style wine, deep cherry-red towards purple, medium-bodied, with chunky tannins, smoky wood and aromas and flavors of ripe berries and plums. Drink up. Score 79.

DICO'S, CABERNET-MERLOT, 2002: A medium-bodied blend of 85% Cabernet Sauvignon and 15% Merlot, this soft, simple, country-style wine has a ripe black cherry flavor, somewhat coarse tannins and a vague hint of sweet cedarwood. Drink up. Score 78.

DICO'S, CABERNET-MERLOT, 2001: Medium-bodied, with a modest array of cedar and cherry flavors that fade on the too-short finish. Drink up. Score 79.

Ein Teina **

Ein Teina
Cabernet - Syrah
2005

Dry red wine made of
Cabernet Sauvugnon and Syrah
14.5%vol   Ein Teina Winery   750Ml
Golan Hights

Founded by Yotam Ben-Tzvi on Moshav Givat Yoav on the southern Golan Heights, this small winery released its first wines in 2004. First year's releases were of 900 bottles, and in 2006 production was about 2,500 bottles. The winery relies on Cabernet Sauvigon, Merlot and Syrah grapes from the southern Golan

EIN TEINA, TALIA'S BLEND, 2005: A ruby-towards-garnet blend of Cabernet Sauvignon, Merlot and Syrah. Medium to full-bodied, with soft tannins integrating with spicy wood. Bold aromas and flavors of blackberries and currants, those on a background of mocha and orange peel, with gentle peppery notes that run through to a long ripe finish. Drink now–2009. Score 89.

EIN TEINA, CABERNET SAUVIGNON-SYRAH, 2005: Medium-bodied, with soft, near-sweet tannins and hints of spicy wood. On first attack raspberry and currant fruits on a lightly earthy background, those yielding to hints of figs and cigar tobacco. Drink now–2009. Score 88.

Ella Valley ★★★★

Located on Kibbutz Netiv Halamed Hey in the Jerusalem Mountains, the winery has vineyards that might well serve as a model of efficiency and beauty anywhere in the world. Cultivation started in 1997 in the Ella and Adulam Valleys in the Judean Hills, and now includes Cabernet Sauvignon, Cabernet Franc, Merlot, Shiraz, Pinot Noir, Petite Sirah, Chardonnay,

Sauvignon Blanc, Semillon and Muscat grapes. Under the supervision of French-trained winemaker Doron Rav Hon, the winery released its first wines, 90,000 bottles, from the 2002 harvest. Production from the 2006 vintage was about 150,000 bottles and projected production for 2010 is 300,000 bottles.

Wines are released in three series: Vineyard's Choice, Ella Valley Vineyards and Ever Red, the first two destined for moderately long cellaring and the third for early drinking.

Vineyard's Choice

VINEYARD'S CHOICE, CABERNET SAUVIGNON, 2005: Full-bodied, with moderately firm tannins, a gentle wood influence, and fine balance. Blended with 10% of Merlot, this soft, round wine opens with near-sweet berries and spices, those yielding to reveal lush currant and blackberry aromas and flavors. Drink from release–2013. Tentative Score 90–92. K

VINEYARD'S CHOICE, CABERNET SAUVIGNON, 2003: Blended with 3% of Cabernet Franc and aged in oak for 17 months, this is a deep and brooding wine. Dark royal-purple, full-bodied, with ripe, rich fruits showing harmony and finesse. Layers of currants, juicy cherries and tempting oak shadings. Drink now–2011. Score 91. K

VINEYARD'S CHOICE, CABERNET SAUVIGNON, 2002: Dark garnet towards royal-purple in color, reflecting its 18 months in *barriques* with generous but not imposing sweet-and-spicy cedarwood. Full-bodied, with soft, mouth-coating tannins and an appealing array of black fruits, those supported by hints of Mediterranean herbs and vanilla. On the long finish a nice rising of red cherries. Drink now–2009. Score 90. K

VINEYARD'S CHOICE, MERLOT, 2005: Deep and dark, with block-buster tannins that promise to soften with time to show the wine's complexity and balance. A tempting array of black cherry, blackberry and currant flavors all coming together in a long finish. Drink now–2012. Score 91. K

VINEYARD'S CHOICE, MERLOT, 2004: Dark, deep and firmly tannic but with balance that bodes well for the future. Reflecting 16 months in oak with spicy and sweet-cedar notes, those opening to reveal raspberry, currant, chocolate and herbal notes that linger on a long finish. Drink now–2012. Score 91. K

VINEYARD'S CHOICE, MERLOT, 2003: Full-bodied and firmly struc-tured, with dark black cherry, berry, anise and spice flavors that stand up nicely to the tannins and moderate oak influences. Needs time but promises to soften and develop beautifully. Drink now–2010. Score 90. K

VINEYARD'S CHOICE, MERLOT, 2002: Developing beautifully. Full-bodied, with firm mouth-coating tannins and—as in its youth—a complex array of plum, currant and berry fruits, those supported now by black olives and a hint of smoked bacon on the long finish. Drink now–2009. Score 92. K

VINEYARD'S CHOICE, CABERNET SAUVIGNON-MERLOT, 2005: Dark garnet towards purple, deeply aromatic, a full-bodied blend of 60% Cabernet Sauvignon and 40% Merlot. Muscular and tannic at this time but with balance and structure that bode well for the future. Currant, cherry and berry fruits with generous hints of toasty oak on an appealing base of exotic spices. Overtones of cedar come in on the long finish. Best 2009–2013. Tentative Score 90–92. K

VINEYARD'S CHOICE, MERLOT-CABERNET SAUVIGNON, 2004: A blend of 60% Merlot and 40% Cabernet Sauvignon, oak-aged for 16 months. Showing generous oak, firm but well-integrating tannins, plums and black cherries on a spicy and harmonious background and with hints of vanilla that rise on the moderately long finish. Drink now–2009. Score 88. K

Ella Valley Vineyards

ELLA VALLEY VINEYARDS, CABERNET SAUVIGNON, 2006: Medium to full-bodied, ruby towards royal-purple in color, with soft tannins well balanced by spicy wood. On the nose and palate red currants, wild berries and hints of pepper, all leading to a generously fruity finish. Best 2009–2012. Tentative Score 89–91. K

ELLA VALLEY VINEYARDS, CABERNET SAUVIGNON, 2005: Dark royal-purple, medium to full-bodied, with tannins and wood in fine balance with fruits. On first attack black currants, blackberries and a light earthy overlay, those opening to reveal spicy oak and hints of dark cocoa. Long, generous and elegant. Drink from release–2011. Tentative Score 89–91. K

ELLA VALLEY VINEYARDS, CABERNET SAUVIGNON, 2004: Full-bodied, ripe and complex, with soft tannins integrating nicely and showing currant and red plums along with intimations of anise, black pepper and oak. On the finish hints of earthiness and freshly tanned leather. Well crafted. Drink now–2012. Score 91. K

ELLA VALLEY VINEYARDS, CABERNET SAUVIGNON, 2003: Dark garnet, aged for 14 months in oak, this well-crafted red's once firm and chunky tannins are now integrated nicely and showing generous aromas and flavors of blackberries, black cherries, stony minerals and spices. Drink now–2009. Score 90. K

ELLA VALLEY VINEYARDS, CABERNET SAUVIGNON, 2002: Dark garnet toward purple, this medium to full-bodied wine shows rich, ripe currant, plum, cherry, anise and mint aromas and flavors. Generous and long, but with a light bitterness that runs through to the finish. Drink up. Score 88. K

ELLA VALLEY VINEYARDS, MERLOT, 2006: Medium to full-bodied, this dark ruby-towards-garnet wine is showing gripping tannins in fine balance with hints of spicy, vanilla-rich wood. On the nose and palate a tempting array of cherry, red and purple berries and cassis, all with an attractive earthy-mineral overlay. Drink from release–2011. Tentative Score 90–92. K

ELLA VALLEY VINEYARDS, MERLOT, 2005: Dark and brooding, with still-gripping tannins, this dense wine offers up generous currant and black cherry aromas and flavors. Showing muscular elegance. Drink now–2012. Score 92. K

ELLA VALLEY VINEYARDS, MERLOT, 2004: A Merlot firm enough in tannins that it needed 5% of Cabernet Sauvignon to soften it somewhat. Supple and with good balance between spicy wood and fruit, this full-bodied red is showing black cherry, currant and cedary oak. Drink now–2011. Score 90. K

ELLA VALLEY VINEYARDS, MERLOT, 2003: Medium to full-bodied, deep garnet in color, with tannins now integrating nicely. Supple and elegant, with plum, blackberry, currant and berry fruits going to hints of cedar and spices on the long finish. Drink now–2009. Score 90. K

ELLA VALLEY VINEYARDS, SYRAH, 2006: Dark, almost impenetrable garnet, medium to full-bodied, deeply aromatic and on the palate plum, blackberry and black cherry fruits. Finishes with minerals, spices and a hint of smoked bacon. Intricate and complex. Best starting in 2010. Tentative Score 90–92. K

ELLA VALLEY VINEYARDS, SHIRAZ, 2004: Full-bodied, dark, rich and complex with an array of spicy, smoky and meaty plum, berry, currant and anise notes set off nicely by near-sweet tannins. Well balanced and flavorful. Drink now–2009. Score 89. K

ELLA VALLEY VINEYARDS, PINOT NOIR, 2006: Pure and delicious. Dark cherry-red, medium-bodied, with soft, well-integrating tannins and appealing raspberry, red plum and cherry flavors supported by sweet spices. Gains intensity in the glass and ends with a long finish. Drink from release–2011. Tentative Score 90–92. K

ELLA VALLEY VINEYARDS, PINOT NOIR, 2005: Showing soft tannins, gentle spicy oak and a generous array of cherry, red currant and raspberry fruits, and sweet spices. Long and elegant. Drink now–2012. Score 91. K

ELLA VALLEY VINEYARDS, CABERNET FRANC, 2006: With blackberry, black cherry, tobacco and steely-mineral notes, the wine calls to mind the Loire Valley. Medium to full-bodied, with soft, mouth-coating tannins, all leading to a fresh, round, ripe and lightly spicy finish. Drink from release–2011. Tentative Score 89–91. K

ELLA VALLEY VINEYARDS, CABERNET FRANC, 2005: Blended with 12% of Merlot, dark garnet, medium to full-bodied, with appealing vegetal aromas on first attack, those opening to reveal gently spicy cedarwood, blackberries, red currants and generous hints of herbaceousness and white chocolate that come in on the long finish. Drink now–2010. Score 90. K

ELLA VALLEY VINEYARDS, CABERNET FRANC, 2004: Garnet towards inky black, medium to full-bodied, with austere tannins. Reflecting its

12 months in oak with appealing vanilla and cinnamon, lead pencil, cherry, currant and wild berry fruits. Opens slowly on the palate but then shows long and generous, with well-tempered doses of smoke and tobacco. Drink now–2009. Score 91. K

ELLA VALLEY VINEYARDS, CABERNET FRANC, 2003: Blended with 15% of Cabernet Sauvignon, this almost impenetrably dark garnet, oak-aged, full-bodied red shows firm tannins and generous wood influence, those balanced nicely by a generous array of black fruits, coffee, vanilla and tobacco, all leading to a long leathery finish. Drink now. Score 91. K

ELLA VALLEY VINEYARDS, CABERNET SAUVIGNON-SYRAH, 2005: Dark purple, full-bodied, with soft tannins, this blend of 65% Cabernet Sauvignon and 35% Syrah is young, generous and remarkably lively, with cherry, raspberry and plum aromas and flavors, those with overlays of cedarwood, freshly cut herbs and spices. Drink now–2010. Score 89. K

ELLA VALLEY VINEYARDS, CABERNET SAUVIGNON-SYRAH, 2004: Deep garnet towards purple, this full-bodied blend of 70% Cabernet Sauvignon and 30% Shiraz reflects its 13 months in oak with spices and vanilla. With tannins settling in nicely now, showing generous blackberry and black cherry fruits, those supported by hints of spicy cedar and herbs and, creeping in comfortably on the long finish, a hint of grilled meat. Drink now–2010. Score 89. K

ELLA VALLEY VINEYARDS, MERLOT-PETIT SYRAH, 2006: Deep purple, medium to full-bodied, with somewhat chunky tannins that give the wine a few sharp edges but showing appealing plum and black currant fruits. An appealing country-style quaffer. Drink from release–2011. Tentative Score 85–87. K

ELLA VALLEY VINEYARDS, CHARDONNAY, 2006: Medium to full-bodied, medium-gold in color, with fresh grapefruit, nectarine, apple and crisp mineral aromas and flavors, those lingering nicely on a crisply clear finish. Drink now–2009. Score 90. K

ELLA VALLEY VINEYARDS, CHARDONNAY, 2005: Medium to full-bodied and aromatic, opening with green apples and figs, those yielding to lush pears and summer fruits. Focused with a long mineral and toasted white bread finish. Drink now–2009. Score 90. K

ELLA VALLEY VINEYARDS, CHARDONNAY, 2004: Deeply aromatic, reflecting ten months in oak with hints of smoke and spices. Soft and round, with generous pear, melon, citrus and mineral aromas and flavors that develop a near creamy note on the finish. Complex and long. Drink now. Score 90. K

ELLA VALLEY VINEYARDS, CHARDONNAY, 2003: Ripe and complex, with spicy pear, apple and hazelnut notes. Reflecting its ten months *sur lie*, this deep gold wine fills the palate with complex and long-lingering flavors, and just the right hints of toasted white bread and yeast. A good dose of oak here but that well integrated. Drink up. Score 91. K

ELLA VALLEY VINEYARDS, SAUVIGNON BLANC, 2006: Light gold in color, freshly aromatic, this medium-bodied white has a fine crispness supplied by natural acidity. On the nose and palate lively citrus, nectarine and light floral aromas and flavors. Drink now–2009. Score 90. K

ELLA VALLEY VINEYARDS, SAUVIGNON BLANC, 2005: Aromatic, with gentle hints of spicy wood and steely minerals underlying generous grapefruit, guava and nectarine aromas and flavors, those lingering nicely to a long, lightly grassy finish. Drink now. Score 90. K

ELLA VALLEY VINEYARDS, MUSCAT DESSERT, 2003: Medium-bodied, unabashedly sweet but with fine balance between sugar, acidity and alcohol. On the nose and palate aromas and flavors of honeyed summer fruits, stewed pears, sesame seeds and spring flowers. Generous, mouth-filling and long. Drink now–2009. Score 90. K

Ever Red

EVER RED, 2005: A blend of 45% each Cabernet Sauvignon and Merlot and 10% Petite Sirah. Dark garnet towards royal-purple, medium-bodied, with soft, well-integrated tannins and appealing currant, berry and spicy overlays. Drink now–2009. Score 87. K

EVER RED, 2004: A medium-bodied blend of Cabernet Sauvignon, Merlot and Petite Sirah (60%, 33% and 7% respectively), with gentle tannins and an appealing array of plum and currant fruits, all with just a hint of spiciness that lingers nicely. Drink now. Score 88. K

EVER RED, 2003: Deep purple, medium-bodied, this blend of Cabernet Sauvignon and Merlot opens in the glass to reveal gentle wood, soft tannins and appealing currant and wild berry fruits, and chocolate. A lightly spicy finish. Drink up. Score 87. K

Erez **

Founded in 2003 by Erez Sadon,
this boutique winery is located
in Rehelim in the Shomron, and
has vineyards on Mount Bracha
at an elevation of 840 meters.
The winery is currently producing about 8,000 bottles annually,
those primarily from Cabernet
Sauvignon, Merlot and Chardonnay grapes.

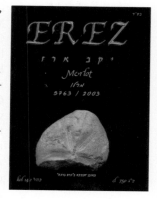

EREZ, CABERNET SAUVIGNON,
2003: Dark garnet towards royal-
purple in color, with firm tannins
and generous wood, but those in good balance with fruits and acidity.
On the nose and palate black fruits, Oriental spices and vanilla. Drink
now. Score 85.

EREZ, MERLOT, 2003: Aged in *barriques* for 18 months, dark garnet,
medium-bodied, with soft tannins. Appealing and clean blackberry
and black cherry fruits and hints of spices, but those perhaps a bit
overshadowed by too-generous wood. Drink now. Score 85.

Essence **

Located in the community of Ma'aleh Tsvia in the Western Galilee, the winery was founded by Yaniv Kimchi, Eitan Rosenberg and Itzhak Avramov, and released its first wines in 2001. Grapes, including Cabernet Sauvignon and Merlot, are raised in the winery's organic vineyards at the foothills of Mount Kamon, and the wines are made in accordance with international organic standards. The winery's output is currently about 5,000 annually.

ESSENCE, CABERNET SAUVIGNON, RESERVE, 2005: Dark ruby towards garnet, medium to full-bodied, with chunky country-style tannins and generous spicy wood. Opens to reveal berry, black cherry and cassis fruits. Drink now. Score 85.

ESSENCE, CABERNET SAUVIGNON, 2004: Garnet-red, medium-bodied, with firm tannins integrating nicely. On the nose and palate berry and currant fruits with hints of toasted oak. Drink now. Score 85.

ESSENCE, CABERNET SAUVIGNON, 2003: Deep ruby towards garnet, medium-bodied, with chunky tannins, spicy cedarwood and aromas and flavors primarily of ripe berries. Pleasant but somewhat one dimensional. Drink up. Score 84.

ESSENCE, MERLOT, 2005: Oak-aged for 14 months, with firm tannins and generous wood, this medium-bodied red opens in the glass to show berry and cherry fruits. Short and one dimensional. Drink now. Score 84.

ESSENCE, MERLOT, 2003: Cloudy purple in color, with chunky tannins that seem not to want to integrate and stingy black fruits dominated by an overly alcoholic finish. Drink up. Score 79.

ESSENCE, ELECTRUM, 2004: Dark royal-purple, medium to full-bodied with soft tannins integrating nicely with spicy wood. A blend of equal parts of Cabernet Sauvignon and Merlot with forward black-berry, currant and tobacco notes that linger nicely. Drink now–2009. Score 86.

ESSENCE, ELECTRUM, 2003: Medium-bodied, with generous oak, this blend of Cabernet Sauvignon and Merlot shows soft but chunky country-style tannins and appealing blackberry and cassis aromas and flavors. Drink now. Score 84.

Flam *****

MERLOT
VINTAGE 2001
RESERVE

PRODUCED AND
BOTTLED BY FLAM
BROS. HAGEFEN LTD
I S R A E L
750 ML 13.5% ALC. BY VOL.

Located in a state-of-the-art facility not far from the town of Beit Shemesh at the foothills of the Jerusalem Mountains, the Flam winery has produced consistently excellent and exciting wines since its first releases from the 1998 vintage. Established by brothers Golan and Gilad Flam; Golan, having trained and worked in Australia and Tuscany, is the winemaker; Gilad is in charge of the business aspects. The winery is currently producing age-worthy varietal Cabernet Sauvignon and Merlot wines in their Reserve and Superiore series; a second wine, Classico, which is a blend of Cabernet Sauvignon and Merlot that is meant for relatively early drinking; and a label for white wine, Flam. Production from the 2004 and 2005 vintages was of 55,000 bottles and the prediction for 2006 is about 75,000 bottles. Grapes come primarily from vineyards over which the winery has full control in the Judean Mountains and the Galilee. Experimental plantings are now underway with Petit Verdot and Cabernet Franc grapes.

Reserve

RESERVE, CABERNET SAUVIGNON, 2006: Not yet a final blend but already showing deep royal-purple, full-bodied, with soft, near-sweet tannins integrating nicely with wood, natural acidity and fruits. On the nose and palate layer after layer of black cherries, currants, raspberries, bay leaf and sweet spices all coming together nicely in a long and generous finish. Best from 2009. Tentative Score 91–93.

RESERVE, CABERNET SAUVIGNON, 2005: Blended with 6% each of Merlot and Petite Verdot and oak-aged for 18 months, this deep garnet, full-bodied red's chewy tannins are now integrating nicely but still showing generous wood. On the nose and palate a complex and elegant array of blackcurrant, black cherry, anise and Mediterranean herbs and on the long finish hints of vanilla and sage. Firm but yielding and lingering long on the palate. Best 2009–2013. Score 93.

RESERVE, CABERNET SAUVIGNON, 2004: Deep garnet towards black, full-bodied, with once searing tannins now integrating nicely. This blend of 88% Cabernet Sauvignon and 12% of Merlot reflects its 18 months in *barriques* with spicy wood and tannins in fine balance with natural acidity and currant, plum, and blackberry fruits. On the long finish hints of mint and spices. Best 2008–2012. Score 91.

RESERVE, CABERNET SAUVIGNON, 2003: This full-bodied, dark garnet-towards-inky purple wine, blended with 7% of Merlot, was oak-aged for about 14 months. Generous black currant and cherry fruits come together elegantly with mineral, herbal and light earthy aromas and flavors, all with a hint of smoky-toasty oak. Super-smooth tannins and a long finish. Best 2009–2014 .Score 93.

RESERVE, CABERNET SAUVIGNON, 2002: Made from Cabernet Sauvignon grapes from the Upper Galilee and blended with a small amount of Merlot from Karmei Yosef, this elegant, deep garnet-towards-black wine shows good integration between wood, soft tannins, sweet cedar and generous currant and ripe red fruits. A long fruity and lightly herbal finish. Drink now–2009. Score 91.

RESERVE, CABERNET SAUVIGNON, 2001: Dark royal-purple toward garnet, with deep extraction, but still showing a remarkable softness. A full-bodied, distinctly Mediterranean red with excellent balance between wood, tannins and fruit. Traditional Cabernet black currants are well set off by cherries, berries, spices and hints of black olives and leather. Drink now. Score 93.

RESERVE, CABERNET SAUVIGNON, 2000: Well focused, this deep purple, medium to full-bodied blend of 90% Cabernet Sauvignon and 10% Merlot spent 15 months in oak casks. A wine so deep you feel you can get lost in it, with flavors and aromas of red currants, ripe red fruit and delicious spices. Drink now–2009. Score 94.

RESERVE, CABERNET SAUVIGNON, 1999: As dark garnet in color today as during its youth, this deep and profound oak-aged blend of 85% Cabernet Sauvignon and 15% Merlot has intense berry, mint and cassis aromas and flavors, along with ample hints of spicy oak. On the outer cusp of its peak but still elegant and refined, with silky tannins and a succulent finish. Drink now. Score 94.

RESERVE, CABERNET SAUVIGNON, 1998: Aged in new oak casks for 14 months, this delicious blend of 85% Cabernet Sauvignon and 15% Merlot may be somewhat past its peak but is as assertive, rich and lush today as it was during its youth. Spicy and peppery tones overlay deep aromas and flavors of currants, black cherries and plums, along with floral and chocolate accents and a clean, long finish. Drink up. Score 88.

RESERVE, MERLOT, 2006: Still in embryonic form but already showing dark garnet towards royal-purple, full-bodied, with near-sweet, gripping and nicely yielding tannins. A gentle hand with the wood and fine balancing acidity highlight berry, plum and orange peel notes, those well supported by hints of Oriental spices. Needs time to show its elegance. Best from 2010. Tentative Score 91–93.

RESERVE, MERLOT, 2005: Dark garnet towards royal-purple, medium to full-bodied, reflecting its 18 months in oak with soft, mouth-coating tannins and spicy wood. Look for a tempting light earthiness that supports blackberries, currants, and a touch of spiciness that weaves its way through the wine and then lingers nicely on a long, elegant finish. Drink now–2012. Score 92.

RESERVE, MERLOT, 2004: Dark garnet with orange and green reflections. Made entirely from Merlot grapes, full-bodied and tannic. On first attack peppery wood reflecting 16 months in oak, that opening slowly to reveal firm mouth-coating tannins, then showing a tempting array of currant, berry and black cherry fruits, those backed up nicely by spices and, on the long finish, a hint of crème Anglaise. Continuing to develop nicely. Drink now–2012. Score 92.

RESERVE, MERLOT, 2003: Blended with 7% Cabernet Sauvignon, dark, deep and intense, with soft, almost sweet tannins and layer after layer of berry, black cherry, anise and spice aromas and flavors that linger nicely on the palate. The once-marked wood influence is now receding and the wine is showing soft, round and long. Drink now–2012. Score 92.

RESERVE, MERLOT, 2002: Deep royal-purple and full-bodied, this dark, rich and luxurious wine has an array of flavors that open in the glass to reveal black cherries, currants, mocha and herbs. Once-firm tannins now integrated nicely and showing a careful hand with smoky oak. On the long spicy finish, anise and light tar overtones. Drink now–2009. Score 91.

RESERVE, MERLOT, 2001: Subdued and elegant, this full-bodied wine shows smooth, well-integrated tannins together with delicious plum, black cherry and light olive fruits, all coming together with smoky oak. An appealing, almost sweet herbal finish adds to the charm of the wine. Drink now. Score 92.

RESERVE, MERLOT, 2000: Aged for 15 months in small oak casks, the wine shows deep and concentrated black fruits overlaid with generous mocha, chocolate and vanilla aromas and flavors, as well as a pleasing sensation of herbaceousness that comes in on the long finish. With smooth tannins and excellent balance, a mouth-filling, ripe and elegant wine. Drink now–2009. Score 91.

RESERVE, MERLOT, 1999: Darkening in color but showing no signs of browning, this medium to full-bodied wine has silky tannins and remarkably harmonious aromas and flavors of cassis, violets, plums and toasty oak. With soft, almost caressing tannins, the wine is fully mature but continues to show rich, with flavors that linger on and on. Drink now. Score 91.

RESERVE, SYRAH, 2005: Dark garnet in color, with hints of dusty wood on first attack, those yielding to appealing plum, wild berry and mint. Full-bodied and chewy but soft and elegant. Drink from release–2010. Tentative Score 90–92.

RESERVE, SYRAH, 2004: Youthful royal-purple, aged in French and American *barriques*, this aromatic, medium to full-bodied wine shows firm but yielding tannins, gentle wood and a tempting array of berry and plum fruits, those backed up by hints of oriental spices, chocolate and light earthiness. Drink now–2010. Score 90.

RESERVE, SYRAH, 2003: Aged in oak for about ten months, this deep purple wine shows tempting earthy, mineral aromas and flavors, those backed up nicely by berries, currants and spices. Drink now–2009. Score 91.

RESERVE, CHARDONNAY-SAUVIGNON BLANC, 2004: Unoaked and retaining the fresh and unalloyed aromatic flavors of both varieties (70% Chardonnay, 30% Sauvignon Blanc), this crisply dry, medium-bodied wine shows delicious citrus, pear and summer fruit aromas and flavors, those with tempting overlays of melon, herbs and flowers. Harmonious and expressive. Drink up. Score 90.

Superiore

SUPERIORE, 2005: A blend of 82% Syrah and 18% Cabernet Sauvignon. After 12 months in oak, this dark ruby-red is medium to full-bodied, with fine-grained tannins and lively cherry, raspberry and cassis fruits, those supported nicely by hints of herbs, cedar and spring flowers. Drink now–2010. Score 90.

SUPERIORE, 2004: A blend of 80% Syrah and 20% Cabernet Sauvignon showing toasty oak, smoke and generous but soft tannins, those matched nicely by spicy plum, berry and black cherry fruits. A long, round and elegantly near-sweet finish. Drink now–2010. Score 90.

SUPERIORE, 2003: A blend of 77% Syrah and 23% Cabernet Sauvignon, each fermented separately in French oak before blending. Medium to full-bodied, with soft tannins and a generous earthy-herbal Syrah background coming together nicely with plum, tobacco and blackberry fruits. Round, long, and elegant. Calls to mind a Rhone Cornas. Drink now. Score 90.

Classico

CLASSICO, 2006: Aged in French and American oak for 6 months, this full-bodied, softly tannic blend of Cabernet Sauvignon and Merlot in equal parts shows a generous array of currant, berry and black cherry fruits on a background of Mediterranean herbs. Generous and mouth-filling. Drink now–2010. Score 90.

CLASSICO, 2005: A dark ruby-towards-royal-purple, medium-bodied blend of Cabernet Sauvignon and Merlot in equal parts. Aged in *barriques* for six months and showing a hint of spicy oak and near-sweet tannins, those yielding to blackberry and currant fruits. Soft and round. Drink now–2009. Score 90.

CLASSICO, 2004: A blend of 50% each Cabernet Sauvignon and Merlot, those aged in oak separately for six months. Earthy and herbal on first attack, but that yielding quickly to black cherries, blackberries and currants and, on the finish, hints of tobacco and bittersweet chocolate. Round, generous and elegant. Drink now. Score 90.

CLASSICO, 2003: A medium-bodied blend of equal parts of Cabernet Sauvignon and Merlot, with soft, already well-integrated tannins, a well-balanced dose of wood and aromatic red berries and currants all coming together nicely with light smoky vanilla and a hint of spices. Drink up. Score 90.

Flam

FLAM, SAUVIGNON BLANC-CHARDONNAY, 2006: Light gold with tints of green, unoaked to highlight the natural acidity and fruit flavors, this aromatic, medium-bodied blend of 60% Sauvignon Blanc and 40% Chardonnay opens with aromas and flavors of grapefruit and citrus flowers, those going to vibrant stony minerals and lime. Ripe, vivacious and lively, with hint of passion fruit and freshly cut hay on the finish. Drink now–2009. Score 91.

FLAM, CHARDONNAY-SAUVIGNON BLANC, 2005: Golden-straw in color, this unoaked blend is a fascinating combination of freshness and crisp fruitiness complexity. On the nose and palate tropical fruits, melon, citrus and freshly cut spring flowers, those matched on the long finish by hints of guava and minerals. Drink now. Score 90.

Gad *

Located on Moshav Sdot Micha in the Ella Valley, this boutique winery was founded by Amir Baruch in 2000. Production, primarily from Cabernet Sauvignon, Merlot, Syrah and Petite Sirah grapes from vineyards in Carmei Yosef, is currently about 10,000 bottles annually.

GAD, CABERNET SAUVIGNON, RESERVE, 2006: Dark but not clear garnet in color, with gripping tannins and searing alcohol, already oxidizing and showing Port-like aromas and flavors. Lacks balance or charm. Score 65. K

GAD, CABERNET SAUVIGNON, 2006: Dark ruby, with too-generous dusty and smoky oak reflecting the simultaneous use of oak barrels and oak chips for five months. Muddy flavors hold back whatever fruits may be lurking here. Score 70. K

GAD, CABERNET SAUVIGNON, RESERVE, 2005: An oak-aged blend of 90% Cabernet Sauvignon and 10% Merlot. Medium-bodied, with coarse tannins and a far too generous dose of wood on the palate and nose. Lacks balance. Score 72. K

GAD, CABERNET SAUVIGNON, 2005: Garnet-red, with chunky, country-style tannins and spicy berry-black cherry fruits. Lacks depth, breadth or length. Drink up. Score 78. K

GAD, MERLOT, 2005: Dark ruby-red, light to medium-bodied, with chunky tannins, a few berry, cherry fruits and a too herbal finish. One dimensional. Drink up. Score 76. K

GAD, BLEND, 2005: A pot pourri of Cabernet Sauvignon, Merlot, Syrah, Petite Sirah and Argaman grapes. Medium-bodied, with flabby tannins, far too acidic and not fruity enough. Score 70. K

Galai ✶✶

Sigalit and Asaf Galai established this small winery at Moshav Nir Akiva in the northern part of the Negev Desert in 2002. The winery has vineyards containing Cabernet Sauvignon and Merlot as well as experimental sections of Cabernet Franc, Shiraz and Zinfandel. Current production is about 9,000 bottles annually.

GALAI, CABERNET SAUVIGNON, 2005: Dark garnet and medium-bodied, with firm but yielding tannins and light smoky oak. On the nose and pallet generous black currant, red and black berries and a hint of white pepper that comes in on the finish. Drink now. Score 85. K

GALAI, CABERNET SAUVIGNON, 2004: Dark ruby towards royal-purple, medium to full-bodied, with chunky country-style tannins. Appealing currant, plum and smoky oak flavors but somewhat one-dimensional. Drink now. Score 85. K

GALAI, CABERNET SAUVIGNON, 2003: Deep garnet in color, with firm tannins integrating nicely, this soft and round medium-bodied wine is a blend of Cabernet Sauvignon, Merlot and Cabernet Franc (85%, 11% and 4% respectively). Well balanced, with appealing black fruits and a moderately long finish. Drink up. Score 86. K

GALAI, MERLOT, 2005: The best wine to date from this small winery. Deep garnet in color, with soft, mouth-coating tannins and light spicy cedarwood in good balance with berry, black cherry and plum notes and on the moderately long finish nice hints of Mediterranean herbs. Drink now–2009. Score 87. K

GALAI, MERLOT, 2004: Medium to full-bodied, with firm tannins integrating nicely and an appealing array of berry, cherry and plum, those matched nicely by hints of spices and smoke. A bit of bitterness creeps in on the finish. Drink up. Score 84. K

GALAI, MERLOT, 2003: Dark ruby towards garnet, this medium-bodied wine blended with 15% Cabernet Sauvignon spent 13 months in oak. There are some nice berry and cherry flavors here but with flabby tannins and high acidity the wine fails to come together. Drink up. Score 83. K

GALAI, CABERNET SAUVIGNON-SHIRAZ, 2004: Deep purple, medium-bodied, with soft, mouth-coating tannins and gentle spicy wood influences highlighting berry, plum and mineral notes. Drink now. Score 85. K

GALAI, CABERNET SAUVIGNON-SHIRAZ, 2003: Aged for 20 months in oak, this medium to full-bodied blend of 67% Cabernet Sauvignon and 33% Shiraz offers appealing currant, plum and earthy-mineral aromas and flavors, all leading to a moderately long finish. Drink now. Score 85. K

Galil Mountain ★★★★

With its physically beautiful state-of-the-art winery located on Kibbutz Yiron in the Upper Galilee, this joint venture between the Golan Heights Winery and the *kibbutz* has vineyards located in some of the best wine-growing areas of the Upper Galilee, including Yiron, Meron, Misgav Am, Yiftach and Malkiya. Winemaker Micha Vaadia produces distinctly *terroir*-based wines in two series. The first label, Yiron, is a blend of Cabernet Sauvignon and Merlot, and the second, Galil Mountain, contains varietal releases of Cabernet Sauvignon, Merlot, Pinot Noir, Syrah, Sangiovese, Chardonnay and Sauvignon Blanc. Production from the 2000 vintage was about 300,000 bottles. Since then the winery has grown to an output of 650,000–700,000 bottles annually and expects to produce 1,000,000 bottles from the 2007 vintage.

Yiron

YIRON, 2004: A blend of 72% Cabernet Sauvignon, 25% Merlot and 3% Syrah. Intense garnet towards royal-purple, full-bodied, with firm, near-sweet tannins integrating nicely with smoky and vanilla-tinged wood. Opens with wild berries on the nose and palate, those yielding to black cherry, cassis and spices and finally on the long finish a tantalizing hint of bitterness. Best 2009–2013. Score 91. K

YIRON, 2003: Full-bodied, with mouth-coating tannins and spicy wood in fine proportion. Deep ruby towards royal-purple in color, showing appealing blackberry, black cherry and currant fruits, those with light earthy-herbal overtones. Long, mouth-filling and elegant. Drink now–2010. Score 90. K

YIRON, 2002: A medium to full-bodied oak-aged blend of 54% Cabernet Sauvignon and 46% Merlot. Deeply aromatic, dark purple toward black in color, with still-firm tannins well integrated. Shows abundant black currant, plum, black cherry and berry fruits as well as sweet cedarwood. A generous and mouth-filling finish with an appealing light herbal-earthy overtone. Drink now–2009. Score 90. K

YIRON, 2001: Dark garnet, showing somewhat more full-bodied than in its youth, this blend of 78% Cabernet Sauvignon and 22% Merlot offers still-generous tannins and oak but those in fine tune with blackberry, currant and black cherry fruits. Also on the nose and palate gentle spiciness and now showing hint of tobacco and dark chocolate. Throwing a bit of sediment now but maturing with grace. Drink up. Score 90. K

YIRON, SYRAH, 2004: Dark royal-purple with orange and green reflections, opening with a rich fruity and floral nose. Full-bodied, with bold but soft tannins integrating nicely with spicy wood and showing black fruits, dusty wood and light meaty and earthy overlays. Long and deep. Drink now–2012. Score 91. K

YIRON, SYRAH, 2003: Full-bodied, showing soft tannins with just enough grip to catch the attention, those yielding nicely to light spicy wood. Dark garnet in color, aromatic, with blackberries, purple plums and hints of white pepper and chocolate as well as a light meaty-earthy sensation that comes in on the round and comfortably medium-long finish. Drink now–2012. Score 91. K

Galil Mountain

GALIL MOUNTAIN, CABERNET SAUVIGNON, 2006: Super-dark garnet, showing moderate spicy and vanilla input and near-sweet tannins from the oak aging. On the nose and palate blackberries and blueberries, currants and, coming in from mid-palate, hints of earthiness and freshly turned mushrooms. Best from 2009. Score 90. K

GALIL MOUNTAIN, CABERNET SAUVIGNON, 2005: Deep garnet with orange reflections, medium to full-bodied, with appealing near-sweet tannins and spicy wood integrating nicely to reveal aromas and flavors of black currants, wild berries and minerals all lingering nicely on the palate. Drink now–2009. Score 89. K

GALIL MOUNTAIN, CABERNET SAUVIGNON, 2004: Dark garnet-red, with near-sweet tannins already integrating nicely, and traditional Cabernet currant, berry and light herbal aromas and flavors. Approaching elegance. Drink now. Score 88. K

GALIL MOUNTAIN, CABERNET SAUVIGNON, 2003: Inky-black, full-bodied, with muscular tannins that have started to soften and with good balance and excellent structure. Tempting currant, cranberry and rhubarb aromas and flavors make this a long, round and quietly elegant wine. Drink now. Score 89. K

GALIL MOUNTAIN, MERLOT, 2006: Medium to full-bodied, with still-gripping tannins but already showing fine balance and structure. On the nose and palate plums, cranberries, wild berries and orange peel notes backed up nicely by a light vegetal hint. Long and generous. Drink now–2010. Score 90. K

GALIL MOUNTAIN, MERLOT, 2005: Deep, almost inky black-garnet, full-bodied, with firm but comfortably yielding tannins. Ripe berry, currant, green pepper and light herbal aromas and flavors, those coming together in a deep and complex *terroir*-driven wine. Drink now–2009. Score 89. K

GALIL MOUNTAIN, MERLOT, 2004: Dark ruby towards garnet, medium-bodied, with soft tannins, and with berry and plum fruits, all on a light peppery background. Round and smooth. Drink now. Score 88. K

GALIL MOUNTAIN, MERLOT, 2003: Medium to full-bodied and rich in currant, berry and grapefruit peel aromas and flavors, smoky overlays and generous soft tannins, this unoaked wine promises to develop nicely. Drink now. Score 88. K

GALIL MOUNTAIN, SHIRAZ, 2006: Dark garnet, medium to full-bodied, with soft tannins integrating nicely and showing a generous array of berry, black cherry and plum fruits, those on a lightly spicy and herbal background. Drink now–2009. Score 88. K

GALIL MOUNTAIN, PINOT NOIR, 2006: Dark cherry-red towards garnet, this medium-bodied wine, still relatively firm shows tannins but reveals fine balance and a complex array of red berry, cherry, blueberry and spices, supported nicely by light toasty vanilla and, on the finish, a hint of minerality. Drink now–2010. Score 89. K

GALIL MOUNTAIN, PINOT NOIR, 2005: Deep ruby towards garnet, medium-bodied, reflecting ten months in oak with light spicy wood and now comfortably softening tannins. Concentrated aromas and flavors of black cherries, berries, currants, spring flowers and minerals. Drink now–2010. Score 90. K

GALIL MOUNTAIN, PINOT NOIR, 2004: Dark ruby towards garnet in color, with firm tannins well balanced with wood, those needing time to come together with red berries and plums, black cherries, light herbal notes and, on the finish, fresh strawberries. Long and elegant. Drink now–2009. Score 90. K

GALIL MOUNTAIN, PINOT NOIR 2003: This lightly oaked, medium-bodied wine continues to show soft tannins and appealing currant, purple plum and berry fruits. The once light meaty-herbal hints are now turning to lightly dusky cigar-box aromas. Drink now. Score 87. K

GALIL MOUNTAIN, SANGIOVESE, 2005: Dark, almost impenetrable garnet in color, rich, complex and with remarkable finesse for a pure Sangiovese. On the nose and palate plum, cherry, blackberry, anise, currants and wild berries. Drink now–2009. Tentative Score 91. K

GALIL MOUNTAIN, BARBERA, 2006: Bright ruby, medium-bodied, with impressive concentration, depth and complexity and generous fruits to support the soft tannins, lively acidity and moderate oak. On the nose and palate blackberry, violets and bittersweet chocolate supported nicely by hints of black pepper and minerals, and, on the long finish, a rising cassis fruitiness. Drink from release–2011. Tentative Score 90–92. K

GALIL MOUNTAIN, SHIRAZ-CABERNET SAUVIGNON, 2005: Dark and concentrated, full-bodied, showing a light herbal and spicy oak nose and opening to reveal currant, blackberry and black cherry fruits, all coming together in a long, round, elegant finish. Drink now–2012. Score 90. K

GALIL MOUNTAIN, SHIRAZ-CABERNET, 2004: Deep royal-purple, this medium to full-bodied blend of 64% Shiraz and 36% Cabernet Sauvignon shows remarkably smooth tannins and a generous array of blackberry and blueberry fruits, those set off nicely by hints of green peppers and a light influence of vanilla. Generous and mouth-filling. Drink now–2009. Score 89. K

GALIL MOUNTAIN, SHIRAZ-CABERNET, 2003: Dark garnet, medium-bodied, with soft tannins and showing smooth and supple aromas and flavors of creamy currants, black cherries and coffee. Distinctly New World in style. Drink now. Score 87. K

GALIL MOUNTAIN, ROSÉ, 2006: Rose-petal pink in color, opens quietly but quickly in the glass to reveal aromas and flavors of fresh cherries, raspberries and strawberries, all on a crisp, clean background. Drink up. Score 88. K

GALIL MOUNTAIN, ROSÉ, 2005: A blend of 65% Sangiovese, 22% Cabernet Sauvignon and 13% Syrah. On the nose and palate, strawberries, wild berries, spices and a hint of mint that comes in on the finish. Medium-bodied and crisp with a 13.5% alcohol content. Perhaps the best rosé ever from Israel. Drink up. Score 90. K

GALIL MOUNTAIN, CHARDONNAY, 2006: Light golden-straw in color, this medium-bodied white is aromatic, with bare hints of spicy oak highlighting green apple, melon, citrus and lightly spicy fragrances and flavors. Crisp and well balanced. Drink now. Score 88. K

GALIL MOUNTAIN, CHARDONNAY, 2005: Golden-straw with orange reflections, medium-bodied, with fine balance and an appealing array of citrus, apple and melon aromas and flavors. Crisp and refreshing. Drink now. Score 88. K

GALIL MOUNTAIN, SAUVIGNON BLANC, 2006: Light straw in color, light to medium-bodied, this unoaked wine shows refreshing crisp acidity with overtones of citrus, citrus peel and light but tantalizing hints of freshly mown grass. Not complex, but a most pleasant quaffer. Drink now. Score 88. K

GALIL MOUNTAIN, SAUVIGNON BLANC, 2005: Delicious! Medium-bodied, pale greenish-yellow, with a generous citrus nose and on the palate, passion fruit, flinty minerals and the hint of an English rose garden after a summer shower. Crisp, lively and elegant. Drink up. Score 91. K

GALIL MOUNTAIN, VIOGNIER, 2006: Lightly golden with greenish tinges, this medium-bodied white opens with a lively and spicy nose, then reveals enticing aromas and flavors of peaches, nectarines, pears and apples backed up by spring flowers and minerals, all complemented by hints of white pepper that play nicely on the palate. Delicious. Drink now–2009. Score 90. K

Gat Shomron *

Founded by Avigdor Sharon and Limor Nachum on the settlement of Karnei Shomron, not far from Kfar Saba, in 2003, this small winery released its first wines from that harvest in 2005, and is currently producing about 6,000 bottles annually of oak-aged Cabernet Sauvignon, Merlot and Chardonnay.

GAT SHOMRON, CABERNET SAUVIGNON, 2005: Medium-bodied, with chunky, country-style tannins and skimpy aromas and flavors of spicy berries and black cherries. One dimensional. Drink now. Score 82. K

GAT SHOMRON, CABERNET SAUVIGNON, 2004: Garnet-red, with chunky tannins and a few currant, berry and plum fruits. Drink up. Score 80. K

GAT SHOMRON, CABERNET SAUVIGNON, 2003: Dark ruby towards garnet, with somewhat overgenerous tannins and oak, ripe plum and berry fruits. Drink up. Score 82. K

GAT SHOMRON, MERLOT, 2005: Garnet towards purple, with soft tannins and spicy oak opening in the glass to reveal berry and plum fruits. A simple entry-level wine. Drink now. Score 80. K

GAT SHOMRON, MERLOT, 2004: A somewhat cloudy garnet-red, with firm tannins and very generous oak hiding whatever black fruit flavors try to make themselves felt. Drink up. Score 79. K

GAT SHOMRON, MERLOT, 2003: Garnet-red, medium-bodied, with chunky country-style tannins and generous oak set off nicely by aromas and flavors of plums, cassis and sweet herbs. Drink up. Score 84. K

GAT SHOMRON, CHARDONNAY, 2005: Golden-straw colored, with tart pineapple and citrus flavors. Floral with a hint of sweetness. Drink up. Score 78. K

GAT SHOMRON, CHARDONNAY, 2004: Medium-bodied, light golden in color, with aromas and flavors of pineapple, citrus and spring flowers. Somewhat alcoholic and coarse on the palate. Drink up. Score 82. K

Gesher Damia *

Founded in 1999 by Moshe Ka-
plan in the town of Pardes Han-
nah on the northern Coastal
Plain, this small winery receives
Cabernet Sauvignon, Mer-
lot, Argaman, Petite Shiraz,
Gewurztraminer and Chardonnay grapes from Gush Etzion,
the Jerusalem Hills and the center of the country. Production
is currently about 6,000 bottles
annually.

GESHER DAMIA, CABERNET SAUVIGNON, 2005: Ruby towards
garnet, light to medium-bodied, with almost unfelt tannins, spicy oak
and a few blackberry fruits. Drink up. Score 78.

GESHER DAMIA, CABERNET SAUVIGNON, 2004: Dark ruby, medium-
bodied, with chunky tannins, smoky oak and skimpy black fruits. Drink
up. Score 79.

GESHER DAMIA, CABERNET SAUVIGNON, 2003: Deep ruby, medium-
bodied, with still-gripping tannins, generous sweet and smoky oak and
a few berry-cherry fruits. Drink up. Score 78.

GESHER DAMIA, MERLOT, 2005: Medium-bodied, with almost unfelt
tannins and stewed plum and berry fruits. Drink up. Score 78.

GESHER DAMIA, MERLOT, 2004: Medium-bodied, with soft, near-
sweet tannins and blackberry, cherry and cassis fruits, those on a lightly
spicy background. Drink now. Score 80.

Ginaton **

Founded in 1999 by Doron Cohen and Benju Duke on Moshav Ginaton on the Central Plain not far from the city of Lod, the winery draws Cabernet Sauvignon, Muscat and Chardonnay grapes from Karmei Yosef and Kerem Ben Zimra. The first commercial releases were 3,000 bottles from the 2000 vintage. Current annual production is about 5,500 bottles.

GINATON, CABERNET SAUVIGNON, 2005: Youthful royal-purple, medium-bodied, with still-firm tannins needing a bit of time to integrate in order to show the lightly spicy black fruits that are present. Drink now–2009. Score 85.

GINATON, CABERNET SAUVIGNON, 2004: Garnet towards royal-purple, medium-bodied, with soft tannins integrating nicely to show blackberry and currant fruits on a light spicy background. Drink now. Score 84.

GINATON, CABERNET SAUVIGNON, HAR BRACHA, NUMBERED SERIES, 2003: Reflecting its 18 months in oak with generous spicy and smoky cedar and moderately firm tannins. Medium to full-bodied, with some black fruits. Lacking complexity. Drink now. Score 84.

GINATON, CABERNET SAUVIGNON, KEREM BEN ZIMRA, 2003: Clear ruby towards purple, medium-bodied, with soft, almost unfelt tannins. Aromas and flavors of berries, cassis and black cherries on a lightly herbaceous background. Drink up. Score 84.

GINATON, MERLOT, 2005: This medium-bodied wine shows generous, spicy and vanilla-rich oak with soft tannins. Opens slowly to reveal plum, blackberries and black cherry fruits that linger nicely. Not complex but easy to drink. Drink now–2009. Score 85.

GIATON, MERLOT, 2004: Oak-aged for 18 months, this blend of 80% Merlot and 20% Petite Syrah shows very generous smoky oak and gripping tannins, those holding back the black fruits that struggle to make themselves felt. Drink now. Score 84.

GINATON, MERLOT, KEREM YOSEF, 2003: Medium-bodied, with soft, well-integrated tannins and appealing aromas and flavors of blackberries and purple plums on a lightly spicy background. Drink up. Score 84.

GINATON, SHIRAZ, 2003: Developed in oak for 18 months, medium to full-bodied, with firm tannins just starting to yield and revealing berry, black cherry and plum fruits on a lightly spicy and herbal background. Drink now. Score 84.

GINATON, CABERNET SAUVIGNON-MERLOT, 2003: Aged for 14 months in oak, a somewhat sharp and chunky country-style wine but showing appealing red berry and cassis aromas and flavors. Drink now. Score 84.

GINATON, CABERNET SAUVIGNON-SHIRAZ, 2003: Dark garnet, medium-bodied, with soft tannins and currant, plum and meaty-earthy aromas and flavors. Simple but appealing. Drink now. Score 84.

GINATON, CABERNET SAUVIGNON-MERLOT-PETITE SIRAH, 2003: Medium-dark garnet in color, with chunky tannins and a hint of country-style coarseness. A few wild berry, currant and leafy aromas and flavors. Drink up. Score 82.

Givon *

Established by Nir Ernesti and Shuki Segal in the village of Givon Hachadasha, north of Jerusalem in the Judean Mountains, and relying on Cabernet Sauvignon and Merlot grapes from nearby vineyards, this winery released its first wines from the 2002 vintage. Current production is about 5,000 bottles annually.

GIVON, CABERNET SAUVIGNON, 2005: Somewhat cloudy dark garnet, medium to full-bodied, with chunky tannins and generous currant, berry and black cherry fruits. A simple country-style wine. Drink now. Score 84.

GIVON, CABERNET SAUVIGNON, 2004: Dark cherry-red, medium bodied, with soft tannins and appealing black cherry and plum fruits. Not typical for the variety but an acceptable quaffing wine. Drink now. Score 83.

GIVON, CABERNET SAUVIGNON, 2003: Medium-bodied, with soft tannins and simple but appealing flavors of berries and black cherries but faulted somewhat by a too-generous acidity. Drink up. Score 78.

GIVON, MERLOT, 2005: Garnet towards purple, with soft tannins and spicy wood, this medium-bodied wine is showing appealing plum berry and cherry fruits. Drink now. Score 83.

GIVON, MERLOT, 2004: Medium-bodied, low in tannins and on the simple side, with only skimpy berry and plum fruits. Drink up Score 80.

GIVON, NEBBIOLO, 2005: Cherry-red towards garnet, medium-bodied with a floral nose and generous berry, cherry and red plum fruits. Drink now. Score 83.

GIVON, NEBBIOLO, 2004: Dark cherry-red, medium-bodied, with soft tannins and appealing raspberry and cherry fruits. A simple quaffer Drink now. Score 82.

Golan Heights Winery *****

From the moment they released their first wines in 1984, there has been no doubt that the Golan Heights Winery was and is still today largely responsible for placing Israel on the world wine map. The winery, with its state-of-the-art facilities located in Katzrin on the Golan Heights, and fine vineyards on the Golan and in the Upper Galilee, is owned by eight of the *kibbutzim* and *moshavim* that supply them with grapes. Maintaining rigorous control over the vineyards and relying on a combination of New and Old World knowledge and technology, senior winemaker Victor Shoenfeld and his staff of winemakers, all of whom trained in California or France, produce wines that often attain excellence.

The winery has three regular series, Yarden, Gamla and Golan, the wines in the first two series often being age-worthy while those in the Golan series are meant for early drinking. There is also the top-of-the-line Katzrin series that includes a red Bordeaux-style blend that is released only in years considered exceptional, and a Chardonnay that has been released annually since 1995.

The winery is currently producing more than six million bottles annually and of this production nearly thirty percent is destined for export. Among the regularly released varietal wines are Cabernet Sauvignon, Merlot, Pinot Noir, Gamay, Sangiovese, Sauvignon Blanc, Chardonnay, Johannisberg Riesling, Muscat Canelli and Gewurztraminer, and the winery is currently cultivating experimental plantings of Nebbiolo and Malbec. The winery also produces sparkling Blanc de Blanc and Brut, which are made in the traditional *Champenoise* method, Heightswine (a play on the words Ice Wine) and several dessert wines.

Katzrin

KATZRIN, 2004: Not yet a final blend but already showing potential elegance. Dark, youthful garnet towards royal-purple in color, full-bodied, with generous but not dominant oak and still-firm tannins, those in fine balance with blackberry, currant and cherry fruits and, on the background, peppery and herbal overtones. A super-long, fruity and tannic finish. Showing balance and structure that bode well for the future. Best 2009–2018. Tentative Score 91–93. K

KATZRIN, 2003: A dark garnet, full-bodied blend of 83% Cabernet Sauvignon, 14% Merlot and 3% Cabernet Franc, with soft tannins and smoky oak integrating nicely. Opens with black currant and berry fruits, those yielding to come together with peppery and herbal aromas and flavors culminating in a long blueberry and chocolate finish. Best 2010–2018. Score 93. K

KATZRIN, 2000: Elegant, ripe and bold with concentrated tannins softening nicely and showing fine balance and structure. On the nose and palate blackberries, currants, black cherries and plums, those opening in layers together with overlays of spicy oak and a hint of cigar tobacco. Best 2009–2015. Score 92. K

KATZRIN, 1996: Vibrant and complex, with an array of aromas and flavors that include currants, cherries and plums overlaid by smoky oak, chocolate, spices and tobacco, this full-bodied, young tannic red is only now beginning to reveal its charms. Excellent integration between fruit, tannins and oak indicates that the wine will continue to develop beautifully. Drink now–2015. Score 93. K

KATZRIN, 1993: Deep, broad, long and complex, this full-bodied Cabernet-Merlot blend continues to live up to its promise. Abundant tannins are well balanced by wood and fruits that include cassis, black cherries and orange peel, along with generous overlays of milk chocolate and toasty oak. Elegant and graceful. Drink now–2012. Score 94. K

KATZRIN, 1990: A blend of 90% Cabernet Sauvignon and 10% Merlot, this deep, elegant, full-bodied wine has a dark garnet color and excellent balance between fruits, wood, acidity and tannins. Look for a complex array of aromas and flavors, including black currants, cherries, vanilla, cloves and chocolate. Lingers long on the palate. Drink now–2010. Score 95. K

KATZRIN, CHARDONNAY, 2004: Dark golden-yellow, full-bodied and concentrated. Developed in new oak for ten months, notably yeasty on first attack but that yielding beautifully to a buttery, oak-rich texture and opening to reveal nutty, fig, pear, tropical fruits and butterscotch, all on a spicy background. Rich, long and complex. Drink now–2012. Score 92. K

KATZRIN, CHARDONNAY, 2003: Rich, ripe, concentrated and complex with generous layers of figs, tangerines, summer fruits and hazelnuts. Generous but not imposing oak on the finish makes it especially elegant as does a hint of butterscotch that comes in on the long finish. Drink now–2010. Score 92. K

KATZRIN, CHARDONNAY, 2002: As full-bodied and complex as in its youth but now maturing nicely and reflecting only the barest hint of smoky oak, that serving as a backdrop for summer fruits, pears and citrus. Look as well for roasted nuts, minerals and a hint of cream that play nicely on the palate. Drink now. Score 91. K

KATZRIN, CHARDONNAY, 2000: Aged for ten months *sur lie*, this full-bodied, elegant and complex white still maintains a young and enthusiastic deep golden color and has layers of aromas and flavors that include poached pears, apples and passion fruit. Intense and concentrated, it shows tantalizing hints of spices, vanilla and oak, all culminating in a long finish. Drink now. Score 90. K

Yarden

YARDEN, CABERNET SAUVIGNON, ELROM VINEYARD, 2006: Still in embryonic form, but already showing full-bodied, with firm, near-sweet tannins and spicy oak integrating nicely. On the nose and palate currants, berries and spices, those opening to light earthy-herbal aromas and flavors. Tannins and fruits rise on the finish. Best starting in 2011. Tentative Score 91–93. K

YARDEN, CABERNET SAUVIGNON, 2006: Opulent and ripe, full-bodied, with generous black currant, blackberry and plum fruits supported by rich oak, generous, soft mouth-coating tannins along with spices and light earthy overtones. Best 2010–2018. Tentative Score 91–93. K

YARDEN, CABERNET SAUVIGNON, 2005: Brooding dark ruby-red, full-bodied, with near-sweet tannins and spicy oak wrapped around black currants, berries, spices and a hint of dark chocolate. Look as well for enchanting hints of citrus peel and vanilla on the long finish. Fine balance and structure bode well for the future. Best 2010–2018. Tentative Score 91–93. K

YARDEN, CABERNET SAUVIGNON, EL ROM VINEYARD, 2004: Full-bodied, with gripping but well-integrating tannins and wood in fine balance with fruits and acidity. On first attack, berry and black cherry fruits, those yielding to currants, plums, and tantalizing hints of freshly turned earth, toasted bread and tobacco. Needs a bit of time to show its elegance. Drink from release–2015. Score 93. K

YARDEN, CABERNET SAUVIGNON, 2004: Deep, dark, and brooding. Generous smoky oak and tannins now settling down to reveal rich currant, berry and plum fruits along with hints of asphalt, earthiness and spices. Drink now–2013. Score 91. K

YARDEN, CABERNET SAUVIGNON, EL ROM VINEYARD, 2003: Dark ruby towards purple, full-bodied, with caressing tannins and a moderate oak influence. Opens with currants and minerals, goes to meaty, earthy and herbal aromas and flavors, and then to spices and a long and elegant fruity finish. Firmly structured with excellent grip and complexity. Best 2010–2020. Score 95. K

YARDEN, CABERNET SAUVIGNON, 2003: Aged in French oak for 18 months and showing generous but gentle wood influence. Soft mouth-coating tannins support generous blackberry, back cherry and plum fruits and, on the long finish, hints of Oriental spices and a light herbal-tobacco sensation. Best 2009–2014. Score 93. K

YARDEN, CABERNET SAUVIGNON, 2002: Dark garnet towards royal-purple, full-bodied, with firm tannins and spicy oak yielding nicely to reveal flavors and aromas of red currants and berries on first attack, those giving way to layers of sweet cedar, vanilla, leather and, on the long finish, a hint of anise. Generous and elegant. Drink now–2012. Score 92. K

YARDEN, CABERNET SAUVIGNON, ELROM VINEYARD, 2001: Dark, almost impenetrable garnet-purple, full-bodied, with finely-tuned balance between generous well-integrated tannins and judicious oak, this exquisite wine shows complex tiers of aromas and flavors of red currants, berries, and spices on the first attack, those opening to include light earthy and herbal overlays. Plush and opulent, with a long, complex finish. Among the best ever made in Israel. Drink now–2013. Score 95. K

YARDEN, CABERNET SAUVIGNON, 2001: This delicious, full-bodied red has good balance between wood, tannins and fruits. With plum, wild berry and currant fruits, and reflecting its 18 months in oak with appealing overlays of vanilla, cedar and cocoa. Drink now–2010. Score 91. K

YARDEN, CABERNET SAUVIGNON, 2000: Full-bodied, still youthful, with firm tannins and generous oak well balanced by currants and what at one moment feels like plums and another like black cherries, all matched nicely with vanilla and an appealing herbal overlay followed by a long finish. Drink now–2010. Score 92. K

YARDEN, CABERNET SAUVIGNON, 1999: With once-firm tannins now softening and showing fine balance between wood and fruits, the wine is opening beautifully. Deep royal-purple toward garnet in color with delicious aromas and flavors of black berries and cherries on a background of vanilla and sweet cedar wood, as well as a hint of freshly roasted coffee on its long finish. Drink now. Score 92. K

YARDEN, CABERNET SAUVIGNON, 1998: Full-bodied, deep in color and remarkably intense, with aromas and flavors of currant, plum, black cherry, vanilla and lightly toasted oak as well as excellent balance between fruits, wood and tannins. On the long finish mineral-earthy overtones and an appealing hint of anise. Maturing beautifully. Drink now. Score 91. K

YARDEN, CABERNET SAUVIGNON, 1997: This traditional Yarden blend of 94% Cabernet Sauvignon, 5% Merlot and 1% Cabernet Franc is now fully mature but continues to show an overall firm structure and good balance between soft tannins, fruits, wood and acidity. Plenty of Cabernet currants along with blackberries and plums on the first attack, those yielding to gentle overlays of spices and Mediterranean herbs. Not for further cellaring. Drink up. Score 89. K

YARDEN, CABERNET SAUVIGNON, 1996: A blend of 98% Cabernet Sauvignon and 2% Cabernet Franc, this concentrated and intense medium to full-bodied wine with sweet tannins is now showing plum, currant and cherry fruits, those complemented nicely by vanilla and anise on the mid-palate, and appealing herbal sensations on the finish. Drink now. Score 91. K

YARDEN, CABERNET SAUVIGNON, 1995: The wine needs time to open in the glass but doing so it reveals luscious layers of aromas and flavors of black currants, plums, tobacco and vanilla. Full-bodied, with concentrated but well-integrated tannins, and a hint of raspberries on the long finish. Fully mature and not for further cellaring. Drink up. Score 92. K

YARDEN, CABERNET SAUVIGNON, 1994: As 1994 was not a great vintage year in Israel, this wine never attained the heights of the best of this series. Medium-bodied, it shows flavors of stewed prunes, black fruits and floral-earthy overtones. Fully mature. Drink up. Score 87. K

YARDEN, CABERNET SAUVIGNON, 1993: This royal-purple, full-bodied, concentrated, powerful wine is in its maturity and has now attained enviable levels of roundness, depth and complexity along with impeccable balance and an elegant bouquet. Silky tannins that give the wine just the right bite, flavors that unfold comfortably on the palate. Drink now. Score 94. K

YARDEN, CABERNET SAUVIGNON, 1992: Full-bodied, with fully integrated tannins and abundant black fruits, vanilla and appealing herbal, earthy, and tobacco overlays, this well-balanced and generous wine shows a moderately long, near-sweet finish. Past its peak. Drink up. Score 88. K

YARDEN, CABERNET SAUVIGNON, 1991: Deep purple and medium to full-bodied, the wine continues to reveal traditional Cabernet aromas and flavors of black currants, cedarwood and black cherries along with herbal-mineral overtones on the finish. Past its peak. Drink up. Score 87. K

YARDEN, CABERNET SAUVIGNON, 1990: When young, this superb wine showed almost massive tannins and intensity, but due to its excellent structure and good balance the wine has maintained its rich concentration along with its traditional black currant, oak and vanilla aromas and flavors, those overlaid by aromatic cedar, leather and to-bacco, and a remarkably long finish. Drink up. Score 92. K

YARDEN, MERLOT, ODEM VINEYARD, 2006: Made from organically raised grapes. Deep, dark and mysterious, as the wine is still in its pre-natal state, but already showing sweet, smoky and spicy oak well matched by mouth-coating tannins. Opens to reveal sweet black cherries, those followed by blackberries and currants and hints of Mediterranean herbs. Best from 2009. Tentative Score 90–92. K

YARDEN, MERLOT, ODEM VINEYARD, 2005: Saturated ruby towards royal-purple, full-bodied and intense, this wine was made from organically raised grapes. Opens with an attack of black cherry syrup, that settling down quickly to reveal cherries, berries and cassis along with bitter chocolate and spices. On the long finish gripping tannins rise together with an appealing hint of licorice. A simultaneously muscular and elegant wine. Best from 2009. Tentative Score 91–93. K

YARDEN, MERLOT, 2005: Still in embryonic form but showing the potential for a medium to full-bodied spicy red, with currant and plum aromas and flavors, and overlays of smoke and herbaceousness. Long and elegant. Drink from release–2011. Tentative Score 89–91. K

YARDEN, MERLOT, ORTAL VINEYARD, 2004: Dark ruby towards garnet, this elegant and exquisite wine has firm but not aggressive tannins and generous but not intrusive wood, those yielding beautifully to subtle layers of blackberry, plum and currant aromas and flavors, with hints of red licorice coming nicely into play on the long and harmonious finish. Drink now–2013. Score 93. K

YARDEN, MERLOT, 2004: Dark garnet towards purple, medium to full-bodied, with tannins and wood integrating nicely and showing a generous array of berry, cassis and plum fruits, those supported by minerals, sweet cedarwood and, rising on the medium-long finish, a spicy overlay. Drink now–2010. Score 89. K

YARDEN, MERLOT, 2003: This soft, smooth and polished wine shows tempting ripe cherry and currant fruits, those supported nicely by layers of Mediterranean herbs, vanilla and light hints of smoky oak. Complex, long and elegant. Drink now–2010. Score 90. K

YARDEN, MERLOT, 2002: Dark garnet, with once-firm tannins well integrated with now gently spicy wood. Showing plum and berry fruits on herbal, citrus peel and white chocolate notes. Still drinking nicely but not for further cellaring. Drink now. Score 88. K

YARDEN, MERLOT, ORTAL VINEYARD, 2001: Deeply aromatic, reflecting its 14 months in mostly new French barrels with generous spicy oak, that in harmony with ample but seamless tannins, all coming together in a plush and luxurious wine. Full-bodied, showing appealing aromas and flavors that open in layer after layer, those including blackberries, near-jammy plums, chocolate, fresh herbs and, on the long finish, a rising hint of Oriental spices. Drink now–2014. Score 94. K

YARDEN, MERLOT, 2001: Dark, almost inky purple in color, continuing to show the generous spicy wood that it did in its youth but with the tannins now soft and well integrated. On the nose and palate ripe plums and blackberries complemented by chocolate, spices and vanilla. On the long finish a hint of earthiness that is on the rise. Not for further cellaring. Drink now. Score 89. K

YARDEN, MERLOT, 2000: Somewhat less full-bodied than in its youth but still rich and tempting. Generous in plum, berry and black cherry fruits as well as in overlays of chocolate, with a hint of citrus peel on its finish. Drink now–2009. Score 90. K

YARDEN, SYRAH, 2006: Still in its infancy but already showing commendable complexity, with aromas and flavors of plums, boysenberries, freshly turned earth, pepper and roast game meat. Full-bodied with tangy acidity and firm tannins that need time to settle down but showing fine balance and structure, those boding well for the future. Best from 2009. Tentative Score 88–90. K

YARDEN, SYRAH, ORTAL, 2005: Made from grapes from the Ortal vineyard. Deeply aromatic, full-bodied, with soft tannins integrating nicely and showing a gentle hand with spicy oak. Opens on the nose and palate with raspberries and sweet oak, those merging to wild berries, pepper and hints of Oriental spices and smoked meat, all lingering nicely. Best from 2009. Tentative Score 89–91. K

YARDEN, SYRAH, ORTAL, 2004: Moderately dark ruby, medium to full-bodied, with tannins integrating nicely with spicy wood. Opens with a burst of almost jammy aromas of raspberries and kirsch liqueur, those yielding beautifully to blackberry, cherry and plum fruits. In the background generous hints of anise and Oriental spices and at this stage a vague but tantalizing note of spiced meat. Drink now–2012. Score 91. K

YARDEN, SYRAH, 2003: Dark garnet in color, with soft tannins and generous but unimposing spicy and vanilla-rich oak coming together nicely with near-sweet berry, peach pit and plum fruits. In the background, holding well into the long finish, violets and a light earthiness. Drink now–2012. Score 90. K

YARDEN, SYRAH, 2002: Reflecting its 18 months in oak, this medium to full-bodied red is showing generous, soft tannins and spicy oak highlighting layers of berries, cherries, plums and spices along with distinctive aromas and flavors of chocolate, vanilla and anise. On the long finish hints of spring flowers and espresso. Drink now–2010. Score 91. K

YARDEN, SYRAH, 2001: Medium to full-bodied, with its tannins integrating with spicy wood and vanilla, and continuing to show fine balance and structure. On the nose and palate an appealing array of black cherries, plums, licorice and hints of earthiness that come in on the generous finish. Drink now–2009. Score 90. K

YARDEN, SYRAH, 2000: Deep, almost inky purple in color, this softly tannic, medium to full-bodied wine features aromas and flavors of red currants, plums and spices and, reflecting its 18 months in oak, is showing tobacco, herbs and an appealing light meaty-earthy sensation. Long and mouth-filling. Drink now–2009. Score 91. K

YARDEN, PINOT NOIR, 2006: Intense ruby towards garnet, medium to full-bodied, with well-focused cherry fruits at the core, those opening to reveal plums, dark chocolate and espresso coffee, all leading to a long blackberry-rich finish. Generous, balanced, and long, with wood and tannins integrating nicely. Best from 2009. Tentative Score 90–92. K

YARDEN, PINOT NOIR, 2005: Promises to be the best Pinot Noir yet from the winery. Dark ruby, full-bodied enough to be thought of as fleshy and with spicy wood and gentle tannins in fine balance with acidity and fruits. Opens with near-sweet, liqueur-like berry aromas and flavors, those yielding in the glass to reveal a crisply dry wine on which you will feel hints of kirsch, dark chocolate and lightly smoked meat, all climaxing in a long and generous blackberry finishing. Best from 2009. Tentative Score 91–93. K

YARDEN, PINOT NOIR, 2004: This medium to full-bodied, dark garnet wine is showing a complex array of aromas and flavors. Opens with blackberries and roasted pine nuts, those going to plums and black cherries that offer up an intriguing hint of anise and ending in a long and generous finish on which the fruits rise again. Drink now–2012. Score 90. K

YARDEN, PINOT NOIR, 2003: Garnet-red, medium to full-bodied, with soft, mouth-coating tannins and a moderate hand with spicy oak. On the nose and palate forward but elegant black cherry, blackberry, and cassis fruits supported nicely by hints of lightly spicy floral and earthy notes. Drink now–2011. Score 91. K

YARDEN, PINOT NOIR, 2002: Medium to full-bodied, with soft, near-sweet tannins and fine balance between wood and fruit. On the nose and palate red berries, cherries, violets and cassis, those matched nicely by hints of espresso coffee and vanilla. Drink now. Score 90. K

YARDEN, MOUNT HERMON RED, 2006: A blend this year of Merlot, Cabernet Sauvignon, and Cabernet Franc (45%, 40% and 15% respectively). Dark cherry-red, medium-bodied, with soft, almost unfelt tannins and generous berry and black cherry fruits. Aromatic and straightforward. Drink now. Score 84. K

YARDEN, MOUNT HERMON RED, 2005: As nearly always, this dark cherry-red, medium-bodied blend of Merlot, Cabernet Sauvignon and Cabernet Franc offers soft tannins that make the wine ready to drink in its youth. A few berry, currant and black cherry fruits here but those a bit too subdued. An entry-level wine. Drink up. Score 84. K

YARDEN, CHARDONNAY, 2006: Lightly golden in color, with ripe apple, citrus and spices, opening to a touch of charred oak. Medium-bodied, but light, crisp and rich on the palate and showing fine balance along with a long and lively finish. Drink now–2010. Score 89. K

YARDEN, CHARDONNAY, ODEM ORGANIC VINEYARD, 2005: Ripe and floral, with aromas and flavors of apricots, citrus and figs set off nicely by hints of ginger and pears that come in on the long and complex finish. Drink now–2009. Score 90. K

YARDEN, CHARDONNAY, 2005: Full-bodied, bright gold in color, with nutty, floral and woody notes highlighting ripe tropical fruits, pears and citrus. On the background a nice hint of white pepper, all leading to a long finish. Drink now. Score 89. K

YARDEN, CHARDONNAY, ODEM ORGANIC VINEYARD, 2004: Rich and complex, full-bodied and creamy, with ripe apricot, citrus and pear fruits backed up nicely by an appealing spicy note. The oak here is generous but not offensive. Drink now–2009. Score 91. K

YARDEN, CHARDONNAY, ODEM ORGANIC VINEYARD, 2003: Lightly burnished gold in color, rich and elegant, with ripe pear, honeysuckle and melon flavors coming together beautifully with generous oak, minerals and nutmeg. On the long finish a hint of hazelnuts. Drink now–2009. Score 90. K

YARDEN, CHARDONNAY, 2003: Drinking beautifully now. Showing medium to full-bodied, with a complex array of apricot, pear and fig fruits on first attack, those yielding comfortably to citrus, pineapple, minerals and spicy oak. Drink now–2009. Score 90. K

YARDEN, CHARDONNAY, ODEM ORGANIC VINEYARD, 2002: Maturing gracefully and showing a bright golden-straw color. Ripe and complex flavors of pears, tropical fruits, hazelnuts and spices opening on the palate to reveal flinty and floral overtones along with generous but well-integrated oak and a long, creamy finish. Drink now. Score 92. K

YARDEN, CHARDONNAY, 2002: Deeper gold now than in its youth, the once generous oak is nicely integrated and showing a hint of caramel. Full-bodied with pear, hazelnut and citrus notes backed up nicely by nutty and mineral aromas and flavors. Drink up. Score 89. K

YARDEN, CHARDONNAY, 2001: Fully mature, showing dark gold now, less acidity and more buttery than in its youth but still drinking very nicely. On the nose and palate ripe pears, citrus peel, toasty bread and vanilla, all lingering nicely. Drink up. Score 89. K

YARDEN, CHARDONNAY, 2000: Mature, but still plenty of fruit here. Medium to full-bodied, with pears, figs, apples and citrus on the nose and palate, those supported nicely by hints of vanilla and spring flowers and a light hint of smoky wood. Drink up. Score 89. K

YARDEN, SAUVIGNON BLANC, 2006: Medium-bodied, light golden-straw in color, with grapefruit, yellow plum, apricot and floral aromas and flavors. Lively, dry and pleasant, with a hint of pineapple arising on the finish. Drink now–2009. Score 88. K

YARDEN, SAUVIGNON BLANC, 2005: Well balanced and aromatic, with a personality bursting with spices, herbs and peppery wood, those matched nicely by pear, apple, melon and mineral aromas and flavors. Drink now. Score 89. K

YARDEN, SAUVIGNON BLANC, 2004: Light straw in color, medium-bodied, with straightforward aromas and flavors of lemon, lime, and ripe peaches. Marred somewhat by unwanted hints of bitterness and earthiness that develop on the palate. Drink up. Score 85. K

YARDEN, VIOGNIER, 2006: Showing traditional Viognier traits of peaches, pears, apples, white flowers and minerals, those backed up nicely by hints of citrus and lively acidity. This clean, fresh and long white shows many of the best traits of the white wines of Condrieu. Promises to be the best Israeli Viognier to date. Drink from release–2010. Tentative Score 90–92. K

YARDEN, VIOGNIER, 2005: Aged partly in *barriques*, partly in stainless steel and reflecting a gentle hand with spicy wood. Lively gold in color, full-bodied, with nectarines, peaches, kiwis and hints of citrus that play nicely on the palate together with aromas and flavors of spring flowers. Drink now. Score 90. K

YARDEN, VIOGNIER, 2004: Lightly golden in color, with classic Viognier apricot, citrus, litchi and peach fruits on the nose and palate, those set off by a hint of coconut and a gentle spiciness. Aromatic, harmonious and long. Drink now. Score 91. K

YARDEN, VIOGNIER, 2003: The winery's first Viognier, released only in limited quantities. Fermented partly in new oak and partly in stainless steel, this medium-bodied rich and ripe wine shows spring flowers, vanilla, and orange blossoms on a background of pineapple, nectarine and apricots, all complemented by lively acidity. Drink up. Score 88. K

YARDEN, JOHANNISBERG RIESLING, 2003: Medium-bodied, semi-dry, with a light golden-straw color and appealing summer fruits well balanced by good acidity. On the moderately long finish look for green apples and a hint of spiciness. Drink up. Score 87. K

YARDEN, JOHANNISBERG RIESLING, 2002: Pale yellow toward gold in color, this medium-bodied semi-dry wine shows appealing aromas and flavors of peaches and apricots along with a long mineral-laden finish. Plenty of natural acidity setting off the light sweetness makes it a good choice as an aperitif. Drink now. Score 89. K

YARDEN, JOHANNISBERG RIESLING, 2001: Even though this wine is categorized as semi-dry, it has just the barest hint of sweetness on the palate. Lively, well balanced and delicious, the wine has tempting aromas and flavors of peaches, apples and citrus. Drink up. Score 87. K

YARDEN, GEWURZTRAMINER, 2006: A medium-dry, medium-bodied white with just enough acidity to keep it lively. Floral and spicy aromas and flavors matched nicely by apricot, grapefruit and litchi fruits, all highlighted by an appealing hint of petrol. Drink now–2009. Score 88. K

YARDEN, GEWURZTRAMINER, 2005: Silky and spicy on the palate, with grapefruit, summer fruits and spices. Medium-dry, with an appealing hint of rose petals on the finish. Drink now. Score 86. K

YARDEN, GEWURZTRAMINER, 2004: Perhaps the most representative Gewurztraminer released by the winery, semi-dry but crisp, medium-bodied but mouth-filling, with traditional litchi and tropical fruits set off nicely by an appealing spiciness. Well balanced and generous. Drink now. Score 88. K

YARDEN, GEWURZTRAMINER, 2003: An appealing semi-dry, medium-bodied white with litchi, summer fruits and spices but lacking the acidity that might have made it more refreshing. Best as an aperitif. Drink up. Score 86. K

YARDEN, MOUNT HERMON WHITE, 2006: A straightforward white with citrus, pineapple and tropical fruits. Drink now. Score 83. K

YARDEN, MOUNT HERMON WHITE, 2005: Medium-bodied, a simple entry-level dry wine with citrus and pineapple fruits. Drink up. Score 82. K

YARDEN, NOBLE SEMILLON, BOTRYTIS, 2004: Golden in color, with fine concentration and balance and developing deep honeyed botrytis-impacted spices and funkiness. On the nose and palate dried apricots, orange peel, toasty oak, and tropical fruits that come in towards the long caressing finish. Drink now–2018. Score 92. K

YARDEN, NOBLE SEMILLON, BOTRYTIS, 2003: Deep and rich, with a concentrated personality of citrus peel, honeyed peaches, botrytis spice. Generously sweet, with fine balancing acidity and a long sweet and caressing finish on which tropical fruits and butterscotch arise. Drink now–2015. Score 91. K

YARDEN, NOBLE SEMILLON, BOTRYTIS, 2002: Golden towards subdued orange in color, medium to full-bodied and showing generous botrytis influence. Honeyed sweetness complemented nicely by aromas and flavors of orange peel and apricots. Soft, round and creamy on the palate, with good balancing acidity and hints of heather and white pepper on the moderately long finish. Drink now–2015. Score 90. K

YARDEN, NOBLE SEMILLON, BOTRYTIS, 2001: This lively, golden, medium-bodied dessert white offers up unabashed honeyed sweetness along with aromas and flavors of orange marmalade, pineapple and ripe apricots that meld comfortably into a soft, almost creamy texture. Plenty of balancing natural acidity and a medium-long finish boasting hints of spring flowers and spices. Promises to darken and attain greater complexity and depth in the future. Drink now–2010. Score 90. K

YARDEN, HEIGHTSWINE, 2006: This dessert wine is made entirely from Gewurztraminer grapes treated to sub-freezing temperatures at the winery. Showing varietal typicity with litchis, apricots and tropical fruits, all on a spicy background. Now starting to develop the floral and honeyed characteristics of an ice wine. Drink from release–2012. Tentative Score 88–90. K

YARDEN, HEIGHTSWINE, 2005: Made entirely from Gewurztraminer grapes frozen at the winery. Pale gold in color, with a complex nose and palate that offers up pineapple, citrus, litchi, orange peel and floral aromas and flavors, those with a light hint of sea water that adds to the wines charm and complexity. Drink now–2012. Score 91. K

YARDEN, HEIGHTSWINE, 2004: Made as always from Gewurztraminer grapes by the process of cryoextraction in the winery, this year offering its usual share of elegance and richness. Deep gold with a bronze overlay, with apricots, peaches and spices on the nose and palate set to a honeyed and floral background. Drink now–2010. Score 91. K

YARDEN, HEIGHTSWINE, 2003: As always, a tantalizing dessert wine, light to medium-bodied with delicate honeyed apricot and peach aromas and flavors, good balancing acidity and an elegant, lingering finish. Drink now. Score 90. K

YARDEN, HEIGHTSWINE, 2002: Light gold in color, medium-bodied, with excellent balance. Plenty of natural acidity to back up the sweetness and keep it lively while allowing the peach, apricot, and quince fruits to make themselves nicely felt. Honeyed and floral, generous and round. Drink now. Score 90. K

YARDEN, HEIGHTSWINE, 2001: Well balanced, generous and elegant, this honeyed dessert wine has a lively golden color and offers up a generous array of yellow peaches, apricots, melon, orange marmalade and quince, all on a floral and just-spicy-enough background. Drink now. Score 91. K

YARDEN, HEIGHTSWINE, 2000: A deliciously honeyed dessert wine, now showing pear and quince fruits together with traditional Gewurztraminer spices and litchis. As the wine develops in the glass look for hints of ripe apricots and white peaches. Generously sweet but with fine balancing acidity to keep it lively. Drink now. Score 92. K

YARDEN, HEIGHTSWINE, 1999: The first ice-wine made by the winery and showing still remarkably youthful and graceful. Sweet, with generous mineral and floral overtones, now showing lightly honeyed tones and in addition to the peach, apple and tropical fruits of its youth appealing hints of citrus peel and litchis. Drink now. Score 89. K

YARDEN, MUSCAT DESSERT WINE, 2005: Light straw in color, this medium-bodied, brandy-reinforced wine shows appealing dried apricot and peach fruits, those with a citrus honey overlay and finely balanced acidity to keep the wine lively. Drink now–2009. Score 88. K

YARDEN, MUSCAT DESSERT WINE, 2003: Reinforced lightly with brandy, this floral wine shows tempting aromas and flavors of citrus and summer fruits. Good balance between generous sweetness, acidity and fruits. Drink now. Score 87. K

YARDEN, MUSCAT DESSERT WINE, 2002: Lightly reinforced with brandy, a floral wine, rich with citrus peel, pineapple and white peach aromas and flavors. Smooth and round, with generous sweetness and good balancing acidity to keep it fresh and lively. Drink up. Score 87. K

YARDEN, BLANC DE BLANCS, 2001: The best Blanc de Blancs to date from the winery. Made from Chardonnay grapes by the traditional *methode Champenoise*, this medium-bodied sparkling wine shows just the right balance between yeasty sour-dough bread, peaches, citrus and minerals. With a generous mousse and sharp, well-focused bubbles that go on and on, this crisp and sophisticated wine goes on to a long and mouth-filling finish. Drink now–2011. Score 92. K

YARDEN, BLANC DE BLANCS, 2000: Made entirely from Chardonnay grapes in the traditional method of Champagne, this tempting sparkling wine shows appealing summer fruits, citrus and kiwis, those on a background of minerals and just a hint of yeast. A somewhat short mousse but sharp bubbles that linger nicely. Score 89. K

YARDEN, BLANC DE BLANCS, 1999: Made by the traditional *methode Champenoise*, just yeasty enough to enchant, with rich citrus, peach and tropical fruits along with a hint of mineral crispness. Sharp bubbles, a long mousse and a long and tempting near-creamy finish. Drink now–2009. Score 90. K

YARDEN, BLANC DE BLANCS, 1998: Ripe and vibrant with crisp apple and citrus aromas and flavors along with hints of vanilla, toasted white bread and nuts. The mousse is somewhat short but the bubbles are long-lasting and the nutty-grapefruit finish lingers nicely. Drink now. Score 90. K

YARDEN, BLANC DE BLANCS, 1997: Made entirely from Chardonnay grapes in the traditional *Champenoise* method, this lovely and sophisticated sparkling wine has just the right hint of yeast on a background of delicious citrus, white peach, spring flowers and mint. Sharp, concentrated bubbles, a long-lasting mousse and a lingering nutty finish. Drink now. Score 90. K

YARDEN, BLANC DE BLANCS, 1996: Made entirely from Chardonnay grapes, this medium-bodied sparkling wine is simultaneously rich and subdued. With concentrated long-lasting bubbles, a bouquet of dried and exotic fruits, spring flowers and the barest hints of coffee beans and herbs, this remains a refined, fresh and vibrant wine. Drink up. Score 91. K

YARDEN, BRUT, N.V.: Made in the traditional *Champenoise* method from a blend of Chardonnay and Pinot Noir grapes, this wine shows good balance, an abundance of citrus and white peach fruits, nutty flavors, just the right hints of yeast and sharp, long-lasting bubbles. Score 89. K

Gamla

GAMLA, CABERNET SAUVIGNON, 2004: Oak-aged for 12 months, this traditional Bordeaux blend is showing good balance between soft tannins, spicy oak and berry, cherry and currant fruits, those matched nicely by hints of white pepper and anise on the moderately long finish, Drink now–2010. Score 89. K

GAMLA, CABERNET SAUVIGNON, 2003: Soft and round, this medium to full-bodied blend of Cabernet Sauvignon, Cabernet Franc and one percent Malbec shows black currants and black cherries with spicy and herbal overlays. On the generous finish hints of vanilla and light earthiness. Drink now. Score 88. K

GAMLA, CABERNET SAUVIGNON, 2002: The usual Gamla Bordeaux blend of Cabernet Sauvignon, Merlot and Cabernet Franc. Medium to full-bodied, a gentle touch of oak, soft tannins and appealing black currant, blackberry and vanilla aromas and flavors. Drink up. Score 87. K

GAMLA, CABERNET SAUVIGNON, 2001: Medium to full-bodied, oak-aged for about 12 months, showing soft tannins and still remarkably youthful currant and berry fruits, those matched by hints of spices and, on the moderately long finish, intimations of tobacco and chocolate. Drink now–2009. Score 88. K

GAMLA, CABERNET SAUVIGNON, 2000: Perhaps singing its swan song, this medium to full-bodied, 12-month oak-aged blend of 85% Cabernet Sauvignon, 11% Merlot and 4% Cabernet Franc is still lively, its dark garnet color barely fading around the rim. Showing berry, black cherry and ripe plum fruits, those with appealing spicy and toasty oak overlays. Not for further cellaring. Drink up. Score 88. K

GAMLA, MERLOT, 2004: Reflecting 12 months in French oak with spices and fresh herbs. Medium to full-bodied, this dark ruby towards garnet wine has soft, integrated tannins and appealing berry, black cherry and cassis fruits backed up by a light hint of espresso coffee that comes in on the finish. Round and generous. Drink now–2009. Score 88. K

GAMLA, MERLOT, 2003: Deep garnet, medium to full-bodied, with still-firm tannins but with balance and structure that bode well for the future. Generous berry, currant and plum fruits here, with overlays of sweet cedar, hints of milk chocolate and an appealing herbaceous overlay. Drink now–2009. Score 89. K

GAMLA, MERLOT, 2002: Dark ruby towards garnet, medium to full-bodied, with tannins well balanced by spicy wood, black plum and wild berry fruits. Not overly complex. Drink up. Score 85. K

GAMLA, MERLOT, 2001: Elegant, well balanced and supple, this deep garnet medium-bodied wine offers up tempting berry and plum fruits, those complemented nicely by aromas and flavors of milk chocolate, vanilla and sweet cedarwood. Drink up. Score 89. K

GAMLA, MERLOT, 2000: Lean and with still-taut tannins, this deep royal-purple-toward-garnet wine is more in the country-style than one usually anticipates from the Golan Heights Winery. Somewhat coarse and earthy, the wine shows plenty of plum and blackberries, and hints of orange peel and mint to carry it. Drink up. Score 87. K

GAMLA, PINOT NOIR, 2004: Cherry-red, medium-bodied, lightly oaked with berry, black cherry and floral aromas. Soft, round tannins integrating nicely, leading to a medium-long and generously fruity finish. Drink now. Score 87. K

GAMLA, PINOT NOIR, 2003: Dark cherry-red towards garnet, medium-bodied, reflecting its seven months in oak with a hint of spicy wood. Well balanced, smooth and ripe, with cherry, raspberry and cola aromas and flavors on a lightly spicy background. Long and rich, with soft, well-integrated tannins. Drink now. Score 88. K

GAMLA, PINOT NOIR, 2002: Light colored and medium-bodied, this smooth wine shows aromas and flavors of currants, berries and spring flowers as well as gentle overlays of oak and a hint of chocolate on the finish. Drink up. Score 86. K

GAMLA, SANGIOVESE, 2005: Tempting aromas and flavors of sweet oak, berry and tea, those on a full-bodied and chewy background with a medium-long finish. Drink from release. Tentative Score 88–90. K

GAMLA, SANGIOVESE, 2004: Its firm tannins now settled in, this soft, round red shows fine balance with gentle wood and fruits. On the nose and palate wild berries, black cherry, licorice and violets, all coming together nicely. Drink now–2009. Score 88. K

GAMLA, SANGIOVESE, 2003: Dark garnet, medium-bodied, with soft tannins integrating nicely, and appealing spicy plum, berry and violet aromas and flavors. Soft, round, moderately long and although lacking great complexity, very appealing. Drink now. Score 89. K

GAMLA, SANGIOVESE, 2002: In its youth boasting good concentration and generous black fruits but now just a bit past its peak, its black cherry and plum fruits tainted by earthiness and a hint of oxidation on the rise. Drink up. Score 85. K

GAMLA, CHARDONNAY, 2006: Golden-straw in color, with light hints of spicy wood highlighting peach, citrus and tropical fruits. Drink now. Score 87. K

GAMLA, CHARDONNAY, 2005: Tempting citrus, summer fruits and light spices on a crisp, mineral-rich background. Drink now. Score 87. K

GAMLA, CHARDONNAY, 2004: Light gold, medium-bodied, with generous summer fruit, citrus and citrus flower aromas and flavors, those on a lightly spicy background. Good balancing acidity to keep it lively. Drink up. Score 87. K

GAMLA, SAUVIGNON BLANC, 2006: Light golden-straw, medium-bodied, packed with minerals, melon and summer fruits. Drink now. Score 87. K

GAMLA, SAUVIGNON BLANC, 2005: Fresh and crisp, with minerals and a hint of citrus peel leading to rich melon, citrus and tropical fruit aromas and flavors. Drink now. Score 87. K

GAMLA, SAUVIGNON BLANC, 2004: Light straw in color, medium-bodied, with appealing pear, tropical fruit and melon flavors, those with a nice hint of spiciness and a light herbaceousness. Drink up. Score 87. K

GAMLA, SAUVIGNON BLANC, 2003: Light golden-straw colored, medium-bodied, with generous aromas and flavors of tropical fruit, melon and a light overlay of grassiness. Good balancing acidity makes for a refreshing drink. Drink up. Score 86. K

GAMLA, WHITE RIESLING, 2006: Light gold in color, medium-bodied, with moderate sweetness set off nicely by acidity. On the nose and palate citrus, summer fruits and a hint of passion flower. Drink now. Score 87. K

GAMLA, WHITE RIESLING, 2004: Frankly sweet even though categorized as semi-dry, the wine has enough natural acidity to keep it lively and to highlight tempting citrus, pineapple and apricot flavors. Look for a hint of mint on the moderately long finish. Drink now. Score 87. K

Golan

GOLAN, CABERNET SAUVIGNON, 2005: Ruby towards garnet, medium-bodied, with soft tannins. Showing wild berry and black currant fruits and reflecting its six months in American oak with light spiciness and vanilla. Soft, round and easy to drink. Drink now. Score 85. K

GOLAN, CABERNET SAUVIGNON, 2004: Dark ruby, medium-bodied, with soft tannins, gentle wood, and currant and berry fruits. Fresh and fruity. Drink up. Score 85. K

GOLAN, CABERNET SAUVIGNON, 2003: Ruby-red towards purple in color, medium-bodied, with light oak and tannins and spicy berry-cherry aromas and flavors. Drink up. Score 86. K

GOLAN, MERLOT, 2005: Light to medium-bodied, with soft tannins and moderate acidity to keep it lively. Showing generous berry, cherry and cassis fruits. Not complex but easy to drink. Drink now. Score 85. K

GOLAN, MERLOT, 2004: The first Merlot release in the Golan series. Nothing overly complex here and not meant for cellaring but a pleasant, medium-bodied wine, with soft tannins and lively plum, currant and berry fruits, those on a lightly spicy background. Drink up. Score 85. K

GOLAN, GAMAY NOUVEAU, 2005: Made from Gamay Noir grapes, treated to carbonic maceration and bottled within weeks after completion of the harvest. Light in body, lively dark cherry towards purple in color, with scarce tannins and an abundance of wild berry, cherry, and even citrus peel and apple aromas and flavors. Drink up. Score 85. K

GOLAN, SION CREEK, RED, 2005: Light to medium-bodied, with almost unfelt tannins and fruity enough to make one think more of fruit juice than of fine wine. Drink up. Score 80. K

GOLAN, SION CREEK, RED, 2004: A simple-entry-level wine, light to medium-bodied, with soft tannins, a floral aroma and a berry-cherry personality. Drink up. Score 80. K

GOLAN, CHARDONNAY, 2005: Light golden-straw in color, with aromas and flavors of citrus, green apples and pineapple. Not complex but as always, a pleasant quaffer. Drink now. Score 85. K

GOLAN, CHARDONNAY, 2004: As always, a lively, clean and refreshing wine, medium-bodied with aromas of citrus, citrus peel and green apples. Drink up. Score 86. K

GOLAN, MOSCATO, 2006: Made from Muscat Canelli grapes, this white is generously sweet, with good balancing acidity, and remarkably floral on the nose, much in the style of Moscato d'Asti. Look for aromas and flavors of green apples, ripe white peaches, tropical fruits and a hint of grapefruit, all with a nice fizziness. Not complex but delicious. Drink now. Score 86. K

GOLAN, MOSCATO, 2005: As it has been since 1999, light, fresh, lightly *frizzante*, generously sweet but with good balancing acidity and appealing pineapple, lemon and lime aromas and flavors. A simple but fun wine. Drink up. Score 86. K

GOLAN, SION CREEK RED, 2006: Light to medium-bodied, soft and round with a few basic floral and red berry fruits. Somewhat too acidic but an acceptable entry-level wine. Drink up. Score 80. K

Greenberg ✶✶✶✶

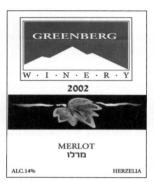

Located in Herzliya, not far from Tel Aviv, this micro-winery owned by Motti Greenberg is now producing about 1,000 bottles annually. First wines were released from the 2003 vintage, using Cabernet Sauvignon, Merlot and Shiraz grapes from the Karmei Yosef vineyards at the foothills of the Jerusalem Mountains.

GREENBERG, CABERNET SAUVIGNON, 2006: Dark garnet towards royal-purple, lithe and open-textured. Soft tannins and spicy wood integrating nicely to show currant and blackberry fruits, those with hints of espresso coffee and eucalyptus on the long finish. Best from 2010. Tentative Score 89–91.

GREENBERG, CABERNET SAUVIGNON, 2005: Aged in oak for 12 months and racked four times before blending 85% Cabernet Sauvignon with 10% of Merlot and 5% Shiraz. Dark ruby towards garnet, medium to full-bodied, with generous, soft tannins and light spicy wood opening to show black currant, blackberry and spicy notes. On the finish a hint of eucalyptus. Drink now–2009. Score 88.

GREENBERG, CABERNET SAUVIGNON, 2004: Medium-bodied, with still-firm tannins and generous smoky oak, those opening in the glass to reveal currant, black cherry and berry fruits on a light vanilla background. Drink now. Score 87.

GREENBERG, CABERNET SAUVIGNON, 2003: Deep garnet toward purple, this medium to full-bodied red is a fine first effort, the wine showing generous but well-integrating tannins, and black currant and wild berry fruits with moderate overlays of spicy oak, vanilla and a light herbaceousness. Drink up. Score 86.

GREENBERG, MERLOT, 2006: Dark, almost impenetrable garnet, a plush wine showing layers of raspberry, blackberry and fig aromas and flavors, those complemented by spices, minerals and a hint of lead pencil. Bodes for elegance. Best from 2010. Tentative Score 89–91.

GREENBERG, MERLOT, 2005: Garnet towards royal-purple, this medium to full-bodied blend of 85% Merlot, 10% Cabernet Sauvignon and 5% Shiraz opens with generous, near-sweet tannins and spicy wood, those coming together nicely to show blackberry, black cherry and spicy aromas and flavors. Drink now–2009. Score 87.

GREENBERG, MERLOT, 2004: Medium to full-bodied, with soft tannins integrating nicely and light spicy wood highlighting currant, berry and citrus peel aromas and flavors. Drink now. Score 86.

GREENBERG, MERLOT, 2003: Medium-bodied, with soft, sweet tannins. Blackberry and cherry fruits are complemented nicely by spiciness and hints of vanilla and eucalyptus. Drink now. Score 87.

GREENBERG, SHIRAZ, 2006: Complex and supple, with layers of spices, wild berries, anise and leather, all coming together beautifully. A firm tannic grip here that carries through to the long finish. Best from 2010. Tentative Score 91–93.

GREENBERG, SHIRAZ, 2005: Deep purple, with soft tannins and light spicy wood influences, this is a medium to full-bodied blend of 85% Shiraz, 10% Merlot and 5% Cabernet Sauvignon. On the nose and palate black fruits matched nicely by hints of saddle leather and earthiness. Generous and moderately long. Drink now–2009. Score 89.

GREENBERG, SHIRAZ, 2004: Dark, cloudy, garnet-red, this medium-bodied wine shows black fruits and light earthy aromas and flavors that linger nicely. Drink now. Score 86.

GREENBERG, SHIRAZ, 2003: This tempting medium-bodied wine shows floral and earthy aromas and flavors matched well by moderate tannins, wood and appealing black fruits. Mouth-filling and long. Drink up. Score 87.

GREENBERG, ANIN, 2005: A blend of one-third each of Cabernet Sauvignon, Merlot and Shiraz, aged in oak separately for 12 months before blending. Medium to full-bodied, dark garnet, with firm tannins needing time to integrate but already showing berry, black cherry and cassis fruits, those on a lightly earth and mineral background. Best 2009–2012. Score 88.

GREENBERG, APPOLONIA, 2005: A blend of 60% Shiraz and 20% each of Merlot and Cabernet Sauvignon, this medium to full-bodied red opens with floral and tarry notes on the nose, those yielding in the glass to ample black fruits, spices and hints of cigar tobacco. Complex, generous and long. Best 2009–2012. Score 89.

GREENBERG, ANIN, 2004: A medium-bodied, dark garnet-towards-royal-purple blend of 50% Merlot and 25% each Shiraz and Cabernet Sauvignon. Soft, well-integrated tannins highlight forward berry, black cherry and cassis aromas, those with an appealing spicy hint on the finish. Drink now. Score 87.

Gush Etzion ✶✶✶

Located at the Gush Etzion Junction near Jerusalem, the winery is owned largely by vintner Shraga Rozenberg and partly by the Tishbi family, and has its own vineyards in the Jerusalem Mountains providing Cabernet Sauvignon, Merlot, Pinot Noir, Shiraz, Cabernet Franc and Petit Verdot as well as Chardonnay, Viognier and Johannisberg Riesling grapes. First releases were in 1998 of 3,000 and the winery currently produces about 30,000 bottles annually. A new winery is now under construction with the potential for future production of up to 100,000 bottles.

GUSH ETZION WINERY
Cabernet Sauvignon 70% Merlot 30%
2000 | Judean Hills

Bottle No. **2890** of 7900   13% Alcohol by Volume 750 ml Ⓤᴾ

GUSH ETZION, CABERNET SAUVIGNON, 2002: Deep royal-purple, full-bodied, with generous soft tannins and spicy oak well balanced by ripe currants and cassis. Appealing overlays of chocolate and tobacco on the long finish. Drink now. Score 88. K

GUSH ETZION, CABERNET SAUVIGNON, 2001: Dark, almost inky garnet toward royal-purple, this full-bodied wine shows excellent balance between generous but soft tannins, just the right touch of smoky-spicy oak and elegant black currant and wild berry fruits and spices along with Mediterranean herbs and green olives coming in toward the finish. Drink now. Score 87. K

GUSH ETZION, CABERNET SAUVIGNON, 2000: Deep ruby, medium to full-bodied wine with generous tannins and wood blending well with currant, plum and herbal aromas and flavors. Look for light hints of spices and smoky wood as well. Drink up. Score 86. K

GUSH ETZION, CABERNET SAUVIGNON-MERLOT, 2000: Medium to full-bodied, this country-style wine shows chunky tannins, plenty of wood, plum and black cherry fruits, all with hints of dill and other Mediterranean herbs. Drink up. Score 85. K

GUSH ETZION, CHARDONNAY, 2005: Light-straw colored, this un-oaked white shows tempting tropical and citrus fruits on a light mineral background. Fresh, crisp and refreshing. Drink now. Score 86. K

GUSH ETZION, CHARDONNAY, ORGANIC, 2003: Light golden-straw in color, medium-bodied, with generous balancing acidity and apple and peach fruits. Lightly *frizzante* which may indicate that a second fermentation is taking place in the bottle, and with a somewhat odd spearmint flavor. Drink up. Score 85. K

Gustavo & Jo ★★★★

Located in the village of Kfar Vradim in the Western Galilee, and drawing on grapes from the Golan Heights and the Upper Galilee, this small winery was founded in 1995 by Gideon Boinjeau and produced only Cabernet Sauvignon wines until the release of a first white in 2005. Pro-duction of two series,

Premium and Gustavo & Jo, averages 3,000 bottles annually. Starting with the 2006 vintage, all the wines will be kosher.

Premium

PREMIUM, CABERNET SAUVIGNON, 2004: Deep ruby towards garnet, medium to full-bodied, with firm tannins that need time to integrate but already showing fine balance and structure. Aromas and flavors of blackberries, currants, near-sweet cedarwood and white pepper lead to a long tobacco and chocolate-rich finish. Drink now–2012. Score 91.

PREMIUM, CABERNET SAUVIGNON, 2003: Dark garnet towards black, full-bodied, with firm tannins integrating nicely, those well balanced by spicy wood and black currant, blackberry and cassis fruits all on a background of minty-chocolate. Long and complex. Drink now–2012. Score 91.

PREMIUM, CABERNET SAUVIGNON, 2002: Deep garnet towards black, full-bodied, with still firm but well-integrating tannins. Excellent balance between wood, tannins and an appealing array of black and red fruits, those yielding to spices, chocolate and mint. Long and complex. Drink now–2012. Score 91.

PREMIUM, CABERNET SAUVIGNON, 2001: Full-bodied, with once-firm tannins now integrating nicely and continuing to show the fine balance and structure of its youth. On the nose and palate currant, black cherry and plum fruits, those backed up nicely by hints of Mediterranean herbs and a gentle overlay of mint. Drink now. Score 91.

PREMIUM, CABERNET SAUVIGNON, 2000: Full-bodied and with its once-firm tannins now well integrated, the wine reveals a complex set of aromas and flavors that include currants, wild berries, leather and spices. Deep, rich, and bordering on elegance. Drink up. Score 90.

Gustavo & Jo

GUSTAVO & JO, CABERNET SAUVIGNON, 2004: Medium-dark garnet in color, with grapes primarily from the Upper Galilee, this spicy, generously oaked and tannic wine shows fine balance and structure and appealing black fruits. Hints of licorice and green olives come together nicely on a long and mouth-filling finish. Drink now–2012. Score 90.

GUSTAVO & JO, CABERNET SAUVIGNON, 2003: Dark garnet towards black, full-bodied, with still-firm tannins well balanced by spicy wood and black currant, blackberry and cassis fruits all on a background of minty-chocolate. Long and complex. Drink now–2010. Score 89.

GUSTAVO & JO, CABERNET SAUVIGNON, 2002: This deep inky purple, full-bodied, still-young red has firm, somewhat tight tannins and a tempting array of currant and black cherry fruits, those coming together nicely with spicy oak, eucalyptus and generous hints of chocolate and tobacco on the long finish. Long, complex and mouth-filling. Drink now. Score 88.

GUSTAVO & JO, CABERNET SAUVIGNON, 2001: Dark purple toward garnet, full-bodied, with distinct Cabernet aromas and flavors including black currants, black cherries, and a generous hint of mint on firm but well-integrated tannins, the wine shows good balance between wood and tannins and has a long, appealing herbal finish. Drink now. Score 89.

GUSTAVO & JO, CABERNET SAUVIGNON, 2000: Full-bodied, well rounded, with already soft tannins and good black currant, plum and cherry aromas and flavors that linger very nicely on the palate, the wine also shows an appealing overlay of oak. Drink up. Score 89.

GUSTAVO & JO, CABERNET SAUVIGNON, 1999: Deep, almost impenetrable garnet, full-bodied, with now silky soft tannins and a ripe and complex core of currants, berries, leather and spices. On the long finish hints of dried herbs and espresso coffee. Drink up. Score 89.

GUSTAVO & JO, CABERNET SAUVIGNON, 1998: Medium to full-bodied, with fine balance between gently spicy, smoky wood and now silky smooth tannins. With still youthful black currant and berry fruits, those matched by appealing olive and earthy streaks that run through to the long finish. Drink up. Score 90.

GUSTAVO & JO, CABERNET SAUVIGNON, 1997: Full-bodied and complex but now moving gracefully from maturity to old age. Tannins fully integrated, showing some appealing black currant and berry flavors but those turning a bit acidic after a short while in the glass. Drink up. Score 88.

GUSTAVO & JO, FUMÉ BLANC, SHANI, 2005: Developed partly in 300 liter Burgundy-style barrels, this medium to full-bodied, lightly golden, Sauvignon Blanc-based wine features grassiness with a light but appealing pungency. Crisp and fresh. Drink now. Score 89.

Gvaot ★★★

Founded by Shivi Drori and Amnon Weiss on the settlement of Shiloh in the Shomron region, with vineyards at an altitude of 700–900 meters above sea level, this boutique winery released its first wines from the 2005 vintage. Production in 2005 was for 5,000 bottles and for 2006 17,500 bottles, those of Cabernet Sauvignon, Merlot and Chardonnay grapes. The winery is currently releasing wines in two series: one upper-level, Masada, and the other mid-level, Herodion.

Masada

MASADA, CABERNET SAUVIGNON, 2006: Made from grapes that had partly dried on the vines, cold-fermented before being transferred to oak barrels. Medium-bodied, with a vague hint of sweetness set off nicely by aromas and flavors of ripe berries and black cherries and, on the moderately long finish, a touch of eucalyptus. Drink from release. Tentative Score 86–88. K

MASADA, MERLOT, 2006: Dark, almost impenetrable garnet in color, full-bodied, firm and concentrated, opening with peppery cedarwood, that yielding comfortably to blackberry and spicy and earthy aromas and flavors. Needs time to soften but has a distinct personality and a long-lingering finish. Best from 2009. Tentative Score 89–91. K

MASADA, MERLOT, 2005: Dark royal-purple with orange reflections, this wine reflects its 18 months in *barriques* with spicy oak and mouth-coating near-sweet tannins in fine balance with minty, herb-scented cherry and berry flavors, those with overlays of milk chocolate and mint. Full-bodied, with fine tannins and a caressing finish. Drink now–2010. Score 90. K

MASADA, CHARDONNAY-CABERNET SAUVIGNON, 2005: A blend of Chardonnay and Cabernet Sauvignon (75% and 25% respectively), the Cabernet with minimal skin contact yielding a rather unique *blanc de noirs*. Full-bodied, with a texture of cream and glycerin, showing a surprising but appealing array of citrus, pear and wild berry fruits. A complex and 'interesting' wine but not for long cellaring. Drink now. Score 86. K

Herodion

HERODION, CABERNET SAUVIGNON, 2005: A blend of 85% Cabernet Sauvignon and 15% Merlot, reflecting sweet and spicy cedarwood from its 14 months development in French oak, the wood in good balance with soft, gently mouth-coating tannins and fruits. Medium to full-bodied, aromatic, and showing deep currant, black cherry and dark red fruits. Finishes with a touch of heat but that will integrate nicely in time. Best starting in 2009. Score 88. K

HERODIAN, RED, 2005: Dark garnet in color, medium-bodied, with soft tannins and gentle oak integrating nicely, this blend of 60% Cabernet Sauvignon and 40% Merlot was aged in French oak for 12 months. Aromatic, round and soft, with appealing aromas and flavors of blackberry and purple plum fruits, those supported by hints of spice and chocolate. Drink now. Score 87. K

Hakerem **

Founded in 2001 by Isaac Herskovitz and located in Beit-El near Hebron, this winery produces Cabernet Sauvignon and Merlot wines, drawing on grapes from various vineyards. The winery sometimes releases more than one wine under the same label. Annual production is currently about 6,000 bottles.

HAKEREM, CABERNET SAUVIGNON, 2005: Somewhat cloudy dark garnet, medium to full-bodied, with chunky and firm country-style tannins tending to hide the black fruits that are present. Simple and one dimensional. Drink now. Score 82. K

HAKEREM, CABERNET SAUVIGNON, 2004: Deep ruby towards garnet, medium-bodied, with firm tannins and too generous hints of spicy oak and earthiness with aromas and flavors of currants and black cherries. Drink now. Score 84. K

HAKEREM, CABERNET SAUVIGNON, 2003: Medium-bodied, with soft, nicely integrated tannins and plum, cherry, berry and spice notes, this smooth wine ends with an appealing fruity finish. Drink now. Score 86. K

HAKEREM, CABERNET SAUVIGNON, 2002: Maturing now, its once dark garnet color now with generous hints of adobe brick, this medium to full-bodied oak-aged wine shows softened tannins and generous vanilla and smoky aromas and flavors, those well balanced by black fruits and hints of herbs and tobacco. Drink up. Score 86. K

HAKEREM, MERLOT, 2005: Medium-bodied, with somewhat coarse tannins and an overriding earthy note that tends to hide whatever fruits may be hidden. Drink up. Score 75. K

HAKEREM, MERLOT, 2004: Medium-bodied, with plum, berry and currant fruits but marred by unclean earthy overtones, the wine is somewhat one dimensional. Drink up. Score 80. K

HAKEREM, MERLOT, 2003: Dark garnet toward purple, this medium-bodied, gently oaked wine shows good balance between soft tannins and ripe berry and currant fruits, along with a nice herbal-spicy finish. Drink now. Score 86. K

KAKAREM, MERLOT, 2003 (SECOND EDITION): Dark ruby towards garnet, medium-bodied, with soft tannins and aromas and flavors of a stewed fruit compote. Drink up. Score 79. K

Hamasrek ✳✳✳

HAMASREK

2002

CHARDONNAY
שרדונה

Alc 12.5% Vol 750 ml. Prod & Bot.
By HAMASREK Winery, ISRAEL.

Established by brothers Nachum and Hanoch Greengrass in 1999 on Moshav Beit Meir in the Jerusalem Mountains, this kosher boutique winery draws on grapes from their own area as well as from Zichron Ya'akov and the Upper Galilee. In 2000 the winery released 5,000 bottles of Merlot and Chardonnay and since then the winery has added Cabernet Sauvignon and Gewurztraminer to their line. Current production is about 20,000 bottles.

HAMASREK, CABERNET SAUVIGNON, 2005: Dark garnet, medium to full-bodied, with near-sweet tannins and spicy wood well balanced by blackberry, currant and black cherry fruits. On the moderately long finish hints of freshly turned earth and tobacco. Drink now–2009. Score 86. K

HAMASREK, CABERNET SAUVIGNON, 2003: Deep ruby towards garnet, medium to full-bodied, with firm tannins and generous wood but those yielding nicely to show black currant and plum fruits on a lightly spicy background. Drink now. Score 86. K

HAMASREK, MERLOT, 2004: Generous spicy oak and tannins in this dark royal-purple wine, those somewhat holding back the berry and black cherry aromas and flavors. Drink now. Score 84. K

HAMASREK, MERLOT, 2003: Made entirely from Merlot grapes, this red reflects its 18 months in *barriques* with dusty-smoky oak, and under that currant and blackberry flavors that never quite make it to the surface. Drink now. Score 83. K

HAMASREK, MERLOT, 2002: Dark royal-purple, medium-bodied and with soft, well-integrating tannins opening to reveal generous blackberry, black cherry and cassis aromas and flavors. Drink up. Score 86. K

HAMASREK, THE KING'S BLEND, JUDEAN HILLS, N.V.: A blend of Cabernet Sauvignon, Merlot and Zinfandel grapes from the 2004 and 2005 vintages. Dark garnet, medium to full-bodied, with soft tannins integrating nicely and showing generous berry, black cherry and herbal aromas and flavors. Lingers nicely. Drink now–2009. Score 86. K

HAMASREK, THE KING'S BLEND, JUDEAN HILLS, N.V.: A blend of Cabernet Sauvignon, Merlot and Zinfandel grapes from the 2003 and 2004 vintages. Medium to full-bodied, with chunky tannins, a strong influence of the wood and only bare hints of black fruits. Flat and one dimensional. Drink up. Score 80. K

HAMASREK, CHARDONNAY, 2006: Dark gold, medium-bodied, developed partly in oak and partly in stainless steel. Citrus peel, guava and tropical fruits here along with a hint of spices. Good balancing acidity. Drink from release–2009. Score 86. K

HAMASREK, CHARDONNAY, 2005: Golden-straw with a green tint, medium-bodied, with hints of spices and vanilla from the oak in which it was partially aged. Citrus peel, guava and pear flavors. Drink up. Score 85. K

HAMASREK, GEWURZTRAMINER, 2005: Light golden-straw in color, off-dry, with good balancing acidity and appealing litchi and ripe summer fruits. Drink now. Score 86. K

HAMASREK, GEWURZTRAMINER, 2004: Although defined as semi-sweet, the wine shows deep sweetness set off nicely by natural acidity. Rich and soft but not flabby, with aromas and flavors of spices, honey, litchis and peaches, all coming together in a long finish. Drink now. Score 88. K

Hans Sternbach **

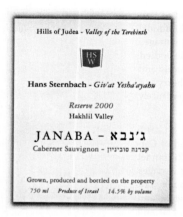

Hills of Judea - *Valley of the Terebinth*

HS
W

Hans Sternbach - *Giv'at Yesha'ayahu*

Reserve 2000
Hakhlil Valley

JANABA - ג'נבא

Cabernet Sauvignon - קברנה סוביניון

Grown, produced and bottled on the property
750 ml   *Produce of Israel*   14.5% *by volume*

Founded by Gadi and Shula Sternbach in Moshav Givat Yeshayahu in the Judean Hills, the Domaine Hans Sternbach's first release was of 1,800 bottles from the 2000 harvest. With a new winery located on the moshav and relying primarily on Cabernet Sauvignon grapes from its own nearby vineyards, production from the 2003 vintage was about 3,000 bottles and from the 2004 and 2005 vintages about 10,000 bottles. The winery produces three series: Janaba Reserve, Nachal Hakhlil and Emek Ha'ella.

Janaba Reserve

JANABA RESERVE, CABERNET SAUVIGNON, HAKHLIL VALLEY, 2006: Dark garnet towards royal-purple, full-bodied with still-firm tannins holding back the fruits somewhat, but showing good balance and structure. Opens to reveal currant and blackberry fruits on a spicy and lightly herbal background. Drink from release. Tentative Score 84–86.

JANABA RESERVE, CABERNET SAUVIGNON, HAKHLIL VALLEY, 2005: Youthful, dark royal-purple, medium to full-bodied, with firm tannins still controlling the wine but already showing black currant, wild berry and spicy oak aromas and flavors. Drink from release–2009. Score 84.

JANABA RESERVE, CABERNET SAUVIGNON, 2003: 100% Cabernet Sauvignon, this deep garnet towards royal-purple, medium to full-bodied oak-aged red shows firm tannins and generous oak that yield only partly to black currant and wild berry fruits. Marred by a bit of unwanted residual sugar. Drink up. Score 82.

Nachal Hakhlil

NACHAL HAKHLIL, 2006: Dark royal-purple in color, this oak-aged blend of 70% Cabernet Sauvignon and 30% Merlot is showing medium to full-bodied, with firm tannins opening to reveal generous currant, blackberry and Mediterranean herbs. Drink from release. Tentative Score 85–87.

NACHAL HAKHLIL, CABERNET SAUVIGNON, 2005: An oak-aged blend of 80% Cabernet Sauvignon and 20% Merlot. Medium to full-bodied, with somewhat coarse tannins not yet wanting to yield but showing appealing black fruits and a medium-long finish. Drink now. Score 85.

NACHAL HAKHLIL, CABERNET SAUVIGNON, 2004: Oak-aged for 21 months. Dark garnet towards royal-purple, medium to full-bodied, with chunky country-style tannins. On the nose and palate spicy oak tends to dominate the black fruits. Drink now. Score 84.

NACHAL HAKHLIL, CABERNET SAUVIGNON, 2003: Deep garnet, medium to full-bodied, with firm, chunky tannins and aromas and flavors of currants and berries, this blend of 90% Cabernet Sauvignon and 10% Petite Sirah reflects its 12 months in oak with spicy and vanilla overtones. Drink now. Score 85.

Socho Valley

SOCHO VALLEY, CABERNET SAUVIGNON, 2004: Made entirely of Cabernet Sauvignon grapes and aged in French oak for one year. Cloudy ruby towards purple in color, with black fruits almost completely buried beneath barnyard aromas. Drink up. Score 74.

Emek Ha'ella

EMEK HA'ELLA, 2005: An unoaked blend of 80% Cabernet Sauvignon and 20% Merlot. Light in body, with soft tannins and berry-cherry fruits. A simple quaffer. Drink up. Score 81.

EMEK HA'ELLA, CABERNET SAUVIGNON, VALLELLA CLASSICO SUPERIORE, 2002: Like the Valpolicella Classico Superiore, this wine is also made by the *ripasso* method, but unfortunately, Cabernet Sauvignon grapes are not appropriate for the method. Light cherry-colored, light to medium-bodied, the wine shows far too bitter overtones to the plum flavors that are here and therefore lacks balance. Drink up. Score 79.

Hatabor ✶✶

Located in the village of Kfar Tabor in the Lower Galilee, this winery was founded by Shimi Efrat in 1999 and released its first wines from the 2002 harvest. Grapes come primarily from nearby vineyards, and production is currently about 7,000 bottles annually.

HATABOR, CABERNET SAUVIGNON, 2005: Full-bodied, with almost searing tannins and far too generous wood hiding the fruits that struggle to make themselves felt. Drink up. Score 78.

HATABOR, CABERNET SAUVIGNON, 2004: Dark purple, medium-bodied, with chunky tannins opening to reveal black fruits, spices and a light herbal note. Drink up. Score 81.

HATABOR, CABERNET SAUVIGNON, 2003: Garnet towards purple, medium-bodied, with soft tannins and appealing currant, cassis and cherry fruits backed up nicely by a hint of spiciness. Drink up. Score 80.

HATABOR, MERLOT, 2005: Deep royal-purple, medium to full-bodied, with firm tannins yielding somewhat in the glass to reveal raspberry, cassis and herbal aromas and flavors. Drink now. Score 84.

HATABOR, MERLOT, 2004: Ruby towards garnet, medium-bodied, with chunky tannins and spicy wood. A country-style wine that opens to show plum and black cherry fruits on a herbal and black olive background. Drink up. Score 80.

HATABOR, MERLOT-CABERNET SAUVIGNON, 2005: Medium-bodied, with soft tannins and a gentle wood influence. Showing appealing black and red berry as well as black cherry fruits. A good quaffer. Drink now. Score 85.

HATABOR, CHARDONNAY, 2006: Medium-bodied, with lively acidity and appealing citrus and tropical fruits. Simple but easy to drink. Drink up. Score 84.

HATABOR, CHARDONNAY, 2005: Light golden–straw in color, light to medium-bodied, with melon, citrus and tropical fruits. A simple but pleasant quaffer. Drink up. Score 84.

HATABOR, CHARDONNAY, 2004: Golden-straw in color, medium-bodied, with appealing citrus, tropical fruit and pear aromas and flavors. Drink up. Score 82.

HATABOR, SAUVIGNON BLANC, 2006: Light golden-straw, light-bodied with generous acidity. Showing grapefruit and tropical fruits. Drink up. Score 82.

HATABOR, SAUVIGNON BLANC, 2004: Light straw in color, light to medium-bodied, with crisp acidity backing up citrus and light grassy aromas and flavors. Drink up. Score 80.

Hevron Heights **

Located in Kiryat Arba, not far from the heart of the city of Hebron, this winery was founded in 2001 by a group of French investors and initially produced about 150,000 bottles per year, the target audience largely being observant Jews abroad. The winery reports current production of about 600,000 bottles annually, and produces a line of varietal and blended wines of Cabernet Sauvignon, Merlot, French Colombard, Sauvignon Blanc, and Malbec grapes, drawing largely on grapes from the Judean Hills as well as vineyards near Hebron. The winery has a broad and somewhat confusing labeling system with a large number of series and brands including Hevron Heights, Noah, Hevron, Tevel, Efron's Cave, Shemesh, Pardess, Judea and Jerusalem Heights, some of which are also produced as private labels.

Hevron Heights

HEVRON HEIGHTS, CABERNET SAUVIGNON, KIDRON, 2004: Dark garnet, this medium to full-bodied wine reflects its 12 months exposure to oak with spices and soft tannins. On the nose and palate black fruits and hints of pepper and star anise. Neither complex nor long but an acceptable entry-level wine. Drink now. Score 84. K

HEVRON HEIGHTS, CABERNET SAUVIGNON, GIDEON, 2004: Deep garnet towards purple, medium to full-bodied, with firm and chunky country-style tannins. On the nose and palate blackberries, plums and a hint of orange peel. Turns almost sweet on the finish. Drink now. Score 83. K

HEVRON HEIGHTS, CABERNET SAUVIGNON, SDEH CALEV, 2003: Deep garnet, medium to full-bodied, with soft tannins and currant and berry fruits matched by hints of spices and mint. Drink up. Score 84. K

HEVRON HEIGHTS, CABERNET SAUVIGNON, JUDEAN HEIGHTS, 2002: Deep garnet going to brick-brown, medium to full-bodied, with firm, somewhat chunky country-style tannins opening in the glass to reveal currant, berry, and black cherry fruits. On the finish look for hints of earthy minerals and mint. Drink up. Score 83. K

HEVRON HEIGHTS, CABERNET SAUVIGNON, GIDEON, 2002: Dark inky purple and medium-bodied, the wine has chunky tannins, too much acidity and an overbearing influence of what appears to be oak. Overripe and cloying. Drink up. Score 78. K

HEVRON HEIGHTS, CABERNET SAUVIGNON, ISAAC'S RAM, 2002: Medium-bodied, ruby towards garnet in color, with soft, near-sweet tannins and appealing berry, black cherry and currant fruits overlaid by hints of cigar tobacco and Oriental spices. Drink up. Score 82. K

HEVRON HEIGHTS, MERLOT, JUDEAN HEIGHTS, 2002: Dark garnet, medium-bodied, with soft tannins, a judicious hand with wood and appealing black fruits backed up by light overlays of Mediterranean herbs and, on the finish, a hint of white chocolate. Drink now. Score 85. K

HEVRON HEIGHTS, MERLOT, PARDESS, 2002: Dark ruby towards garnet, medium-bodied, with well-integrated near-sweet tannins and appealing cassis, wild berry and citrus peel fruits, those supported by light hints of spices, tobacco and bittersweet chocolate. Drink now. Score 83. K

HEVRON HEIGHTS, SYRAH, RESERVE, 2004: Dark royal-purple, medium to full-bodied, with firm tannins integrating nicely. On the nose and palate plums, blackberries, and spices with a moderately long earthy-mineral finish. Drink now. 86. K

HEVRON HEIGHTS, SYRAH, RESERVE, 2003: Medium to full-bodied, with gripping tannins and generous acidity, this red reflects its 12 months in oak with spices and smoke, and opens on the palate to reveal plum, berry and cassis fruits. Drink up. Score 85. K

HEVRON HEIGHTS, ARMAGEDDON (*MEGIDDO IN NORTH AMERICA*), 2002: An unfiltered blend of 80% Cabernet Sauvignon, 15% Merlot and 5% Syrah, aged in new French oak for 24 months. To my palate the wine has been so vastly different from tasting to tasting that it defies a firm description or consistent scoring. Overall, it continues to reflect generous sweet and smoky wood and gripping tannins. At this most recent tasting, the tannins and wood seem to finally be integrating, allowing the black currant, red and black berries and ripe red plum aromas and flavors to show. Drink now. Scores range from 80–86. K

HEVRON HEIGHTS, MAKAPELAH, 2002: A blend of 70% Cabernet Sauvignon, 26% Merlot and 4% Marsanne, oak-aged for more than 20 months. This dark garnet going to adobe-brown wine is full-bodied, almost thick in texture, with chunky tannins and generous wood tending to hide the plum and blackberry fruits that never fully make their way to the surface. Drink up. Score 82. K

HEVRON HEIGHTS, MAKAPELAH, 2001: Dark garnet going to brown, this blend of Cabernet Sauvignon, Merlot and Syrah was oak-aged for 20 months. Showing black currant and blackberry fruits, those with overlays of earthy minerals and tobacco. Fully mature. Drink up. Score 84. K

HEVRON HEIGHTS, SPECIAL RESERVE, 2002: Developed in French and American oak for 20 months, this blend of Cabernet Sauvignon, Merlot and Shiraz (65%, 25% and 10% respectively) shows full-bodied, with gripping tannins and generous spicy and smoky wood. Opens to reveal plum, wild berry and cassis fruits, those leading to a moderately long and generously peppery finish. Drink now–2009. Score 85. K

HEVRON HEIGHTS, TRIPLE RED, EFRON'S CAVE, 2003: Dark garnet, this medium-bodied, unoaked blend of one-third each Cabernet Sauvignon, Merlot and Syrah offers up soft tannins and forwards berry-cherry fruits. Drink up. Score 79. K

HEVRON HEIGHTS, TRIPLE PLUM, EFRON'S CAVE, 2003: A light to medium-bodied one-dimensional blend of Cabernet Sauvignon, Merlot and Syrah (35%, 35% and 30% respectively) with forward plum and black cherry fruits. Drink up. Score 78. K

HEVRON HEIGHTS, SAUVIGNON BLANC FUMÉ, SHEMESH, 2004: Straw-colored, medium-bodied, with smoky oak and appealing citrus peel, tropical fruits, light herbal and grassy aromas and flavors. Not complex but pleasant. Drink now. Score 84. K

HEVRON HEIGHTS, WHITE, EFRON'S CAVE, 2003: Unoaked Sauvignon Blanc, light in color and body with refreshing citrus and herbal-mineral aromas and flavors. A simple entry-level wine. Drink up. Score 80. K

HEVRON HEIGHTS, MOSCATO, SHEMESH, 2004: Light, lively golden-straw in color, light in body, with moderate sweetness and distinctly floral on the nose and with an abundance of citrus and tropical fruits. Drink now. Score 83. K

Noah

NOAH, CABERNET SAUVIGNON, TEVEL, 2004: Medium-bodied, softly tannic, with black cherry, blackberry, cedar and bell pepper notes along with a smoky oak finish. Drink up. Score 84. K

NOAH, MERLOT, TEVEL, 2004: Medium-bodied, with soft tannins, hints of wood and generous berry, cherry and currant fruits. Drink up. Score 84. K

NOAH, PETITE SIRAH, GEDEON, 2005: Dark purple, medium-bodied, with chunky and somewhat coarse tannins, this distinct country-style wine shows skimpy berry and black cherry fruits, all with a not-entirely-wanted sweet aftertaste. Drink up. Score 78. K

NOAH, CABERNET SAUVIGNON-MERLOT, TEVEL, 2004: A blend of 60% Cabernet Sauvignon and 40% Merlot. Medium-bodied, with soft tannins and gentle wood. On the nose and palate berry, black cherry and cassis fruits, those with hints of eucalyptus and espresso coffee. Drink now. Score 85. K

NOAH, CABERNET SAUVIGNON-MERLOT, TEVEL, 2002: Medium-bodied, with soft tannins and perhaps too generous acidity but with appealing aromas and flavors of currants and wild berries. Drink now. Score 83. K

NOAH, SHIRAZ-CABERNET SAUVIGNON, 2004: Garnet towards purple, medium-bodied, with soft tannins and gentle wood influences integrating nicely and showing appealing berry, black cherry and cassis fruits. Round and crisp. Drink now. Score 85. K

NOAH, CABERNET-MERLOT, BLUSH WINE, MESSOPY, 2005: Dark-tinted pink, with raspberry, cassis, herbal and mineral aromas and flavors. Medium-bodied, somewhere between dry and off-dry. Drink up. Score 80. K

NOAH, SAUVIGNON BLANC, TEVEL, 2005: Unoaked, light to medium-bodied, with a few citrus and tropical fruits but with an unwanted hint of sweetness. Drink up. Score 81. K

NOAH, MUSCAT DESSERT, 2005: Golden-yellow in color, not so much full-bodied as it is thick. Unabashedly sweet and flowery, with apricot, peach and nutty aromas and flavors, but lacking balancing acidity. Drink up. Score 79. K

Kadesh Barnea ✶✶

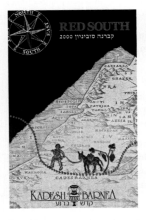

This Negev Desert winery was established in 1999 by Alon Tzadok on Moshav Kadesh Barnea and has its own vineyards near the ruins of the Byzantine city of Nitzana, just north of the Egyptian border. Releases to date have included only Cabernet Sauvignon and Merlot-based wines, but the winery is now developing further vineyards containing Petit Verdot, Shiraz, Cabernet Franc, Sauvignon Blanc and Chardonnay grapes. Production for the 2004 and 2005 vintages was about 5,000 bottles and in 2006 the winery made a major jump to 25,000 bottles. The wines have been kosher since the 2002 vintage.

The winery is one of the first in the country to be conducting experiments with making wines from vines irrigated by the brackish water that underlies much of the Negev desert, though these have not yet resulted with any releases.

KADESH BARNEA, CABERNET SAUVIGNON, 2006: Garnet towards royal-purple, medium-bodied, with soft tannins and spicy oak. On the nose and palate forward berry, currant and black cherry fruits. Not complex but promises to be a good quaffer. Drink from release. Tentative Score 82–84. K

KADESH BARNEA, CABERNET SAUVIGNON, ALON, 2005: Developing in American oak, this red is already showing generous wood balanced by soft, near-sweet tannins and good acidity. Aromatic, opening to reveal berry, cherry and cassis fruits, those matched by hints of bell peppers and chocolate. Drink from release. Tentative Score 84–86. K

KADESH BARNEA, CABERNET SAUVIGNON, GILAD, 2005: Showing generous spicy wood and firm tannins that need time to integrate, this red opening slowly in the glass to reveal berry, black cherry and earthy-tobacco notes. Drink now–2008. Score 85. K

KADESH BARNEA, CABERNET SAUVIGNON, 2004: Medium-dark garnet, medium-bodied, with chunky, country-style tannins. Blended with 15% Merlot, an easy-to-drink quaffer with berry and black cherry fruits. Drink now. Score 83. K

KADESH BARNEA, CABERNET SAUVIGNON, RED SOUTH, 2003: Medium to full-bodied, as firmly tannic now as in its youth, with hints of black cherry and plum fruits, those coming together with hints of green olives, herbs and chocolate. Drink up. Score 84. K

KADESH BARNEA, MERLOT, ALON, 2006: Dark royal-purple, this medium to full-bodied wine shows gripping, near-sweet tannins that yield slowly to reveal generous wild berry, currant and spices on first attack, those in turn opening to Mediterranean herbs and an appealing hint of black olives. Drink from release–2009. Tentative Score 84–86. K

KADESH BARNEA, MERLOT, ALON, 2005: Deep garnet towards royal-purple, medium-bodied, opening with a light medicinal aroma but that passes quickly to reveal aromas and flavors of berries, black cherries and plums. High acidity and chunky tannins make this a country-style wine, best for early drinking. Drink from release. Tentative Score 83–85. K

KADESH BARNEA, MERLOT, GILAD, 2005: Blended with 15% Cabernet Sauvignon and aged in oak for ten months, this bright garnet, medium-bodied wine shows soft tannins, spicy oak and appealing plum, currant and tobacco. Somewhat acidic. Drink now. Score 85. K

KADESH BARNEA, MERLOT, 2004: Medium-bodied, with chunky, country-style tannins, this red reflects its 14 months in *barriques* with spicy and smoky oak. On the nose and palate red currant, raspberry and plum fruits, those with light herbal and licorice overlays. Drink now. Score 84. K

KADESH BARNEA, MERLOT, RED SOUTH, 2003: Generous black cherry, cedar and spice flavors but somewhat tannic and going sweet on the finish. Drink up. Score 80. K

KADESH BARNEA, GILAD, 2005: A blend of 80% Merlot and 10% each Shiraz and Petit Verdot. Dark garnet, medium to full-bodied with near-sweet tannins integrating nicely. Opens in the glass to reveal aromas and flavors of plums, blueberries and currants, those with overlays of white pepper and mint. Drink now–2009. Score 85. K

KADESH BARNEA, CABERNET SAUVIGNON-MERLOT, GILAD, 2004: A medium-bodied blend of 50% each of Cabernet Sauvignon and Merlot. Sweet vanilla from the wood and near-sweet tannins here opening to reveal ripe plum and blackberry fruits. Drink up. Score 84. K

Kadita ★★★★

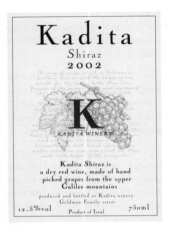

Jonathan Goldman made wines at his home in Bikta Bekadita in the Upper Galilee for several years before he released his first commercial output of 600 bottles in 2001, a blend of Cabernet Sauvignon and Merlot. Grapes are currently drawn from the winery's own nearby vineyards and from Kerem Ben Zimra. Annual production is currently 4,000 bottles.

KADITA, CABERNET SAUVIGNON, 2006: Full-bodied, intense and concentrated, showing deep, almost inky purple, with still-firm tannins and spicy wood in fine balance with natural acidity and fruits. Opens with aromas and flavors of raspberries and minty chocolate, those yielding to black currants and red plums and finally to a long fruity finish with hints of white chocolate. Best starting in 2009. Tentative Score 89–91.

KADITA, CABERNET SAUVIGNON, 2005: Deep royal-purple, full-bodied, with firm tannins and spicy oak integrating nicely. On the nose and palate an array of blackberry, currant and black cherry fruits matched handsomely by hints of roasted herbs, green olives and, on the long finish, a hint of black licorice. Best from 2009. Tentative Score 90–92.

KADITA, CABERNET SAUVIGNON, 2004: Youthful, deep royal-purple, full-bodied, with generous soft tannins integrating nicely with concentrated black fruits, Mediterranean herbs, eucalyptus and hints of spicy cedarwood from the oak barrels. Long, concentrated and mouth-filling. Drink now–2009. Score 90.

KADITA, CABERNET SAUVIGNON, 2003: A blend of grapes from two vineyards, one with volcanic soil, one with red soil, this still youthful deep royal-purple wine shows full body, firm tannins promising to integrate nicely and a tempting array of black currant and wild berry fruits, those on a long, spicy tobacco and chocolate finish. Drink now–2009. Score 89.

KADITA, MERLOT, 2006: Dark cherry-red towards garnet, medium to full-bodied, with soft, mouth-coating tannins and a gentle wood influence. Showing red and black berries, cassis and just the right hint of herbaceousness. Long and generous. Best from 2009. Tentative Score 89–91.

KADITA, MERLOT, 2005: Full-bodied, deep and aromatic, with black pepper highlighting cherry, currant, chocolate and light licorice aromas and flavors, all lingering on the generous finish. Drink from release–2012. Tentative Score 91–93.

KADITA, MERLOT, 2004: Full-bodied and aromatic, with firm but already well-integrating tannins, and showing a tempting array of blueberry, raspberry and purple plum fruits, those on a background of chocolate and Mediterranean herbs. Drink now. Score 89.

KADITA, MERLOT, 2003: Full-bodied, concentrated, and intense, with soft tannins well balanced by near-sweet and smoky oak. Look for aromas and flavors of black cherries, blackberries and cassis as well as for hints of mocha and cigar tobacco on the long finish. Drink now. Score 88.

KADITA, SHIRAZ, 2004: Rich, ripe and generous, full-bodied, with liberal but refined tannins. On the nose and palate plum, blueberry, black cherry and gentle spices, all coming together with lively acidity. Powerful and graceful with flavors that linger on and on. Drink now–2010. Score 91.

KADITA, SHIRAZ, 2002: Made from grapes from a largely untended vineyard, this intense and concentrated wine is blended with 10% Cabernet Sauvignon and aged in French oak for 20 months. Medium to full-bodied, with firm but well-integrating tannins and an appealing array of plum, berry and cassis fruits all on a background of generous black pepper, light earthiness and herbaceousness. Drink now. Score 89.

KADITA, CABERNET SAUVIGNON-MERLOT, 2005: Dark garnet, opening slowly to reveal a firm and remarkably concentrated wine with a complex set of aromas and flavors, those including cassis, blackberries, anise, tobacco, and espresso coffee, all still tightly wound. On the finish an unusual combination of super-firm tannins and an explosion of fruits. Best from 2009. Tentative Score 90–92.

KADITA, CABERNET-MERLOT, 2004: Deep garnet, medium to full-bodied, with soft, caressing tannins and ripe blackberry, plum, currant and herbal aromas and flavors on first attack, those yielding very nicely to hints of coffee, tobacco and earthiness. Drink now–2009. Score 90.

KADITA, CABERNET SAUVIGNON-MERLOT, 2003: Dark ruby toward garnet, medium to full-bodied, showing generous, ripe berry and plum fruits and soft tannins, all balanced by vanilla, spices and herbal overtones. Drink now. Score 87.

Karmei Yosef ✶✶✶✶

Founded in 2001 by Ben-Ami Bravdo and Oded Sho-sheyov, both professors of oenology at the Hebrew University of Jerusalem, the winery sits in the heart of a vineyard at Karmei Yosef on the western slopes of the Judean Mountains. This small winery released 2,800 bottles of its first wine in 2001 and current production is about 26,000 bottles annually.

Among the varieties under cultivation in the winery-owned vineyards are Cabernet Sauvignon, Merlot, Chardonnay, Carignan, French Colombard, Emerald Riesling and Muscat of Alexandria grapes.

KARMEI YOSEF, CABERNET SAUVIGNON, BRAVDO, 2006: Deep youthful purple, medium to full-bodied, with soft, gently mouth-coating tannins showing fine balance with wood, acidity and fruits. On the nose and palate an array of minty cherry, raspberry and cassis, those with light spicy overtones adding depth. Best from 2009. Tentative Score 90–92.

KARMEI YOSEF, CABERNET SAUVIGNON, BRAVDO, 2005: Dark garnet towards royal-purple, medium to full-bodied, with soft tannins integrating nicely and showing generous but well-proportioned ripe blackberries, currants, lead pencil and sweet herbal aromas and flavors. Intense, with tannins and fruit rising on a long finish. Drink now–2012. Score 91.

KARMEI YOSEF, CABERNET SAUVIGNON, BRAVDO, 2004: Medium to full-bodied with soft, near-sweet tannins and spicy wood well balanced by black currant, wild berry and black cherry fruits. Round, generous and long. Drink now–2012. Score 91.

KARMEI YOSEF, CABERNET SAUVIGNON, BRAVDO, 2003: A well-balanced, well-structured blend of 80% Cabernet Sauvignon and 20%

Merlot. Still young but already showing ripe, generous and mouth-filling aromas and flavors of plums, currants, black cherries and berries, with hints of minty spice and wood. Elegant and graceful wine. Drink now–2010. Score 91.

KARMEI YOSEF, CABERNET SAUVIGNON, BRAVDO, 2002: This blend of 90% Cabernet Sauvignon and 10% Merlot is full-bodied and tight but well focused and lively, and has a leathery base with a complex array of ripe aromas and flavors of currants, black cherries and a tantalizing hint of anise. Look for an appealing intimation of bitterness that makes itself felt on the long fruity finish. Drink now. Score 90.

KARMEI YOSEF, CABERNET SAUVIGNON, BRAVDO, 2001: Deep garnet toward purple, this oak-aged, unfiltered blend of 85% Cabernet Sauvignon and 15% Merlot shows fine balance between soft, well-integrated tannins, natural acidity, wood, and a tempting array of currant, blackberry and black cherry fruits, those on a background of toasted nuts, black licorice and Mediterranean herbs. Mouth-filling and long. Drink now. Score 91.

KARMEI YOSEF, MERLOT, BRAVDO, 2006: Still in its infancy, developing in French and American oak, but already showing almost impenetrable dark purple in color, with gripping tannins, those in fine balance with spicy wood. Opening to reveal a generous core of plums, blackberries, currants, and exotic spices that yield on the long finish to blueberries and mocha. Best 2009–2013. Tentative Score 90–92.

KARMEI YOSEF, MERLOT, BRAVDO, 2005: After developing for 12 months in French and American oak, this dark-ruby-towards garnet wine is showing medium to full-bodied, with near-sweet tannins and dusty wood highlighting intense currant, blackberry, black cherry and mocha aromas and flavors. A hint of unwanted sweetness creeping in on the finish. Drink now–2010. Score 89.

KARMEI YOSEF, MERLOT, BRAVDO, 2004: Oak-aged for 12 months, with 10% of Cabernet Sauvignon blended in, this medium-bodied red shows appealing smoky oak and moderately firm tannins well balanced with cassis, blueberry and black cherry fruits. On the long finish hints of anise, sweet cedar, sage and tobacco. Drink now–2010. Score 90.

KARMEI YOSEF, MERLOT, BRAVDO, 2003: A rich, generous Merlot, with minty and licorice accents to ripe blackberry, currant and anise flavors. Soft tannins balanced well by gentle wood. Drink now–2009. Score 90.

KARMEI YOSEF, MERLOT, BRAVDO, 2002: Ripe, bold, well focused and delicious, with layer after layer of blueberry, plum and currant fruits, this medium-bodied wine boasts soft tannins along with hints of mocha and Mediterranean herbs that seem to dart in and out on the palate, all culminating in a long, near-sweet finish. Drink up. Score 90.

KARMEI YOSEF, CHARDONNAY, BRAVDO, 2006: Fermented partly on its lees in new French and American oak and partly in stainless steel, this deeply golden white shows a green tint, and is bursting with layers of figs, apples, apricots, melon and light cedary oak. Rich, with mineral flavors that linger nicely on the finish. Drink now–2009. Score 89.

KARMEI YOSEF, CHARDONNAY, BRAVDO, 2005: A bright and generous wine, light gold in color, medium to full-bodied, with light hints of spice-tinted wood and layers of citrus, citrus peel, nectarine and melon fruits, all lingering nicely on the finish. Elegant. Drink now–2010. Score 90.

KARMEI YOSEF, CHARDONNAY, BRAVDO, 2004: Light gold in color, medium to full-bodied, this crisply dry white shows hints of flinty minerals and spicy oak, with concentrated but elegant aromas and flavors of citrus, citrus peel, figs, melon and green apples, those lingering nicely in a mineral finish. Drink now. Score 90.

Katlav ★★★

Owner-winemaker Yossi Yittach founded this small winery on Moshav Nes Harim in the Jerusalem Mountains in 1996, and released his first wines from the 2000 vintage. The winery, now located in a new structure, draws on Cabernet Sauvignon, Merlot and Syrah grapes from local vineyards. Production for 2005 was 10,000 bottles; due to a small harvest, 2006 production was limited to about 8,500 bottles; and plans are to release 15,000 bottles from the 2007 vintage.

KATLAV, CABERNET SAUVIGNON, RESERVE, 2005: Dark garnet, medium to full-bodied, with soft tannins integrating nicely and showing good balance with spicy oak. Black currant and blackberry fruits, those well supported by hints of black pepper and Mediterranean herbs. Potentially the best wine to date from Katlav. Drink from release. Tentative Score 86–88. K

KATLAV

Cabernet Sauvignon
2003

750 ml. 14.5 Alc.
Katlav Winery, Nes Harim 99885, Israel

KATLAV, CABERNET SAUVIGNON, 2006: Deep ruby towards garnet, medium-bodied, with crisp acidity, soft tannins and hints of spicy cedar and sandalwood. On the nose and palate plums, red cherries and raspberries, leading to a medium-long finish. Drink from release. Tentative Score 84–86. K

KATLAV, CABERNET SAUVIGNON, 2005: Oak-aged for 18 months, garnet towards royal-purple in color, with soft tannins and toasty wood. Medium-bodied, with a basic berry, cherry and light spicy personality. Drink from release. Tentative Score 84–86. K

KATLAV, CABERNET SAUVIGNON, 2004: Medium to full-bodied, dark royal-purple in color, with tannins and spicy wood integrating nicely to show black currant, blackberry and spicy plum aromas and flavors that linger nicely. Drink now. Score 86. K

KATLAV, CABERNET SAUVIGNON, 2003: Dark garnet towards royal-purple, medium to full-bodied with still-firm tannins, the wine shows good balance between wood and fruits. On the nose and palate cassis, wild berries, spices and a welcome hint of smoke on a moderately long finish. Drink now. Score 86. K

KATLAV, CABERNET SAUVIGNON, 2002: Dark purple, this medium-bodied oak-aged wine, a blend of Cabernet Sauvignon with a small amount of Shiraz, offers up generous aromas and flavors of currants and wild berries, those complemented by a hint of spiciness. Somewhat one dimensional. Drink up. Score 81. K

KATLAV, MERLOT, 2006: Garnet towards royal-purple, medium to full-bodied, with soft tannins promising to integrate nicely with light oak. Showing dried currants and berries, those overlaid with spices and mint and a tantalizing hint of earthy bitterness. Drink from release. Tentative Score 85–87. K

KATLAV, MERLOT, 2005: Medium-bodied, with soft tannins and gentle wood, this round and easy-to-drink wine offers red and black berries and cherries backed up by hints of earthy minerals. Drink from release. Tentative Score 84–86. K

KATLAV, MERLOT, 2004: Dark garnet, with a bit of browning at the rim. Soft, mouth-coating tannins and spicy wood together with blackberry, red currant and herbal overlays. Showing age in the slight medicinal edge creeping in. Drink up. Score 84. K

KATLAV, SYRAH, 2005: Medium to full-bodied, with traditional Syrah leathery, meaty and spicy notes, those highlighting red plum and cassis aromas and flavors. Drink from release. Tentative Score 86–88. K

KATLAV, CABERNET SAUVIGNON-MERLOT, WADI KATLAV, 2004: An oak-aged blend of 60% Cabernet Sauvignon and 40% Merlot. Dark garnet, with soft near-sweet tannins, light, spicy wood and blackberry and black cherry fruits that linger nicely. Drink now. Score 85. K

KATLAV, CABERNET SAUVIGNON-MERLOT, WADI KATLAV, 2003: A deep garnet blend of 60% Cabernet Sauvignon and 40% Merlot. Full-bodied, with firm tannins now softening and opening in the glass to reveal tempting currant, plum and berry fruits. Drink now. Score 86. K

Katz *

Founded by Jossi Katz in 2001 and located on Moshav Mesi-lat Tzion in the foothills of the Judean Mountains, this small winery is currently producing about 5,000 bottles annually and plans to grow to an output of about 20,000.

KATZ, MESILAT TZION, 2004: A vaguely off-dry, distinctly alcoholic and far too generously oaked blend of Cabernet Sauvignon, Merlot and Petite Sirah. Lacks charm. Score 70.

KATZ, RENOIR, DRY RED RESERVE, 2004: Dark royal-purple in color, this blend of Cabernet Sauvignon, Merlot and Petite Sirah (55%, 42% and 3% respectively) shows medium-bodied, with firm tannins and far too many sharp edges. An unwelcome medicinal hint hides the black fruits. Drink up. Score 74.

KATZ, RENOIR, DRY RED RESERVE, 2003: A country-style blend of 55% Cabernet Sauvignon, 45% Merlot and 5% Syrah, which was oak-aged for 24 months. Medium-bodied, with chunky tannins, a bit of coarse-ness, and only skimpy black fruits. Drink up. Score 72.

KATZ, MATISSE, 2004: Made with no sulfites or other chemical addi-tives, this sweet blend of Cabernet Sauvignon, Merlot and Petite Sirah (50%, 41% and 9% respectively) shows some plum, raisin and caramel flavors and aromas. One dimensional and far too alcoholic. Score 68.

Kfir **

Founded in 2003 by Meir Kfir in the village of Gan Yavne in the southern Coastal Plain, this small winery was originally known as Gefen Adderet and changed its name to Kfir in 2006. Although producing only about 8,000 bottles annually, it releases a large variety of labels, those from Cabernet Sauvignon, Merlot, Cabernet Franc, Sangiovese, Nebiolo, Syrah, Petite Sirah, Zinfandel, Malbec, Viognier, Riesling, Gewurztraminer and Chardonnay grapes from the vineyards of Karmei Yosef, the Jerusalem Mountains and the Galilee.

KFIR, BARBERA, 2005: 86% Barbera with 14% Cabernet Sauvignon blended in to add backbone, this medium-bodied, oak-aged, garnet-towards-deep royal-purple wine shows soft tannins integrating nicely with acidity, spicy wood and appealing berry and currant fruits. On the long and generous finish a hint of smoky tobacco. Drink now–2009. Score 87.

KFIR, CABERNET FRANC, 2005: Made entirely from Cabernet Franc grapes and aged in *barriques* for 12 months, this medium-bodied and softly tannic wine opens with sweet cherries on the nose and palate. This light hint of sweetness remains throughout, complemented from mid-palate on by currants and a light herbal overlay. Drink now. Score 85.

KFIR, SHIRAZ, BAR, 2005: Ruby towards garnet, medium-bodied, with chunky, near-sweet tannins. Showing basic plum and black cherry fruits, those with a hint of Oriental spices. Drink now. Score 84.

KFIR, SHIRAZ, BAR, 2004: A medium-bodied blend of 86% Shiraz, 10% Cabernet Franc, and 4% Cabernet Sauvignon, with light, near-sweet tannins and appealing plum, black cherry and wild berry fruits leading to a medium-long finish. Drink now–2007. Score 86.

KFIR, GILAD, 2005: Dark garnet towards royal-purple, this oak-aged blend of Sangiovese, Zinfandel, Nebbiolo, and Barbera grapes (64%, 26%,8% and 2% respectively) has a distinctly Italian character. Medium to full-bodied, with soft tannins integrating nicely, it shows appealing raspberry, cherry and red currant fruits overlaid with hints of black olives and anise, all with a light spicy oak overlay. Drink now. Score 88.

KFIR, SYRAH-PETITE SIRAH, 2005: Deep royal-purple in color, this oak-aged blend of 58% Syrah and 42% Petite Sirah shows generous but not dominating spicy wood and still-firm tannins needing time to settle down. Opening to reveal a full-bodied, nicely round wine, with plum, wild berry and black cherry fruits on a spicy background. Drink now–2009. Score 87.

KFIR, HOD, 2004: This garnet-towards-royal-purple blend of 64% Cabernet Sauvignon and 36% Merlot is medium to full-bodied, with chunky, country-style tannins integrating well. Showing black and red berries, cassis and some spicy aromas and flavors. Drink now. Score 86.

KFIR, AVICHAI, TEVA, 2003: A medium-bodied blend of 79% Merlot, 13% Cabernet Sauvignon and 8% Petite Sirah. Dark garnet, with soft tannins and appealing aromas and flavors of plums, black cherries and currants all on a lightly spicy background. Drink now. Score 86.

KFIR, ZOHARA, TEVA, 2004: A somewhat clumsy blend of Sangiovese, Nebbiolo, Merlot, Cabernet Sauvignon, Cabernet Franc and Shiraz. Dark cherry-red, medium to full-bodied, with soft, near-sweet tannins and aromas and flavors of blackberries, currants and black cherries, matched nicely by hints of pepper, tar and light earthiness. Drink now. Score 84.

KFIR, ZOHARA, TEVA, 2003: Deep ruby towards garnet, this medium-bodied blend of Cabernet Sauvignon, Merlot and Argaman (68%, 22% and 10% respectively) shows light tannins and a fresh, lightly spicy berry-cherry personality. Drink now. Score 84.

KFIR, CABERNET FRANC, DESSERT WINE, 2004: Generously sweet, with good balancing acidity. Medium-full on the palate, maintaining the blackberry, and greenness of the variety. Appealing but perhaps best as an aperitif. Drink now. Score 86.

KFIR, GALIA, BAR, 2005: Call this deep pink and unusual blend of white Riesling and red Petite Sirah grapes (70% and 30% respectively) blush, or call it rosé as you like. Light to medium-bodied, floral, with a combination of strawberry and cassis liqueur aromas and flavors, a pleasant quaffer, best served very well chilled. Drink up. Score 85.

KFIR, CHARDONNAY, TEVA, 2005: Lightly golden in color, medium-bodied, with fine balance between light spicy oak, acidity and fruits. On the nose and palate, pear, melon and citrus backed up by a handsome mineral note that lingers nicely on the palate. Drink now. Score 88.

KFIR, CHARDONNAY, TEVA, 2004: With a distinct smoky-spicy overlay from the oak chips with which the wine was developed, that tending to overshadow the pear and melon aromas and flavors that remain somewhat muted throughout. Drink now. Score 83.

KFIR, VIOGNIER, BAR, 2005: Light golden-straw in color, with generous fresh acidity keeping it lively. Aromas and flavors of peaches, melon, citrus and freshly cut hay. Not representative of the variety but appealing and refreshing. Drink up. Score 84.

KFIR, WHITE NIGHTS, TEVA, 2005: An off-dry blend of 85% Gewurztraminer and 15% Riesling, showing mango, pineapple and citrus peel aromas and flavors. With good acidity to keep it lively and refreshing. A pleasant aperitif. Drink now. Score 84.

Kleins *

Founded in 2004 by Yom-Tov Klein, this winery is set in the old city of Hebron, and is producing wines from Merlot, Cabernet Sauvignon, Chardonnay, Sauvignon Blanc and other grapes, though none of them indicate either the grape variety or the vintage year on their labels. Production is currently about 110,000 bottles annually.

KLEINS, DRY RED, N.V.: Dark garnet, with hints of browning, and distinctly barnyard aromas that hide whatever fruits may be trying to make themselves felt. Score 60. K

KLEINS, SEMI-DRY WHITE, N.V.: Crisply floral on the nose, but on the palate overly sweet, without balancing acidity and only the skimpiest of lemon and lime aromas and flavors. Score 68. K

KLEINS, YASMIN DESSERT, RED, N.V.: Super-sweet, coarse, alcoholic, oxidized and caramelized. Score 55. K

KLEINS, YASMIN DESSERT, WHITE, N.V.: Golden-straw in color, heavy on the palate and cloyingly sweet with overripe peach fruits. Score 60. K

KLEINS, PORT WINE, ANATOT, N.V.: Pale ruby in color, medium-bodied and with burned rubber and muddy aromas and flavors. Score 55. K

La Terra Promessa ***

Parma-born Sandro Pelligrini comes from a family of winemakers, and he and his wife Irit founded this small winery in 1998 at their home on Moshav Shachar on the fringes of the northern Negev Desert. The winery relies on Cabernet Sauvignon and Merlot grapes from the Upper Galilee and Ramat Arad, as well as from a vineyard near the winery with Shiraz, Zinfandel, Sangiovese and Petite Sirah. The winery is currently producing about 4,500 bottles annually, in four series: the premium Rubino and La Crime Riserva and the regular La Crime and La Terra Promessa.

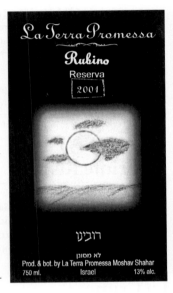

Rubino Riserva

RUBINO RISERVA, 2004: Dark garnet towards royal-purple, full-bodied, with generous caressing tannins in fine balance with wood, natural acidity and fruits. On the nose and palate black currants, blackberries and ripe plums, all with a hint of black truffles that makes itself felt on the finish. Drink from release–2010. Tentative Score 87–89.

RUBINO RISERVA, 2003: Reflecting its 24 months in *barriques* with generous spicy oak. Full-bodied, softly tannic and well balanced, this blend of 60% Cabernet Sauvignon and 40% Merlot offers up aromas and flavors of black currants, plums, and black cherries matched nicely by hints of cocoa and mint on the moderately long finish. Drink now. Score 87.

RUBINO RISERVA, 2002: A blend of 60% Cabernet Sauvignon and 40% Merlot, oak-aged in used French *barriques* for 24 months. Full-bodied, with spicy wood balanced nicely by soft tannins and on the nose and palate black cherries, currants and berries. Long and generous. Drink up. Score 87.

RUBINO RISERVA, 2001: A lightly oak-aged, dark garnet towards purple, medium to full-bodied blend of Cabernet Sauvignon and Merlot, with soft tannins now integrating nicely, hints of smoky oak from the wood and generous aromas and flavors of currant, wild berries and plums. A moderately long, just spicy enough finish adds charm. Drink up. Score 88.

RUBINO RISERVA, 2000: Deep garnet-red, medium to full-bodied, with tannins now well integrated, showing an appealing herbal overlay over currant and plum fruits. Moderately long and mouth-filling. Drink up. Score 87.

La Crime Riserva

LA CRIME RISERVA, 2004: A dark garnet, medium to full-bodied of 45% each Sangiovese and Cabernet Sauvignon and 10% Cabernet Franc. Reflecting 24 months in *barriques* with generous dusty oak and tannins, those yielding slowly in the glass to reveal an appealing array of plums, blackberries and a light leathery note. Drink now. Score 87.

La Crime

LA CRIME, 2005: Showing medium-bodied, with generous black fruit, tobacco and chocolate. Long, round and well-balanced. Drink now–2009. Score 86.

LA CRIME, 2004: Syrah, Sangiovese and Cabernet Franc come together nicely in this medium to full-bodied blend, showing gentle oak, soft tannins, and an appealing overlay of bitterness that highlights plum, berry, and lightly meaty-earthy aromas and flavors. Drink now. Score 88.

LA CRIME, 2003: A blend of 45% each Syrah and Sangiovese and 10% Cabernet Franc. Dark, deep and rich, full-bodied with muscular tannins but those well balanced by smoky wood and generous berry-cherry and earthy aromas and flavors. Drink up. Score 86.

La Terra Promessa

LA TERRA PROMESSA, CABERNET SAUVIGNON, 2005: Garnet-red, medium-bodied, with soft tannins and an appealing hint of sweet herbs backing up plum and currant fruits. Lacking complexity. Drink now. Score 86.

LA TERRA PROMESSA, CABERNET SAUVIGNON, 2004: Deep ruby towards garnet in color, aged in oak for ten months, with soft tannins already integrating nicely. Aromas and flavors of currants, berries and cherries are matched by spicy wood and light minerals that linger comfortably in the background. Drink now. Score 87.

LA TERRA PROMESSA, CABERNET SAUVIGNON, 2003: Medium to full-bodied, dense royal-purple towards black in color, with firm tannins now starting to integrate, this wine shows a gentle hand with the wood, and currant and black cherry fruits on a lightly spicy and herbal background. Drink now. Score 87.

LA TERRA PROMESSA, CABERNET SAUVIGNON, 2002: Dark garnet toward purple, this medium-bodied red has firm and chunky country-style tannins, those matched nicely by plum, berry and black cherry fruits and light spiciness. Drink up. Score 85.

LA TERRA PROMESSA, CABERNET SAUVIGNON, 2001: An appealing deep purple, this medium-bodied wine has soft tannins and soft, smoky oak to match currant, wild berry and light herbal aromas and flavors that linger nicely on the palate. Drink up. Score 86.

LA TERRA PROMESSA, MERLOT, 2005: This somewhat weak ruby-red wine is medium-bodied, with soft tannins and appealing berry, cherry and currant fruits. A simple quaffer. Drink now. Score 84.

LA TERRA PROMESSA, MERLOT, 2004: Aged eight months in French oak *barriques*, this deep royal-purple towards-garnet-wine is medium-bodied with soft tannins and a basic cherry-berry personality, that backed up by hints of spices and earthiness. Drink now. Score 86.

LA TERRA PROMESSA, MERLOT, 2003: Made entirely from Merlot grapes, with eight months in oak, this calls to mind a Tuscan Merlot. Medium-bodied, unfiltered, with soft, sweet and already well-integrating tannins. Good plum, berry and black cherry fruits and a light hint of spices that linger nicely on the palate. Drink up. Score 87.

LA TERRA PROMESSA, SYRAH, 2005: Medium-dark garnet, medium to full-bodied, with appealing smoky oak and earthiness opening to reveal tempting black fruits and minerals. Generous and long. Drink now–2009. Score 87.

LA TERRA PROMESSA, SYRAH, 2004: Deep inky purple and medium to full-bodied, reflecting 16 months in oak with firm tannins and generous smoky wood, those in fine balance with plums, red berries, and spices, all leading to a long smoked-meat finish. Drink now–2009. Score 88.

LA TERRA PROMESSA, SYRAH, 2003: Dark and spicy, with firm tannins and generous oak in fine balance with wild berry, currant and cherry fruits, all of those with hints of anise and a light anise-leathery edge on the finish. Drink now. Score 88.

LA TERRA PROMESSA, PRIMITIVO, 2005: Made entirely from Primitivo grapes and aged for 12 months in 400 liter oak casks, this bright garnet wine shows soft, near-sweet tannins, spicy oak and ripe raspberry, cassis and cherry aromas and flavors. Drink now. Score 86.

LA TERRA PROMESSA, ZINFANDEL, 2004: Deep garnet, medium-bodied, with tannins that have softened nicely and light wood influences. On the nose and palate violets, hints of meatiness and an appealing light touch of Brett to complement blackberry, cherry and cassis fruits. Round and easy to drink. Drink now. Score 86.

LA TERRA PROMESSA, ZINFANDEL, 2003: Inky purple in color, with generous acidity well balanced by wood and a fine array of wild berry, cherry and cassis aromas and flavors, all of which linger nicely on the palate. Drink up. Score 85.

LA TERRA PROMESSA, EMERALD RIESLING, 2005: Crisply dry and refreshing. On the nose and palate enough minerals and citrus peel that you might think you were drinking a Petit Chablis. A good choice for everyday quaffing. Drink up. Score 85.

Lachish **

Established on Moshav Lachish on the Central Plain by Oded Yakobson, Oscar Meisels and Gai Rosenfeld, this small winery relies entirely on Cabernet Sauvignon and Shiraz grapes from their own vineyards. Current production is about 3,000 bottles annually.

LACHISH, CABERNET SAUVIGNON, 2005: Garnet towards royal-purple, medium to full-bodied, a somewhat coarse but pleasing country-style wine with generous black fruits, spices and hints of Mediterranean herbs. Drink now. Score 84.

LACHISH, CABERNET SAUVIGNON, 2004: Medium to full-bodied, with chunky, firm tannins that yield slowly in the glass to show ripe blackberry and currant fruits. Drink now. Score 84.

LACHISH, CABERNET SAUVIGNON, 2003: Dark ruby towards garnet, medium-bodied, with light oak influences and chunky country-style tannins. Appealing currant and berry fruits overlaid with light spices and a hint of herbaceousness. Drink up. Score 84.

LACHISH, MERLOT, 2002: Garnet-red with soft tannins integrated nicely, and appealing berry, black cherry and cassis fruits backed up by hints of spices and earthiness. Somewhat past its peak. Drink up. Score 84.

LACHISH, SHIRAZ, 2004: Medium to full-bodied, with soft, mouth-coating tannins and spicy wood yielding in the glass to reveal plum, berry and citrus peel aromas and flavors. Drink now. Score 84.

LACHISH, SHIRAZ, 2003: Deep royal-purple in color, showing soft tannins and a hint of spicy wood, along with aromas and flavors of ripe plums, wild berry and freshly picked mushrooms. Drink up. Score 84.

Latroun *

Located in an idyllic setting at the foothills of the Judean Mountains midway between Jerusalem and the coast, the Trappist monks at this monastery have been producing wine since their arrival from France in the 1890s. With over 400 dunams of land adjoining the monastery planted in grapes, the winery was the first to introduce Gewurztraminer, Riesling, Pinot Noir and Pinot Blanc grapes to the country and is currently producing about 300,000 bottles annually from twenty varieties of grapes.

LATROUN, CABERNET SAUVIGNON, 2006: Medium-bodied, with soft tannins and forward black fruits. Drink now. Score 83.

LATROUN, CABERNET SAUVIGNON, 2005: Light to medium-bodied, soft, round and fruit-forward, a simple but pleasant quaffer. Drink now. Score 82.

LATROUN MERLOT, 2006: Ruby towards garnet, medium-bodied, with soft tannins, this is a pleasant, country-style wine with berry and black cherry fruits. Drink now. Score 82.

LATROUN, MERLOT, 2005: This simple, country-style wine is dark ruby, medium-bodied, with chunky tannins, and some berry, plum and near-sweet cassis aromas and flavors. Drink up. Score 81.

LATROUN, PINOT NOIR, 2005: Bright ruby towards garnet, medium-bodied, with soft tannins and gentle wood. Showing spicy berry-cherry aromas and flavors. Drink up. Score 82.

LATROUN, PINOT NOIR, 2004: Dark ruby, medium-bodied, with soft tannins. An odd sour aroma and flavor tend to hide the plum and berry fruits here. Drink up. Score 79.

LATROUN, CHARDONNAY, 2006: Light golden-straw, light in body, with grapefruit and tropical fruits. Drink up. Score 83.

LATROUN, CHARDONNAY, 2005: Light to medium-bodied, with generous pineapple, apple and melon aromas and flavors. Drink up. Score 82.

LATROUN, SAUVIGNON BLANC, 2005: Light straw in color, light to medium-bodied, with citrus and herbal aromas and flavors. One dimensional and short. Drink up. Score 75.

LATROUN, PINOT BLANC, 2006: Light in color and body, a simple white with citrus and pineapple flavors. Drink up. Score 78.

Lavie **

Located in the community of Ephrata not far from Jerusalem, the first wine of Asher Bentolila and Yo'av Guez was from the 2002 vintage. Drawing largely on grapes from the Jerusalem Mountains, the winery is currently producing about 3,000 bottles annually.

LAVIE, CABERNET SAUVIGNON, 2005: Garnet to purple, medium-bodied, with soft, near-sweet tannins and vanilla-tinged wood influences, those yielding to spicy currant, berry and black cherry fruits. Drink now–2009. Score 85. K

LAVIE, CABERNET SAUVIGNON, 2004: Medium-bodied, with soft tannins and a light hand with oak aging. Aromas and flavors of black currants and blackberries matched nicely by light spicy and herbal notes. Drink now. Score 85. K

LAVIE, CABERNET SAUVIGNON, 2003: Medium-bodied, with firm tannins that seem not to want to yield and holding back the plum and berry fruits that struggle to make themselves felt. Drink up. Score 84. K

LAVIE, CABERNET SAUVIGNON, 2002: Deep purple, this medium-bodied oak-aged wine shows clean and appealing aromas and flavors of blackberries, currants and spices on the first attack, those then complemented by light overtones of spices and green olives. Past its peak. Drink up. Score 80. K

Levron *

Established by Segal and Yehuda Levron, with the winery located in their Haifa home, first releases are from the 2004 vintage. Drawing on Merlot and Cabernet Sauvignon grapes from Kerem Ben Zimra and the Gush Chalav area in the Galilee, the winery is currently producing 4,000 bottles annually and plans to expand to 6,000.

LEVRON, CABERNET SAUVIGNON, 2005: Dark ruby towards garnet, medium-bodied, with chunky tannins giving the wine a distinct country style. Opens to reveal blackberry, currant and spices. Drink now. Score 84.

LEVRON, CABERNET SAUVIGNON, 2004: Medium-dark garnet, medium-bodied, with soft tannins and ripe plum, berry and smoky oak flavors. Drink now. Score 84.

LEVRON MERLOT, 2005: Dark ruby, medium-bodied, with soft tannins and appealing berry, cherry and spicy notes. A good quaffer. Drink now. Score 85.

LEVRON, MERLOT, 2004: Reflecting eight months aging in used oak barrels, this medium-bodied wine shows soft tannins, hints of vanilla and a pleasant berry-black cherry personality. Drink now. Score 85.

Maccabim★★

Founded in 2002 by Eytan Rosenthal, Gari Hochwald, Yo'av Heller and Ami Dotan in the community of Maccabim, at the foothills of the Jerusalem Mountains, and drawing grapes from that area as well as from the Galilee and the Ella Valley, this start-up winery's first release was of 1,200 bottles in 2002. Now producing Cabernet Sauvignon and Merlot wines, the winery releases 4,500 bottles annually.

MACCABIM, CABERNET SAUVIGNON, 2005: Medium to full-bodied, with soft, near-sweet tannins and spicy wood integrating nicely. On the nose and palate currant, red berry and spices all leading to a medium-long finish. Score 85. K

MACCABIM, CABERNET SAUVIGNON, 2004: Deep garnet, medium to full-bodied, with spicy oak and soft tannins highlighting currant, black cherry and plum fruits. Drink now. Score 85. K

MACCABIM, CABERNET SAUVIGNON, 2003: Dark ruby towards garnet, medium-bodied, with gentle oak influences and appealing currant and wild berry fruits. On the moderately long finish look for hints of spices and vanilla. Drink now. Score 84. K

MACCABIM, CABERNET SAUVIGNON, BIN 9, 2002: Dark cherry red toward garnet, this medium-bodied, lightly oaked red shows soft tannins and appealing cherry-berry and currant fruits along with hints of spicy oak. Refreshing and pleasant. Drink up. Score 84. K

MACCABIM, MERLOT, 2005: Dark royal-purple, medium to full-bodied, with firm tannins and spicy wood. Needs a bit of time to show its blackberry and currant fruits. Best from 2009. Score 86. K

MACCABIM, MERLOT, 2004: Medium-bodied, with soft tannins and hints of spicy wood, those showing blueberry, blackberry and black cherry fruits. Drink now. Score 84. K

MACCABIM, MERLOT, 2003: Garnet-red, medium-bodied, with soft tannins integrating nicely to reveal cassis, plum and berry fruits on a lightly herbal background. Drink now. Score 84. K

Maor ***

Established by Danny Maor on Moshav Ramot on the Golan Heights, the winery's first release was of 3,200 bottles from the 2003 vintage. Current production is about 5,000 bottles annually, drawing on grapes from the Golan Heights and the Upper Galilee, those including Cabernet Sauvignon, Merlot, Syrah, and Cabernet Franc.

MAOR, CABERNET SAUVIGNON, 2005: Blended with 15% Merlot and 3% Cabernet Franc, this generously oaked, dark garnet wine shows aromatic and tempting. Soft tannins give the wine a round, well-balanced personality, that flushed out by traditional currant, berry, black cherry and light herbal aromas and flavors. On the long finish a hint of freshly roasted coffee. Drink from release–2010. Tentative Score 87–89.

MAOR, CABERNET SAUVIGNON, CLASSIC, 2004: Blended with 20% of Merlot, this deep ruby-towards-garnet wine is medium-bodied, with soft tannins integrating nicely with spicy wood. Look for aromas and flavors of raspberries, red plums and cranberries, those supported nicely by hints of freshly turned earth and green olives. Drink now–2009. Score 88.

MAOR, CABERNET SAUVIGNON, 2004: Dark garnet, medium to full-bodied, with generous but not dominating wood and firm tannins well balanced by fruits and acidity. On the nose and palate currants, wild berries and vanilla, all lingering nicely. Drink now. Score 87.

MAOR, CABERNET SAUVIGNON, 2003: Deep garnet towards royal-purple, medium to full-bodied and concentrated, with rather firm tannins and a somewhat heavy hand with the oak, the wine shows aromas and flavors of very ripe plums and berries as well as hints of sweet herbs, mocha and chocolate in the background. Drink now. Score 85.

MAOR, SYRAH, 2006: Dark garnet towards royal-purple in color, with generous but soft tannins and hints of spicy wood. Well balanced and showing appealing red plum, cassis, herbal and chocolate aromas and flavors, all leading to a generous and mouth-coating finish. Drink from release–2011. Tentative Score 87–89.

MAOR, SYRAH, 2005: Dark garnet in color, with solid but yielding tannins and spicy oak, those in fine balance with fruits and acidity. Opens to show plum, currant, tar, tobacco and mineral notes, leading to a long and chocolate-tinted finish. Best yet from the winery. Drink now–2010. Score 89.

MAOR, CABERNET SAUVIGNON-MERLOT, 2006: Dark ruby towards garnet, medium to full-bodied, with soft tannins, fine concentration and a complex array of black and red fruits, those complemented by generous hints of Mediterranean herbs and, on the long finish, an appealing hint of freshly unearthed mushrooms. Best 2009–2011. Tentative Score 88–90.

MAOR, SYRAH-MERLOT, 2006: Deep purple towards inky black in color, firm and well focused and capturing the traditional herbaceousness of Merlot and the minty, berry and meaty flavors of Syrah. Concentrated but soft and round. Drink from release–2010. Tentative Score 88–90.

Margalit ★★★★★

Among the first boutique wineries in the country, and the first to capture the imagination of sophisticated wine lovers. Founded in 1989, it was first located on Moshav Kfar Bilu near the town of Rehovot, and since 1994 has been set in a larger winery near the town of Hadera, at the foothills of Mount Carmel. Father and son team Ya'ir and Assaf Margalit are most renowned for their Bordeaux-style reds that are released in both a regular and a reserve series. In his role as a physical chemist, Ya'ir Margalit has published several well-known textbooks. Assaf, who studied in the agriculture faculty of Hebrew University at Rehovot, also trained in California.

Margalit's earliest release, in 1989, was of 900 bottles of Cabernet Sauvignon. More recent releases, including Cabernet, Merlot, Petite Sirah and Syrah, are made primarily of grapes from their own vineyards in Kadita in the Upper Galilee, while the Cabernet Franc is grown in their Binyamina vineyard. The winery offers three series, the top of the line Special Reserve and Margalit, and, starting with the 2003 harvest, Enigma, a Bordeaux-style blend. All of Margalit's wines are meant for long cellaring. Production, including the occasional Chardonnay, currently varies at between 17,000–21,000 bottles annually.

Special Reserve

SPECIAL RESERVE, CABERNET SAUVIGNON, 2006: Cabernet Sauvignon blended with about 25% of Margalit's special Petite Sirah. Full-bodied, dense and intense, but at the same time round and yielding, offering up chocolate-covered cherries, cassis, wild berry and kirsch, those balanced nicely by spicy-cedary oak. Long, complex and destined for elegance. Best 2009–2015. Tentative Score 92–94.

SPECIAL RESERVE, CABERNET SAUVIGNON, 2005: A blend of 85% Cabernet Sauvignon and 15% of Margalit's special Petite Sirah. Deep garnet towards inky black, remarkably concentrated and intense; still firmly tannic at this stage but with fine balance and structure. As the wine develops in the bottle look for a glorious array of currant, black berry and plums on the first attack, those melding into hints of coffee dusky spices and smoky notes. On the super-long finish, the tannins recede to let the fruits and a hint of espresso coffee rise to the surface Perhaps Margalit's longest-lived wine. Best 2009–2022. Score 94.

SPECIAL RESERVE, CABERNET SAUVIGNON, 2004: A limited edi tion of 600 bottles, this full-bodied blend of 86% Cabernet Sauvignon and 14% Petite Sirah shows fine bal ance between tannins that are now integrating nicely, hints of sweet oak and generous but subdued black cur rant, plum and chocolate aromas and flavors. Drink now–2012. Score 91.

SPECIAL RESERVE, CABERNET SAUVIGNON, 2003: Rich, ripe and concentrated, with layer after layer of dark plum, currant, anise, mocha black cherries and sage. An oak-aged blend of Cabernet Sauvignon and Petite Sirah (87% and 13% respectively), this distinctly Old World wine has excellent balance between wood, lively acidity and well-integrated tannins. Complex and long. Drink now–2013. Score 93.

SPECIAL RESERVE, CABERNET SAUVIGNON, 2002: This blend of 80% Cabernet Sauvignon, 12% Petite Sirah and 8% Cabernet Franc is remark ably concentrated, intense, and heavy enough to chew, but through its muscles shows great elegance. Ripe currants, spices and cedar flavors on a complex leathery core and a long, intense finish make this a wine difficult to match with food but excellent on its own or with fine, aged cheeses. Drink now–2012. Score 93.

SPECIAL RESERVE, CABERNET SAUVIGNON, 2001: Dense and con centrated, this firmly tannic, full-bodied and rich blend of 85% Cabernet Sauvignon and 15% of Margalit's very special Petite Sirah needs time to develop, but as it does look for multiple layers of currants, wild ber ries, plums and black cherries along with toasty oak, minerals and just the right hints of earthiness and sage on the very long finish. Drink now–2012. Score 91.

SPECIAL RESERVE, CABERNET SAUVIGNON, 2000: Delicious, com plex and so deep in color that it is almost black, this remarkably full bodied, deep and concentrated blend of 80% Cabernet Sauvignon, 15%

Petite Sirah and 5% Merlot boasts earthy currant, sage, black cherry and cedary oak flavors. As it develops look for coffee and tobacco notes. Drink now–2010. Score 93.

SPECIAL RESERVE, CABERNET SAUVIGNON, 1999: Harmonious, dense and tannic, this full-bodied and elegant blend of 87% Cabernet Sauvignon and 13% Carignan offers tempting spices and ripe fruit aromas and flavors of currants, plums, chocolate and coffee. Drink now–2012. Score 93.

SPECIAL RESERVE, CABERNET SAUVIGNON, 1998: This blend of 90% Cabernet Sauvignon and 10% remarkably concentrated Petite Sirah offers up a luxurious mouthful of ripe black cherry, currant, anise and plum flavors. Dark, hearty, rich and tannic, the wine is now beginning to turn silky and polished and has a long, mouth-filling finish. Drink now. Score 92.

SPECIAL RESERVE, CABERNET SAUVIGNON, 1997: A blend of 85% Cabernet Sauvignon and 15% of the very special Petite Sirah that Margalit has managed to isolate and cultivate, this ripe, complex and full-bodied red has a lovely balance between currant, black cherry, spice, chocolate and cedary oak flavors, all of which seem to burst forth and blend together on the palate. Its once rough tannins are now integrating nicely and the wine shows a long, mouth-filling finish. Drink now. Score 93.

SPECIAL RESERVE, CABERNET SAUVIGNON, 1995: Having lost its youthful rough edges, this full-bodied, harmonious and mature wine shows now well-integrated tannins blending nicely with deep oak, tobacco, cherry and spicy flavors. Drink up. Score 91.

SPECIAL RESERVE, CABERNET SAUVIGNON, 1994: From a problematic vintage, and thus lacking the concentration and intensity felt in the 1993 wine, but still showing tempting currant, plum and berry aromas and flavors, those on a background of smoky oak and fresh forest. Somewhat past its peak. Drink up. Score 89.

SPECIAL RESERVE, CABERNET SAUVIGNON, 1993: Deep violet toward garnet and showing first hints of browning, this remains one of Margalit's finest efforts. A blend of Cabernet Sauvignon with 15% of deep and smooth Petite Sirah, this full-bodied wine boasts multiple layers of black currants, dried fruits and vanilla as well as violets and plums. Even though somewhat past its peak, this seductive, tempting and well-structured wine continues to offer ample charms. Drink up. Score 92.

Margalit

MARGALIT, CABERNET SAUVIGNON, 2006: Almost inky black in color, offering a generous mouthful of currant, cherry, blackberry and blueberry fruits, those matched by layers of sweet spices. Big, broad and intense but yielding on the palate to show grace and elegance, and closing with a long, fruity finish. Best 2009–2015. Tentative Score 92–94.

MARGALIT, CABERNET SAUVIGNON, 2005: Deep garnet towards royal-purple, medium to full-bodied, with soft but gripping tannins and fine balance and structure. Opens with red currant, raspberry and red plum fruits, those yielding to blueberries and appealing earthy-herbal overtones with gentle spicy wood on the long finish. Best 2009–2015. Score 93.

MARGALIT, CABERNET SAUVIGNON, 2004: Dark garnet towards royal-purple with orange reflections, this well-balanced, medium to full-bodied wine is showing generous currant and berry fruits, those matched nicely by spicy wood, dark chocolate and espresso coffee. Long and luxurious. Drink now–2012. Score 92.

MARGALIT, CABERNET SAUVIGNON, 2003: Full-bodied and intense, but rich and well balanced, this blend of 88% Cabernet Sauvignon and 12% Cabernet Franc, both from the Kadita vineyard, is loaded with complex earthy currant, black cherry, anise and mocha aromas and flavors, those well set off by generous but smooth tannins. Look for an appealing leathery sensation on the long finish. Drink now–2012. Score 91.

MARGALIT, CABERNET SAUVIGNON, 2002: This full-bodied, well-balanced blend of 85% Cabernet Sauvignon, 8% Merlot and 7% Cabernet Franc is concentrated, its once-firm tannins softening now and showing tempting aromas and flavors of black currants, berries and game meat, together with a long finish. Complex and sophisticated. Drink now–2009. Score 92.

MARGALIT, CABERNET SAUVIGNON, 2001: This dark, dense and richly flavored oak-aged blend of 90% Cabernet Sauvignon and 10% Merlot offers generous currant, blackberry, sage and mineral aromas and flavors. Still firm tannins, those integrating nicely now, and a long finish with tempting coffee, dark chocolate and hints of licorice and mint. Drink now–2012. Score 91.

MARGALIT, CABERNET SAUVIGNON, LOT 37, 2001: Vastly different in style from every other Margalit wine released, this wine was aged in *barriques* for two years, in contrast to all of Margalit's other wines, aged for only one. The black currants that typify so many of this winery's wines have been replaced here by plums, and the oft-searing tannins that sometimes take years to integrate are already soft and now showing a sweet and dusty nature. Drink now–2012. Score 92.

MARGALIT, CABERNET SAUVIGNON, 2000: This full-bodied, still tannic blend of 88% Cabernet Sauvignon and 12% Merlot had some rough edges in its youth but has now come fully into its own. Look for an abundance of raspberry, black cherry, sage, and spicy aromas and flavors, all with delicious leathery, cedarwood overtones. Drink now. Score 91.

MARGALIT, CABERNET SAUVIGNON, 1999: A blend of 84% Cabernet Sauvignon, 12% Merlot and 4% Petite Sirah, this oaked, full-bodied, ripe and complex wine shows good balance between wood and ripe cherry and berry flavors that come together in a long finish. Drink now. Score 92.

MARGALIT, CABERNET SAUVIGNON, 1998: A blend of 90% Cabernet and 10% Merlot, this chewy, full-bodied red is packed with spicy currant and blueberry flavors alongside notes of pepper and cola for additional dimension. Still showing firm tannins, but not for further cellaring. Drink up. Score 91.

MARGALIT, CABERNET SAUVIGNON, 1997: Deep garnet-purple, this full-bodied blend of 85% Cabernet Sauvignon, 13% Merlot and 2% Petite Sirah has a complex core of currant, spices and cedar flavors along with hints of anise, tobacco and ripe cherries. Good balance, now well-integrated tannins and a long finish. Fully mature and not for further cellaring. Drink up. Score 88.

MARGALIT, CABERNET SAUVIGNON, 1996: Full-bodied but neither as tannic nor as heavy as some of Margalit's earlier efforts. Deep garnet-red now, this distinctly Bordeaux-style red shows good balance between fruits, tannins and acidity, and is fleshy, elegant and long. Fully mature now. Drink up. Score 91.

MARGALIT, CABERNET SAUVIGNON, 1995: Medium to full-bodied, with soft and well-integrated tannins and generous aromas and flavors of black fruits, coffee and tobacco along with earthy-herbal notes, this well-balanced and well-structured wine offers up a generous mouthful. Not meant for further cellaring. Drink up. Score 91.

MARGALIT, MERLOT, 2006: Full-bodied, with near-sweet tannins and ripe blackberry, plum and berry fruits complemented nicely by spicy oak. Concentrated and elegant, with hints of dark chocolate on the long finish. Best 2009–2012. Tentative Score 91–93.

MARGALIT, MERLOT, 2005: Inky purple in color, offers up generous near-sweet oak, black cherries, blackberries and currants on first attack, those yielding to red plums and jammy raspberries. Dark and brooding at this time, with the tannins rising on the long finish. Best 2009–2014. Score 93.

MARGALIT, MERLOT, 2004: Fresh, ripe and generous, with appealing blackberry, plum, cassis, mocha and vanilla aromas and flavors finishing with a hint of grilled herbs. Medium to full-bodied, with soft tannins, a gently spicy wine that lingers nicely. Drink now–2009. Score 90.

MARGALIT, MERLOT, 2002: Full-bodied, deep purple toward inky black in color and blended with 10% Cabernet Sauvignon to add backbone, this ripe, bold and delicious wine shows well-integrated tannins that give it a welcome softness, those matched nicely by aromas and flavors of plums, currants and black cherries, and a long spicy and cedar-flavored finish. Drink now–2012. Score 92.

MARGALIT, MERLOT, 2001: This complex, intense and well-balanced 85% Merlot and 15% Cabernet Sauvignon blend has abundant soft tannins and plenty of earthy and mineral notes overlaying spicy currant, wild berry and coffee aromas and flavors. Look for a long, lingering finish with an array of hazelnuts, coffee and anise. Drink now–2010. Score 91.

MARGALIT, MERLOT, 2000: Remarkably tannic for a Merlot, this full-bodied wine which also contains 10% of Cabernet Sauvignon grapes is rich, ripe and concentrated, with layer after layer of currants, plums and black cherries, all with generous hints of tobacco, smoky oak and vanilla. Drink now. Score 92.

MARGALIT, MERLOT, 1999: With smooth tannins and rich flavors that fill the mouth and then linger nicely, this well-balanced, full-bodied, bold, ripe and delicious wine shows layer after layer of plum, currant, and black cherry flavors as well as a long finish on which you will find nice herbal overtones. Drink now. Score 90.

MARGALIT, MERLOT, 1998: A full-bodied blend of 87% Merlot, 10% Cabernet Sauvignon and 3% Petite Sirah, with layers of ripe, spicy black cherry, currant, plum and mineral aromas and flavors. This rich, smooth, elegant, complex and now mature wine has remarkable depth and concentration. Drink up. Score 90.

MARGALIT, MERLOT, 1997: Bold, ripe and delicious, with multiple layers of plum, currant and black cherry aromas and flavors, smooth, nicely polished tannins, and a rich, deep finish. Fully mature. Drink up. Score 91.

MARGALIT, CARIGNAN, 1999: A delightful surprise because Carignan rarely produces a fine wine on its own. This full-bodied wine which also contains 5% of Cabernet Sauvignon grapes to round it out is still surprisingly closed when first poured, but given time to open in the glass bursts with raspberry and chocolate flavors and an almost floral bouquet. Drink now. Score 90.

MARGALIT, CABERNET FRANC, 2006: Youthful royal-purple, medium to full-bodied, with rich black currant, cherry and blackberry fruits matched nicely by floral and light earthy aromas and flavors, all coming to a long, caressing finish. Drink from release–2012. Tentative Score 90–92.

MARGALIT, CABERNET FRANC, 2005: Dark cherry towards garnet and full-bodied, this round and polished wine shows abundant blackberry, currant and black cherry fruits, those matched nicely by hints of spices and cedarwood, all leading to a long, generously tannic finish. Faithful to the variety and destined for elegance. Drink now–2012. Score 92.

MARGALIT, CABERNET FRANC, 2004: Deeply fragrant, this full-bodied wine was blended with 12% Cabernet Sauvignon. Silky-smooth tannins, black and red fruits, hints of tobacco and chocolate come together on a long, mouth-filling finish with an appealing hint of freshly turned earth. Drink now–2009. Score 90.

MARGALIT, CABERNET FRANC, 2003: Almost impenetrable deep purple, full-bodied, with excellent balance between soft, luxurious tannins and a tempting array of dark plum, wild berry and herbal aromas and flavors. Oak-aged, with the addition of 10% Cabernet Sauvignon, the wine is mouth-filling and long, showing a tantalizing hint of mint on the finish. Drink now–2010. Score 90.

MARGALIT, CABERNET FRANC, 2002: This deep royal-purple, full-bodied, concentrated Cabernet Franc with 12% Cabernet Sauvignon blended in, shows aromas and flavors of spicy plums and earthiness on first attack that yield to an array of currant, anise, chocolate and sweet cedar, all coming together in a long mouth-filling finish. The wine has soft tannins, generous oak, plenty of acidity and overall good balance. Drink now–2010. Score 92.

MARGALIT, CABERNET FRANC, 2001: This full-bodied, heavily oaked blend of 90% Cabernet Franc and 10% Cabernet Sauvignon is at the same time seductive, well balanced and supple. The wine has generous cherry, anise and currant fruits along with spicy and toasty aromas and flavors and a generous hint of mocha. The long finish boasts earthy and cedarwood flavors typical of the best wines made from this variety. Drink now. Score 90.

Enigma

ENIGMA, 2006: A medium to full-bodied, subtle and round, softly tannic blend of 60% Cabernet Sauvignon and 20% each Cabernet Franc and Merlot. Opens with red currants and red plums, goes to black cherries and a pleasing light spiciness and closing with a long fruity and persistent finish. Drink from release–2012. Tentative Score 90–92.

ENIGMA, 2005: This medium to full-bodied blend of Cabernet Sauvignon, Cabernet Franc and Merlot (60%, 22% and 18% respectively) shows generous cassis, raspberry, and cherry fruits, those matched nicely by caressingly soft tannins, lightly spicy oak and chocolate, all coming together elegantly on a long and mouth-filling finish. Drink now–2013. Score 93.

ENIGMA, 2004: A blend of 60% Cabernet Sauvignon, 21% Cabernet Franc and 19% Merlot. A Bordeaux blend but with the clear Margalit signature, with generous but near-sweet soft tannins and a moderate hand with the wood. Even now showing dark purple plum and currant fruits, those matched nicely by spices and a hint of red licorice that creeps in on the long finish. Drink now–2012. Score 93.

ENIGMA, 2003: Fully living up to its earlier promise, this Bordeaux blend of 70% Cabernet Sauvignon, 18% Merlot and 12% Cabernet Franc is showing remarkably rich, ripe and polished. Round and approachable, with a complex array of currant, plum and wild berry aromas and flavors, those well focused and long and matched by a gentle spiciness that runs through to the long finish. Drink now–2010. Score 92.

Meishar ★★★

Founded in 1991 by Ze'ev and Chaya Smilansky on Moshav Meishar in the southern coastal plains, this small winery relies entirely on its own vineyards of Cabernet Sauvignon, Merlot, Shiraz and Muscat grapes and currently produces about 9,000 bottles annually of red wines in a Reserve and a Meishar series.

Reserve

RESERVE 730, CABERNET SAUVIGNON, 2004: Full-bodied, this red reflects its 18 months in oak with firm tannins and sweet cedar notes, those integrating nicely with black cherries, ripe currants, and light chocolate mousse flavors that sneak in quietly on the finish. Drink now–2010. Score 89.

RESERVE 730, CABERNET SAUVIGNON, 2003: Dark garnet, medium to full-bodied, with soft tannins complementing black currant and blackberry fruits, all on a spicy and lightly smoky background. Long and generous. Drink now–2009. Score 88.

RESERVE 730, CABERNET SAUVIGNON, 2002: Medium to full-bodied, dark garnet-red, with still-firm tannins but those starting to integrate nicely to reveal aromas and flavors of smoky oak, all well balanced with black fruits, Oriental spices and hints of chocolate and cigar tobacco on the moderately long finish. Drink now. Score 87.

RESERVE 730, CABERNET SAUVIGNON, 2001: Dark cherry-red toward garnet, this medium to full-bodied Cabernet was blended with 4% of Merlot to round it out. Its generous tannins balanced nicely with wood and fruits, the wine shows aromas and flavors of red currants and berries together with smoky oak and anise, as well as chocolate and mocha on the long finish. Drink now. Score 89.

RESERVE, CABERNET SAUVIGNON, 2000: Medium to full-bodied, with a rich array of berry, currant and plum fruits on a spicy oak background, the wine has good balance and tannins that are integrating nicely, as well as a long near-sweet finish. Drink up. Score 89.

RESERVE, 730, MERLOT, 2005: Showing dark and spicy, with an enchanting earthy character that highlights cherry, blackberry and spice aromas and flavors. Long and mouth-filling. Drink now–2010. Score 89.

RESERVE, 730, MERLOT, 2004: Made entirely from Merlot grapes, showing medium to full-bodied along with a gentle hand with the oak and generous earthy-herbal overtones, those in fine balance with ripe currant and blackberry fruits. On the long finish hints of Oriental spices and grilled meat. Drink now–2010. Score 89.

Meishar

MEISHAR, CABERNET SAUVIGNON, 2005: Dark garnet towards royal-purple, medium to full-bodied, with fine balance between still firm but already integrating tannins, spicy wood and well-focused currant, dark plum and black cherry fruits. Hints of ground pepper and anise that linger nicely. Drink now–2010. Score 90.

MEISHAR, CABERNET SAUVIGNON, 2004: Dark garnet, medium to full-bodied, with generous but soft tannins and smoky oak opening nicely to reveal aromas and flavors of black currants, purple plums, white chocolate and spices. Long and mouth-filling. Drink now–2009. Score 89.

MEISHAR, CABERNET SAUVIGNON, 2003: Medium to full-bodied, with soft tannins and appealing currant and black cherry fruits set off nicely by hints of vanilla and spices. Drink now–2009. Score 89.

MEISHAR, CABERNET SAUVIGNON, 2002: Deep garnet in color with a hint of browning, full-bodied, with tannins almost fully absorbed and showing light chocolate and caramel hints over the currant and now hyper-ripe plum aromas and flavors. Not meant for further cellaring. Drink up. Score 86.

MEISHAR, CABERNET SAUVIGNON, 2001: Deep garnet, with generous but well-integrated tannins balanced nicely by smoky oak, this medium-bodied red offers up appealing plum, black cherry and black currant aromas and flavors. Look as well for a hint of Oriental spices on the finish. Drink up. Score 88.

MEISHAR, CABERNET SAUVIGNON, 2000: This firm, intense and well-balanced red reveals currant and toasty oak flavors on a not overly imposing background of herbs and earthiness. Drink up. Score 88.

MEISHAR, MERLOT, 2005: Medium-dark garnet, medium-bodied and with silky tannins allowing raspberry, blackberry and cassis fruits to show through nicely, those complemented by generous hints of cocoa and a light earthy-graphite sensation that lingers nicely. Potentially elegant. Drink now–2010. Score 88.

MEISHAR, MERLOT, 2004: Dark royal-purple in color, this gently oak-aged medium-bodied wine was blended with 13% of Cabernet Sauvignon. Long, soft and round with plum and blackberry fruits backed up by hints of nutmeg and freshly turned earth. Drink now. Score 87.

MEISHAR, MERLOT, 2003: Dark brick-red, medium to full-bodied, with tannins integrating nicely and showing a generous array of blackberry, plum and black cherry fruits on a background of red licorice and chocolate. Drink now. Score 88.

MEISHAR, SHIRAZ, 2005: Ripe and generous, with gamy and leathery notes that intertwine nicely with berry, black cherry, plum and smoky aromas and flavors. Round and long, with a hint of earthiness on the long finish. Drink now–2009. Score 89.

MEISHAR, SHIRAZ-MERLOT-CABERNET SAUVIGNON, #41, 2004: Dark garnet, medium-bodied, with sweet cedar and spicy oak overtones highlighting blackberries, black cherries and an array of herbs and spices. Look for hints of minerals and anise on the crisp finish. Drink now–2009. Score 89.

MEISHAR, SHIRAZ-MERLOT-CABERNET SAUVIGNON, #41, 2003: A blend of 40% each of Shiraz and Merlot and 20% Cabernet Sauvignon. Aged in oak for eight months, medium-bodied, showing good balance between near-sweet tannins, spicy oak and fruits. On the nose and palate ripe plums, black currants and blackberries matched by hints of earthiness and tobacco. Long and generous. Drink now–2010. Score 90.

MEISHAR, TACSUM, 2003: Perhaps the winemakers were in a playful mood when they named this wine by spelling "Muscat" backward. Made from Muscat Canelli grapes that were sun-dried and then frozen before pressing, this is a wine as much in the Italian *appasimento* style as it is an ice wine. Not so much full-bodied as it is "thick", the wine shows unabashed sweetness and a dark, burnished bronze color. Good balancing acidity and flavors of apricots, ripe peaches and honeydew melon keep it lively. Drink now–2009. Score 89.

Meister *

Founded by Ya'akov Meister in Rosh Pina in the upper Galilee and drawing on Cabernet Sauvignon, Merlot, Shiraz and Carignan grapes from his own and other Galilee vineyards, this small winery released its first wines to the market with 2,000 bottles in 2003. Current production is about 6,000 bottles.

MEISTER, CABERNET SAUVIGNON, 2006: A funky, muddy wine, with charred herbs, tar and searing tannins that end with a chalky aftertaste. Tentative Score 58–60.

MEISTER, CABERNET SAUVIGNON, 2005: Cloudy in color, with coarse tannins, an unwanted sweetness and a far too-generous dusty oak that hides the fruits that try to make themselves felt. Score 68.

MEISTER, MERLOT, 2006: Dry and bitter, with green earthy and tobacco ash aromas and flavors. Tentative Score 63–65.

MEISTER, MERLOT, 2005: Deep garnet in color, without any of the varietal traits of Merlot, this red shows medium-bodied and softly tannic with skimpy blueberry fruits. A bit too much of Brett here gives the wine a somewhat muddy taste. Score 70.

MEISTER, SHIRAZ, 2006: Medium-bodied, with barnyard aromas and flavors of slightly sour stewed plums and cherries that lead to an earthy and balsamico finish. Tentative Score 55–57.

MEISTER, CARIGNAN, 2006: Medium-bodied, with spicy oak, weedy and vegetable aromas and flavors that hide the black fruits struggling without much success to make themselves felt. Tentative Score 68–70.

Miles **

Founded by vintner Eyal Miles in 2001 on Moshav Kerem Ben Zimra in the Upper Galilee, with its own vineyards containing Cabernet Sauvignon, Merlot, Sauvignon Blanc and Gewurztraminer, this winery is currently producing 6,000 bottles annually.

MILES, CABERNET SAUVIGNON, 2005: Oak-aged for 15 months, deep ruby towards garnet, medium to full-bodied, with chunky, country-style tannins that are showing nicely with black fruits and a light earthy-mineral finish. Drink now. Score 85.

MILES, CABERNET SAUVIGNON, 2004: Dark garnet, medium to full-bodied, with soft tannins and spicy wood balanced by appealing currant, berry and black cherry fruits as well as generous hints of Mediterranean herbs. Drink now. Score 85.

MILES, CABERNET SAUVIGNON, 2003: A medium-bodied, quaffing wine, garnet towards purple in color, with soft tannins, red fruits and a near-sweet finish. Drink now. Score 83.

MILES, CABERNET SAUVIGNON, 2002: Aged in oak for 14 months, this medium to full-bodied deep garnet wine shows chunky tannins, generous wood, and currant, berry and pepper aromas and flavors, those somewhat hidden under earthy and herbal notes. A pleasant country-style wine. Drink up. Score 84.

MILES, MERLOT, 2005: Deep garnet, medium-bodied with soft, mouth-coating tannins and near-sweet oak. A blend of 88% Merlot and 12% Cabernet Sauvignon opening to reveal blackberry, blueberry and currant fruits, all on a lightly spicy background. Drink now–2009. Score 86.

MILES, MERLOT, 2004: Medium-bodied, with firm tannins integrating nicely and well balanced with generous blueberry, black cherry and cassis fruits. A generous hint of spiciness adds charm to the moderately long finish. Drink now. Score 85.

MILES, MERLOT, 2003: Garnet towards royal-purple, medium-bodied with soft, well-integrated tannins and not at all complex but rewarding aromas and flavors of blackberries, black cherries and plums. Drink up. Score 83.

MILES, RED-DOME, 2005: A blend of 60% Cabernet Sauvignon and 40% Merlot, oak-aged for 15 months and showing soft tannins and dusty wood nicely balanced with black fruits and hints of mint. Drink now–2009. Score 86.

MILES, SAUVIGNON BLANC, 2006: Light gold with a green tint, medium-bodied, showing citrus, guava and pineapple fruits. Refreshing and lively. Drink now. Score 85.

MILES, SAUVIGNON BLANC, 2004: Light straw-colored, medium-bodied with citrus, green apple and pineapple fruits. A bit past its peak. Drink up. Score 84.

MILES, SAUVIGNON BLANC, 2003: A light straw-colored medium-bodied white with appealing apple, grapefruit, and pineapple fruits, a gentle hint of spring flowers and good balancing acidity to add liveliness. Not complex but pleasant. Drink up. Score 85.

MILES, GEWURZTRAMINER, 2004: Light golden-straw with a hint of bronze, medium-bodied and with good balancing acidity to show off the appealing, spicy tropical fruits. Drink up. Score 86.

MILES, GEWURZTRAMINER, DESSERT, 2004: Light golden, medium-bodied, with moderate sweetness set off nicely by refreshing acidity. On the nose and palate tropical fruits and honeyed apricots. Somewhat one dimensional but very pleasant. Drink up. Score 86.

Miller **

Established in 2003 by Dan Ashkenazi in the community of Sha'arei Tikva on the western slopes of the Samarian Mountains, this small winery is currently producing 7,000 bottles annually, relying primarily on Cabernet Sauvignon and Merlot grapes from local vineyards and vineyards in the Galilee.

MILLER, CABERNET SAUVIGNON, 2005: This dark cherry-red wine is unoaked and medium-bodied, with soft tannins and simple but pleasant raspberry and cherry aromas and flavors. Drink now. Score 80. K

MILLER, MERLOT, 2005: Ruby towards garnet, this medium-bodied, unoaked country-style wine has appealing berry, black cherry and cassis aromas and flavors. Drink now. Score 83. K

MILLER, ASHTORET, 2005: This unoaked blend of Cabernet Sauvignon and Merlot is light to medium-bodied, with raspberry, cherry and currant fruits. Drink now. Score 82. K

Mony ***

Located in the foothills of the Jerusalem Mountains on the grounds of the Dir Rafat Monastery, the winery was operated for many years by the resident monks. About five years ago, control of the vineyards and winery passed to the Ertul family, long-time vintners for the monastery. Grapes in the vineyards include Cabernet Sauvignon, Cabernet Franc, Merlot, Zinfandel, Shiraz, Carignan, Argaman, Petite Sirah, Chardonnay, Semillon, Emerald Riesling and other varieties. Annual production is about 22,000 bottles. The winery is currently producing wines in two series, the upper-level Reserve and the regular Mony, and from the 2005 vintage, the wines have been kosher.

Reserve

RESERVE, CABERNET SAUVIGNON, 2004: Garnet to royal-purple, medium-bodied, with spicy oak and soft tannins opening to reveal blackberry, black cherry and cassis fruits. Drink now. Score 85.

RESERVE, CABERNET SAUVIGNON, 2003: Medium-bodied, with gentle oak and soft tannins. Showing generous ripe currant and wild berry flavors with a spicy hint in the background. Drink up. Score 83.

RESERVE, CABERNET SAUVIGNON, 2002: Medium to full-bodied, with soft tannins and a marked but pleasant influence of smoky oak well balanced by generous currant, berry and herbal aromas and flavors. A light spiciness on the moderately long finish. Somewhat past its peak. Drink up. Score 82.

RESERVE, MERLOT, 2004: Medium to full-bodied, with gripping tannins only now starting to integrate. Opens slowly in the glass to show black and red berries and purple plums on a background of spices and licorice. Drink now. Score 85.

RESERVE, MERLOT, 2003: Deep royal-purple, medium-bodied, with berry and cherry fruits and a hint of spicy oak on the moderately long finish. Drink up. Score 85.

RESERVE, MERLOT, 2002: Dark garnet-red, medium to full-bodied, with still-firm tannins but those set off nicely by spicy-smoky oak and generous currant and berry aromas and flavors. Drink up. Score 84.

RESERVE, SHIRAZ, 2003: Deep cherry towards garnet in color, with firm tannins, generous spicy wood and vanilla. On the nose and palate a basically black cherry-plum personality, that with hints of leather, chocolate and licorice that come in on the medium-long finish. Drink now. Score 84.

RESERVE, CHARDONNAY, 2004: With eight months in oak, this medium-bodied, golden-straw colored wine shows good balance between wood, acidity and fruits. Generous tropical fruits, citrus peel and melon aromas and flavors along with a hint of spices to add complexity. A bit past its peak. Drink up. Score 84.

Mony

MONY, CABERNET SAUVIGNON, 2005: Lightly oaked, this deep ruby wine is medium-bodied, with soft tannins and appealing red fruits. Not complex but appealing. Drink now. Score 85. K

MONY, CABERNET SAUVIGNON, 2004: With only three months in oak, this medium-bodied red shows soft tannins and nice hints of spices and vanilla on a background of black fruits. Marred by an increasingly strong barnyard aroma. Drink up. Score 80.

MONY, CABERNET SAUVIGNON, 2003: Deep garnet-red, medium to full-bodied, with firm but well-integrating tannins and with traditional Cabernet aromas and flavors of currants, berries and a hint of spicy cedarwood. Well balanced and moderately long. Drink up. Score 85.

MONY, MERLOT, 2005: Ruby-red, light to medium-bodied, with soft tannins and appealing currant and berry fruits. Drink up. Score 80. K

MONY, MERLOT, 2004: Light in body, with almost unfelt tannins and berry, strawberry and cherry aromas. Drink up. Score 80.

MONY, MERLOT, 2003: Dark ruby towards garnet, medium to full-bodied, with firm tannins that need time to open to reveal the berry, black cherry and currant flavors that lie underneath as well as spicy oak and light herbal overlays. Drink up. Score 85.

MONY, SHIRAZ, 2003: Dark cherry towards garnet red, with chunky, country-style tannins and reflecting its 12 months in oak with spices and hints of vanilla. Aromas and flavors of currants, black cherries and plums backed up by a hint of freshly tanned leather. An entry-level wine. Drink up. Score 84.

MONY, CHARDONNAY, 2005: Light straw in color and medium-bodied, this lightly oak-aged white shows some apple and pineapple aromas but leaves a sensation of flatness on the palate. Drink up. Score 79. K

MONY, MUSCAT OF ALEXANDRIA, 2004: Light straw in color, light to medium-bodied, not complex but with appealing floral and citrus flower aromas and flavors on a lightly honeyed background. Drink up. Score 84.

Na'aman ✶✶

Founded by Rami and Betina Na'aman on Moshav Ramot
Naftali in the Upper Galilee, this small winery released their
first wines from the 2004 vintage. With their own vineyards
containing Cabernet Sauvignon, Merlot, Cabernet Franc,
Petit Verdot and Shiraz grapes, releases from 2004 were just
under 1,000 bottles and in 2006 about 4,000 bottles.

NA'AMAN, CABERNET SAUVIGNON, 2006: Deep purple, medium
to full-bodied, with soft but mouth-coating tannins, gently spicy
wood and natural acidity all well in balance. On the nose and palate
red berries, currants and orange peel, those supported by light hints
of cedarwood and spicy herbaceousness. Drink from release–2010.
Tentative Score 86–88.

NA'AMAN, CABERNET SAUVIGNON, 2005: Dark garnet towards royal-
purple, medium to full-bodied, with still-firm tannins and generous
wood, but those integrating nicely. Showing black currant, blackberry
and briar aromas and flavors with hints of roasted coffee in the background. Drink now. Score 85.

NA'AMAN, CABERNET SAUVIGNON, 2004: Medium to full-bodied,
with chunky, country-style tannins and reflecting its 12 months in
barriques with dusty and near-sweet cedar. On the nose and palate appealing blackberry and currant fruits, those with a light herbal overlay.
Drink up. Score 84.

NA'AMAN, MERLOT, DEEP PURPLE, 2005: Indeed deep purple in
color, but with little charm beyond that, as medicinal and barnyard
aromas and coarse tannins hide whatever fruits may be hiding here.
Tentative Score 72–74.

NA'AMAN, CABERNET FRANC, 2006: Medium to full-bodied, with
firm tannins, this dark cherry-red wine shows an array of blackberry,
huckleberry, currant, black licorice and Mediterranean herbs, all lingering nicely. Drink from release–2010. Tentative Score 85–87.

NA'AMAN, CABERNET SAUVIGNON-MERLOT, KING CRIMSON, 2005: A medium-bodied, softly tannic bend of 75% Cabernet and 25% Merlot, this wine shows spicy wood, cherry and red currant aromas and flavors, those with an appealing, light herbal undertone. Drink now. Score 85.

NA'AMAN, CABERNET SAUVIGNON-MERLOT, 2004: A lightly oak-aged blend of 75% Cabernet and 25% Merlot, with soft tannins integrated nicely and showing currant and berry fruits. Straightforward and not complex but easy to drink. Drink up. Score 84.

NA'AMAN, 50/50, 2004: Dark garnet, medium-bodied, with chunky country-style tannins and perhaps too-generous wood. On the nose and palate currant and cherry fruits. Marred somewhat by a light medicinal hint that fails to fade. Drink up. Score 80.

NE'EMAN, PINK FLOYD, 2006: This simple but appealing rosé is light to medium-bodied and crisply dry, with strawberry, raspberry and cassis aromas and flavors. Drink up. Score 84.

Nachshon ***

Founded in 1996 on Kibbutz Nachshon in the Ayalon Valley at the foot of the Jerusalem Hills, the winery, now under the supervision of winemaker Shlomi Zadok, raises its own Cabernet Sauvignon, Merlot, Shiraz, Cabernet Franc and Argaman grapes and produces about 17,000 bottles annually. Until 2003 the winery produced wines in four series, Ayalon, Sela, Pushkin and Nachshon.

Ayalon

AYALON, CABERNET SAUVIGNON, 2004: Dark garnet, full-bodied, with firm tannins and sweet cedarwood integrating nicely to show black currant and berry fruits on a light herbal background. On the finish a hint of dark chocolate. Drink now. Score 86.

AYALON, CABERNET SAUVIGNON, 2003: Made entirely from Cabernet Sauvignon grapes, this deep garnet wine was aged first for 25 months in new *barriques* and then for an additional 12 months in old ones. Medium to full-bodied, and showing near-sweet tannins and hints of sweet cedarwood complemented nicely by spicy berry and currant fruits. Drink now. Score 87.

AYALON, CABERNET SAUVIGNON, 2002: Developed for two years in oak, this deep garnet blend of 66% Cabernet Sauvignon and 34% Merlot shows good balance between soft tannins, smoky wood and berry, currant and black cherry fruits. Drink up. Score 85.

AYALON, MERLOT, 2004: Deep cherry-ruby red, medium-bodied, with soft tannins, aromas and flavors of raspberries and cherries, the wine is gently oaked, well rounded and nicely balanced. Drink now. Score 86.

AYALON, MERLOT, 2002: Dark royal-purple in color, this blend of 66% Cabernet Sauvignon and 34% Merlot shows generous, sweet cedarwood, currants, and plums, all with an appealing overlay of Mediterranean herbs. Somewhat past its peak. Drink up. Score 84.

AYALON, SYRAH, 2006: Garnet towards royal-purple in color, this round and generous blend of 90% Syrah and 10% Cabernet Sauvignon is medium-bodied, with soft tannins, and shows raspberry, leathery and meaty aromas and flavors. Drink from release–2010. Tentative Score 86–88.

AYALON, SYRAH, 2005: Blended with 15% Cabernet Sauvignon, this dark royal-purple, oak-aged wine opens with a light but tantalizing herbal nose and goes on to show black cherries, cassis and blackberries, those backed up nicely by hints of tobacco and licorice. Drink from release–2010. Tentative Score 86–88.

AYALON, SYRAH, 2004: Youthful royal-purple in color and already showing a nice touch of sweet cedarwood, with firm but nicely yielding tannins. Aromas and flavors of currants, red berries, plums and hints of vanilla-scented oak. Good balance between tannins and wood ensures medium-term aging. Drink now. Score 87.

AYALON, SYRAH, 2003: Medium-bodied, deep ruby in color, with soft tannins integrating well and ripe purple plum, blackberry and cherry fruits. Good balance between wood, tannins and acidity and an appealing spicy-earthy finish. Drink now. Score 87.

AYALON, CABERNET FRANC, 2006: Dark garnet, this medium to full-bodied softly tannic blend of 90% Cabernet Franc and 10% Cabernet Sauvignon shows complex currant, plum, cedarwood and tobacco aromas and flavors. Well balanced and round, with an appealing finish highlighted by spicy oak and orange peel. Drink from release–2010. Tentative Score 87–89.

AYALON, CABERNET FRANC, 2005: Cabernet Franc, blended with 7–8% each of Merlot and Petit Verdot. Oak-aged partly in French, partly in American barrels, the wine opens with a light, somewhat pungent, aroma but that passes in a few moments to reveal plum, currant and citrus peel. Full-bodied, with firm tannins needing time to settle down. Drink from release–2010. Tentative Score 86–88.

AYALON, CABERNET-MERLOT, 2004: A blend of almost equal parts of Cabernet Sauvignon and Merlot with a small amount of Cabernet Franc, this dark, medium to full-bodied wine shows a generous hand on the oak, but that may well settle down with time. Beyond that, dusty tannins and good purple plum and black currant aromas and flavors. Drink now–2009. Score 86.

Sela

SELA, FRENCH BLEND, 2006: Dark royal-purple in color, this oak-aged blend of 57% Syrah, 20% Merlot, 13% Cabernet Franc and 10% Cabernet Sauvignon opens with a slightly musky aroma which passes quickly to reveal soft tannins integrating nicely and an array of berry, black cherry and cassis fruits, those on a lightly meaty background. Drink from release–2009. Tentative Score 85–87.

SELA, FRENCH BLEND, 2005: Medium-dark garnet with silky tannins, this blend of Syrah, Cabernet Sauvignon, Cabernet Franc and Petit Verdot (41%, 33%, 16% and 10% respectively) shows an appealing array of wild berries, currants and plums, those on a gently spicy background. Rich, round and moderately long. Drink from release–2009. Tentative Score 87–89.

SELA, FRENCH BLEND, 2004: A blend of 30% each of Syrah and Cabernet Sauvignon and 20% each of Cabernet Franc and Merlot. Oak-aged for 18 months, the wine is showing spicy wood, firm tannins and aromas and flavors of black fruits along with hints of herbs and green olives. Drink now. Score 87.

SELA, FRENCH BLEND, 2003: A blend of Cabernet Sauvignon, Merlot, Cabernet Franc and Syrah (37%, 33%, 25% and 5% respectively), this smooth and round full-bodied red was aged in mostly new French oak for 16 months. Soft tannins well balanced by smoky oak and aromas and flavors of plums, cherries and raspberries. Drink up. Score 86.

Pushkin

PUSHKIN, 2006: A deep garnet, oak-aged blend of 59% Merlot, 22% Cabernet Franc, and 19% Cabernet Sauvignon. Medium to full-bodied, with still-gripping tannins that need time to allow underlying blackberries, currants and spices to make themselves better felt. Drink from release. Tentative Score 85–87.

PUSHKIN, 2005: This blend of Cabernet Sauvignon, Merlot, Cabernet Franc and Syrah (43%, 42%, 11% and 4% respectively) was aged partly in French *barriques* for six to eight months and partly in stainless steel tanks. Medium-bodied, with soft tannins and aromas of spicy wood, raspberries and cassis. A good quaffer. Drink now. Score 85.

Nachshon

NACHSHON, ROSÉ, 2006: Made from Argaman grapes and blended with 3% Emerald Riesling, the best feature of this dry little wine is its pleasant pinkish color. As one might anticipate from this grape variety, minimal fruits, minimal aroma, minimal flavor and minimal acidity. Drink up. Score 78.

Nahal Amud *

Established by Avi Abu in 1998 and located on Moshav Kfar Shamai near Sefad in the Upper Galilee, the winery draws on grapes from its own vineyards, those including Cabernet Sauvignon, Cabernet Franc, Merlot and Petite Sirah. Current production is about 5,000 bottles annually.

NAHAL AMUD, CABERNET SAUVIGNON, 2005: Garnet towards purple, medium-bodied, with chunky, somewhat coarse tannins, minimal fruits and an excessive earthy overlay. Drink up. Score 72. K

NAHAL AMUD, CABERNET SAUVIGNON, 2004: Medium-bodied, with coarse tannins and far-too-generous and not entirely clean earthy overlays and only the skimpiest of black fruits. Drink up. Score 75. K

NAHAL AMUD, CABERNET SAUVIGNON, 2003: Developed partly in oak barrels and partly in glass demijohns, this unfiltered country-style wine is more heavy than full-bodied and is lacking balance between its chunky tannins, high acidity and overripe fruits. Drink up. Score 72. K

NACHAL AMUD, MERLOT, 2005: Dark garnet with a hint of browning, medium-bodied, with firm tannins and an underlying sweetness to stewed red fruits. Score 70. K

NAHAL AMUD, MERLOT, 2003: Dark but not fully clear royal-purple, medium-bodied, with searing tannins and aromas and flavors that call to mind cherry liqueur. Score 68. K

NAHAL AMUD, CABERNET SAUVIGNON-MERLOT-SHIRAZ, 2003: Dark garnet, medium to full-bodied, firmly tannic, with plum and currant fruits pushed into the background by unwanted medicinal and earthy aromas and flavors. Drink up. Score 79. K

Nashashibi *

Founded in 2001 by brothers Munir and Nashashibi Nashashibi, the winery is located in the village of Eehbelin in the heart of the Carmel Mountains, on a site where wine has been made since Roman times. Currently production is about 12,000 bottles annually of Cabernet Sauvignon, Merlot and Chardonnay in two series, Special Reserve and Nashashibi. Grapes come from the Upper Galilee as well as from the winery's own vineyards at the foothills of the Carmel Mountains.

Special Reserve

SPECIAL RESERVE, CABERNET SAUVIGNON, 2005: Dark garnet and medium-bodied, with firm tannins starting to integrate. Showing generous smoke and spices from the wood casks in which it aged. On the nose and palate currants and berries. Drink from release. Score 80.

SPECIAL RESERVE, CABERNET SAUVIGNON, 2004: Garnet towards purple, medium-bodied, with firm tannins and spicy oak. An overlay of moldy barnyard aromas hide the fruits. Score 60.

SPECIAL RESERVE, CABERNET SAUVIGNON, 2003: Dark ruby towards garnet, medium to full-bodied, with stale, moldy, barnyard aromas and flavors that hide the fruits. Score 60.

SPECIAL RESERVE, MERLOT, 2004: Medium-bodied, with almost unfelt tannins, this dark cherry-red-towards-purple wine reflects its 14 months of aging with generous smoky oak. Not much in the way of fruits here. Drink up. Score 80.

Nashashibi

NASHASHIBI, CABERNET SAUVIGNON, 2005: Medium to full-bodied, dark garnet in color, this country-style wine is somewhat chunky on the palate but showing appealing black fruits and spices. Drink now. Score 84.

NASHASHIBI, CABERNET SAUVIGNON, 2004: Medium-dark garnet, medium-bodied, with chunky tannins. The once appealing aromas and flavors of spicy oak, cassis and blackberries now turning musky, with hints of barnyard. Drink up. Score 70.

NASHASHIBI, CABERNET SAUVIGNON, 2003: Garnet-red but browning at the rim, with unyielding tannins and only skimpy black fruits. Drink up. Score 74.

Natuf **

CABERNET
SAUVIGNON
2001

CONT. 750 ml   12.5 ALC. by VOL

Founded by Meir Akel and Ze'ev Cinamon on Moshav Kfar Truman in the Central Plains, not far from Ben Gurion Airport, this winery draws on grapes from the Ayalon Valley, and its releases have been primarily of Cabernet Sauvignon. Current production is about 4,500 bottles annually.

NATUF, CABERNET SAUVIGNON, 2005: Deep garnet and medium to full-bodied, with near-sweet tannins and spicy oak in good balance with currant, blackberry and blueberry fruits. On the moderately long finish an appealing hint of freshly picked mushrooms. Drink now–2009. Score 86.

NATUF, CABERNET SAUVIGNON, 2004: Dark ruby, medium to full-bodied, with firm tannins integrating nicely with smoky wood and forward cassis, black cherry and berry fruits, those matched by hints of sweet herbs. Drink now. Score 86.

NATUF, CABERNET SAUVIGNON, 2003: Ruby towards garnet-red, medium-bodied, with chunky tannins and aromas and flavors of ripe berries, plums and cassis as well as a bare hint of sweet chocolate on the finish. An appealing country-style wine. Drink now. Score 85.

NATUF, CABERNET SAUVIGNON, 2002: A pleasant country-style wine, medium to full-bodied with chunky tannins, firm texture, and appealing cassis, berry and plum fruits. Drink up. Score 85.

Neot Smadar *

This small winery, the south-ernmost in the country, is lo-cated on an oasis on Kibbutz Neot Smadar in the Jordan Valley, 60 kilometers north of Eilat. The winery released its first wines from the 2001 vintage and since its incep-tion has relied entirely on organically raised grapes of Cabernet Sauvignon, Mer-lot, Chardonnay, Sauvignon Blanc and Muscat Canelli, all grown in vineyards on the *kibbutz*. Due to the unique climate conditions, theirs is invariably the earliest harvest in the country. The winery is currently produc-ing about 4,000 bottles annually.

קברנה סוביניון
Cabernet Sauvignon
2002

יין אורגני אדום יבש
Organic Dry Red Wine

13% Alc. By Vol. 750 ml.
Prod. & bot. By Neot Semadar Wine Cellars

נאות סמדר
אורגני מן המדבר

NEOT SMADAR, CABERNET SAUVIGNON, 2005: Dark ruby in color, medium-bodied, with soft tannins and a few berry and cherry fruits. Drink up. Score 76.

NEOT SMADAR, CABERNET SAUVIGNON, 2004: Medium-bodied, with soft tannins and lightly spicy oak. Nicely balanced and showing berry and cherry aromas and flavors. Not typical of the variety but a pleasant quaffer. Drink up. Score 80.

NEOT SMADAR, MERLOT, 2005: Light to medium-bodied, somewhat diluted on both nose and palate and with only skimpy black fruits. Drink up. Score 76.

NEOT SMADAR, MERLOT, 2004: Deep royal-purple, medium-bodied, with soft tannins and appealing aromas and flavors of blackberries, minerals and spices. Drink up. Score 83.

NEOT SMADAR, MERLOT, 2003: Medium to full-bodied, deep royal purple in color and with generous mineral, herbal and green olive overlays. Somewhat atypical for Merlot, this wine has good balance and depth, and a surprisingly long and tannic finish. Drink up. Score 78.

NEOT SMADAR, CABERNET SAUVIGNON-MERLOT, 2003: This blend of 85% Cabernet and 15% Merlot is still somewhat tannic and rough because of its youth, but showing good balance and a promise to reveal nice currant, berry and herbal aromas and flavors. Drink up. Score 84.

NEOT SMADAR, CHARDONNAY, 2006: Gold towards bronze in color, medium-bodied, with tropical fruits, grapefruit and light spices in the background. Drink up. Score 80.

NEOT SMADAR, CHARDONNAY, 2005: Dark straw in color, medium bodied, with generous acidity and minerality backing up tropical fruits and melon aromas and flavors. Not complex but refreshing and appealing. Drink up. Score 80.

NEOT SMADAR, SAUVIGNON BLANC FUMÉ, 2006: Light golden straw, light to medium-bodied, with spicy peach and citrus fruits. Drink up. Score 80.

Noga *

Owned by the Harari family and located between Gedera and Moshav Kidron on the Southern Plains, the winery released its first 2,000 bottles from the 2004 vintage. It currently produces two wines, Noga and Tom, both blends of Cabernet Sauvignon and Merlot.

NOGA, 2005: This blend reflects its oak-aging with spicy and vanilla-rich overtones and soft tannins. On the nose and palate black cherry and berry fruits. One dimensional and short. Drink now. Score 79.

NOGA, 2004: A dark royal-purple blend of 80% Merlot and 20% Cabernet Sauvignon, oak-aged for 12 months. Medium to full-bodied, with generous smoky wood, medicinal aromas, and a potent alcoholic nose that dominates and hides the black fruit. Drink up. Score 78.

TOM, 2005: Garnet-red, this oak-aged blend of Cabernet Sauvignon and Merlot shows medium-bodied, with soft tannins and spicy oak yielding to reveal wild berry fruits. A pleasant quaffer. Drink now. Score 83.

TOM, 2004: Dark garnet towards purple, this blend of 80% Cabernet Sauvignon and 20% Merlot was aged in oak for 12 months. Medium to full-bodied, with currant and berry fruits buried under firm tannins and a far too strong sense of alcohol. Drink now. Score 78.

Odem Mountain ✳✳✳

Founded by the Elfasi family in 2003, the winery is situated in a modern facility on Moshav Odem in the northern Golan Heights. It relies primarily on grapes grown in its own vineyards—one of which is organic—supplemented by grapes from other vineyards on the Golan and in the Upper Galilee. Currently producing wines based on Cabernet Sauvignon, Merlot, Shiraz and Cabernet Franc, the winery is considering future releases of Sauvignon Blanc and Pinot Noir. Production for 2003 was 6,500 bottles and for 2004, 2005 and 2006 about 30,000 bottles. The wines will be kosher starting with the 2007 vintage.

The top-of-the-line series are Alfasi and Reserve, the mid-range series are Nimrod and Odem Mountain, and there is a special label, Volcanic, for wines made from organic grapes.

Alfasi

ALFASI, 2005: An oak-aged blend, this year of 70% Cabernet Sauvignon and 30% Merlot. Medium to full-bodied, with soft tannins integrating nicely and unfolding on the palate to show a generous array of currant and berry fruits, those supported by hints of sweet herbs and green olives. Drink from release–2010. Tentative Score 88–90.

ALFASI, CABERNET-MERLOT, 2004: This oak-aged blend of 60% Cabernet Sauvignon and 40% Merlot shows fine balance between still-firm tannins and spicy wood, those yielding in the glass to reveal black fruits, sweet herbs and, on the long finish, hints of green olives and anise. Best 2008–2011. Score 91.

Reserve

RESERVE, CABERNET SAUVIGNON, 2005: Deep garnet towards royal-purple, medium to full-bodied, with generous, soft tannins and spicy wood in good balance with blackberry, currant and cassis fruits On the moderately long finish, hints of cedar and freshly cut herbs Drink now–2010. Score 90.

RESERVE, CABERNET SAUVIGNON, 2004: Dark garnet towards inky black, full-bodied, with soft tannins and a moderate oak influence in fine balance with black currant and blackberry fruits, those supported by hints of herbs and sweet cedar. Drink now–2009. Score 89.

RESERVE, CABERNET SAUVIGNON, 2003: Dark ruby towards garnet, medium to full-bodied, with generous tannins and wood influence now starting to integrate. Needs time in the glass to open but when it does look for appealing black fruits, spices and chocolate leading to a long finish. Drink now. Score 87.

RESERVE, MERLOT, 2005: Dark ruby towards garnet, medium-bodied, with soft tannins and smoky, vanilla-laded wood, those integrating nicely to show an appealing range of black fruits. Deep and long. Drink now–2009. Score 88.

RESERVE, MERLOT, 2004: Oak-aged for 15 months, this almost inky-dark purple wine is medium to full bodied, with abundant but not dominating spicy wood. Opens to show wild berries, cassis, black cherries and appealing hints of chocolate that linger nicely. Generous and mouth-filling. Drink now. Score 88.

RESERVE, MERLOT, 2003: Dark-almost impenetrable garnet towards purple in color, this medium to full-bodied wine reflects its 15 months in new and used oak *barriques* with firm tannins and smoky oak. Look for aromas and flavors of currants, plums and blueberries, those with hints of tobacco and vanilla on the finish. Drink up. Score 87.

RESERVE, CABERNET SAUVIGNON-MERLOT, 2005: Deep ruby towards garnet, medium-bodied, with soft tannins integrating nicely with spicy and vanilla-rich wood. On the nose and palate, berry, black cherry and cassis, those backed up by sweet herbs and a hint of anise. Moderately long and complex. Drink now–2010. Score 89.

Nimrod

NIMROD, CABERNET SAUVIGNON, 2005: Medium to full-bodied, this dark cherry-red-towards-garnet wine is reflecting its ten months in oak with soft, mouth-coating tannins and hints of smoke. On the nose and palate black currants, blackberries and black cherries, all lingering nicely. Drink now. Score 87.

NIMROD, CABERNET SAUVIGNON, 2004: Medium to full-bodied, with soft tannins integrating nicely, and a pleasant hint of oak from its 18 months in *barriques*. Flavors and aromas of black fruits along with hints of anise and chocolate. Round and generous. Drink now. Score 86.

NIMROD, CABERNET SAUVIGNON, 2003: Garnet towards purple, medium-bodied, with soft tannins and sweet cedarwood. Black cherry, currant and hints of spices on the moderate finish. Drink up. Score 85.

NIMROD, MERLOT, 2005: Garnet towards purple, reflecting ten months in oak with spicy and vanilla overlays and showing appealing berry and cassis fruits. Medium-bodied, with soft tannins integrating nicely and with a moderately long finish. Drink now. Score 87.

NIMROD, MERLOT, 2004: Deep ruby towards purple, medium-bodied, with soft, well-integrated tannins and a gentle hand with the wood. Black currants, berries and a nice hint of spiciness on the nose and palate. Drink up. Score 85.

NIMROD, CABERNET SAUVIGNON-MERLOT, 2004: Dark ruby towards garnet, medium-bodied, with soft tannins and generous but not overpowering oak. Currant, blackberry and plum fruits with a nice hint of dark chocolate on the finish. Drink now. Score 86.

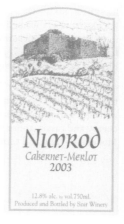

Odem Mountain

ODEM MOUNTAIN, CABERNET SAUVIGNON, 2005: Dark ruby towards garnet, medium-bodied, with soft tannins integrating nicely and well balanced by spicy oak. On the tangy nose and palate, traditional Cabernet black currant and wild berry fruits. Drink now–2009. Score 86.

ODEM MOUNTAIN, CABERNET SAUVIGNON, 2004: Medium to full-bodied and deep garnet in color. Firm tannins just starting to recede and now balanced nicely by smoky oak and aromas and flavors of black currants, plums and chocolate. Drink up. Score 86.

ODEM MOUNTAIN, CABERNET SAUVIGNON, 2003: Deep royal-purple, medium-bodied and reflecting its six months in oak with an overlay of spices and vanilla. Look for aromas and flavors of black currants and blackberries on a background of citrus peel and chocolate. Drink up. Score 85.

ODEM MOUNTAIN, MERLOT, 2006: Medium-dark garnet, medium-bodied, with soft tannins. Showing generous berry and black cherry fruits but somewhat on the acidic side and lacking depth. Drink from release. Tentative Score 83–85.

ODEM MOUNTAIN, MERLOT, 2005: Dark ruby towards garnet, medium-bodied, with soft tannins and gentle spicy oak influences. Look for aromas and flavors of blueberries, cranberries and cassis. Not complex but a good quaffer. Drink now–2009. Score 85.

ODEM MOUNTAIN, MERLOT, 2004: Dark garnet towards purple, medium to full-bodied, with firm tannins already integrating nicely and generous ripe plum, black cherry and berry fruits backed up nicely by hints of spices and vanilla. Drink up. Score 86.

ODEM MOUNTAIN, CABERNET SAUVIGNON-SYRAH, 2006: This blend of 70% Cabernet and 30% Syrah is showing spicy, floral and earthy aromas and flavors on first attack, those opening to reveal currant, berry and black cherry fruits. Finishing with appealing leathery and cigar-box hints. Drink from release–2009. Tentative Score 85–87.

Volcanic

VOLCANIC, CABERNET SAUVIGNON, 2005: Garnet-red, medium-bodied, softly tannic and generously fruity, this unoaked blend of 87% Cabernet Sauvignon and 13% Merlot was made from organically grown grapes. On the nose and palate blackberry and currant fruits, a hint of wood and abundant acidity that makes the wine refreshing but somewhat one dimensional. Drink now. Score 85.

VOLCANIC, CABERNET SAUVIGNON, 2004: Fermented partly in stainless steel and then allowed to undergo malolactic fermentation in French oak *barriques*, this medium to full-bodied deep garnet blend of Cabernet Sauvignon and Merlot shows primarily herbal aromas and flavors when first poured, but then opens nicely in the glass to reveal currant and purple plum fruits. Drink up. Score 86.

VOLCANIC, CHARDONNAY, 2006: Aged for five months in new French oak, this light gold wine shows an aromatic nose and light wood influences. Opens in the glass to reveal citrus, pineapple and ripe melon fruits, those supported nicely by hints of flinty minerals. Drink now. Score 87.

VOLCANIC, CHARDONNAY, 2005: Developed *sur lie* in French *barriques* for five months, this light golden-straw wine is medium-bodied and opens slowly in the glass to reveal appealing aromas and flavors of pineapple and tropical fruits, those backed up by a light spicy oak influence. Drink up. Score 87.

Pelter ✶✶✶✶

Established in 2002 on Kibbutz Ein Zivan on the Golan Heights by Tal Pelter, who studied oenology and worked at several wineries in Australia, the winery plans to move soon to nearby Kibbutz Merom Golan. Drawing on Cabernet Sauvignon, Merlot, Cabernet Franc, Shiraz, Petit Verdot, Grenache, Semillon and Chardonnay grapes from the Golan, the Upper Galilee and the Jerusalem Mountains, the winery, one of only four in the country to produce a sparkling wine, releases wines in two series: T-Selection and Pelter. Production from the 2002 vintage was about 4,000 bottles and current production is about 30,000 bottles annually.

T-Selection

T-SELECTION, CABERNET SAUVIGNON, 2004: Dark, dense and concentrated, this spicy and complex red shows muscular and earthy currants and blackberries, backed up by herbal and spicy oak, all with a generous dose of firm tannins. Turns smooth and polished as it opens to reveal tempting mineral, sage and cedar flavors. Long and generous, with a promise for true elegance. Drink now–2012. Score 92.

T-SELECTION, SHIRAZ, 2005: Dark crimson in color, opening with generous vanilla on the nose, this full-bodied, round and elegant wine shows a generous array of plum and currant fruits, freshly tanned leather and an appealing earthy-herbaceousness. The soft but gripping tannins linger well into the long finish. Drink now–2012. Score 91.

T-SELECTION, SHIRAZ, 2004: Developed for 18 months in French oak, and showing fine balance and structure. Full-bodied, deeply tannic and concentrated enough to be thought of as chewy, but under that, red currants, plums and red berries along with black pepper, rosemary, thyme and a very appealing hint of peppermint. Drink now–2012. Score 91.

T-SELECTION, CABERNET FRANC, 2005: This full-bodied wine reflects its 14 months in new French oak with spicy wood and mouth-coating tannins, both integrating nicely. A generous array of black fruits on first attack, those opening to reveal overlays of fresh Mediterranean herbs, and finally, on the long finish, espresso coffee, dark chocolate and the barest but tantalizing hint of crushed raspberries. Best 2009–2013. Score 92.

T-SELECTION, CABERNET FRANC, 2004: Dark purple towards black in color, lush and elegant with a rich array of ripe raspberry, plum and berry fruits, those matched nicely by herbal and chocolate aromas and flavors. Firm tannins, especially on the finish but with just the right levels of French oak influence and both balance and structure that bode well for the future. Drink now–2012. Score 91.

T-SELECTION, CABERNET FRANC, 2003: Oak-aged for 14 months in new French *barriques*. Smooth, rich and supple, with ripe plum, currant and berry fruits together with an array of mocha, tobacco and espresso coffee, all complemented nicely by a hint of vanilla-scented oak. Finishes tannic so give this one some time to show its elegance. Drink now–2012. Score 90.

T-SELECTION, SHIRAZ-GRENACHE, 2005: Dark garnet towards inky purple, full-bodied, with firm tannins integrating nicely. Reflecting its 14 months in French *barriques* with spicy cedar, this blend of 60% Shiraz and 40% Grenache shows concentrated purple plum, blackberry and citrus peel notes on a background of what at one moment seems to be sweet herbs and at the next turns to licorice. Drink now–2014. Score 92.

T-SELECTION, SHIRAZ-GRENACHE, 2004: Medium-dark garnet towards purple, full-bodied, with generous tannins well balanced by the influence of aging in French oak casks for 14 months. Distinctive, ripe and luxurious, with near-sweet plum, blueberry and citrus peel intertwined beautifully with spicy, herbal and pomegranate aromas and flavors. Drink now–2014. Score 92.

T-SELECTION, SHIRAZ-GRENACHE, 2003: Almost impenetrably purple towards black in color, this rich, big and juicy wine is absolutely loaded with blackberry and plum fruits, those set off nicely by hints of cloves, coffee, citrus peel and black pepper, all on super-soft tannins. Generous, long and mouth-coating, a harmonious wine that will develop nicely in the bottle. Drink now–2012. Score 91.

Pelter

PELTER, CABERNET SAUVIGNON-SHIRAZ, 2005: Deep ruby towards garnet, full-bodied, with a generous backbone of wood and tannins, those integrating nicely. On the nose and palate black currants, blackberries, raspberries and cherries, all supported by appealing earthy and herbal notes. Deep, long and smooth. Drink now–2012. Score 91.

PELTER, CABERNET SAUVIGNON-SHIRAZ, 2004: Aged in American oak for 18 months, this blend of 50% each of Cabernet Sauvignon and Shiraz shows a medium-dark garnet color, a strong acidic backbone and appealing spices and vanilla from the wood, none of which hold back layers of blackberry, cherry, herbal and earthy aromas and flavors. Good concentration, ripeness and smoothness lead to a long and generous finish. Drink now–2012. Score 91.

PELTER, CABERNET SAUVIGNON-SHIRAZ, 2003: Deep ruby towards garnet, medium-bodied, with good balance between soft, well-integrating tannins, vanilla and herbal overtones and appealing currant, blackberry and red plum fruits. Long, but with a hint of bitterness that creeps in on the finish. Drink now. Score 86.

PELTER, QUARTO, LIMITED EDITION, 2005: A rich Bordeaux blend of Cabernet Sauvignon, Merlot, Cabernet Franc and Petit Verdot. Deep royal-purple, full-bodied, with still-firm tannins just starting to settle down. Opens to show berry and cassis fruits on a lightly spicy background, with a long red fruit finish. Best 2009–2012. Score 90.

PELTER, TRIO, 2005: A blend this year of 80% Cabernet Sauvignon and 10% each Merlot and Cabernet Franc, this medium to full-bodied wine reflects its 14 months in oak with moderate smoky, almost musky, aromas and soft tannins integrating nicely. Opens to show a tempting array of cassis, berry and black cherry fruits, those leading to a long, lightly spicy finish. Drink now–2012. Score 91.

PELTER, TRIO, 2004: A blend of 90% Cabernet Sauvignon with 5% each of Merlot and Cabernet Franc. Deep ruby towards garnet, medium to full-bodied, showing a rich core of berry and currant flavors, those with herbal and cedar overlays, all on a background of supple tannins. Long and generous. Drink now–2012. Score 91.

PELTER, CABERNET SAUVIGNON-MERLOT-CABERNET FRANC, 2003: Medium to full-bodied, round and generous with silky soft tannins allowing us to focus on blueberry, plum, cola and light herbal-spicy notes, all leading to a long and satisfying finish. Drink now–2010. Score 90.

PELTER, CABERNET-MERLOT-CABERNET FRANC, 2002: Dark garnet, medium to full-bodied, and with an appealing berry-black cherry personality. Soft tannins, overall good balance, and a mouth-filling finish. Drink now. Score 86.

PELTER, CABERNET SAUVIGNON-SHIRAZ, 2003: Dark ruby, medium to full-bodied, with soft tannins integrating nicely. On the nose and palate berry, currant, plum and tobacco aromas, those opening in the glass to reveal hints of espresso and chocolate. Drink now–2009. Score 88.

PELTER, CABERNET SAUVIGNON-SHIRAZ, 2002: Medium-bodied, dark garnet in color, this oak-aged blend of 65% Cabernet Sauvignon and 35% Shiraz shows appealing herbal and leathery overlays, those nicely highlighting black currant, plum and spicy oak aromas and flavors. Drink now. Score 87.

PELTER, CHARDONNAY, 2006: Unoaked, this light to medium-bodied white is showing fine acidity to keep it lively. Light golden-straw in color and aromatic with crisp peach, citrus and flinty minerals. Drink now–2009. Score 89.

PELTER, CHARDONNAY, UNOAKED, 2005: Lovely! Fresh and lively, with generous but not at all overbearing acidity and showing appealing peach, apricot and tropical fruits on a background that tantalizes with hints of freshly cut grass. Drink now. Score 90.

PELTER, SAUVIGNON BLANC, 2006: Light damp-straw in color and unoaked, with fine balancing acidity to set off refreshing aromas and flavors of tropical fruits, white peaches, green apples, and, as in the previous release, a hint of celery. Drink now. Score 90.

PELTER, SAUVIGNON BLANC, 2005: Blended with 10% of Semillon, unoaked, as are all of Pelter's whites, this crisp and delicious wine offers up bright and generous aromas and flavors of guava, grapefruit, green apples and, lurking in the background, a nearly unconscious hint of celery. Drink now. Score 91.

PELTER, SAUVIGNON BLANC, 2004: Crisp, clean and straightforward, this light golden-straw wine is medium-bodied, with good balancing acidity allowing appealing citrus, melon and light grassiness to show through. Drink up. Score 87.

PELTER, SEMILLON, 2006: Fermented partly in stainless steel and partly in *barriques* for three months, this straw-colored wine opens with citrus peel and pear aromas and flavors, those going to melon and green apples, all with an appealing spicy overlay. Drink now–2009. Score 90.

PELTER, SEMILLON, 2003: Partly fermented in stainless steel, and partly in *barriques* for two months. Perhaps the very first truly successful local dry Semillon, with herbal and pepper aromas, and flavors of citrus, pears and green apples, all leading to a long and spicy finish. Drink now. Score 91.

PELTER, BLANC DE BLANC BRUT, N.V.: A sparkling wine made by the Champenoise method with Chardonnay grapes entirely from the 2003 vintage despite its categorization as non-vintage. Gentle yeast and hints of toasted white bread with sharp bubbles that go on and on. Fresh, aromatic, well focused and intense, with grapefruit and lime fruits backed up by hints of cloves, ginger and roasted nuts. Drink now–2010. Score 90.

Psagot ★★★

2005
Viogner
ויוניה

750 ml. Vol. 13.5

Located in the northern Jerusalem Mountains, overlooking Wadi Kelt (Nachal Prat), the winery was founded by Na'ama and Ya'akov Berg, who planted their first vineyards in 1998. The oak *barriques* used by the winery are stored in a cave containing ancient pressing facilities, which maintains 90% humidity and temperatures up to 18 degrees Celsius. Relying on Cabernet Sauvignon, Merlot, Cabernet Franc, Viognier and Chardonnay grapes, the winery's top-of-the-line wine is a Bordeaux blend named Edom. Regular varietal wines are produced in the Psagot series and there is also a Port-style wine. 2006 production was 45,000 bottles, and the anticipated release from the 2007 vintage is about 65,000 bottles.

Edom

EDOM, 2005: Deep garnet in color, this blend of Cabernet Sauvignon and Merlot opens with a rich vanilla and white chocolate nose, then settles down in the glass to reveal aromas and flavors of black cherries, plums and currants. Medium to full-bodied, with soft but mouth-coating tannins, a good touch of spicy cedarwood and on the finish an appealing earthy minerality. Drink now–2009. Score 88. K

EDOM, 2004: This blend of 75% Cabernet Sauvignon and 25% Merlot reflects its 14 months in *barriques* with firm but nicely integrating tannins, spicy and vanilla-rich oak and, on the nose and palate, blackberries, currants and an appealing hint of freshly turned earth. A solid effort, with a long berry-rich finish. Drink now. Score 87. K

Psagot

PSAGOT, CABERNET SAUVIGNON, 2005: Dark, almost impenetrable garnet with green and purple reflections, this medium to full-bodied wine reflects its 13 months in French *barriques* with a moderate touch of spicy oak and firm tannins that are in fine balance with blackberry, black cherry and cassis fruits. On the moderately long finish look for appealing hints of sweet herbs and tobacco. Drink now–2010. Score 88. K

PSAGOT, CABERNET SAUVIGNON, 2004: Generous oak and firm, country-style tannins open to reveal blackberry, black cherry and currant fruits along with hints of tobacco and herbs. Well balanced and moderately long. Drink now. Score 85. K

PSAGOT, MERLOT, 2005: Full-bodied with silky tannins, this smooth and round wine shows generous cherry and berry fruits and just the right hint of spicy oak. Drink now–2009. Score 88. K

PSAGOT, MERLOT, 2004: Aged in French and American oak barrels for 13 months, this dark garnet, oaky and distinctly plummy wine shows medium-body, soft tannins and a hint of spiciness. Drink now. Score 86. K

PSAGOT, ROSÉ, 2006: Light to medium-bodied, this rose-petal pink wine is made from Cabernet Sauvignon grapes blended with 7% of Viognier to round it out, and offers appealing red berry, strawberry and cassis fruits on a lively background. A refreshing quaffer. Drink now. Score 86. K

PSAGOT, CHARDONNAY, 2006: Light gold in color, opening with a slight medicinal aroma that quickly fades away to reveal a tempting but not at all typical Chardonnay. On the nose and palate primarily pear and kumquat fruits, those on a background of peach pits and bitter almonds. On the moderately long finish a hint of tropical fruits. Drink now. Score 86. K

PSAGOT, CHARDONNAY, RESERVE, 2004: Aged for ten months in 300 liter French oak barrels, this crisp and lively wine shows appealing aromas and flavors of citrus and tropical fruits on first attack, those yielding nicely to pear and vanilla on the finish. Drink now. Score 87. K

PSAGOT, VIOGNIER, 2006: Light to medium-bodied, opening with a floral nose and going on to aromas and flavors of summer fruits, green apples, and pears, all with a generous mineral note in the background. Drink now. Score 88. K

PSAGOT, VIOGNIER, 2005: Medium-bodied, crisply dry, with floral and mineral overlays showing peach, melon and pear fruits. Long and generous. Drink now. Score 87. K

Ra'anan **

Established by Ra'anan Margalit in 1994 on Moshav Ganei Yochanan in the Southern Plains, the winery utilizes Cabernet Sauvignon, Merlot and Chardonnay grapes from its own vineyards, located nearby, as at Karmei Yosef. Current production is about 8,000 bottles annually.

RA'ANAN, CABERNET SAUVIGNON, RESERVE, 2005: Dark garnet, medium-bodied, with gripping tannins, generous sweet cedarwood and black fruits. Drink now. Score 80.

RA'ANAN, CABERNET SAUVIGNON, RESERVE, 2004: With its chunky and somewhat coarse tannins, this is a country-style wine but one with charm, showing currant, plum and wild berry aromas and flavors. Drink up. Score 82.

RA'ANAN, CABERNET SAUVIGNON, RESERVE, 2003: A country-style wine. Medium-bodied, with chunky and firm tannins but those yielding in the glass to reveal smoky wood, black plums and cassis flavors. Drink up. Score 80.

RA'ANAN, MERLOT, 2005: Garnet to purple, medium-bodied, with soft, near-sweet tannins and hints of spices, licorice and earthy minerals supporting berry and cassis aromas and flavors. Drink now. Score 84.

RA'ANAN, MERLOT, 2003: Medium-bodied, with soft tannins and hints of spicy oak. Aromas and flavors of black cherries and wild berries. Drink up. Score 83.

RA'ANAN, MERLOT-CABERNET SAUVIGNON, 2003: Garnet towards purple in color, with soft tannins integrating nicely and on the nose and palate spicy cedar, berry and cassis fruits. Drink up. Score 84.

Ramim **

Founded in 1999 on Moshav Shachar in the Southern Plains by Nitzan Eliyahu and producing first wines from the 2000 harvest, the winery draws grapes from three self-owned vineyards, in Kfar Yuval and Safsufa, both on the Lebanese border, and on Moshav Shachar. Red varieties include Cabernet Sauvignon, Merlot, Sangiovese, Cabernet Franc, Syrah from France and Shiraz from Australia, as well as early plantings of Barbera, and Nebbiolo. White varieties include Zinfandel, Chardonnay, Gewurztraminer, Riesling, Semillon and Muscat.

The winery, which relies on Hungarian, French and American oak barrels, releases wines in four series: Special Reserve, Reserve, Ramim and Yuval. Production in 2002 was 22,000 bottles, in 2003, 55,000 bottles, and in 2005 and 2006 jumped to about 80,000 bottles. The wines have been kosher since the 2003 vintage.

Special Reserve

SPECIAL RESERVE, CABERNET SAUVIGNON, 2003: Dark garnet, medium to full-bodied, with firm tannins and generous spicy wood influences, those somewhat holding back the currant and blueberry fruits that are here. One dimensional and short. Drink now. Score 84. K

SPECIAL RESERVE, CABERNET SAUVIGNON, 2002: This blend of 85% Cabernet Sauvignon, 10% Merlot and 5% Cabernet Franc is best described as wood-driven, the smoky oak and tannins so dominant that they all but suppress whatever black fruits struggle to make themselves felt. Drink up. Score 83.

SPECIAL RESERVE, MERLOT, 2002: Dark, almost impenetrable garnet towards black, aged in barrels for a lengthy 29 months, now so dominated by wood that it is difficult to find either the tannins or the fruits here. Past its peak. Drink up. Score 79.

Reserve

RESERVE CABERNET SAUVIGNON, 2003: Deep ruby towards garnet, with firm but yielding tannins and a moderate hand with spicy oak. Opens to reveal forward berry, black cherry and cassis fruits on a background of Mediterranean herbs. Round and moderately long. Drink now. Score 85. K

RESERVE, CABERNET SAUVIGNON, 2002: Aged for 15 months in 400 liter Hungarian oak barrels, this deep cherry-red-toward-garnet wine shows solid tannins, those well balanced by vanilla and spiciness from the wood and a generous array of black currant and blackberry fruits. Drink up. Score 84.

RESERVE, MERLOT, 2003: Not complex but tasty and straightforward, with spicy cedarwood, blackberries and hints of tea, with the tannins rising on the finish. Drink now. Score 84. K

RESERVE, MERLOT, 2002: Aged for 14 months in new Hungarian oak barrels, the wine shows a few off aromas when first poured, but those fade quickly in the glass making place for aromas and flavors of plums and black cherries, vanilla and sweet cedar. Somewhat acidic. Drink up. Score 82.

Ramim

RAMIM, CABERNET SAUVIGNON, SHACHAR, 2005: A medium-bodied, modest wine with spicy wood and ripe and earthy plum, herb and sage notes, those fading somewhat on the finish. Drink now–2009. Score 85. K

RAMIM, CABERNET SAUVIGNON, SHACHAR, 2004: Dark garnet, medium to full-bodied, with chunky, somewhat country-style tannins, this oak-aged red shows generous spicy wood on first attack but that yielding to blackberry and currant fruits. Somewhat one dimensional and short. Drink now. Score 84. K

RAMIM, CABERNET SAUVIGNON, SHACHAR, 2003: Oak-aged in 165 liter Hungarian oak barrels, this medium-bodied red shows firm but well integrated tannins and an array of currant and plum fruits on a spicy background with appealing herbal hints coming in on the finish. Drink now. Score 85. K

RAMIM, CABERNET SAUVIGNON, SHACHAR, 2002: Oak-aged for 15 months and with the addition of 6% Merlot, this dark ruby-towards-garnet wine shows medium-body, soft near-sweet tannins and aromas and flavors of raspberries and cassis on a background of spices and smoky oak. Drink up. Score 83.

RAMIM, MERLOT, SHACHAR, 2005: Deep garnet, medium to full-bodied, with firm tannins, perhaps too-generous smoky oak, and only skimpy berry-cherry aromas and flavors Drink now. Score 82. K

RAMIM, MERLOT, SHACHAR, 2004: Garnet towards purple, medium-bodied with still firm and gripping tannins that seem not to want to settle down. Once past the tannins appealing berry, black cherry and cassis aromas and flavors. Drink up. Score 84. K

RAMIM, MERLOT, SHACHAR, 2003: Aged in small oak casks, with just-firm-enough tannins balanced nicely by vanilla and spices from the wood, the wine shows good spicy plum and black cherry fruits as well as hints of tobacco and cocoa on the long finish. Drink up. Score 83. K

RAMIM, SANGIOVESE, 2003: Aged in 165 liter Hungarian oak barrels, this deep garnet-toward-royal-purple, medium-bodied red has generous but soft and well-integrated tannins, but hardly any aromas, and flavors of plum, berry and cassis that fade too quickly. Drink up. Score 82. K

RAMIM, CABERNET FRANC, 2004: Deep ruby towards garnet, with gripping tannins settling in nicely, and with aromas and flavors of plums, wild berries and wood-inspired spices and vanilla. Drink now. Score 85. K

RAMIM, CABERNET FRANC, 2003: This dark ruby-toward-garnet, medium to full-bodied oak-aged red shows appealing black fruit, cassis and spicy flavors but hardly any aromas. Drink up. Score 84. K

RAMIM, BARBERA, PSAGOT, 2003: Aged in small barrels for one year, medium-bodied, with soft tannins nicely integrated with smoky oak and appealing currant, cherry, berry and earthy notes. Drink up. Score 84. K

RAMIM, CABERNET SAUVIGNON-MERLOT, 2005: Medium-bodied, with mineral and cedar notes complementing berry and cherry flavors. A pleasant quaffer. Drink now. Score 85. K

RAMIM, CABERNET SAUVIGNON-MERLOT, 2004: A deep garnet, medium-bodied blend of 55% Cabernet Sauvignon and 45% Merlot, aged in oak for about six months. Soft tannins and good balance with aromas and flavors of ripe berries and plums as well as hints of sweet cedar and vanilla. Drink now. Score 86. K

RAMIM, CABERNET SAUVIGNON-MERLOT, 2003: Aged in small oak barrels for six months, this blend of Cabernet Sauvignon, Merlot, Pinot Noir and Syrah (54%, 31%, 8% and 7% respectively) has dark purple color, medium body, soft tannins and berry, currant and plum fruits on a lightly earthy-vanilla background. Somewhat short on the finish. Drink up. Score 85. K

RAMIM, WHITE RIESLING, SHACHAR, 2004: Semi-dry, light and fruity, with generous acidity to keep it lively. Flavors of citrus and tropical fruits. Drink up. Score 83. K

RAMIM, RIESLING, SHACHAR, 2003: Light to medium-bodied, semi-dry, and with skimpy citrus and summer fruits. A bit flat. Drink up. Score 80. K

RAMIM, CHARDONNAY DESSERT WINE, 2003: Appealing in its youth but now falling apart and showing oily, earthy and herbal aromas. Drink up. Score 75. K

RAMIM, CHARDONNAY, DESSERT ICE, 2003: Showing dramatically better than at an earlier tasting, almost as if my palate was discerning two different wines. Medium-bodied, dark golden in color, with generously sweet kiwi, pineapple and citrus fruits backed up by gentle acidity. At its best served icy-cold. Drink now. Score 84. K

RAMIM, CABERNET FRANC, DESSERT ICE, 2003: Strawberry colored, light to medium-bodied, tutti-fruity in flavor, unabashedly sweet, without balancing acidity and with barnyard aromas and flavors that linger too long on the palate. Score 50. K

Yuval

YUVAL, CABERNET SAUVIGNON, 2003: Medium-bodied, with gripping tannins and generous wood but those yielding nicely to reveal currant, berry and herbal aromas and flavors. A rather standard but pleasant wine. Drink up. Score 83. K

YUVAL, MERLOT, 2003: Deep cherry towards garnet-red, medium-bodied with soft tannins, this is a smooth, well-balanced wine showing lightly spicy berry, cherry and plum flavors and aromas. Somewhat internationalized in style. Drink up. Score 85. K

YUVAL, CABERNET SAUVIGNON-MERLOT, 2003: Deep ruby towards garnet, medium-bodied, and with soft tannins and moderate oak. On the nose and palate currants, plums and berries leading to a medium-long finish. Drink up. Score 83. K

Ramot Naftali **

Founded on Moshav Ramot Naftali in the Upper Galilee in 2003 by vintner Yitzhak Cohen working with wine-maker Tal Pelter, this small winery owns vineyards planted with Cabernet Sauvignon, Merlot, Shiraz, Petit Verdot and Malbec. Production from the 2003 vintage was 1,300 bottles and 7,500 bottles will be released from the 2006 vintage.

RAMOT NAFTALI, CABERNET SAUVIGNON, 2006: Made entirely from Cabernet Sauvignon grapes, this garnet-towards-purple, medium to full-bodied red is showing soft tannins and generous berry, black cherry and currant fruits and, on the background, hints of spices and earthiness that linger nicely. Drink from release–2009. Tentative Score 86–88.

RAMOT NAFTALI, CABERNET SAUVIGNON, 2005: Deep purple, medium to full-bodied, with firm tannins yielding nicely. Richly aromatic and with fine balance between black cherry, currant and wild berry fruits, dusty herbs, and a hint of green olives. Well focused. Drink now–2010. Score 88.

RAMOT NAFTALI, CABERNET SAUVIGNON, RESERVE, 2004: Dark but somewhat cloudy garnet in color, with firm tannins that seem not to want to yield and generous oak influence that tends to hide the currant and berry fruits here. Drink now–2009. Score 84.

RAMOT NAFTALI, CABERNET SAUVIGNON, RESERVE, 2003: Dark ruby towards garnet, medium to full-bodied, reflecting 18 months in French oak with generous wood but in good balance with tannins and fruit. On first attack, tobacco and espresso, those yielding to aromas of ripe berries and currants. Drink now–2009. Score 87.

RAMOT NAFTALI, MERLOT, 2006: Dark garnet with orange reflections, medium to full-bodied, with gentle wood influences and soft tannins nicely balanced with aromas and flavors of dark plums and currants, grilled herbs and toasty notes. Drink from release–2009. Tentative Score 84–86.

RAMOT NAFTALI, BARBERA, 2006: Dark cherry-red, medium-bodied, with soft tannins and gentle wood. On the nose and palate red berries, cherries and hints of spices, vanilla and minerals leading to a mouth-filling fruity finish. Drink from release–2009. Tentative Score 85–87.

RAMOT NAFTALI, DUET, 2005: This lightly oak-aged blend of Merlot and Cabernet Sauvignon (65% and 35% respectively) is medium-bodied, with soft tannins and hints of sweet cedarwood highlighting youthful berry and black cherry fruits. Not complex but very appealing. Drink now. Score 86.

Recanati ★★★★

Established in 2000, this modern winery located in the Hefer Valley in the north part of the Sharon region relies on grapes from their own as well as contract vineyards, primarily in the Upper Galilee. Under the supervision of California-trained winemaker Lewis Pasco, the winery currently produces wines in several series: the top-of-the-line Special Reserve wines, which are often blends of Cabernet Sauvignon and Merlot; and two varietal series, Reserve and Recanati, which now include Cabernet Sauvignon, Merlot, Syrah, Petite Sirah, Chardonnay and most recently Sauvignon Blanc. The winery also has a popularly priced series named Yasmine. Production in 2002 was 230,000 bottles, in 2003, 500,000 and since then about 700,000 annually.

Special Reserve

SPECIAL RESERVE, 2006: Already showing the potential for being the darkest and most strikingly full-bodied release in this series. Generous tannins still making themselves felt but yielding to show currant, blackberry and kirsch aromas and flavors on a tasty oak background. Best from 2009. Tentative Score 89–91. K

SPECIAL RESERVE, 2005: Deep royal-purple, full-bodied, with firm, still rough-edged tannins but those merely needing time to integrate and show the wine's fine balance and structure. A big, rich and bold wine, with concentrated layers of currant, blackberry, anise and cedary oak flavors. Drink from release–2012. Tentative Score 90–92. K

SPECIAL RESERVE, 2004: A blend of 92% Cabernet Sauvignon and 8% Merlot, with generous but not exaggerated toasty oak and soft tannins, those integrating nicely and opening to reveal a rich array of currant, blackberry and black cherry fruits, with gentle overlays of mint and chocolate. As the wine develops look for a hint of cigar tobacco on the long finish. Drink now–2012. Score 93. K

SPECIAL RESERVE, 2003: This deep, broad, gently tannic blend of 72% Cabernet Sauvignon and 28% Merlot combines Cabernet currants, cassis and spicy-herbal overtones with typical Merlot softness. Good balance between wood, tannins and fruits, and a long finish. Drink now–2012. Score 92. K

SPECIAL RESERVE, 2001: As in its youth, deep garnet towards royal-purple, full-bodied, with fine balance between well-integrated soft tannins, spicy and mocha-rich oak, and currant, blackberry and ripe red plum fruits. Some variation between bottles but that primarily in fruit intensity. Drink now. Score 90. K

SPECIAL RESERVE, 2000: Aged 18 months in new French oak, this full-bodied mature blend of 50% each of Cabernet Sauvignon and Merlot now shows soft tannins in good balance between fruits and smoky oak. On the nose and palate tempting currants, black cherries and vanilla and on the long finish herbal, earthy and leathery notes. Not for further cellaring and with a good deal of variation between bottles. Drink up. Score 90. K

Reserve

RESERVE, CABERNET SAUVIGNON, 2006: Still in embryonic form but already showing dark, youthful purple in color, with generous near-sweet tannins and forward currant, spice and mocha notes. Juicy and long. Drink from release–2010. Tentative Score 87–89. K

RESERVE, CABERNET SAUVIGNON, 2005: Dark and intense but with subtlety and finesse. Soft tannins, a gentle hand with the toasty oak and generous red currant, black cherry and berry fruits, those with appealing hints of mocha. A long and firmly tannic finish. Drink from release–2011. Tentative Score 89–91. K

RESERVE, CABERNET SAUVIGNON, 2004: Dark garnet with orange and purple reflections, this full-bodied wine's tannins are yielding and integrating nicely. Shows generous but well-balanced spicy wood, opening to reveal currant, plum and blackberry fruits, those well supported by light hints of herbs and cedarwood. Drink now–2010. Score 91. K

RESERVE, CABERNET SAUVIGNON, 2003: Super-dark garnet in color, ripe and rich, now showing full-bodied with soft tannins integrating nicely. On the nose and palate an appealing array of currant and berry fruits, those complemented by hints of Oriental spices and toasty oak. Generous. Drink now–2010. Score 90. K

RESERVE, CABERNET SAUVIGNON, 2002: Dark garnet towards royal-purple, full-bodied, with still-firm tannins that yields in the glass to show generous wood, currants, plums and spicy-herbal aromas and flavors. Somehow the elements fail to come together fully. Drink up. Score 87. K

RESERVE, CABERNET SAUVIGNON, 2001: Dark garnet in color, with a bit of clearing around the rim, this wine is as comfortably tannic as it was in its youth and still showing an array of currant, plum and berry fruits. Still elegant but now with an earthy-mineral edge creeping in. Drink up. Score 90. K

RESERVE, MERLOT, 2006: Full-bodied, firm in texture, with the tannins just starting to soften but already showing forward blackberry and plum fruits and developing an appealing mocha hint. Chewy, round and long. Best 2009–2012. Tentative Score 89–91. K

RESERVE, MERLOT, 2005: Smooth, round and generous, rich and spicy, with a fine core of raspberry, cherry and creamy oak backed up by hints of minty chocolate that linger nicely. Good balance between fresh acidity, wood and fruits, and a very long finish. Drink from release–2010. Tentative Score 89–91. K

RESERVE, MERLOT, 2004: Dark garnet, medium to full-bodied, with firm tannins and near-sweet oak integrating well. On the nose and palate black cherries, berries and currants on a tantalizing earthy-herbal background. On the long finish hints of chocolate. Drink now–2010. Score 90. K

RESERVE, MERLOT, 2003: Dark garnet in color, with firm tannins giving a solid backbone. Sweet oak makes itself felt from first attack to the long finish, with layers of currant, black cherry, mocha and chocolate. A concentrated and graceful wine. Drink now–2009. Score 90. K

RESERVE, MERLOT, 2002: Medium-dark garnet, medium to full-bodied, with well-integrated tannins. Showing somewhat heavier wood and herbs than in the past but continuing to show appealing berry, black cherry and bittersweet chocolate. Drink now. Score 88. K

RESERVE, MERLOT, 2001: Dark garnet with a first hint of browning, medium to full-bodied, with soft tannins now integrated. Continuing to show blackberry, currant and chocolate aromas and flavors, and the once gentle herbal aromas and flavors are rising along with first hints of oxidation. Drink up. Score 89. K

RESERVE, SHIRAZ, 2006: Garnet towards royal-purple in color, with still chewy tannins but those surrounding spicy wood and a generous array of blackberry, black cherry, roasted meat and green olive aromas and flavors. Drink from release–2009. Tentative Score 87–89. K

RESERVE, SHIRAZ, 2005: Dark royal-purple in color, with well-focused tannins and moderate spicy wood in fine balance with black cherry, wild berry and cassis fruits, those with just a hint of smoked meat in the background. At this stage the still-firm tannins hold the wine back a bit. Drink from release–2010. Score 89. K

RESERVE, SHIRAZ, 2004: Dark cherry-red towards garnet, supple and round, with black cherry, herbal and beefy aromas and flavors, those coming together with firm tannins and sweet cedarwood. On the long tannic finish, toasted bread and mocha. Drink now–2009. Score 89. K

RESERVE, CABERNET FRANC, 2004: Aromatic, medium to full-bodied, with soft tannins integrating nicely. Showing an appealing array of currant, plums and wild berries, those complemented by light smoky wood, tobacco and refreshing acidity. Drink now–2009. Score 90. K

RESERVE, PETITE SIRAH-ZINFANDEL, 2006: A blend of 88% Petite Sirah and 12% Zinfandel. Youthful royal-purple, its soft, mouth-coating tannins integrating nicely and taking on smoky and dusty wood. Opens to reveal blueberry, pomegranate, mocha and sage notes. Tannic and firm but elegant. Best 2009–2012. Tentative Score 89–91. K

RESERVE, PETITE SIRAH-ZINFANDEL, 2005: Dark and concentrated, its firm, crisp tannins integrating nicely with vanilla-rich spicy oak. On the nose and palate blackberry, raspberry and black cherry fruits, those coming together nicely with hints of minerals and an appealing light earthy note. Long and generous. Drink now–2011. Score 90. K

RESERVE, PETITE SIRAH-ZINFANDEL, 2004: Aged in American oak, this dark garnet blend of 70% Petite Syrah and 30% Zinfandel is packed with ripe blueberry, blackberry, plum, pepper, licorice and mineral aromas and flavors. Generous but not exaggerated oak and tannins, those in fine balance with the fruits. Drink now–2010. Score 90. K

RESERVE, PETITE SIRAH-ZINFANDEL, 2003: A dark garnet blend of 80% Petite Syrah and 20% Zinfandel, aged in American oak. Tannic, concentrated, full-bodied and with expressive spicy plum and black cherry fruits, those matched nicely by spicy, earthy overlays and a light hint of asphalt on the finish. Drink now. Score 89. K

RESERVE, CHARDONNAY, 2003: Deeply golden, smooth and supple, with a pleasant earthy accent to pineapple, hazelnut and mineral notes, this stylish wine offers up appealing oak seasoning, a light buttery note and a round and mouth-filling finish. Drink now. Score 89. K

RESERVE, CHARDONNAY, 2002: Oak-aged for about nine months, still zesty and with a golden color, the wine shows pear and hazelnut, as well as generous buttery-smoky oak aromas and flavors on the finish. Drink up. Score 88. K

Recanati

RECANATI, CABERNET SAUVIGNON, 2005: Dark garnet with orange and purple reflections, this medium to full-bodied wine shows soft tannins and Mediterranean herbs balanced nicely by generous currant, plum and berry. Rich, round and soft. Drink now–2009. Score 88. K

RECANATI, CABERNET SAUVIGNON, 2004: Deep garnet, medium to full-bodied, with near-sweet tannins and generous currant and berry fruits, those backed up by smoky wood and earthiness. Drink now. Score 87. K

RECANATI, CABERNET SAUVIGNON, 2003: Medium-bodied, with soft tannins and appealing berry, currant and plum fruits, all with a hint of spice on the background. Drink now. Score 85. K

RECANATI, CABERNET SAUVIGNON, 2002: Soft tannins, inviting currant and plum flavors, with hints of spices and herbs. This medium to full-bodied wine is just a bit past its peak. Drink up. Score 85. K

RECANATI, MERLOT, 2005: Garnet-red, medium to full-bodied, with generous soft tannins nicely balanced by hints of cedarwood. Firm but lively, with appealing aromas and flavors of red berries, spices and tobacco that linger nicely. Drink now. Score 87. K

RECANATI, MERLOT, 2004: Medium-bodied, soft but concentrated, with a core of currant, blackberry and cherry fruits matched nicely by cedar and anise. Well balanced and with a moderately long finish on which hints of exotic spices make themselves felt. Drink now. Score 88. K

RECANATI, MERLOT, 2003: Smooth, ripe and fruity, with cherry, berry, earthy and herbal aromas and flavors. Young and vibrant, with good balance between tannins and fruits. Drink now. Score 86. K

RECANATI, MERLOT, 2002: Medium-bodied, somewhat on the earthy side, with wild berry and juniper accents along with sweet cedar and spices. Round but a bit tight. Drink up. Score 85. K

RECANATI, SHIRAZ, 2005: Ripe, rich, but more chewy than past releases, this dark garnet-towards-royal-purple wine opens with flowers and crushed fruits on the nose along with aromas and flavors of cherries, blackberries, and freshly ground coffee on first attack, all yielding nicely to spices and sweet cedarwood. Drink now–2011. Score 90. K

RECANATI, SHIRAZ, 2004: Dark royal-purple, medium to full-bodied, with a gentle spicy layer highlighting sweet notes and hints of toast from the American and French barrels in which it developed. Showing plum, blackberry and cherry fruits, those matched nicely by suggestions of thyme and a light meatiness that develops on the lingering finish. Drink now–2010. Score 89. K

RECANATI, SHIRAZ, 2003: This deep ruby-towards-purple, medium-bodied wine shows good balance between near-sweet tannins, wood and appealing aromas and flavors of jammy berry fruits, those with spicy, peppery and licorice overtones. Drink now–2009. Score 89. K

RECANATI, BARBERA, 2006: Aromas and flavors of crushed berries, black cherries and a hint of chocolate liqueur, all supported nicely by lightly toasted oak and velvety tannins. Drink from release. Tentative Score 87–89. K

RECANATI, BARBERA, 2005: Medium-bodied, with good acidity and a light hand with the wood, this wine is generously aromatic and showing aromas and flavors that open with cherry and berry fruits, those yielding to plums, lemon rind and, on the generous finish, an appealing hint of chocolate. Drink now–2009. Score 88. K

RECANATI, BARBERA, 2004: Youthful royal-purple, medium to full-bodied, with fine balance between gently spicy oak, acidity and velvety smooth tannins. Aromas and flavors of blueberries, blackberries, black cherries, plums and earthy minerals along with a hint of white truffles on the long finish. Drink now–2009. Score 90. K

RECANATI, BARBERA, 2003: Fermented in stainless steel and then transferred to *barriques* for nine months, this garnet-towards-deep royal-purple, medium-bodied round wine shows soft tannins nicely integrated with lightly spicy oak, acidity and fruits. On the nose and palate vanilla, plums, cherries and currants. Drink now. Score 88. K

RECANATI, ROSÉ, 2006: This first rosé release of the winery is a blend of 96% Cabernet Franc and 4% Barbera. Rose-petal pink bordering on cherry-red in color, showing fresh berry and strawberry fruits and a touch of crisp minerality. Drink now. Score 87. K

RECANATI, CHARDONNAY, 2006: Lightly oaked, showing simultaneously crisp and creamy, with good balance between wood, acidity and fruits. On the nose and palate citrus, apricots and cinnamon-spiced apples, all lingering nicely. Drink now–2009. Score 89. K

RECANATI, CHARDONNAY, 2005: Following nine months in new and used French, Hungarian and American oak, the wine shows light golden-straw color, and after opening in the glass reveals fresh, crisp aromas of citrus, melon and apples, those backed up by hints of smoked meat and minerality. Drink now. Score 87. K

RECANATI, CHARDONNAY, 2004: Golden-straw in color, medium-bodied, with aromas and flavors of tropical fruits, melon and citrus. Lively, complex, round and long with a light mineral-yeasty finish. Drink now. Score 87. K

RECANATI, SAUVIGNON BLANC, 2006: Light straw in color, this unoaked white shows crisp, fresh acidity that highlights citrus, honeydew, melon and light grassy aromas and flavors. Drink up. Score 87. K

RECANATI, SAUVIGNON BLANC, 2005: A lively straw in color, this unoaked white shows medium body and, on the nose and palate, crisp citrus and summer fruits. Not complex but clean, crisp and refreshing. Drink up. Score 88. K

RECANATI, SAUVIGNON BLANC, 2004: Light straw-colored, medium-bodied, not specially aromatic but with very appealing summer fruits on a grassy, earthy background. Drink up. Score 87. K

Yasmine

YASMINE, RED, 2006: As in the past, a pot pourri of grapes that were exposed to oak chips. Shows dark ruby, light body, soft tannins, a bit too-generous acidity and simple black fruits. Drink now. Score 83. K

YASMINE, RED, 2005: A somewhat hodge podge blend of Cabernet Sauvignon, Merlot, Shiraz and Pinot Noir treated to oak chips while developing. Ruby towards purple, light to medium-bodied, with silky soft tannins and a basically berry-cherry and herbal-chocolate personality. Lacking complexity but a soft, smooth quaffer. Drink up. Score 85. K

YASMIN, WHITE, 2006: A light to medium-bodied blend of Emerald Riesling, French Colombard and Sauvignon Blanc. Not complex but easy to drink with crisp and clean citrus and tropical fruits. Drink up. Score 84. K

YASMIN, WHITE, 2005: Light golden-straw in color, light to medium-bodied, with grapefruit and nectarine aromas and flavors. A good summertime quaffer. Drink up. Score 85. K

Red Poetry **

Established in 2001 by Dubi Tal on Havat Tal on the western slopes of the Judean Mountains, the winery has its own vineyards with Cabernet Sauvignon, Merlot, Cabernet Franc, Petit Verdot, Shiraz, Petite Sirah, Sangiovese, Riesling and Gewurztraminer grapes. The winery releases wines in two series, Reserve and Red Poetry. Current production is 4,500 bottles annually.

Reserve

RESERVE, CABERNET SAUVIGNON, 2004: Dark royal-purple, medium-bodied, with soft tannins. Opens with barnyard aromas but those blow off quickly to reveal appealing blackberry and black cherry fruits. Somewhat short and one dimensional. Drink now. Score 84.

RESERVE, CABERNET SAUVIGNON, 2003: Medium to dark garnet, medium-bodied, with generous spicy oak and still-firm tannins reflecting 20 months in *barriques*. On the nose and palate black currants and plums matched by generous spices and a light herbal finish. Drink now. Score 84.

RESERVE, CABERNET SAUVIGNON, 2002: Dark garnet towards royal-purple, medium-bodied, with firm tannins and generous smoky oak that yield slowly to reveal straightforward but appealing currant, berry and spicy aromas and flavors. Drink up. Score 84.

Red Poetry

RED POETRY, CABERNET SAUVIGNON, 2003: Ruby towards royal-purple, medium-bodied, with soft, near-sweet tannins and generous oak opening to show currant, berry and cherry fruits on a lightly spicy background. Drink now. Score 85.

RED POETRY, CABERNET SAUVIGNON, 2002: Dark garnet, medium-bodied, with near-sweet ripe fruits and with an aroma of decaying mushrooms. Drink up. Score 75.

RED POETRY, MERLOT, 2004: Dusty garnet-red, medium-bodied with rather gripping tannins, this oak-aged wine shows minimal red fruits. Lacking balance and meant for early drinking. Drink now. Score 80.

RED POETRY, MERLOT, 2003: Blended with 10% of Cabernet Franc, garnet towards brick-red, with slight browning at the edges, and black fruits almost hidden by far too-generous acidity. Drink up. Score 72.

RED POETRY, CARIGNAN, ORCA SELECTION, 2004: Dark garnet with orange reflections, a medium to full-bodied blend of 85% Carignan, 10% Merlot and 5% Cabernet Franc. Drying tannins and generous spicy wood in good balance with black fruits, chocolate and licorice. Drink now–2010. Score 88.

RED POETRY, SHIRAZ-CABERNET SAUVIGNON, 2003: Medium to full-bodied, with soft, mouth-coating tannins, the wine reflects its 14 months in *barriques* with hints of smoky oak and vanilla. Opens to reveal plum and blackberry fruits on a generously spicy and lightly leathery background. Drink now–2009. Score 85.

RED POETRY, SHIRAZ-CABERNET SAUVIGNON, 2002: Medium-bodied, with soft, nicely integrating tannins set off well by hints of spicy oak. On the nose and palate blackberry, currant and plum fruits. Drink up. Score 83.

RED POETRY, CABERNET FRANC-MERLOT, SHARONA, 2003: This blend of 60% Cabernet Franc and 40% Merlot is medium-bodied, with chunky, country-style tannins and an overly generous dose of smoky wood. A few spicy berry and currant fruits but short and one dimensional. Drink up. Score 80.

RED POETRY, EHRLICH, 2004: Dark garnet, a medium to full-bodied blend of 40% each Merlot and Shiraz and 10% each of Cabernet Sauvignon and Petite Sirah. Soft tannins integrating nicely with spicy wood and natural acidity. On the nose and palate berries, black cherries, purple plums and hints of cola and leather, all leading to a long finish. Drink now–2009. Score 87.

RED POETRY, MERLOT-SHIRAZ-CABERNET SAUVIGNON, EHRLICH, 2003: This oak-aged blend of the three named grapes (40%, 40% and 20% respectively) is garnet towards purple in color, with spicy and lightly earthy blackberry and plum fruits that linger nicely. Drink now–2009. Score 85.

RED POETRY, CHARDONNAY, 2005: Light golden-straw in color, this light to medium-bodied wine shows only the skimpiest of citrus fruits and an overabundance of acidity. Drink up. Score 79.

RED POETRY, RHINE RIESLING, 2004: Categorized as dry but on the palate half-dry, with perhaps too-generous acidity. Lacking varietal traits but with some clean summer fruits and citrus. An acceptable quaffer. Drink up. Score 83.

Rosh Pina *

Set near the village of Rosh Pina in the Galilee, this small winery was founded by Ya'akov Blum in 2001 and released its first wines in 2002. It draws on grapes from the Galilee, those including Cabernet Sauvignon, Shiraz and Carignan. No wines were released from the 2005 vintage due to damages done to the winery during the 2006 war between Israel and the Hezbollah forces of Lebanon. The winery is currently releasing about 4,000 bottles annually.

ROSH PINA, CABERNET SAUVIGNON, 2004: Medium-bodied, dark brick-red in color, with chunky tannins, this is a simple country-style wine with a few raspberry and plum flavors. Drink up. Score 78.

ROSH PINA, CABERNET SAUVIGNON, 2003: Medium-bodied, with somewhat coarse tannins, but beyond that appealing currant and berry flavors and aromas. Drink up. Score 79.

ROSH PINA, MERLOT, 2004: Garnet-red, medium-bodied, with a few cherry and wild berry fruits but those overpowered by earthy, musty aromas and flavors. Drink up. Score 74.

ROSH PINA, MERLOT, 2003: Coarse enough to be thought of as vulgar, with chunky tannins, far too much acidity and earthy and only bare hints of wild berry fruits. Drink up. Score 70.

ROSH PINA, SHIRAZ, 2003: Dark, but not fully clear garnet in color, with chunky country-style tannins and a bit of coarseness. On the nose and palate black cherry and cassis fruits, those with a somewhat exaggerated earthy character. Drink up. Score 76.

ROSH PINA, CARIGNAN, TEVA, 2004: A few raspberry fruits, but those struggling to be felt against too-dominant horsy, leathery and herbal aromas and flavors. Score 70.

ROSH PINA, CABERNET SAUVIGNON-MERLOT, 2004: Opens with powerful aromas of tobacco, stingy black fruits and an oddly sour cedarwood note and finishes with a distinct barnyard stink. Score 65.

ROSH PINA, CABERNET SAUVIGNON-SHIRAZ, 2003: This blend of 60% Cabernet and 40% Shiraz is light ruby towards brick-red, light to medium-bodied, far too acidic and with chunky country-style tannins. A few berry and black cherry fruits. Drink up. Score 75.

ROSH PINA, ROSÉ, 2006: This off-dry blend of Shiraz and Muscat is dull pale pink in color, with aromas and flavors that at one moment call to mind tutti-frutti chewing gum and at another tinned fruit salad. Drink up. Score 70.

ROSH PINA, CARIGNAN, PNINA DESSERT WINE, 2003: Burnished copper in color, as sweet as treacle, with far too little acidity to make it lively and fruits that are best described as muddy. Score 60.

Rota ***

Founded by Erez Rota on the Negev Heights, this artisanal winery released its first wines in 2002. The winery and its beautifully planted and tended vineyards are set on an isolated farm, surrounded by magnificent desert mountains. Grapes under cultivation are Cabernet Sauvignon, Merlot, Shiraz and Muscat of Alexandria. In addition, the winery also receives grapes from the Ella Valley.

First releases in 2002 were of 1,000 bottles. Production from the 2006 vintage was of 3,000 bottles and plans for the 2007 harvest are for 12,000 bottles.

ROTA, CABERNET SAUVIGNON, 2004: Blended with 5% Merlot, this medium to full-bodied wine is showing soft tannins and gentle spicy wood integrating nicely, with black currant and blueberry fruits, those complemented by hints of black pepper, chocolate and mint. Drink now–2010. Score 90.

ROTA, CABERNET SAUVIGNON, SHUA, 2003: Deep garnet towards purple, medium-bodied, with near-sweet tannins and clean aromas and flavors of plums, black cherries and cassis. Simple but appealing. Drink now. Score 84.

ROTA, MERLOT, 2006: Deep garnet, medium to full-bodied, with firm tannins and spicy French oak integrating nicely. Opens on the palate to show abundant red currant and raspberry fruits, those matched by hints of white pepper and green olives. Generous and long. Drink from release–2011. Tentative Score 87–89.

ROTA, MERLOT, 2004: Dark garnet in color with orange and green reflections, this deeply extracted wine shows mouth-coating tannins and a judicious hand with spicy oak. Opens with a bit of bottle stink but that passes quickly to reveal a deeply aromatic wine with an array of red and black berries, currants, Oriental spices and chocolate, all lingering comfortably on a long, fruity finish. Drink now–2011. Score 89.

ROTA, MERLOT, SHUA, 2003: Dark cherry-red, medium-bodied but somewhat flabby with only skimpy berry fruits making themselves felt. Drink up. Score 82.

ROTA, CABERNET SAUVIGNON-MERLOT, 2006: Deeply aromatic, this dark garnet, medium to full-bodied wine is showing soft, mouth-coating tannins and a moderate hand with spicy oak. On the nose and palate berry, black cherry and cassis fruits, those complemented by hints of pepper, anise and light earthiness. Drink from release–2011. Tentative Score 87–89.

ROTA, CABERNET SAUVIGNON-MERLOT, 2003: Unoaked, medium-bodied and somewhat on the simple side, but with just enough plum, black cherry and herbal aromas and flavors to hold interest. Drink up. Score 82.

ROTA, CABERNET-MERLOT, 2002: With clean aromas and flavors of berries and cherries, this soft, fresh and only moderately tannic wine is pleasant, although lacking complexity. Drink up. Score 83.

Ruth **

Founded by Tal Ma'or and located in Kfar Ruth, adjoining the city of Modi'in, this family-owned winery produced several hundred bottles of wine from the 2002 vintage and current production is 4,000 bottles annually. Grapes, including Cabernet Sauvignon, Merlot and Shiraz are harvested from vineyards on the central plain and in the hills of Jerusalem.

Reserve

RESERVE, CABERNET SAUVIGNON, 2003: Medium-bodied, with chunky, country-style tannins opening slowly to show skimpy black currant and berry fruits. Drink now. Score 82. K

RESERVE, CABERNET SAUVIGNON, 2002: Medium to full-bodied, with generous oak and firm tannins that tend to hide the black fruits and spices that are here. Drink now. Score 82. K

RESERVE, MERLOT, 2003: Medium-bodied, with acidity so puckering that you cannot tell where the sour sensations stop and the citrus peel and sour cherry flavors start. Lacking balance or charm. Drink up. Score 75. K

Ruth

RUTH, CABERNET SAUVIGNON, 2005: Medium-bodied, with soft tannins integrating nicely. Showing appealing blackberry and grape flavors supported nicely by bramble, spice and tobacco notes. Drink now–2009. Score 86. K

RUTH, CABERNET SAUVIGNON, 2004: This dark garnet, medium-bodied wine offers up straightforward cherry, berry and raspberry fruits with hints of spices, licorice and roasted herbs that run throughout. Drink now. Score 86. K

RUTH, CABERNET SAUVIGNON, 2003: Dark ruby towards garnet, medium-bodied, with soft tannins, hints of smoky oak, and berry, cherry and currant fruits that open nicely on the palate. Not complex but generous and satisfying. Drink now. Score 86. K

RUTH, CABERNET SAUVIGNON, 2002: Deep garnet, medium to full-bodied, with soft, well-integrated tannins and generous currant, berry and cherry fruits. Good balance between smoky wood, fruits and a hint of tobacco on the finish. Drink now. Score 87. K

RUTH, MERLOT, 2004: Medium-bodied with chunky tannins, but those well balanced by smoky wood and appealing aromas and flavors of black fruits. Lacking complexity but appealing. Drink now. Score 84. K

RUTH, MERLOT, 2003: A somewhat dusty garnet-red in color, with chunky country-style tannins, this medium-bodied red shows muted aromas and flavors of berries and black cherries. Drink up. Score 84. K

RUTH, CABERNET SAUVIGNON-MERLOT, 2005: Deep garnet towards royal-purple, medium-bodied, with soft tannins integrating nicely and showing appealing currant, berry and spicy aromas and flavors. Drink now. Score 86. K

RUTH, CABERNET SAUVIGNON-MERLOT, 2004: Medium-dark garnet in color, with soft tannins and medium-body. On the nose and palate clean black currant and berry aromas as well as a hint of spices. Drink now. Score 85. K

RUTH, MERLOT-SHIRAZ, 2004: Deep garnet in color, with soft tannins and gentle spicy wood in fine balance with plum, currant and berry fruits, those complemented nicely by hints of eucalyptus and freshly turned earth. Drink now–2009. Score 87. K

RUTH, MERLOT-SHIRAZ, 2003: Dark royal-purple, with generous acidity but scarcely any tannins, this medium-bodied blend of equal parts Merlot and Shiraz was developed in oak for ten months. Appealing aromas and flavors of plums and black berries and, starting on mid-palate, an earthy-herbal overlay. Serve lightly chilled. Drink now. Score 85. K

Salomon ✶✶

Located on Moshav Amikam in the Ramot Menashe forest not far from Zichron Ya'akov, this winery was founded in 1997 by Itamar Salomon. For several years the winery made only small quantities of wine for home consumption, and the first commercial release was from the 2002 vintage. Grapes are currently drawn from the Golan Heights but the winery is planting its own vineyards with Cabernet Sauvignon, Merlot, Cabernet Franc and Shiraz grapes in the Upper Galilee. Production was about 2,500 bottles in 2004 and 5,000 in 2005 and 2006.

SALOMON, CABERNET SAUVIGNON, 2005: Medium-bodied with soft, mouth-coating tannins. Opening to reveal appealing cherry, plum and sandalwood aromas and flavors. Slightly rustic on the finish. Drink now. Score 84.

SALOMON, CABERNET SAUVIGNON, 2004: Medium-bodied, with coarse tannins that seem not to want to settle down and dominating whatever black fruits are lying underneath. Drink now. Score 82.

SALOMON, CABERNET SAUVIGNON, 2003: Dark garnet but not fully clear, and medium-bodied with chunky, somewhat coarse tannins, but under those generous plum and black cherry fruits. Lacking complexity, but pleasant. Drink now. Score 84.

SALOMON, MERLOT, 2005: Medium-bodied, soft and round, with black cherry, grape and light hints of herbs and cocoa. Look for a hint of toasted bread on the finish. Drink now–2009. Score 85.

SALOMON, MERLOT, 2004: Deep garnet, medium-bodied, with soft tannins and generous berry, cherry and cassis fruits. Not complex but appealing. Drink now. Score 84.

SALOMON, MERLOT, 2003: Somewhat over-extracted and showing hyper-ripe, almost sweet fruits, and fairly deep tannins for a Merlot. Simple but pleasant. Drink now. Score 84.

SALOMON, MERLOT-CABERNET SAUVIGNON 2003: Dark ruby towards garnet, medium-bodied, with soft tannins and appealing berry and plum aromas, those with a tempting spicy overlay. Drink now. Score 85.

Saslove ✶✶✶✶

Established by Barry Saslove in 1998 on Kibbutz Eyal in the Sharon region, this boutique winery has vineyards in the Upper Galilee currently planted with Cabernet Sauvignon, Merlot, Syrah, and Sauvignon Blanc grapes, and plans to grow Cabernet Franc, Petit Verdot, and Gewurztraminer grapes in the future. The winery recently opened a new facility primarily for receiving and fermenting grapes in the Upper Galilee, not far from its vineyards. The barrel room and visitor's center remain on Kibbutz Eyal.

Current production of red wines is in three series: Reserved, Adom and Aviv. The winery occasionally produces white wines as well. Under the label "K by Saslove", the winery released kosher wines from the 2003 and 2004 vintages, but that line has been discontinued. Production has grown steadily, from 35,000 bottles in 2002 to about 75,000 bottles from the 2006 vintage.

Reserved

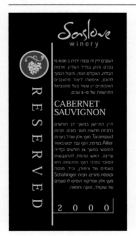

RESERVED, CABERNET SAUVIGNON, 2005: Super-dark garnet, with spicy and dusty wood in fine balance with still-firm tannins, acidity and fruits. On the nose and palate an array of currant, blackberry, and bitter orange peel, those backed up nicely by light earthy, asphalt and licorice hints, all leading to a long finish. Drink from release–2011. Tentative Score 90–92.

RESERVED, CABERNET SAUVIGNON, 2004: Reflecting 27 months in French oak with generous sweet-and-spicy oak, that well balanced by soft, mouth-coating tannins, acidity and fruits. Opens with currants and berries, those yielding to earthy, herbal and tobacco notes and, on the long finish, a hint of mint. Round, generous and long. Drink now–2013. Score 92.

RESERVED, CABERNET SAUVIGNON, 2003: This oak-aged blend of 88% Cabernet Sauvignon and 12% Merlot is dark garnet and medium to full-bodied. Showing generous sweet-and-spicy wood and tannins in fine balance with currant, black cherry and blackberry fruits and a complex array of herbs and spices. On the long finish a hint of raspberry liqueur. An elegant wine. Drink now–2009. Score 91.

RESERVED, CABERNET SAUVIGNON, 2002: Taking on a nose of sweet herbs, this dark garnet, full-bodied mature wine continues to show currant, vanilla and herbal aromas and flavors that come together nicely and lead to a long, rich finish. Drink now. Score 89.

RESERVED, CABERNET SAUVIGNON, 2000: This full-bodied, deep garnet-toward-purple wine is fully mature now but still showing good balance between wood, well-integrated tannins and fruits. Black fruits together with appealing spices, and on the finish a generous overlay of Mediterranean herbs. Drink up. Score 89.

RESERVED, CABERNET SAUVIGNON, 1999: Dark, deep and elegant, this delicious full-bodied wine has sweet plum, black cherry and red currant aromas and flavors, all opening slowly on the palate to join herbs, vanilla and a light hint of mint. Fully mature now. Drink up. Score 90.

RESERVED, CABERNET SAUVIGNON, 1998: Aged in new oak for 21 months, this elegant wine has a generous core of ripe cherries, wild berries, red currants, plums, vanilla and spices. Showing signs of aging. Drink up. Score 88.

RESERVED, MERLOT, 2003: Medium-dark garnet with orange reflections, this medium to full-bodied wine shows generous but well-integrating tannins set off nicely by vanilla and spice notes from the wood and appealing black cherry, plum and berry fruits. Long and mouth-filling. Drink now–2009. Score 89.

RESERVED, SYRAH, 2005: Already showing the potential for a plum and spice-rich nose along with flavors of ripe black fruits and smoked meat, those supported throughout by hints of freshly tanned leather. Drink from release–2011. Tentative Score 90–92.

RESERVED, GEWURZTRAMINER, DESSERT, JASMINE, 2004–2005: Made from Gewurztraminer grapes harvested in 2004 and 2005 in the Upper Galilee, this unabashedly sweet wine seems to have gone seriously wrong. Even though it offers honeyed summer and tropical fruits, it is too alcoholic and has an unwanted medicinal overlay. Score 65.

RESERVED, GEWURZTRAMINER, DESSERT, JASMINE, 2002–2003: A blend of Gewurztraminer grapes from two harvest years that was aged in oak and reinforced to obtain a 14% alcohol content. This frankly sweet wine has good balancing acidity and generous aromas and flavors of litchis, pineapple, ripe peaches and lilacs, as well as a hint of bitterness on the finish that will appeal to some. Drink now. Score 87.

Adom

ADOM, CABERNET SAUVIGNON, 2004: Medium to full-bodied, with soft, mouth-coating tannins in fine balance with spicy and smoky wood and acidity. On the nose and palate traditional Cabernet black currant and blackberry fruits, those matched nicely by light tobacco and chocolate-coated orange peel on the long finish. Drink now–2010. Score 89.

ADOM, CABERNET SAUVIGNON, 2003: Ripe, round and smooth, with soft tannins integrating now with wood and fruits. On the nose and palate tempting black currant, blackberry and cherry fruits, those complemented nicely by hints of vanilla and, on the long finish, Mediterranean herbs. Drink now–2009. Score 90.

ADOM, CABERNET SAUVIGNON, 2002: Full-bodied, and with generous currant and berry fruits, those matched nicely by exotic spices and hints of sweet cedar. Drink up. Score 90.

ADOM, CABERNET SAUVIGNON, 2001: Deep garnet-red, full-bodied, and showing good balance between sweet and smoky wood, soft tannins and generous currant, blackberry and ripe plum fruits. Appealing hints of mint, chocolate and now a tantalizing note of cigar tobacco on the moderately long finish. Drink up. Score 90.

ADOM, CABERNET SAUVIGNON, 2000: Made entirely from Cabernet Sauvignon grapes and aged for 14 months in new and old French and American *barriques*, this attractive red shows currant, berry and smoky oak aromas and flavors. It has good balance, integrated tannins and a medium-long finish. Fully mature. Drink up. Score 88.

ADOM, MARRIAGE, 2004: Dark, almost impenetrable garnet, this medium-bodied, smooth and round blend of Cabernet Sauvignon, Merlot and Shiraz opens with generous spicy-dusty oak on the nose but that yielding nicely to black and red currants, crushed berries and appealing hints of licorice. Drink now–2010. Score 90.

ADOM, MARRIAGE, 2003: Aged in a variety of oak barrels, fermented with different yeasts, this full-bodied blend of Cabernet Sauvignon, Merlot and Syrah (60%, 37% and 35% respectively) is one of Saslove's best efforts to date. Full-bodied and tannic but simultaneously soft, round and elegant, on the nose and palate a basic black currant personality but that matched by a generous array of berry, black cherry, and spices, all lingering nicely on the finish. Drink now–2011. Score 92.

Aviv

AVIV, CABERNET SAUVIGNON, 2006: Medium to full-bodied with firm tannins and smoky wood waiting to integrate, so a bit coarse now but with balance and structure that promise well for the future. As this one develops look for blackberry, purple plum and currant fruits matched by hints of spices, cloves and espresso coffee. Best 2008–2011. Score 88.

AVIV, CABERNET SAUVIGNON, 2005: Dark garnet, medium to full-bodied with firm tannins integrated nicely with a generous array of black currant and blackberry fruits, those with an appealing spicy overlay. Drink now–2009. Score 89.

AVIV, CABERNET SAUVIGNON, 2004: Dark garnet-red, medium to full-bodied, with soft, mouth-coating tannins. Good balance here and a tempting array of currant, plum and spices, those backed up by hints of vanilla and green olives. Drink now. Score 88.

AVIV, CABERNET SAUVIGNON, 2003: Deep garnet-red, medium-bodied, with firm tannins that coat the mouth nicely, those balanced by spicy oak and appealing currant and black cherry fruits. Drink now. Score 87.

AVIV, CABERNET SAUVIGNON, 2002: Dark and tannic, with concentrated sweet cedar and smoke now blended comfortably with berry and currant fruits. Drink up. Score 88.

AVIV, MERLOT, 2005: Medium-bodied, with caressing, near-sweet tannins and a generous array of black fruits backed up nicely by earthy, herbal and chocolate aromas and flavors that linger nicely on the palate. Drink now–2009. Score 90.

AVIV, MERLOT, 2004: Medium to full-bodied, with well-integrating tannins, spicy oak and appealing berry, black cherry and cassis aromas and flavors, those with hints of red licorice, chocolate and Mediterranean herbs. Drink now. Score 88.

AVIV, MERLOT, 2003: Medium-bodied, deep royal-purple towards garnet in color, with soft tannins and light spicy oak set off well by currant, berry and cherry fruits. On the finish hints of white chocolate and mocha. Drink now. Score 87.

AVIV, MERLOT, 2002: Fresh and exuberant, medium to full-bodied, and garnet toward purple in color, the wine was aged for six months in French and American oak and shows tannins that start off firmly but open in the glass to reveal a pleasing berry and black cherry personality, the fruits complemented nicely by spicy chocolate and coffee flavors. Look as well for hints of smoky oak and toasted white bread on the medium-long finish. Drink up. Score 89.

AVIV, MARRIAGE, 2005: A medium to full-bodied blend of Merlot, Cabernet Sauvignon and Syrah (60%, 32% and 8% respectively), showing good balance between soft tannins, wood and fruits. On the nose and palate dark plums, cassis and berries that come together nicely. Soft and caressing. Drink now–2009. Score 88.

AVIV, MARRIAGE, 2004: A blend of 60% Merlot, 36% Cabernet Sauvignon and 4% Syrah, all from the Upper Galilee, developed on oak chips for six months. Dark garnet in color, with soft tannins integrating nicely with vanilla and white pepper, those on a background of blackberries, currants and Mediterranean herbs. Smooth and soft. Drink now. Score 87.

AVIV, MARRIAGE, 2003: This deep royal-purple, full-bodied blend of 60% Merlot, 39% Cabernet Sauvignon and 1% Syrah shows generous but almost sweet tannins coming together nicely with vanilla-rich American oak, spices and appealing berry, currant and black cherry fruits. On the pleasingly long finish look as well for hints of cigar tobacco. Drink now. Score 88.

Saslove

SASLOVE, SAGOL, PRIVATE EDITION, 2000: Dark royal-purple, this medium to full-bodied wine spent 14 months in French oak barrels. With soft, well-integrated tannins, a gentle influence of smoky oak, and generous black currant and plum fruits backed up nicely by Oriental spices, vanilla and chocolate, this is a well-balanced and moderately long wine. Fully mature and somewhat past its peak. Drink up. Score 88.

Sassy *

Sasson Bar-Gig set up this small winery in 2000 in the town of Bat Yam on the outskirts of Tel Aviv. The winery draws on grapes from Gush Etzion and the Golan Heights, and is currently producing about 8,000 bottles annually, the reds aged in oak for about 12 months.

SASSY, CABERNET SAUVIGNON, 2004: A pleasant little country-style wine, medium-bodied, with an herbal edge to currant and cherry fruits. Drink now. Score 84.

SASSY, CABERNET SAUVIGNON, 2003: Medium-bodied, with somewhat coarse tannins and too-generous smoky, dusty oak and on the nose and palate skimpy berry and cherry fruits. Drink up. Score 79.

SASSY, CABERNET SAUVIGNON, 2002: This garnet-red, medium-bodied wine continues to offer very earthy aromas and flavors but also reveals some plum and berry fruits. Drink up. Score 80.

SASSY, MERLOT, 2004: Ruby towards garnet, medium-bodied, with strawberry and red cherry fruits. Drink now. Score 83.

SASSY, MERLOT, 2003: Medium-bodied, with firm tannins and generous wood influence, the wine opens to reveal jam-like aromas and flavors of plums and currants. Drink up. Score 82.

SASSY, PETITE SIRAH, 2003: Dark garnet, medium-bodied, with chunky, country-style tannins and a somewhat sweet, medicinal taste overlaying black fruits. Drink up. Score 74.

Savion ★★★

Founded by Ashi Salmon and Eli Pardess and set on Moshav Messilat Tzion in the Jerusalem Mountains, this micro-winery released its first wine from the 2000 vintage and is currently producing about 2,200 bottles annually. Grapes come primarily from Ramat Dalton and other vineyards in the Upper Galilee, but the winery has new vineyards in which it is raising its own Cabernet Sauvignon, Merlot and Shiraz grapes.

SAVION, CABERNET SAUVIGNON, 2006: Deep royal-purple, firm, concentrated and intense, this medium to full-bodied wine shows generous soft tannins and complex blackberry, currant, tobacco and anise aromas and flavors. Already revealing sharp focus and tannins that firm up on the long, fruity finish. Best 2009–2012. Tentative Score 90–92.

SAVION, CABERNET SAUVIGNON, 2005: Made entirely from Cabernet Sauvignon grapes and aged in American oak, the wine is showing spicy and vanilla-rich wood and chewy tannins. Opens to reveal layers of currant, black cherry, anise, cedarwood and sage. Finishes with tempting berry-cherry flavors. Best 2009–2012. Tentative Score 91–93.

SAVION, CABERNET SAUVIGNON, 2004: Blended with 10% of Merlot and aged for 12 months in primarily French oak. Garnet towards royal-purple, medium to full-bodied, with firm tannins and spicy wood integrating nicely with fruits and acidity. On the nose and palate black currants and berries complemented by herbal and tobacco notes and, on the long finish, a hint of white chocolate. Drink now–2011. Score 89.

SAVION, CABERNET SAUVIGNON, 2003: Intensely deep royal-purple, medium to full-bodied, with gripping tannins well balanced by spicy wood and acidity. On the nose and palate red and black currants and berries, those with appealing hints of sweet herbs, and on the generous finish, a tempting overlay of bittersweet chocolate. Drink now–2009. Score 90.

SAVION, CABERNET SAUVIGNON, 2002: Dark garnet in color, with tannins that are as firm today as in the wine's youth. On the nose and palate primarily currant and plum fruits along with spices. Blended with a small amount of Merlot, the wine is still drinking nicely but is a bit past its peak. Drink up. Score 86.

SAVION, CABERNET SAUVIGNON, 2001: Full-bodied, with good balance between generous but soft tannins and fruits, this blend of 90% Cabernet Sauvignon and 10% Merlot spent 12 months in *barriques*, which is reflected in the hints of smoke, vanilla and cedarwood on a background of currant, plum and berry fruits. A long, just spicy enough finish. Drink now–2009. Score 89.

SAVION, CABERNET SAUVIGNON, 2000: The first wine released by the winery and more dense and herbal in style than later releases. Blended with small amounts of Merlot and Syrah and aged in *barriques* for 12 months, this full-bodied red has maintained its deep inky-purple color and its tannins are now nicely integrated. Opens with spicy berries, those going to currants and ripe plums with generous herbal and espresso coffee overtones. A long mouth-filling finish. Drink now. Score 89.

Sde Boker ✦✦✦

Located on Kibbutz Sde Boker in the heart of the Negev Desert, this small winery was founded in 1998 by former Californian Zvi Remick who studied winemaking at California's Napa Valley College. Relying on Cabernet Sauvignon, Merlot, Carignan and Zinfandel grapes grown in the desert, production currently varies between 3,000–5,000 bottles annually.

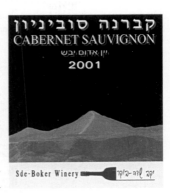

SDE BOKER, CABERNET SAUVIGNON, 2005: Dark garnet towards inky purple, medium to full-bodied, with soft tannins integrating nicely and showing generous but not imposing spicy cedarwood. Look for aromas and flavors of black fruits, Oriental spices and green olives, all lingering nicely. Drink from release–2010. Tentative Score 87–89.

SDE BOKER, CABERNET SAUVIGNON, 2004: Showing dark garnet towards purple, medium to full-bodied, with soft tannins integrating nicely. On the nose and palate traditional Cabernet black currant, blackberry and spices, with hints of smoky wood and vanilla rising on the finish. Drink now–2009. Score 88.

SDE BOKER, CABERNET SAUVIGNON, 2003: Medium to full-bodied, with good balance between wood, soft tannins and tempting black currant, cherry and spicy aromas and flavors. Long and generous. Drink now. Score 88.

SDE BOKER, CABERNET SAUVIGNON, 2001: Dark royal-purple in color, this well-balanced, medium to full-bodied red reflects its 23 months in oak casks with abundant vanilla, toasty oak and cedar flavors, those on the background of currant and berry fruits. Drink now. Score 88.

SDE BOKER, CABERNET SAUVIGNON, 2000: Dark garnet towards purple, with its once ample tannins now fully integrated, this medium-bodied red shows an appealing array of plum and currant fruits, those matched by notes of pepper and black olives as well as a hint of sweetness. Drink up. Score 85.

SDE BOKER, MERLOT, 2005: Bright ruby towards garnet, with soft, gently mouth-coating tannins. Showing a moderate wood influence. On the nose and palate plum, berry and black cherry fruits, those complemented by hints of sweet herbs. Drink from release–2010. Tentative Score 86–88.

SDE BOKER, MERLOT, 2004: Garnet-red, medium-bodied, with firm tannins integrating nicely with spicy wood and aromas and flavors of black fruits, Mediterranean herbs and a hint of tar. Drink now. Score 86.

SDE BOKER, MERLOT, 2003: Dark garnet, medium to full-bodied, with tannins nicely integrated and a generous hint of oak. On the nose and palate red currant, cherry and berry fruits, all on a spicy background. Drink now. Score 88.

SDE BOKER, CARIGNAN, 2005: Blended with 12% of Cabernet Sauvignon, this medium-bodied wine shows still somewhat aggressive tannins waiting to settle down, and appealing aromas and flavors of rose petals, red currants and spices. Drink from release–2009. Tentative Score 85–87.

SDE BOKER, CARIGNAN, 2003: Light to medium-bodied, with a nice chewy sensation and bright and lively on the palate. Showing purple plum and spice flavors that linger nicely. An appealing little wine. Drink up. Score 86.

SDE BOKER, ZINFANDEL, 2004: A generous, hearty rustic wine with lots of personality. Medium-bodied, and on the nose and palate aromas and flavors of black cherries, pomegranate, cola and toasted rye bread. A charmer. Drink now. Score 88.

SDE BOKER, ZINFANDEL, 2003: Medium-bodied with appealing wild berry, cherry and anise flavors that open nicely to a lightly tannic and mineral finish. Not a great Zinfandel but a very nice one. Drink up. Score 87.

SDE BOKER, CABERNET SAUVIGNON-MERLOT, 2006: Deep garnet-red, medium to full-bodied, with spicy aromas and flavors of currants, cherries, anise, herbs and pepper. Well balanced and well focused, with tangy red fruits and smoky oak on the finish. Drink from release–2010. Tentative Score 87–89.

SDE BOKER, ZIN-ZIN, 2005: A sweet but not at all cloying wine made from late-harvested Zinfandel grapes. Opens with aromatic blackberries, raspberries and brambles, those joined by a bit of toasty oak and a hint of mint, all on a lightly tannic, moderately sweet background. Plenty of acidity to keep the wine lively. Drink from release. Score 88.

Sea Horse ★★★★

Ze'ev Dunie founded this boutique winery in 2000 on Moshav Bar Giora in the Jerusalem Mountains after retiring from partnership in the Agur winery, where he had made his first Elul wine. Dunie has his own vineyards planted in Syrah and Zinfandel, and draws on Cabernet Sauvignon from the Upper Galilee. Current planning calls for major enlargement of the winery's own vineyards along with the addition of Mourvedre and Grenache to the winery's repertoire.

The winery has grown from initial production of 1,800 bottles from the 2001 vintage to between 10,000–14,000 bottles annually. Releases include two Cabernet Sauvignon-based wines, Elul and Fellini; two Zinfandel-based wines, Lennon and Take Two; two Syrah-based wines, Camus and Antoine; and in selected years, Munch, which is made entirely from Petite Sirah grapes. There is also one blend, Gaudi, and in barrels from the 2006 vintage are Primitivo and Petit Verdot.

SEA HORSE, ELUL, 2005: A blend of 73% Cabernet Sauvignon, 17% Syrah and 10% Petite Sirah destined for 20 months in French and American oak, this flagship wine of the winery is still in its infancy and showing youthful royal-purple, full-bodied with firm, near-sweet tannins. Opens with currant, kirsch and black cherry fruits, those yielding to hints of licorice, spices and berries, all leading to a long and complex finish. Drink from release–2010. Tentative Score 91–93.

SEA HORSE, ELUL, 2004:, A blend of 85% Cabernet Sauvignon, 12% Syrah and 3% Petite Sirah. Deep, almost impenetrable garnet, full-bodied, with still-firm tannins complemented by spicy oak. On first attack currants and plums, those yielding to red and black berries, a hint of iron, and finally to bittersweet chocolate and Mediterranean herbs, all lingering comfortably. Ripe, round and mouth-filling. Drink now–2010. Score 92.

SEA HORSE, ELUL, 2003: This well-balanced blend of Cabernet Sauvignon, Syrah and Petite Sirah (85%, 10% and 5% respectively) shows rich and quiet elegance. Ripe black cherry, currant and berry fruits overlaid nicely by hints of anise, spicy oak and light earthiness, all culminating in a long and generous finish. Drink now–2010. Score 92.

SEA HORSE, ELUL, 2002: Deep garnet towards royal-purple, this full-bodied blend of 85% Cabernet Sauvignon, 9% Merlot and 6% Syrah, shows generous but soft and well-integrating tannins and jammy currant and berry aromas and flavors set off by spices and toast, all showing appealing overtones of Mediterranean herbs. Plush and elegant, with a long finish that yields bittersweet chocolate. Drink now–2009. Score 91.

SEA HORSE, ELUL, 2001: This full-bodied blend of 70% Cabernet Sauvignon, 28% Merlot and 2% Syrah has settled down, its once chunky tannins now softened and integrating nicely. On the nose and palate currant, black cherry, mineral and herbal aromas and flavors all with a gentle hint of minty-vanilla on the finish. Drink now. Score 91.

SEA HORSE, ELUL, 2000: Fully mature, this oak-aged blend of Cabernet Sauvignon and Syrah (70% and 30% respectively) continues to show fine balance and length. Spicy currant and purple plum fruits here on a lightly herbal finish. Drink up. Score 90.

SEA HORSE, FELLINI, 2005: A blend of 46% each Cabernet Sauvignon and Syrah, those complemented by 8% of Petit Verdot. Developed in French and American oak for 16–18 months, this medium to full-bodied wine shows silky tannins along with cherry, raspberry and licorice aromas and flavors, those opening to reveal a tempting hint of bittersweet chocolate on the finish. Drink now–2011. Score 90.

SEA HORSE, FELLINI, 2004: Super-dark amber towards inky black in color, this blend of equal parts of Cabernet Sauvignon and Syrah developed in oak for 16 months and shows gentle cedar and cigar-box hints that run throughout. On the nose and palate wild berries, currants and a generous hint of citrus peel, those complemented nicely by light earthy and leathery overtones. Mouth-filling, long and generous. Drink now–2009. Score 91.

SEA HORSE, FELLINI, 2003: Generously tannic but with fine balance between the tannins, acidity, wood and fruits. This blend of 60% Syrah and 40% Cabernet Sauvignon was oak-aged for 18 months in French and American oak, and showing forward black currant, blackberry and red plum fruits, those on a spicy and simultaneously near-sweet background. Lingers nicely on the palate. Drink now. Score 90.

SEA HORSE, FELLINI, 2002: This medium to full-bodied blend of 90% Cabernet Sauvignon and 10% Petite Sirah is warm and elegant, and has distinctly Mediterranean aromas and flavors of fresh herbs and spicy vanilla that give an additional dimension to the currant and black cherry fruits. Supple tannins, good balance and concentration come together nicely in this oak-aged blend. Drink up. Score 88.

SEA HORSE, LENNON, 2005: A blend this year of 90% Zinfandel and 5% each Petite Sirah and Carignan. Aged for about 16 months in used American oak barrels, this full-bodied, deep, dark garnet wine is richly aromatic, with soft tannins integrating beautifully with the wood and wild berry, blackberry and sage notes. All coming together nicely in a long spicy finish. Drink now–2010. Score 90.

SEA HORSE, LENNON, 2004: Made from grapes of low-yield Zinfandel vines and blended with 5% Petite Sirah, the wine has good balance between wood, tannins and alcohol, and opens to reveal generous raspberry, plum and cassis fruits, those matched nicely by light peppery, vanilla and minty overtones. Firm and concentrated, lingering nicely on the palate. Drink now–2009. Score 90.

SEA HORSE, LENNON, TETE DE CUVEE, 2004: Made from low-yield organically raised Zinfandel grapes and blended with 5% Petite Sirah, the wine is full-bodied, fruity and with a whopping 15.6% alcohol, but has the balance and structure to carry it. Tightly focused currants, plums and wild berries matched nicely by pepper and mocha from the oak. Drink now–2010. Score 91.

SEA HORSE, LENNON, 2003: A medium to full-bodied blend of 95% Zinfandel and 5% Petite Sirah. With 14 months in American oak, this generously tannic wine shows good concentration of ripe, juicy cherry and wild berry flavors as well as an appealing pepper and anise edge. Drink now. Score 90.

SEA HORSE, TAKE TWO, 2006: This blend of Primitivo Zinfandel and Petite Sirah is deep and dark, with fine intensity and generous firm tannins backing up plum, cherry and chocolate aromas and flavors, those on a medium to full-bodied frame all leading to a long fruity finish. Drink from release–2010. Tentative Score 88–90.

SEA HORSE, TAKE TWO, 2005: A medium-bodied, softly tannic blend of 85% Zinfandel, 10% Petite Sirah and 5% Carignan that was aged for 12 months in primarily American oak. Ripe and round, with light peppery overtones highlighting plum, raspberry and wild berry fruits, those with delicate overlays of sage and minerals. Ripe, round and generous. Drink from release–2010. Score 89.

SEA HORSE, TAKE TWO, 2004: Dark ruby towards garnet, this blend of 88% Zinfandel, 10% Petite Sirah and 2% Cabernet Sauvignon shows light meaty and leathery notes. Smooth and round, with wild berry and cassis fruits that make themselves felt nicely. Drink now. Score 89.

SEA HORSE, TAKE TWO, 2003: A blend of 90% Zinfandel, 9% Petite Sirah and 1% Cabernet Sauvignon, this medium to full-bodied wine reflects its eight months in American oak with good balance between tannins, wood and fruits. A true Zinfandel personality: round and juicy with spicy berry and cherry flavors with a firm tannic edge and a moderately long tar and anise finish. Drink now. Score 89.

SEA HORSE, TAKE TWO, 2002: A blend of 67% Merlot, 25% Cabernet Sauvignon and 8% Petite Sirah that spent eight months in American and French oak. Dark cherry-red and medium-bodied but somewhat light on the palate, the wine has low tannins, lively acidity, and raspberry and black cherry flavors. Drink up. Score 86.

SEA HORSE, CAMUS, 2006: Firm and gripping tannins opening to reveal dense currant and blackberry fruits, those backed up by aromas and flavors of minerals, spices and cigar box. At this stage massive, but with balance and structure that bode well for future elegance. Best 2009–2013. Tentative Score 90–92.

SEA HORSE, CAMUS, 2005: This full-bodied blend of 90% Syrah and 10% Petite Sirah is reflecting its 12 months in French oak with a gentle layer of spicy wood, that well balanced by generous but yielding tannins and on the nose and palate smoky blackberries and currants, Oriental spices and hints of game meat. Soft, round and well focused with the tannins, rising on the long,

ROGOV'S GUIDE TO ISRAELI WINES

supple finish along with appealing hints of leather and black pepper. Best 2009–2011. Score 90.

SEA HORSE, CAMUS, 2004: Dark garnet, medium to full-bodied, this blend of 94% Syrah and 6% Petit Sirah reflects its 12 months in oak with soft tannins, refreshing acidity, and spicy-toasty oak. On the nose and palate black currant, blackberry, tobacco, and a hint of freshly tanned leather with white pepper and cigar tobacco rising on the long finish. Drink now–2010. Score 90.

SEA HORSE, CAMUS, 2003: Full-bodied, with still-firm tannins well balanced by spicy wild berry and cherry fruits, this dark garnet-red Shiraz boasts an appealing leathery edge on the finish. Rich and complex. Drink now–2009. Score 90.

SEA HORSE, CAMUS, 2002: Dark garnet toward royal-purple, this medium to full-bodied red made primarily from oak-aged Shiraz shows deep raspberry flavors with floral accents, but enough tannins to keep it firm. Clean and long, with hints of black pepper and licorice, it has a moderately long, near-sweet finish. Drink up. Score 90.

SEA HORSE, ANTOINE, TETE DE CUVEE, 2005: Made entirely from Syrah grapes, this full-bodied wine spent 16 months in used French barrels and now shows deep garnet-towards royal-purple color with gripping tannins in fine balance with gentle oak. Opens on a decidedly plummy note that yields to blackberries, spices and red licorice. Drink from release–2011. Tentative Score 89–91.

SEA HORSE, ANTOINE, 2004: Showing somewhat less full-bodied than in its youth, with its once-firm tannins now integrating nicely with wood and fruits. Revealing traditional Syrah aromas and flavors of plums, blackberries and licorice, those supported nicely by near-sweet oak and a hint of spiced meat on the long and satisfying finish. Drink now–2009. Score 91.

SEA HORSE, ANTOINE, 2003: Pure Syrah, dark garnet in color, with firm but supple tannins integrated with spicy wood. Showing blackberry, black cherry and currant fruits, those supported by overlays of spices—look especially for a hint of anise—and leathery and light meaty overtones, all leading to a long finish. Drink now–2010. Score 91.

SEA HORSE, MUNCH, 2006: Named as a tribute to artist Edward Munch, this Petite Sirah wine bears a remarkable resemblance to the 2003 release. Full-bodied, with generous tannins integrating nicely, and on the nose and palate berries, currants and black cherry fruits overlaid with peppery and licorice notes. Drink now–2011. Tentative Score 88–90.

334

SEA HORSE, MUNCH, 2005: Made entirely from Petite Sirah grapes from a dry-farmed vineyard, this is an intense and concentrated wine, dense enough to be thought of as chewy, with firm, chunky tannins that need time to integrate. On the nose and palate currants, sur-ripe plums, a hint of citrus peel and an appealing peppery overlay. Drink from release–2011. Tentative Score 90–92.

SEA HORSE, MUNCH, 2003: This 100% Petite Sirah spent 16 months in French and American oak. Exotic, spicy and complex, showing layers of wild berry, plum, currant and black cherry fruits together with a generous peppery overlay and supple tannins. Drink now–2009. Score 91.

SEA HORSE, GAUDI, 2005: Garnet towards purple, this blend of Carignan, Petite Sirah and Cabernet Sauvignon (30%, 30% and 40% respectively) reflects its eight months in oak with medium-body, soft tannins and a personality best described as round. Easy to drink, but with just enough complexities to make it interesting . On the nose and palate plum, currant and wild berries along with hints of spices and licorice. Drink now. Score 88.

Sefad *

Founded by Moshe Alon in 2002 and located in the heart of the old city of Sefad, this winery relies largely on grapes from the Upper Galilee. Production is about 10,000 bottles annually, the wines from Cabernet Sauvignon, Merlot, Cabernet Franc and Gewurztraminer grapes.

SEFAD, CABERNET SAUVIGNON, 2006: Dominated by earthy, compost pile and barnyard aromas that make it impossible to find whatever fruits may be hiding. Score 55. K

SEFAD, CABERNET SAUVIGNON, RESERVED, 2005: Marked by searing tannins, burning alcohol and aromas that call to mind the sewers of Paris. Score 50. K

SEFAD, CABERNET SAUVIGNON, 2004: Stale, with aromas of dirty barnyard and flavors and stewed prunes. Score 55. K

SEFAD, CHARDONNAY, 2006: Despite its youth this bronze-colored wine has gone towards vinegar, that with a distinct aroma of sewage. Score 50. K

Segal ★★★★

Established in the 1950s as Ashkelon Wines and later taking on the name of the family that owned it, Segal was until the mid-1980s one of the more up-market wineries of the country. In 2001 the company was bought out by Barkan Wineries, but kept its name. Under winemaker Avi Feldstein, with quality vineyards in several regions of the Upper Galilee, and operating now in Barkan's state-of-the-art facilities at Kibbutz Hulda, the winery is now producing several excellent wines, including Single Vineyard and Unfiltered wines, both from Cabernet Sauvignon grapes. Other series are Ben Ami, Marom Galil (including those wines labeled *Single* and *Fusion*), Rehasim, the single-vineyard Dovev varietal wines, Batzir and the popular-priced Shel Segal series. The winery relies on Cabernet Sauvignon, Merlot, Argaman, Chardonnay, Sauvignon Blanc, Emerald Riesling, and French Colombard grapes, and current production is about 1.5 million bottles annually, of which nearly one million are in the Shel Segal series.

Single Vineyard

SINGLE VINEYARD, CABERNET SAU-VIGNON, DISHON, 2003: Full-bodied, with generous, firm tannins and smoky wood settling in comfortably. Opening to reveal currant, blackberry, vanilla and hints of tar, all lingering nicely. Drink now–2009. Score 90. K

SINGLE VINEYARD, CABERNET SAU-VIGNON, DISHON, 2002: Layers of jammy berry and strawberry fruits on spicy currants, anise, tar and sweet cedar. A touch of green olive works its way into the finish. Full-bodied and complex with firm but polished tannins. Drink now. Score 89. K

SINGLE VINEYARD, DISHON, 2001: Deep royal-purple in color, with blackberry, black currant and plum fruits, this full-bodied wine was aged in oak for 18 months. Showing good balance between fruits, wood and moderately firm but well-integrating tannins, this complex wine has a long, near-sweet finish. Drink now. Score 91. K

SINGLE VINEYARD, CABERNET SAUVIGNON, DISHON, 2000: Made entirely from Cabernet Sauvignon grapes, this well-balanced, deep garnet-toward-royal-purple wine reflects its 18 months in small oak casks with generous vanilla and smoke on a background of currant, berry, plum and spices. Fully mature. Drink up. Score 90. K

SINGLE VINEYARD, MERLOT, DOVEV, 2003: Developed in French and American *barriques* for 19 months, this wine is showing full-bodied, with firm tannins and spicy wood integrating well and opulent blueberry, currant and plum flavors, those with spicy and floral notes with hints of licorice in the background. Long, smooth, round and polished. Drink now–2011. Score 92. K

SINGLE VINEYARD, MERLOT, DOVEV, 2002: Garnet towards black, medium to full-bodied, soft on the palate despite firm tannins and with tempting aromas and flavors of blackberries, plums and sweet herbs. Drink now. Score 89. K

SINGLE VINEYARD, CHARDONNAY, DOVEV, 2004: Light gold in color, medium-bodied, with crisp minerals in the background yielding nicely to a rich array of spring flowers, summer fruits and melons. Tempting and long. Drink up. Score 90. K

Unfiltered

UNFILTERED, CABERNET SAUVIGNON, 2004: This firm and intense, full-bodied red shows near-sweet, gripping tannins and generous but not dominating oak with good balance between those and the red and black currants, black cherries, sage and spicy cedarwood on the nose and palate. On the long finish a generous overlay of minerals. Drink now–2010. Score 90. K

UNFILTERED, CABERNET SAUVIGNON, 2002: Aged in oak for 18 months, full-bodied, rich and ripe, with fine balance between generous soft tannins and smoky oak. On the nose and palate currants, berries, plums and vanilla, and on the long finish light herbs, black pepper and chocolate. Long, mouth-filling and elegant. Drink now–2009. Score 90. K

UNFILTERED, CABERNET SAUVIGNON, 2001: Dark garnet, full-bodied and reflecting its 22 months in oak with generous vanilla and toasty oak. Concentrated, complex and tannic, the wine shows appealing currant, plum and black cherry fruits, those on a background of Oriental spices, all coming to a long, complex finish. Drink now. Score 89. K

UNFILTERED, CABERNET SAUVIGNON, 2000: Deep garnet and full-bodied, this wine spent 20 months in new French and American oak. Now mature, its currant, red berry and earthy-herbal aromas and flavors are showing overlays of chocolate and mint. Drink up. Score 88. K

UNFILTERED, CABERNET SAUVIGNON, 1999: Full-bodied, and still showing good balance and well-focused black cherry, wild berry and currant fruits along with hints of herbs and spices, but now throwing a generous amount of sediment. Still drinking nicely but picking up a light sweetness and woody notes on the nose. Drink up. Score 89. K

Rehasim

REHASIM, CABERNET SAUVIGNON, DISHON, 2004: Dark, youthful royal-purple in color, intense and concentrated, with a rich array of currant, tobacco, sage and cedarwood aromas and flavors. Fine balance between wood, tannins and acidity yield a ripe and supple Cabernet. Drink now–2010. Score 90. K

REHASIM, CABERNET SAUVIGNON, DISHON, 2003: Full-bodied, with generous, firm tannins and smoky wood now settling in comfortably and opening to reveal currant, blackberry, vanilla and hints of tar, all lingering nicely. Drink now–2009. Score 90. K

REHASIM, CABERNET SAUVIGNON, DOVEV, 2003: Medium to full-bodied, with soft tannins, and layers of blueberries, currants, plums and sweet cedar, those on a generous but not at all offensive background of dusty oak. Rich, round, supple and generous. Drink now–2009. Score 88. K

REHASIM, CABERNET SAUVIGNON, DOVEV, 2002: Pure Cabernet Sauvignon, aged for 20 months in primarily French oak *barriques*, this medium-bodied, soft and round wine offers up enticing aromas and flavors of currants, mocha and minerals, those backed up by chewy but nicely yielding tannins. Worth decanting. Drink now. Score 90. K

REHASIM, MERLOT, DOVEV, 2004: Dark garnet, this medium to full-bodied, herbal, spicy and generously tannic wine shows balance and structure that bode well for its future. Aromas and flavors of black cherries, blackberries and currants matched nicely by spicy oak accents and, on the long finish, hints of espresso and dark chocolate. Drink now–2012. Score 90. K

REHASIM, MERLOT, DOVEV, 2003: Developed in French and American *barriques* for 19 months, this full-bodied red shows firm tannins and spicy wood integrating well. Opulent blueberry, currant plum flavors, those with spices, floral notes and hints of licorice in the background. Long, smooth, round and polished. Drink now–2011. Score 92. K

REHASIM, MERLOT, DOVEV, 2002: Reflecting its 19 months in *barriques* with generous oak but that in fine balance with soft, mouth-coating tannins. On the nose and palate appealing berry, black cherry and cassis fruits, all on a just spicy enough background. Drink up. Score 88. K

Ben Ami

BEN AMI, CABERNET SAUVIGNON, 2005: Dark royal-purple, medium-bodied with generous near-sweet tannins and equally generous smoky wood. Aromas and flavors of currants, blackberries and herbs. Drink now. Score 84. K

BEN AMI, CABERNET SAUVIGNON, 2004: Medium-bodied, with soft tannins and generous hints of smoky wood opening to reveal wild berry, currant and cassis fruits. Drink up. Score 85. K

BEN AMI, CABERNET SAUVIGNON, 2003: Deep garnet towards royal-purple, medium-bodied, with chunky, country-style tannins. Appealing plum and berry fruits are matched nicely by a light herbaceousness. Drink up. Score 85. K

Marom Galil

MAROM GALIL, CABERNET SAUVIGNON, SINGLE, 2004: Made entirely from Cabernet Sauvignon grapes from several Galilee vineyards. Dark garnet in color, with generous spicy and dusty wood influence, the wine is showing red currants, berries, bittersweet chocolate and stony minerals. Needs a bit of time for the elements to integrate. Drink now–2010. Score 88. K

MAROM GALIL, CABERNET SAUVIGNON, SINGLE, 2003: Garnet towards purple, the oak now settling down, this medium to full-bodied red shows firm tannins integrating nicely and good balance between wood, tannins and fruits. On the nose and palate black currant and blackberry fruits supported by hints of earthy herbaceousness. Drink now–2009. Score 87. K

MAROM GALIL, MERLOT, SINGLE, 2004: Medium to full-bodied, with generous oak and firm tannins but with good balance and structure and showing red and black berry fruits, cassis, and hints of spices and eucalyptus on the nose and palate. Look for a candied citrus peel on the finish. Drink now–2009. Score 87. K

MAROM GALIL, MERLOT, SINGLE, 2003: Despite its name, not a single-vineyard wine and not even a single-variety wine, the grapes for this blend of 85% Merlot and 15% Cabernet Franc coming from various vineyards in the upper Galilee. Reflecting 14 months in oak with good balance between spicy wood and now softening tannins and revealing ripe red plums, cassis and citrus peel, all with a light hint of sweetness. Drink up. Score 86. K

MAROM GALIL, MERLOT, 2003: Deep ruby towards garnet, medium-bodied, with soft tannins integrating nicely and currant and wild berry fruits. A bit heavy on the oak. Drink now. Score 87. K

MAROM GALIL, SYRAH, SINGLE, 2005: Blended with 6% of Cabernet Sauvignon, medium to full-bodied, with soft tannins integrating nicely and showing spicy red and black fruits, those complemented by near-sweet tobacco on the finish. Drink now–2009. Score 86. K

MAROM GALIL, RED, FUSION, 2005: A dark ruby towards garnet, medium-bodied and gently tannic blend of Merlot, Cabernet Sauvignon and Cabernet Franc. Soft, round and smooth with aromas and flavors of spicy currants and berries. Drink now. Score 85. K

MAROM GALIL, RED, FUSION, 2004: Ruby towards purple, an uno-aked, medium-bodied and softly tannic blend of 60% Merlot and 20% each of Cabernet Sauvignon and Cabernet Franc. Fresh aromas of black currants and berries as well as a hint of herbaceousness. Drink now. Score 85. K

MAROM GALIL, CABERNET SAUVIGNON-MERLOT, 2003: Dark garnet-red, medium-bodied with somewhat chunky tannins but with generous berry and black cherry fruits. A pleasant quaffer. Drink up. Score 84. K

MAROM GALIL, ROSÉ, 2006: Deep cherry in color, this dry red medium-bodied blend of Tempranillo and Shiraz has generous tutti-frutti and raspberry aromas and flavors. Lacks a bit in acidity. Drink up. Score 85. K

MAROM GALIL, CHARDONNAY, SINGLE, 2004: A lively golden-colored Chardonnay from four different Galilee vineyards, aged partly in oak for seven months. Medium-bodied, with generous oak and lively acidity and aromas and flavors of ripe melons, pineapple and pears matched by a gentle nutty overlay. Drink up. Score 87. K

MAROM GALIL, FUSION, LAVAN, 2005: An unoaked blend of Char-donnay, French Colombard and Sauvignon Blanc. Light golden-straw in color, super-fruity on the nose, medium-bodied, with lively acidity and generous citrus, peach and tropical fruit flavors. Lacking complexity but delightful. Drink up. Score 87. K

MAROM GALIL, FUSION, LAVAN, 2004: A partly oaked blend of Chardonnay and French Colombard, with generous acidity highlighting pineapple, peach and melon aromas and flavors. A good quaffer. Drink up. Score 85. K

MAROM GALIL, MUSCAT DESSERT, 2005: Dark apricot in color, with a few dried fruits, generous sweetness not fully balanced by acidity, and far too alcoholic. Drink now. Score 82. K

Shel Segal

SHEL SEGAL, CABERNET SAUVIGNON, 2005: A simple medium-bodied, soft, round and easy-to-drink red. Drink up. Score 83. K

SHEL SEGAL, CABERNET SAUVIGNON, 2004: Lightly oak-aged, dark ruby towards garnet, medium-bodied, with soft tannins and forward berry, cherry and currant fruits. Drink up. Score 84. K

SHEL SEGAL, DRY RED, 2005: An acceptable country-style little wine, with soft tannins and black berry fruits. Drink up. Score 80. K

SHEL SEGAL, DRY RED, 2004: A simple country-style wine, a bit coarse but with berry and black cherry fruits to make it quaffable. Drink up. Score 80. K

SHEL SEGAL, ROSÉ, 2006: Deep cherry-red in color, this dry, medium-bodied blend of Tempranillo and Shiraz has generous tutti-frutti and raspberry aromas and flavors. Lacks a bit in acidity. Drink up. Score 85. K

SHEL SEGAL, EMERALD RIESLING, 2006: Simple, semi-dry, floral and with citrus and tropical fruits. Drink up. Score 78. K

SHEL SEGAL, EMERALD RIESLING, 2005: Semi-dry, floral on the nose and palate and with basic citrus fruits. Drink up. Score 79. K

SHEL SEGAL, DRY WHITE, 2005: A basic white, with generous acidity and with grapefruit and citrus peel aromas and flavors. Drink up. Score 78. K

Shdema *

Set on Kibbutz Revivim in the Negev Dessert, this small winery released its first wines from the 2004 vintage. Relying on Cabernet Sauvignon and Merlot grapes from their own vineyards and with Shiraz and Petit Verdot soon coming on line, winemaker Omri Kaluski is currently producing about 2,500 bottles annually.

SHDEMA, CABERNET SAUVIGNON, 2005: Dark purple, medium-bodied, with high acidity and coarse, almost stinging tannins, and minimal berry and black cherry fruits that struggle to make themselves felt. Tentative Score 72–74.

SHDEMA, CABERNET SAUVIGNON, 2004: Garnet towards brownish-purple, medium-bodied, with coarse tannins and far too generous smoky wood that hides the fruits. Already showing first signs of oxidation. Score 68.

SHDEMA, CABERNET SAUVIGNON, SDE BOKER, 2005: Not-fully-clear dull garnet, medium-bodied, with soft tannins. Showing muddy and bitter with only stingy black fruits. Tentative Score 74–76.

SHDEMA, MERLOT, 2005: Dull garnet, medium-bodied, with barnyard aromas and showing somewhat watery. Tentative Score 68–70.

SHDEMA, MERLOT, SDE BOKER, 2005: Dark garnet, medium-bodied, with soft tannins, moderate wood influence and appealing currant and berry fruits accompanied by hints of pepper. Drink from release. Tentative Score 83–85.

Sifsaf ∗

Founded by Arik Elbaz on Moshav Safsufa in the Upper Galilee, the winery's own vineyards contain Cabernet Sauvignon, Merlot, Cabernet Franc, Barbera, Nebbiolo, Sangiovese, Syrah, Chardonnay, Viognier and Sauvignon Blanc grapes. Production is about 15,000 bottles annually. Although the labels on the Sifsaf bottles state a given vintage year, the owner/winemaker acknowledges that because labels are expensive, he may at times use the same label for more than one year,

which makes it impossible to know precisely which wine one is tasting or purchasing.

SIFSAF, CABERNET SAUVIGNON, 2005: Medium-bodied, with dusty wood and sour pickle aromas and flavors overpowering whatever fruits might be here. Score 55. K

SIFSAF, CABERNET SAUVIGNON, 2003: Medium-bodied, with aromas of sawdust and dill and only skimpy, dried currant fruits. Score 60. K

SIFSAF, SYRAH, 2005: With odors of iodine and burning rubber and flavors of vinegar, many will consider this an undrinkable wine. Score 50. K

SIFSAF, CHARDONNAY, 2005: Dark gold towards bronze, acidic enough to pucker the lips and with apple vinegar aromas. Score 50. K

SIFSAF, CHARDONNAY, 2004: Medicinal, musty, pungent and unclean aromas and flavors. Score 50. K

SIFSAF, SAUVIGNON BLANC, 2004: Musty, bitter, with distinct iodine aromas and flavors that coat the mouth. Score 50. K

Smadar **

Established by Moty Sela in 1998 and located in Zichron Ya'akov, this winery draws on grapes from nearby vineyards owned by the family, those containing Cabernet Sauvignon, Merlot, Cabernet Franc and Carignan grapes. Production is currently about 5,000 bottles annually.

SMADAR, CABERNET SAUVIGNON, 2005: Deep purple towards black, intense and concentrated, this full-bodied red shows still-firm tannins and generous wood, balanced by fruits, spices and an appealing herbal overlay. On the nose and palate blackberries, black currants and a hint of citrus peel together with vanilla, chocolate and *bouquet garni* aromas and flavors. Drink from release. Tentative Score 86–88.

SMADAR, CABERNET SAUVIGNON, 2004: Blended with 10% of Carignan, this dark royal-purple, medium-bodied red shows generous tannins and wood, those opening to spicy currant and blackberry fruits. Drink now. Score 85.

SMADAR, CABERNET SAUVIGNON, 2003: Dark ruby towards garnet, with its earlier firm tannins and generous wood now integrating nicely and showing appealing currant, wild berry and black cherry fruits with a light hint of toasted herbs that runs through. Drink up. Score 84.

SMADAR, MERLOT, 2005: Dark garnet towards royal-purple, medium to full-bodied, with soft but mouth-coating tannins that highlight appealing purple plum, cassis and blackberry fruits, those with an overlay of Oriental spices. Long and generous. Drink from release. Tentative Score 85–87.

SMADAR, MERLOT, 2004: Blended with 5% each of Cabernet Sauvignon and Carignan, the wine shows garnet-red color, with generous chunky-style tannins opening to reveal blackberry, black cherry and currant fruits on a background of spicy oak. An appealing country-style wine. Drink now. Score 85.

SMADAR, MERLOT, 2003: Dark cherry-red in color, with firm, mouth-coating tannins and spicy wood yielding nicely to black fruits. Needs time in the glass to show its roundness. Drink now. Score 84.

SMADAR, CARIGNAN, 2004: Dark ruby towards garnet, medium to full-bodied, with soft, near-sweet tannins. Showing aromas of berries, black cherries and tobacco. Drink now. Score 85.

Snir **

Founded in 2002 by Danny Stein and located on Kibbutz Snir in the Upper Galilee, the winery relies on Cabernet Sauvignon and Merlot grapes from the Sha'al vineyards. Initial production was of 1,200 bottles and current production is 5,000 bottles annually.

SNIR, CABERNET SAUVIGNON, 2005: Dark royal-purple, medium-bodied, with soft tannins integrating nicely and balanced by a judicious hand with oak and acidity. On the nose and palate currants, blackberries and raspberries, those with light spicy overtones that linger nicely on the finish. Drink from release. Tentative Score 84–86.

SNIR, CABERNET SAUVIGNON, NIMROD, 2004: Dark, but not fully clear royal-purple, aged in oak for one year, medium-bodied, with soft, well-integrating tannins and plum and blackberry fruits on a lightly spicy background. Drink now. Score 83.

SNIR, CABERNET SAUVIGNON, NIMROD, 2002: Dark garnet, medium to full-bodied, with soft tannins. On the nose and palate blackberries and currants along with hints of spices and chocolate. Drink now. Score 86.

SNIR, MERLOT, 2005: Garnet towards purple, medium-bodied, with soft tannins and an appealing array of spicy berries and black cherries. Not complex but a good quaffer. Drink now. Score 84.

SNIR, MERLOT, NIMROD, 2002: Dark purple towards inky black, with its black fruits somewhat hidden under deep layers of bitter herbs and earthiness. Drink up. Score 77.

SNIR, CABERNET SAUVIGNON-MERLOT, NIMROD, 2003: Dark purple, medium-bodied, with generous smoky wood reflecting its 16 months in oak. Showing soft tannins and appealing red currant, raspberry and red plums backed up nicely by a hint of toasted herbs. Drink up. Score 85.

Somek ★★★

2004
SYRAH

75 Cl. 13% Alc. • Zichron - Ya'akov, Israel

Established by Australian-trained winemaker Hilla Ben Gera and vintner Barak Dahan in Rishon Letzion on the southern coastal plain, the winery released its first wines from the 2003 vintage with 1,500 bottles and anticipate future release of 3,000–5,000 bottles annually. The winery relies on its own vineyards, with Merlot, Syrah, Carignan and Chardonnay grapes.

SOMEK, MERLOT, 2003: Dark garnet towards inky-purple, medium to full-bodied, with firm tannins and generous vanilla and spices reflecting its 20 months in *barriques*. Although powerful, the wine is well balanced, with black currants, blackberries and black cherry fruits showing nicely and lingering comfortably on a moderately long and round finish. Drink now. Score 88.

SOMEK, SYRAH, 2004: Mediterranean Syrah, with peppery wild berry, black cherry and plum aromas and flavors, those matched nicely by chewy but yielding tannins, intimations of spicy wood and a beefy hint on the finish. Medium to full-bodied, with the clear potential for elegance. Drink now–2010. Score 89.

SOMEK, CARIGNAN, 2003: Dark garnet, full-bodied, with generous oak reflecting its 20 months in *barriques*, but that in fine balance with soft tannins, fruit and acidity. On the nose and palate black currants, red plums and raspberry fruits together with generous doses of smoky toast and pepper and, on the moderately long finish, hints of vanilla and coffee. Drink now. Score 89.

SOMEK, CHARDONNAY, 2004: Light golden-straw in color, medium-bodied, with generous but not offensive oak influences balanced nicely by crisp acidity. Opens with citrus and citrus flowers, those going to pears, almonds and figs and closing on a near-sweet note. Drink now. Score 87.

Soreq ***

Originally a partnership of Yossi Shacham, his son Nir and Barry Saslove, this small winery was founded in 1994 on Moshav Tal Shachar, which is situated at the foot of the Jerusalem Mountains between the Ayalon and Soreq Valleys. After Saslove left to open his own winery in 1998, Nir Shacham took over as winemaker and has recently taken on full ownership. The winery relies entirely on Cabernet Sauvignon and Merlot grapes grown in its own vineyards, and releases wines in Special Reserve and regular editions. Current production is 5,000 bottles annually.

Special Reserve

SPECIAL RESERVE, CABERNET SAUVIGNON, 2004: Dark garnet towards royal-purple, full-bodied, with generous, somewhat chunky tannins and dusty wood giving the wine a countrified personality. Look for an abundance of currant, berry and black cherry fruits on a background of spicy oak and Mediterranean herbs. Drink from release. Tentative Score 86–88.

SPECIAL RESERVE, CABERNET SAUVIGNON, 2001: Medium to full-bodied, the wine shows generous tannins well balanced by spicy wood and tempting currant, plum and berry fruits along with hints of smoke and chocolate, on a medium-long finish. Drink now. Score 89.

SPECIAL RESERVE, CABERNET SAUVIGNON, 2000: Full-bodied, the wine shows generous, integrated tannins along with rich aromas and flavors of black currant and berry fruits, those complemented nicely by toasted oak and spices. On the long finish hints of chocolate and mint. Fully mature. Drink up. Score 88.

SPECIAL RESERVE, CABERNET SAUVIGNON, 1999: Rich, muscular and full-bodied, but elegant and sophisticated, with currants, black cherries, violets and dried herbs. Fully mature, and somewhat past its peak. Drink up. Score 87.

SPECIAL RESERVE, MERLOT, 2001: Deep garnet-red, medium to full-bodied, with generous soft tannins and generous oaky-vanilla aromas and flavors, those opening to reveal plum and blackberry fruits and a long, moderately sweet finish. Drink up. Score 86.

SPECIAL RESERVE, MERLOT, 2000: Dark garnet towards royal-purple, medium to full-bodied, with good balance between wood, soft tannins and ripe black fruits. Past its peak. Drink up. Score 84.

Soreq

SOREQ, CABERNET SAUVIGNON, 2005: Dark garnet towards purple in color, full-bodied, with firm tannins that need time to integrate but already showing appealing cassis, berry and black cherry fruits leading to a long minty finish. Best from release–2010. Tentative Score 86–88.

SOREQ, CABERNET SAUVIGNON, KEREM YOSEF, 2004: Impenetrably dark garnet, full-bodied and concentrated, with near-sweet tannins and vanilla from the *barriques* in which it developed. On the nose and palate plums, berries and hints of somewhat astringent red licorice. Drink now. Score 87.

SOREQ, CABERNET SAUVIGNON, TAL SHACHAR, 2002: Reflecting its 18 months in *barriques* with generous, sweet cedar and vanilla, the wine shows firm tannins, those balanced well by currant, plum and wild berry fruits and an appealingly long finish rich in espresso and tobacco notes. Drink now. Score 88.

SOREQ, CABERNET SAUVIGNON, TAL SHACHAR, 2001: 100% Cabernet Sauvignon aged for 18 months in French and American oak *barriques*, this medium-bodied red shows basic good balance between wood, soft tannins and somewhat dominating oak as well as plum, black currant and black cherry fruits on a generous smoky background. Drink up. Score 86.

SOREQ, MERLOT, TAL SHACHAR, 2004: Dark garnet towards royal-purple, full-bodied, with softly mouth-coating tannins and hints of vanilla and cinnamon. Opens to reveal currant and berry fruits, those on a lightly spicy background. Long and generous. Drink now–2009. Score 88.

Sraya **

Founded in 2002 by Sraya Ofer and set in the Jordan Valley, this small winery receives Cabernet Sauvignon, Merlot and Shiraz grapes from vineyards in Karmei Yosef and the Ella Valley. First releases were of under 1,000 bottles and currently the winery is releasing about 3,500 bottles annually.

SRAYA, CABERNET SAUVIGNON, 2004: Ruby towards garnet, medium-bodied, with soft tannins integrating nicely and showing red currant and cherry fruits on a spicy, herbal background. On the finish a hint of saddle leather. An appealing quaffer. Drink now. Score 85.

SRAYA, MERLOT, 2004: A round, smooth and easy-going wine, medium-bodied, with soft tannins and forward berry, black cherry and spicy notes. Drink now. Score 85.

Srigim **

Founded by Uriel Harari and Moti Mordechai on Moshav Srigim in the Ella Valley in 2000, this small winery released its first wines from the 2002 harvest. Drawing on grapes from the Judean Mountains, the Ella Valley and Gush Etzion, the winery has chosen to concentrate mainly on Cabernet Sauvignon. Production for the 2004, 2005 and 2006 vintages was 2,500 bottles.

SRIGIM, CABERNET SAUVIGNON, 2005: Very generous dusty oak and still-firm tannins tend to hide the blackberry and currant fruits that may find their way to the surface. Drink from release. Tentative Score 80–82.

SRIGIM, CABERNET SAUVIGNON, 2004: Garnet towards royal-purple in color, this oak-aged wine shows firm tannins and ample oak. On the nose and palate near-jammy blackberry, blueberry and cassis fruits. Drink now. Score 83.

SRIGIM, CABERNET SAUVIGNON, 2003: Aged in oak for one year, this deep royal-purple, full-bodied red offers firm tannins and generous oak, those complemented by super-ripe, almost jammy black plum and berry fruits. Drink up. Score 85.

SRIGIM, CABERNET FRANC, 2005: Developing in new American *barriques*, with generous spicy wood and firm tannins waiting to integrate. Showing some black fruits and a hint of tar. Drink from release. Tentative Score 79–81.

SRIGIM, PETIT VERDOT, 2005: Dark garnet in color, with soft tannins and plum, berry and currant notes. Soft and round. Drink from release. Tentative Score 82–84.

SRIGIM, CABERNET SAUVIGNON-MERLOT, 2005: A blend of 60% Cabernet Sauvignon and 40% Merlot, oak-aged for 13 months. Medium-bodied, soft and round with black fruits and gentle tannins. Lacks complexity but a pleasant entry-level wine. Score 84.

Tabor ****

Founded in 1999 by several grape-growing families in the village of Kfar Tabor in the Lower Galilee, this modern winery draws on white grapes largely from their own vineyards near Mount Tabor and on red grapes from the Upper Galilee. Initial production was of 20,000 bottles and current production is about 650,000 bottles annually.

European-trained winemaker Arieh Nesher is currently releasing wines in three series. The top-of-the-line label is Mes'cha, a series of varietal wines that includes Cabernet Sauvignon, Merlot and Chardonnay, those to be joined shortly by Gewurztraminer. A second label, Adama, reflects the type of soils in the vineyards. In reading the labels it may be useful to know that *adama* translates into soil; *gir* is chalky soil; *terra rossa* is red earth; *charsit* is clay and *bazelet* refers to volcanic soil. There is also a more basic series released under the label Tabor.

Several years ago, the Central Bottling Corporation, which is the local producer of Coca-Cola, bought into Tabor and in 2005 increased its holdings in the winery to 51%. Extensive planting of new vineyards is currently underway.

Mes'cha

MES'CHA, 2003: A blend of Cabernet Sauvignon, Shiraz and Merlot (75%, 15% and 10% respectively), this deep garnet, medium to full-bodied wine reflects its 18 months in oak with tannins and spicy wood integrating and opening to reveal black currant, berry and plum fruits on a background of spicy wood and Mediterranean herbs. Generous, well balanced and long. Drink now–2009. Score 90. K

MES'CHA, 2002: A blend of Cabernet Sauvignon and Merlot, this medium to full-bodied red shows firm but well-integrated tannins with spicy oak and generous currant and wild berry fruits, those matched by hints of spices, earthiness and tobacco on the finish. Drink now. Score 88. K

MES'CHA, CABERNET SAUVIGNON, 2001: Dark garnet-red, medium to full-bodied, with good balance between firm but well-integrated tannins, spicy oak and an appealing array of black currant, plums, smoke and fresh earthy aromas and flavors. Long and mouth-filling. Drink now. Score 90. K

MES'CHA, CABERNET SAUVIGNON, 2000: Full-bodied, concentrated and intense, this deeply tannic, now fully mature wine opens in the glass to show black fruits, cigar tobacco, tar, and earthy aromas and flavors. Drink up. Score 88. K

MES'CHA, CABERNET SAUVIGNON-MERLOT, 2001: A full-bodied blend of 80% Cabernet Sauvignon and 20% Merlot, the wine was aged partly in new oak and partly in one-year-old barrels for 14 months and shows excellent focus and tempting flavors of currants, spices and cedar along with a leathery note that runs throughout. Drink up. Score 89. K

MES'CHA, CHARDONNAY, 2004: Deep gold in color, medium to full-bodied, with appealing pear and citrus flavors along with a hint of mango on a background of spicy oak. Round buttery texture and good balance between wood, acidity and fruits. Drink up. Score 88. K

MES'CHA, RED DESSERT WINE, 2003: Made entirely from Merlot grapes, full-bodied, with generous but not cloying sweetness. Round and soft on the palate with raspberry, plum, blueberry and chocolate notes. Drink now. Score 87. K

Adama

ADAMA, CABERNET SAUVIGNON, BAZELET, 2005: Medium-dark garnet towards purple, this medium to full-bodied blend of 87% Cabernet Sauvignon and 13% Merlot was developed in 2000 liter wood casks and shows generous black currant, blackberry, citrus peel and earthy-mineral aromas and flavors. On the long finish hints of sweet cedar, tobacco and eucalyptus. Drink now–2012. Score 90. K

ADAMA, CABERNET SAUVIGNON, BAZELET, 2004: Dark garnet in color, with deep purple and orange reflections, this medium to full-bodied wine shows good balance between smoky wood, acidity and fruits. On the nose and palate concentrated currant and blackberry fruits matched by espresso and vanilla. Seductive and elegant. Drink now–2010. Score 90. K

ADAMA, CABERNET SAUVIGNON, TERRA ROSSA, 2005: Dark garnet towards royal-purple, medium to full-bodied, with firm, near-sweet tannins integrating nicely and now showing red plums, raspberries and currant fruits, those matched by minerals and light hints of herbaceousness. Round, long and generous. Drink now–2011. Score 89. K

ADAMA, CABERNET SAUVIGNON, TERRA ROSSA, 2004: Dark garnet, medium to full-bodied, with spicy wood, soft tannins integrating nicely and red currant, blackberry and plum on the nose and palate, those backed up by an appealing hint of earthiness that lingers nicely. Drink now. Score 88. K

ADAMA, CABERNET SAUVIGNON, TERRA ROSSA, 2003: Dark royal-purple, almost inky, this medium to full-bodied red is already showing appealing currant, cherry and spice flavors and aromas. Inherent good balance between soft tannins, acidity and fruits and an appealing spicy finish. Drink now. Score 87. K

ADAMA CABERNET SAUVIGNON, TERRA ROSSA, 2002: Dark, tight and firm but well focused and opening nicely in the glass to reveal an array of ripe cherry, currant, spice, anise and lightly toasty oak flavors. Supple and well focused with just the right hints of tannins that come to the fore on the long finish. Drink up. Score 88. K

ADAMA, MERLOT, BAZELET, 2005: Blended with 10% of Cabernet Sauvignon, this medium-bodied red reflects its 12 months in French and American oak with soft tannins and appealing hints of vanilla, white chocolate and spices. On the nose and palate red and black berries, cassis and earthy-minerals. Soft, round and generous. Drink now–2010. Score 90. K

ADAMA, MERLOT, BAZELET, 2004: Dark garnet towards royal-purple, medium to full-bodied, with a moderate wood influence and well-integrated tannins in fine balance with black currant, plum and wild berry fruits. On the moderately long finish, hints of eucalyptus and chocolate. Drink now. Score 88. K

ADAMA, MERLOT, BAZELET, 2003: Reflecting its 12 months in oak with appealing smoky and vanilla overlays and showing tempting black currant, purple plum and berry fruits, this is a distinctly French-style wine, well balanced and generous. Drink now. Score 89. K

ADAMA, MERLOT, BAZELET, 2001: Deep garnet, medium to full-bodied, and reflecting the French and American oak with hints of vanilla and smoke, the wine shows smooth tannins, currant, spice and black cherry flavors, and a rich fruity finish that fans out beautifully on the palate. Aromatic, round and mouth-filling. Drink up. Score 87. K

ADAMA, MERLOT, GIR, 2005: Medium-dark ruby in color, with berries and black currants backed up comfortably by near-sweet tannins and hints of spicy wood, all coming together beautifully. Drink now–2010. Score 89. K

ADAMA, MERLOT, GIR, 2004: Medium-bodied, with gentle spicy oak influences and soft tannins integrating nicely, with raspberry, blackberry, cassis and light earthy overtones. A round, smooth and near-elegant wine. Drink now. Score 89. K

ADAMA, MERLOT, GIR, 2003: Dark garnet, medium-bodied, and somewhat internationalized in style, with soft tannins, hints of sweet cedarwood and forward plum and currant fruits. Light herbal notes on the finish add complexity. Drink now. Score 88. K

ADAMA, MERLOT, GIR, 2002: Dark cherry-red toward garnet, this medium-bodied, lightly oaked wine has a somewhat muted nose but shows very well on the palate, opening to reveal dark plums, currants, smooth tannins and a rich, lingering finish. Drink up. Score 85. K

ADAMA, SHIRAZ, CHARSIT, 2004: Full-bodied, with soft tannins, good hints of smoky oak and sweet cedar, and generous black plums, berries and currants. Still young but promising to be a simultaneously complex and easy-to-drink wine. Drink now. Score 88. K

ADAMA, SHIRAZ, CHARSIT, 2003: Deep garnet, medium to full-bodied, with firm tannins but those well integrated with spicy oak, vanilla and generous red plum and currant fruits. On the long finish, appealing light meaty and herbal overtones. Drink now–2009. Score 89. K

ADAMA, CABERNET FRANC, ROSÉ, CHARSIT, 2006: Mother-of-pearl pink in color, crisply dry, with appealing berry, cherry and currant fruits matched nicely by earthy minerals and tantalizing hints of spearmint and bitterness that come in on the finish. Drink now. Score 88. K

ADAMA, CABERNET FRANC, ROSÉ, CHARSIT, 2005: With a deep pink color of peaches in their first bloom, a medium body and 14% alcohol content, the wine shows appealing currant, red berry and rose petal aromas and flavors, those hinting of earth on the finish. Delicious and crisply dry. Drink up. Score 88. K

ADAMA, CHARDONNAY, BAZELET, 2005: Aged in *barriques* without malolactic fermentation, this is a clean, crisp and fresh, medium-bodied wine, with citrus and peach fruits matched nicely by gentle wood and lively acidity as well as a long finish. Drink now. Score 88. K

ADAMA, CHARDONNAY, BAZELET, 2004: Light gold, medium-bodied, with citrus and tropical fruits on a lightly earthy background. Good balancing acidity keeps the wine lively and hints of earthiness and herbaceousness add complexity. Drink up. Score 88. K

ADAMA, CHARDONNAY, GIR, 2004: Crisp, clean and with abundant minerals on the nose and palate, those matched well by citrus and melon fruits. Calls to mind a Petit Chablis. Drink up. Score 87. K

ADAMA, SAUVIGNON BLANC, GIR, 2006: Bright shining straw in color, medium-bodied and aromatic, this unoaked white shows citrus, citrus peel, white peach and mineral aromas and flavors. Crisp and refreshing. Drink now. Score 87. K

ADAMA, SAUVIGNON BLANC, GIR, 2005: Light straw in color, this un-oaked white starts off with subdued aromas and flavors but given time in the glass opens to reveal crisply dry mineral-rich citrus and nutty aromas and flavors. Round and full of flavor. Drink now. Score 88. K

ADAMA, SAUVIGNON BLANC, GIR, 2004: Unoaked, crisply dry with light herbal and earthy hints on a background of grapefruit, orange peel and minerals. Refreshing and generous. Drink now. Score 88. K

Tabor

TABOR, CABERNET SAUVIGNON, 2006: Dark ruby in color, medium-bodied, this soft, round and fruity red is showing generous berry, black cherry and currant fruits all on a lightly spicy background. Not complex but appealing. Drink now. Score 86. K

TABOR, CABERNET SAUVIGNON, 2005: Medium-bodied, with soft tannins integrating nicely, this unoaked red shows appealing black-berries, currants and spices, all filling the mouth comfortably. Easy to drink and with just enough complexity to hold our attention. Drink now. Score 85. K

TABOR, CABERNET SAUVIGNON, 2004: Dark ruby towards garnet, medium-bodied, with silky-smooth tannins and appealing currant and wild berry fruits. Nothing complex but very pleasant. Drink up. Score 86. K

TABOR, MERLOT, 2006: Soft, smooth and round, with gently mouth-coating tannins and appealing berry, black cherry and currant fruits showing appealing herbal overtones. Drink now. Score 86. K

TABOR, MERLOT, 2005: Ruby towards garnet and medium-bodied, with berry and cherry fruits, this unoaked, soft round wine makes for easy quaffing, although not all will appreciate the hint of sweetness it carries. Drink now. Score 85. K

TABOR, MERLOT, 2003: Medium-bodied, with soft tannins and generous berry and black cherry fruits. Not complex but pleasant. Drink up. Score 85. K

TABOR, SHIRAZ, 2005: This dark garnet-red-towards-royal-purple wine reflects its 12 months in oak with gentle spicy wood and tannins that while still firm show no sharp edges. On the nose and palate plums and blackberries complemented by hints of earthy minerals and, rising on the finish, a hint of raspberries. Drink now. Score 88. K

TABOR, SHIRAZ, 2004: Garnet-red, medium to full-bodied, with tannins and wood integrating nicely and showing berry, plum and light leathery notes leading to a medium-long finish. Drink now. Score 86. K

TABOR, SHIRAZ, 2003: Dark purple in color, the wine opens in the glass to reveal hints of licorice and game together with firm tannins and deep raspberry floral accents. Clean and long, a fine Mediterranean version of Shiraz. Drink up. Score 88. K

TABOR, CHARDONNAY, 2006: Crisp, refreshing and with appealing peach, citrus and citrus peel notes along with a generous mineral overlay. Drink now. Score 88. K

TABOR, CHARDONNAY, 2005: Clean, crisp and refreshing. Medium-bodied, with forward aromas and flavors of citrus and peaches along with crisp minerality. Drink now. Score 87. K

Tanya **

Located in the town of Ofra at the foot of the Hebron Mountains, this winery established by Yoram Cohen released its first wines in 2002. Drawing on Cabernet Sauvignon and Merlot grapes from Gush Etzion and the Golan Heights, the winery produced 6,500 bottles in 2004 and about 15,000 bottles in 2005.

Reserve

RESERVE, CABERNET SAUVIGNON, 2005: Dark ruby towards garnet, medium to full-bodied, with firm tannins and spicy wood opening to reveal currant, berry and black cherry fruits, those with light overtones of fresh herbs. Drink now–2009. Score 85. K

RESERVE, CABERNET SAUVIGNON, 2004: Medium-bodied, softly tannic, with generous but not overpowering smoky oak and appealing aromas and flavors of black currants, berries and dark chocolate, all with a bitter hint that will appeal to some. Drink now. Score 84. K

RESERVE, CABERNET SAUVIGNON, 2003: Dark cherry-red, medium to full-bodied, with firm but already well-integrating tannins and a light influence of oak. Aromas and flavors of currants, plums, Mediterranean herbs and a hint of tobacco. Drink now. Score 84. K

RESERVE, CABERNET SAUVIGNON, 2002: Deep garnet, medium-bodied with firm but well-integrated tannins and a nice hint of wood after four months in small barrels. Opens with barnyard aromas but those fade away to reveal black fruits and herbs. Drink up. Score 84. K

RESERVE, MERLOT, 2005: Deep garnet in color, medium to full-bodied with soft, mouth-coating tannins and a gentle wood influence. On the nose and palate blackberries and cassis fruits supported nicely by hints of chocolate and mint., Drink now–2009. Score 85. K

RESERVE, MERLOT, 2004: Dark garnet towards royal-purple, medium to full-bodied, with soft tannins and generous spicy oak in good balance with black and red berry and black cherry fruits. A pleasant quaffer. Drink now. Score 85. K

RESERVE, MERLOT, 2003: A country-style wine, medium-bodied, with chunky tannins, a distinct smoky oak overlay and very ripe grape and berry aromas and flavors. Drink up. Score 82. K

RESERVE, MERLOT, 2002: Dark cherry-red in color, this wine reflects its seven months in oak with still-firm tannins and very generous toasted-oak aromas and flavors that hide the plum and berry fruits that struggle to make themselves felt. Drink up. Score 83. K

RESERVE, BLEND, 2004: A dark garnet, medium-bodied and softly tannic blend of 70% Cabernet Sauvignon and 30% Merlot. On the nose and palate currants, raspberries and a generous hint of herbaceousness. Drink up. Score 84. K

Teperberg ∗∗∗

Founded in 1870 by the Teperberg family in the Jewish quarter of the old city of Jerusalem, and then relocating outside of the walls, the winery moved to Motza, on the outskirts of the city, in 1964, and there took on the name of Efrat. For much of that time it produced primarily sacramental wines for the ultra-Orthodox community. During the 1990s it also started producing table wines. Starting in 2002, under the supervision of California-trained winemaker Shiki Rauchberger the winery began producing wines destined to appeal to a more sophisticated audience. Now relocated to their newly constructed winery on Kibbutz Tzora at the foothills of the Jerusalem Mountains, the winery has officially changed its name back to Teperberg.

The winery, currently producing about 4 million bottles annually, is now releasing wines in various series. The top-of-the-line wines carry the label of Teperberg Reserve, those followed by Terra, Teperberg Silver, and Israeli. The Collage series has been discontinued. Grapes are drawn from the wineries' own vineyards in the Judean Mountains as well as from other regions. With the exception of the wines in the Reserve, Silver and Terra series, all of the wines are *mevushal*. Target production within the next five years is 7 million bottles annually.

Teperberg Reserve

RESERVE, CABERNET SAUVIGNON, 2005: Dark ruby towards garnet, medium to full-bodied, with soft tannins and gentle smoky wood integrating nicely. Currant and blackberry fruits complemented by hints of cherries, orange peel and light mocha aromas and flavors, all with a hint of Oriental spices rising on the finish. Drink now–2010. Score 88. K

RESERVE, CABERNET SAUVIGNON, 2004: Dark, almost impenetrable garnet, medium to full-bodied, with soft tannins. Reflecting its 12 months in American oak with hints of sweet cedar and vanilla. One the nose and palate currants, berries, sage and espresso coffee and on the finish a hint of asphalt, all coming together nicely. Drink now–2009. Score 87. K

RESERVE, CABERNET SAUVIGNON, 2003: Dark garnet in color, with its once-firm tannins now integrating nicely to show tempting berry, black cherry and currant fruits, those matched by hints of spices, leather and earthiness and, on the generous finish, an appealing overlay of chocolate. Drink now–2009. Score 88. K

RESERVE, MERLOT, 2005: Dark garnet towards purple, medium-bodied, with soft tannins, rich earthiness and red fruits on the nose, those opening to show generous tangy black currants, minerals and cocoa powder, all lingering nicely. Drink from release–2009. Tentative Score 87–89. K

RESERVE, MERLOT, 2004: Medium-dark ruby, medium-bodied, with soft, near-sweet tannins and appealing black currant, cassis and purple plums complemented by hints of chocolate and Mediterranean herbs. Drink now. Score 87. K

RESERVE, CHARDONNAY, 2005: Golden in color with orange tints, showing a moderate hand with spicy oak from its eight months in *barriques*. Subdued when first poured but opens nicely to reveal melon, pear and green apple notes, those on a near-creamy background. Drink now–2009. Score 89. K

RESERVE, CHARDONNAY, 2004: Fermented and developed *sur lie* for six months in new French oak *barriques*, this deep golden, medium-bodied wine shows an appealing array of citrus, peach and pear fruits. Drink up. Score 87. K

RESERVE, CHENIN BLANC, 2005: Golden-straw in color, with a deep herbal, earthy and citrus peel nose opening to reveal a light to medium-bodied lively white with generous orange marmalade, nectarine and cardamom flavors. Drink now. Score 87. K

RESERVE, CHENIN BLANC, 2004: A bit of bottle stink when first opened but that blows off nicely. Golden-straw in color, medium-bodied, reflecting oak treatment with a light creamy overlay on aromas and flavors of peaches, pears, melons and spring flowers, those complemented by a hint of citrus peel on the finish. Drink up. Score 87. K

Silver

SILVER, CABERNET SAUVIGNON, 2006: Dark garnet towards purple, medium to full-bodied, with near-sweet tannins and forward black fruit. Drink now–2010. Score 87. K

SILVER, MERLOT, 2006: Garnet towards purple, medium to full-bodied, with dusty wood and soft tannins coming together nicely with blackberry and berry fruits. Medium-long and generously fruity on the finish. Drink now. Score 86. K

SILVER, SYRAH, 2006: Dark royal-purple in color, reflecting its five months in oak with gentle spices and a hint of toasty wood. Medium-bodied, with soft but mouth-coating tannins opening to reveal purple plum and blackberry fruits, those complemented by a light and appealing earthiness that continues to a medium-long finish. Drink now–2009. Score 88. K

SILVER, SHIRAZ, 2005: Garnet towards purple, medium-bodied, with generous soft tannins. Aromas and flavors of blackberries, licorice and black olives, finishing with a dusty spicy note. Drink now. Score 86. K

SILVER, ZINFANDEL, 2006: Dark garnet in color, medium-bodied, with soft tannins, this semi-dry red shows simple plum and cherry aromas and flavors. Lacks complexity. Drink up. Score 79. K

SILVER, CABERNET SAUVIGNON-MERLOT, 2006: A medium-bodied blend of Cabernet Sauvignon, Merlot and Cabernet Franc (70%, 25% and 5% respectively). Dark garnet, showing spicy wood, soft tannins and an appealing hint of earthiness on the black fruits. Drink now–2009. Score 88. K

SILVER, MERITAGE, 2006: A deep, almost inky-garnet, lightly-oaked blend of Cabernet Sauvignon, Merlot and Cabernet Franc (70%, 25% and 5% respectively). Medium to full-bodied, the wine opens with wild berries and hints of orange peel, those yielding to gentle overtones of vanilla and espresso coffee. Drink now–2009. Score 87. K

SILVER, MERITAGE, 2005: A medium to full-bodied lightly oaked blend of 70% Cabernet Sauvignon, 25% Merlot and 5% Cabernet Franc. Chunky tannins tend to hold back cedar, tobacco, currant and sage aromas and flavors. Perhaps better with time. Drink now–2010. Score 88. K

SILVER, MERITAGE, 2004: Lightly oaked, this dark garnet, medium to full-bodied blend of Cabernet Sauvignon, Merlot and Cabernet Franc offers up spicy oak and black currant, blackberry and orange peel notes. Round and generous. Drink up. Score 87. к

SILVER, MERITAGE, 2003: A full-bodied, softly tannic Bordeaux blend of 50% Cabernet Sauvignon, 40% Merlot and 10% Cabernet Franc. Dark ruby but showing hints of browning, with spicy oak and still appealing plum, currant and berry fruits. Now fully mature. Drink up. Score 85. к

SILVER, CHARDONNAY, 2006: Golden-straw in color, reflecting its six months in new French oak with vanilla, spices and a light buttery overtone. On the nose and palate ripe summer fruits and pears, coming together nicely. Drink now–2009. Score 87. к

SILVER, CHARDONNAY-SAUVIGNON BLANC, 2005: Light straw, medium-bodied, with orange, lemon and apple aromas and flavors. Not complex but a good quaffer. Drink up. Score 85. к

SILVER, EMERALD RIESLING, 2006: Light, shining straw in color, with generous sweetness. Showing floral aromas and flavors of citrus and tropical fruits. Lacks balancing acidity. Drink up. Score 80. к

SILVER, LATE HARVEST WHITE RIESLING, 2006: Delivers a generous mouthful of apricot, raisin, papaya and honey flavors. Generous sweetness here but that given good liveliness by citrus acidity. Fresh, clean and appealing. Drink now–2010. Score 89. к

Terra

TERRA, CABERNET SAUVIGNON, 2005: Dark garnet with purple and orange reflections, this wine shows a gentle hand with spicy oak and soft tannins. On the nose and palate traditional Cabernet black currant and blackberry fruits, those with spice and orange peel overlays and, on the moderately long finish, an appealing hint of cigar tobacco. Drink now–2010. Score 90. к

TERRA, CABERNET SAUVIGNON, 2004: Oak-aged for 12 months, showing soft and round with generous currant, plum and spices but revealing a hint of browning along with a rising herbaceousness. Drinking well but not for further cellaring. Drink up. Score 86. к

TERRA, MERLOT, 2005: Garnet towards royal-purple, medium to full-bodied, with still-gripping tannins but those in fine balance with wood, fruits and acidity. On first attack black fruits and a light earthy overlay, those yielding to raspberries, currants and minerals. On the mouth-filling finish a generous hint of licorice. Drink now–2010. Score 90. к

TERRA, CABERNET SAUVIGNON-MERLOT, 2006: Oak-aged for six months, this garnet-towards-royal-purple blend of 70% Cabernet Sauvignon, 25% Merlot and 5% Cabernet Franc shows an appealing array of blackberry, black cherry and cassis fruits, those on a background of lightly spicy cedar. Round and generous. Drink now–2009. Score 87. K

TERRA, CABERNET SAUVIGNON-MERLOT, 2005: Dark cherry towards garnet-red in color, with soft tannins, just the barest hint of wood, and appealing plum, currant and blueberry aromas and flavors. Not complex but lively and easy to drink. Drink now. Score 85. K

TERRA, ROSÉ, 2006: Rose-petal pink in color, crisply dry and with fine acidity to keep it lively. Showing raspberry, strawberry and cranberry fruits all with a light hint of spiciness that creeps in nicely. Drink up. Score 82. K

TERRA, CHARDONNAY, 2005: Developed *sur lie* in French barrels for three months, this light straw-colored, medium-bodied, and lively white shows straightforward but appealing aromas and flavors of citrus and summer fruits. Drink up. Score 85. K

TERRA, EMERALD RIESLING, 2006: Aromatic, with flowers and freshly mown grass on the nose and showing citrus and mango fruits. Half-dry and finishing with a hint of mint. Drink now. Score 84. K

Israeli

ISRAELI, CABERNET SAUVIGNON, 2006: Medium-bodied with soft tannins, this garnet-towards-purple, country-style blend of 85% Cabernet Sauvignon and Merlot shows simple aromas and flavors of berries, black cherries and spices. Drink now. Score 82. K

ISRAELI, CABERNET SAUVIGNON, 2005: Medium-bodied, soft and round with blackberry, currant and black cherry fruits. An entry-level quaffer. Drink now. Score 84. K

ISRAELI, MERLOT, 2006: Blended with 10% of Shiraz and 5% of Cabernet Sauvignon, a medium-bodied country-style wine with straightforward berry and black cherry aromas and flavors. Drink now. Score 80. K

ISRAELI, MERLOT, 2005: Medium-bodied, with gentle tannins and showing forward plum, raisin and toasty aromas and flavors. A pleasant enough little red. Drink up. Score 83. K

ISRAELI, SHIRAZ, 2006: Made entirely from Shiraz grapes and aged for five months in oak. Ruby towards garnet, medium-bodied, with soft but mouth-coating tannins and with a light earthy overlay on its black fruits. Drink now. Score 80. K

ISRAELI, SHIRAZ, 2005: Soft and round, light and lively, with raspberry, plum and dusty-spicy aromas and flavors that linger nicely. Drink now. Score 85. K

ISRAELI, MERLOT-PETITE SIRAH, 2006: Dark garnet, medium-bodied, with soft tannins, this is a clean, simple wine with blackberry and cherry fruits. Drink up. Score 79. K

ISRAELI, MERLOT-PETITE SIRAH, 2005: Medium-bodied, with soft tannins and hints of spicy wood. Aromas and flavors of currants and blackberries. Simple but appealing. Drink now. Score 85. K

ISRAELI, ZINFANDEL, BLUSH, 2006: A half-dry wine, with a lively pink color but with hardly perceptible fruits hidden by too-generous sweetness. Drink up. Score 75. K

ISRAELI, ZINFANDEL, BLUSH, 2005: Light and fruity, showing cherry, raspberry and citrus. Perhaps a bit on the sweet side. Drink up. Score 82. K

ISRAELI, CHARDONNAY, 2006: Lightly oaked, and light to medium-bodied, this lively straw-colored wine shows appealing citrus, peach and mineral aromas and flavors. Drink now. Score 85. K

ISRAELI, CHARDONNAY, 2005: Pleasant in its extreme youth, but a wine that has aged quickly and badly. Now lacking acidity, showing only minimal fruits and far too much butterscotch. Drink up. Score 76. K

ISRAELI, SAUVIGNON BLANC, 2006: Light straw in color, light to medium-bodied, with only the skimpiest of citrus and tropical fruits and not enough acidity to keep it lively. Drink up. Score 75. K

ISRAELI, SAUVIGNON BLANC, 2005: Light straw in color, medium-bodied, with aromas and flavors of grapefruit, passion fruit, and a light hint of grassiness. An entry-level quaffer. Drink up. Score 84. K

ISRAELI, EMERALD RIESLING, 2006: Half-dry, light and floral, with grapefruit and tropical fruits. Drink up. Score 78. K

ISRAELI, EMERALD RIESLING, 2005: Half-dry, light to medium-bodied, very floral, a fruit cocktail set of flavors and with marked but not overpowering sweetness. Drink up. Score 79. K

Collage

COLLAGE, DRY RED, 2005: A blend of 50% Cabernet Sauvignon and 25% each Shiraz and Petite Sirah. Dark ruby, medium-bodied, with soft, almost unfelt tannins, and simple but clean aromas and flavors of black fruits. Drink up. Score 83. K

COLLAGE, CABERNET SAUVIGNON-PETITE SIRAH, 2005: Light and lively, this ruby-towards-garnet wine is earthy on first attack but this is followed by a lightly spicy berry, black cherry personality. Drink up. Score 83. K

COLLAGE, CHARDONNAY-SEMILLON, 2005: Clean and freshly acidic, with pineapple, tropical and floral aromas and flavors. Drink up. Score 83. K

Tishbi ✶✶✶

Following the initiatives of Baron Edmond de Rothschild, the Tishbi family started to plant vineyards in 1882 on the slopes of Mount Carmel near the town of Zichron Ya'akov and continued to cultivate vines throughout the next hundred years. In 1985, Jonathan Tishbi, a fourth-generation member of the family, launched this family-owned winery in the nearby town of Binyamina, initially named Habaron as homage to Baron Rothschild, and later renamed Tishbi.

With Golan Tishbi serving as senior winemaker, the winery has made the leap from about 750,000 bottles to an output of nearly 1,000,000 annually. Drawing on grapes from their own vineyards as well as from vineyards in the Jerusalem region and the Upper Galilee, the winery produces several series, the top of the-line being the age-worthy varietal Special Reserve wines, the varietal Estate and Vineyards, and the more popularly priced Tishbi. The lower-level Baron series was recently discontinued. The winery also produces a sparkling wine and a Port-style wine.

Special Reserve

SPECIAL RESERVE, CABERNET SAUVIGNON, BEN ZIMRA, 2002: Deep purple in color, ripe, bold and concentrated, the wine has solid and chewy tannins, those well balanced by oak. On the nose and palate spicy currant and berry fruits. Drink now–2009. Score 90. K

SPECIAL RESERVE, CABERNET SAUVIGNON, GUSH ETZION, 2002: Medium to full-bodied, oak-aged for 18 months, well balanced, with soft tannins and aromas and flavors of currant, cherry, plum and wild berry fruits, just the right hints of spicy wood and anise on the medium-long finish. Drink now. Score 88. K

SPECIAL RESERVE, CABERNET SAUVIGNON, BEN ZIMRA, 1999: Ripe and harmonious, this well–balanced, now fully mature wine offers up fresh cherry, spice and plum flavors along with supple tannins, all overlaid by appealing hints of earthiness and herbs. Drink up. Score 88. K

SPECIAL RESERVE, CABERNET SAUVIGNON, SDE BOKER, 1999: Made from grapes grown in the Negev Desert, the wine is not so much earthy or herbal but instead is marked by distinct flavors of green olives and spices. Full-bodied, now fully mature, with well-integrated tannins, it shows ripe and well-focused black cherry and currant flavors along with an appealing, long finish. Drink up. Score 89. K

SPECIAL RESERVE, CABERNET SAUVIGNON, KFAR YUVAL, 1999: With earthy currant and cherry flavors emerging through firm tannins, this rich and concentrated wine is now fully mature and showing the smooth and supple texture promised in its youth. Drink up. Score 88. K

SPECIAL RESERVE, MERLOT, KEREM KFAR YUVAL-GUSH ETZION, 2002: Mature now but still graceful. With a deep, almost inky garnet color and generous but smooth tannins, this supple and well-balanced medium to full-bodied wine shows plums, ripe cherry, chocolate and gentle cedar-oak aromas and flavors along with a sweet and spicy herbal finish. Drink now. Score 90. K

SPECIAL RESERVE, MERLOT, KFAR YUVAL, 2002: Dark ruby towards garnet, full-bodied, with firm but nicely yielding tannins and generous but not imposing oak. On the nose and palate a bare hint of Brett adding an earthy charm to the black cherry, cassis, and mineral aromas and flavors. An appealing hint of dark chocolate on the finish. Drink now. Score 89. K

SPECIAL RESERVE, CABERNET SAUVIGNON-MERLOT-CABERNET FRANC, 2004: Dark garnet, medium to full-bodied, this oak-aged blend is made entirely from grapes harvested at Sde Boker in the Negev. Good balance between still-firm tannins, spicy wood and black fruits, those matched by tobacco and chocolate and a long, lightly minty finish. Drink now–2010. Score 90. K

SPECIAL RESERVE, CHARDONNAY, 2006: Aged in oak for six months, medium-bodied, this golden-straw wine shows light spicy accents running through the appealing citrus, citrus peel and melon aromas and flavors. Lingers nicely. Drink now. Score 87. K

SPECIAL RESERVE, CHARDONNAY, 2005: Medium to full-bodied, appealingly golden in color, with generous but not overpowering oak highlighting creamy aromas and flavors of pears, peaches and vanilla. Drink now. Score 88. K

Estate

ESTATE, CABERNET SAUVIGNON, 2004: Medium to full-bodied, with silky smooth tannins and layers of currant, berry and plum fruits, those matched nicely by hints of spicy wood and a light herbal overlay. Drink now. Score 87. K

ESTATE, CABERNET SAUVIGNON, 2003: Oak-aged for 12 months, this dark garnet, medium to full-bodied wine is showing a gentle spicy oak influence and with appealing black currant and blackberry fruits. A round, medium-long and lightly peppery finish. Drink now. Score 86. K

ESTATE, CABERNET SAUVIGNON, 2001: Garnet towards brick-red, medium-bodied, with soft tannins well integrated, the wine reflects its 18 months in oak with an appealingly spicy finish. Showing currant, berry and plum notes, it is soft, round and generous. Fully mature. Drink up. Score 86. K

ESTATE, MERLOT, 2004: Made from grapes from Sde Boker in the Negev, this soft, medium-bodied wine offers a few berry and spice flavors but shows poor balance and is revealing signs of browning. Drink up. Score 80. K

ESTATE, MERLOT, 2003: Deep garnet-red, medium-bodied, with firm tannins and good balance between lightly smoky wood and plum and currant fruits, all leading to a moderately long finish. Drink now. Score 86. K

ESTATE, MERLOT, 2002: Dark garnet-red, showing more full-bodied than in its youth, but its generous berry, black cherry and currant fruits now receding and yielding increasing sweet-herbal and earthy aromas and flavors. Somewhat past its peak. Drink up. Score 84. K

TISHBI ESTATE

2003

PINOT NOIR
DRY RED WINE

ESTATE, SHIRAZ, 2005: Dark cherry towards garnet in color, medium to full-bodied, with soft tannins integrating nicely. On the nose and palate cherry, raspberry and spicy aromas and flavors on a light earthy background. Drink now–2010. Score 89. K

ESTATE, PINOT NOIR, 2004: Light wood influences and soft tannins, this medium-bodied wine shows berry, plum and light earthy-mineral hints leading to a medium-long finish. A good quaffer. Drink now. Score 85. K

ESTATE, CHARDONNAY, 2006: Crisp and lively, light golden-straw in color, this light to medium-bodied shows appealing citrus, green apple and melon fruits on a flinty-mineral background. Drink now. Score 87. K

ESTATE, CHARDONNAY, 2005: Developed partly in oak, partly in stainless steel, with a crisp and mineral-rich personality. Showing generous citrus, green apple and melon aromas and flavors. Clean, crisp and refreshing. Drink now. Score 86. K

ESTATE, SAUVIGNON BLANC, 2006: Light straw with green tints, this light to medium-bodied white is showing appealing green apple, melon and summer fruits. Good balance between acidity and fruits make the wine lively and refreshing. Drink now. Score 86. K

ESTATE, SAUVIGNON BLANC, 2005: Light, almost watery in color, but given time to open in the glass yields rich aromas and flavors of lightly grassy and herbal notes along with apple and melons. Drink now. Score 85. K

ESTATE, LATE HARVEST RIESLING, 2005: Made from Emerald Riesling grapes, light to medium-bodied, with generous sweetness and appealing floral and summer fruits. Best with fruit-based desserts. Drink now. Score 84. K

ESTATE, LATE HARVEST RIESLING, 2004: Made from Emerald Riesling grapes. Floral on the nose, with ripe peach and apricot fruits. Moderate sweetness set off nicely by acidity makes for a pleasant quaffer. Drink now. Score 85. K

ESTATE, LATE HARVEST RIESLING, 2003: Made from Emerald Riesling grapes, this light to medium-bodied wine offers up simple but lively aromas and flavors of summer fruits and vanilla. Drink up. Score 83. K

ESTATE, WHITE RIESLING, 2004: Light straw-colored, medium-bodied, with tropical and citrus fruits along with a hint of litchis. Not complex but dry, lively and pleasant. Drink now. Score 85. K

ESTATE, WHITE RIESLING, 2003: Golden-straw colored, medium-bodied, with citrus-litchi and traditional and rather marked petrol aromas that often typify Riesling. Dry, well balanced and with a lingering finish. Drink now. Score 87. K

ESTATE, FRENCH COLOMBARD, LATE HARVEST, 2004: Aged in brandy barrels, flowery and cloying, with far too much residual sugar and not enough balancing acidity. Drink up. Score 78. K

Vineyards

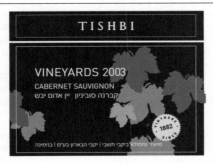

VINEYARDS, CABERNET SAUVIGNON, 2006: Medium-bodied, with soft tannins and forward berry, currant and cherry fruits. Not complex, but a good quaffer. Drink now. Score 85. K

VINEYARDS, CABERNET SAUVIGNON, 2005: Garnet-red with orange and purple reflections, medium-bodied, with caressing soft tannins and generous black currant, blackberry and orange peel aromas and flavors on a lightly spicy background. Drink now. Score 87. K

VINEYARDS, CABERNET SAUVIGNON, 2004: Dark cherry-red, medium-bodied, with soft, almost unfelt tannins, and cassis, blueberry and plum flavors all on a somewhat sweet finish. Drink now. Score 84. K

VINEYARDS, CABERNET SAUVIGNON, 2003: Medium-bodied, with moderate tannins integrating nicely and appealing currant and berry fruits. Not complex but pleasant. Drink up. Score 85. K

VINEYARDS, MERLOT, 2006: Garnet towards purple, medium-bodied, with soft tannins and appealingly spicy berry and black cherry fruits. Drink now. Score 85. K

VINEYARDS, MERLOT, 2005: Deep garnet towards purple, medium-bodied, with generous soft tannins integrating nicely and showing appealing raspberry, red currant and cherry fruits, those on a lightly spicy and herbal background. Round and medium-long. Drink now–2009. Score 87. K

VINEYARDS, MERLOT, 2004: Dark cherry-red towards purple, medium-bodied, with soft tannins and forward plum and black cherry fruits. Look as well for hints of smoky oak and Mediterranean herbs. Drink up. Score 85. K

VINEYARDS, SAUVIGNON BLANC, 2006: Light to medium-bodied, with hints of figs, grass, lime and sweet peas. Not complex but friendly, with a nice mineral-rich finish. Drink now. Score 86. K

VINEYARDS, SAUVIGNON BLANC, 2005: This light straw-colored, light to medium-bodied wine shows appealing citrus and green apple aromas and flavors and nice balancing acidity to keep it lively. Not complex but a nice quaffer. Drink up. Score 85. K

VINEYARDS, WHITE RIESLING, 2006: Light and fresh, with apple, honeysuckle and citrus notes leading to a crisp finish. Drink now. Score 84. K

VINEYARDS, EMERALD RIESLING, 2006: Light in body, off-dry, with floral and citrus aromas and flavors. Good acidity to balance the light sweetness. Drink now. Score 84. K

VINEYARDS, EMERALD RIESLING, 2005: Pale golden-straw in color, light to medium-bodied, this semi-dry white offers up appealing citrus and light herbal aromas and flavors. Best served well chilled or even with an ice-cube. Drink up. Score 83. K

VINEYARDS, EMERALD RIESLING, 2004: Semi-dry, with grapefruit and green apple fruits and a reasonable level of sweetness. An acceptable entry-level wine. Drink up. Score 84. K

VINEYARDS, FRENCH COLOMBARD, 2006: Light golden-straw in color, light to medium-bodied, with citrus and tropical fruits on a floral background. Drink up. Score 83. K

VINEYARDS, DRY MUSCAT, 2005: A pleasant dissonance between the sweet floral nose and the crisply dry green apple and grapefruit flavors. A good entry-level wine. Drink up. Score 85. K

VINEYARDS, SWEET RED MUSCAT, 2004: Made from Muscat Hamburg grapes reinforced with brandy, this medium-bodied, lightly tannic dessert wine shows raspberry and cherry fruits. Drink now. Score 83. K

Tishbi

TISHBI, CABERNET SAUVIGNON-PETITE SIRAH, 2005: Dark ruby-red, with soft tannins and an appealing array of raspberry, cassis and black cherry fruits. A good quaffer. Drink now. Score 85. K

TISHBI, CABERNET SAUVIGNON-PETITE SIRAH 2004: Cherry-red, fresh, lively and with soft tannins and berry-cherry fruits. Drink up. Score 84. K

TISHBI, SAUVIGNON BLANC, 2004: Light golden-straw in color, a simple but pleasant little wine with grapefruit, passion fruit and spicy pear aromas and flavors. Drink up. Score 83. K

TISHBI, FRENCH-RIESLING, 2006: Semi-dry, with a floral nose. Showing aromas and flavors of citrus and melon. Good acidity keeps it lively. Drink now. Score 82. K

TISHBI, FRENCH-RIESLING, 2005: An off-dry blend of French Colombard and Emerald Riesling with summer fruits, melon and citrus aromas and flavors. Best as an aperitif. Drink up. Score 82. K

TISHBI, MUSCAT OF ALEXANDRIA, 2006: Semi-dry, floral, with aromas and flavors of ripe peaches. A simple quaffer. Drink up. Score 83. K

TISHBI, MUSCAT OF ALEXANDRIA, 2005: Lightly golden in color, floral on the nose, semi-dry, and light on the palate, showing spicy summer fruits. Drink up. Score 82. K

Tulip ★★★

Located on Kfar Tikva near the town of Kiryat Tivon, not far from Haifa, this winery is an effort of the Yitzhaki family. The winery currently draws on Cabernet Sauvignon and Syrah grapes from the Alma vineyard and other locations in the Upper Galilee, as well as Cabernet Sauvignon, Merlot, Cabernet Franc and Petit Verdot from Karmei Yosef and Mata vineyards near Jerusalem. Currently in development are vineyards planted in red varieties near Mount Meron.

The winery is currently releasing wines in four series: varietal Grand Reserve and Reserve; blended wines, Mostly; and single-variety wines, Just. The winery also releases a Port-style reinforced red wine.

Grand Reserve

GRAND RESERVE, 2004: This blend of Cabernet Sauvignon and Merlot reflects its 30 months in oak with a heavy, somewhat sweetish wood and firm tannins. Beneath those and making their way slowly to the surface are blackberry, kirsch and dark chocolate aromas and flavors. Earlier experience with the Grand Reserve has shown that given time, the wood may recede. Drink now. Score 86.

GRAND RESERVE, CABERNET SAUVIGNON, 2003: Oak-aged for 30 months, but with the once-heavy wood now integrating nicely with soft tannins and opening to reveal appealing black currant and berry fruits, those with overlays of dark chocolate and sweet herbs. Drink now. Score 88.

GRAND RESERVE, CABERNET SAUVIGNON, 1999: Medium to full-bodied, with surprisingly moderate tannins and wood influence considering its 32 months in old oak *barriques,* the wine shows currant, raspberry and black cherry fruits but lacks complexity and is now beginning to age. Drink up. Score 80.

Reserve

RESERVE, CABERNET SAUVIGNON, 2005: Made from grapes from two different vineyards, this full-bodied red is showing still-firm tannins that need time to integrate, but fine balance between those, spicy wood and fruits. Opens to reveal blackberry, currant and light leathery notes, all on a generously peppery and vanilla-rich background. Long and juicy. Drink now–2011. Score 88.

RESERVE, CABERNET SAUVIGNON, 2004: Dense royal-purple towards black, full-bodied, deeply tannic, with generous wood influence but good balance and structure. On the nose and palate generous spices to highlight black currant, chocolate and a light overlay of cigar tobacco. Drink now–2009. Score 89.

RESERVE, CABERNET SAUVIGNON, 2003: Deep garnet towards black, medium to full-bodied and reflecting 14 months in small oak barrels with firm tannins, vanilla, spicy wood and appealing black fruits. Drink now. Score 89.

RESERVE, SYRAH, 2006: Dark garnet with orange and violet reflections, this full-bodied red is lithe and well focused. Opens with a surprising but pleasing root beer note which holds through the long finish as a background to plum, blackberry and leathery notes. Well balanced, long and generous. Drink from release–2011. Tentative Score 89–91.

RESERVE, SYRAH, 2005: Blended with 10% of Cabernet Sauvignon and oak-aged for 14 months, this medium to full-bodied wine shows soft, near-sweet tannins integrating beautifully Fine balance here between spicy wood, black and red berries, plums and a generous hint of bitter sweet chocolate. On the long finish light and appealing hints of earthiness and tobacco. Drink now–2010. Score 90.

RESERVE, SYRAH, 2004: Full-bodied, with generous dusty-smoky oak. Now-soft tannins well balanced with black fruits, chocolate and earthy-herbal aromas and flavors. Generous and moderately long. Drink now–2010. Score 88.

RESERVE, BORDEAUX BLEND (TENTATIVE NAME), 2005: 70% Cabernet Sauvignon rounded out by Merlot, Cabernet Franc and Petit Verdot. Full-bodied, with soft, caressing tannins in fine balance with lightly spicy French oak. Opens with blackberry and chocolate notes, those yielding to currants and plums. A long and generous finish. Drink from release–2010. Tentative Score 89–91.

Mostly

MOSTLY, MERLOT, 2004: Garnet towards royal-purple, this medium-bodied blend of 77% Merlot and 23% Cabernet Sauvignon shows soft tannins integrating nicely, a judicious hand with oak, and appealing red currant and wild berry fruits. Soft, round, generous and moderately long. Drink now. Score 87.

MOSTLY, SHIRAZ, 2006: A medium to full-bodied blend of 65% Shiraz, 20% Cabernet Sauvignon, 10% Merlot and 5% Petit Verdot. Firm but juicy and well focused, this dark garnet wine opens slowly in the glass to reveal plum, blueberry and sweet spices, with the soft tannins coating the mouth nicely and highlighting the flavors. Best 2009–2012. Tentative Score 88–90.

MOSTLY, SHIRAZ, 2005: Dark garnet, this blend of 60% Shiraz, 20% each of Cabernet Sauvignon and Merlot shows medium-bodied, soft, round and well balanced, filling the mouth nicely. On the nose and palate blackberries, plums and gently spicy oak from its 14 months in *barriques*. Look for hints of Mediterranean herbs and freshly turned earth on the moderately long finish. Drink now–2009. Score 87.

MOSTLY, SHIRAZ, 2004: Dark ruby towards garnet in color, this blend of Shiraz and Cabernet Sauvignon (75% and 25% respectively) was aged primarily in new barrels. Medium to full-bodied, with plum, currant and berry fruits backed up by appealing hints of earthiness and freshly tanned leather. Drink now. Score 87.

MOSTLY, CABERNET FRANC, 2005: A gently oak-aged blend of 80% Cabernet Franc, 15% Merlot and 5% Cabernet Sauvignon. Dark garnet towards purple, medium to full-bodied, with soft tannins integrating nicely and showing generous plum, berry and light earthy aromas and flavors. Drink now–2009. Score 87.

MOSTLY, CABERNET FRANC, 2004: Dark royal-purple, medium to full-bodied, with gripping tannins and generous wood but under those black currants, plums and an appealing light earthiness. Drink now–2009. Score 86.

MOSTLY, SAUVIGNON BLANC, 2004: Dark straw in color, portions of this medium-bodied blend of Sauvignon Blanc and Chardonnay (75% and 25% respectively) were oak-fermented and aged *sur lie* before the final blend was made. Generous melon, pear and citrus fruits backed up nicely by light herbaceousness. Drink up. Score 87.

Just

JUST, CABERNET SAUVIGNON, 2006: Dark, almost impenetrable garnet, full-bodied and concentrated, with generous, soft tannins yet maintaining the roundness that has come to typify the Tulip wines. Opens slowly in the glass to reveal black currant, wild berry and kirsch, those backed up by spicy wood and appealing hints of herbaceousness on the long finish. Drink now–2010. Score 88.

JUST, CABERNET SAUVIGNON, 2005: Dark garnet, this medium-bodied wine's soft tannins are integrating nicely with hints of the oak in which it was aged for six months. On the nose and palate plums, cassis and berries along with intimations of vanilla and tobacco on a moderately long finish. Drink now–2009. Score 88.

JUST, CABERNET SAUVIGNON, 2004: Dark royal-purple, this wine was developed in French and American oak for eight months. Showing good balance between spicy wood, soft, well-integrating tannins and wild berry and currant fruits. On the finish hints of vanilla and Mediterranean herbs. Drink now. Score 86.

JUST, MERLOT, 2006: Medium bodied, with silky tannins, this soft, round red shows appealing berry, black cherry and currant fruits on a light background of spicy oak and eucalyptus. Drink now–2009. Score 86.

JUST, MERLOT, 2005: Reflecting 12 months in oak with soft, slightly chunky tannins and hints of spices. Dark garnet, medium to full-bodied, opening in the glass to show blueberries, black cherries and from mid-palate on hints of chocolate and a light earthiness. On the finish a pleasing herbaceousness. Drink now–2009. Score 87.

JUST, MERLOT, 2004: Medium-dark ruby, medium-bodied, with soft tannins and black fruits complemented by hints of chocolate and espresso coffee. Well balanced and moderately long. Drink now. Score 86.

JUST, SHIRAZ, 2005: Oak-aged for about 12 months, medium-bodied, with still-firm tannins, those in good balance with spicy wood and earthy, plum and spicy aromas and flavors. Drink now. Score 85.

JUST, SAUVIGNON BLANC, 2005: Light and lively, with aromas and flavors of apples and melons along with light grassy and citrus peel notes. Drink up. Score 85.

JUST, SAUVIGNON BLANC, 2004: Light straw-colored, light to medium-bodied, clean, crisp and refreshing, with pineapple, green melon and citrus fruits on a generously acidic and spicy background. Drink up. Score 86.

Tzora ✴✴✴✴

Set on Kibbutz Tzora at the foothills of the Jerusalem Mountains and overlooking the Soreq Valley, this *kibbutz*-owned winery released its first 1,500 bottles from the 1993 vintage. Production in 2004 was about 60,000 bottles, in 2005 it was reduced to about 30,000 bottles but in 2006 rose again, this time to a high of 70,000 bottles.

Ronnie James, who has been the winemaker since the winery's inception, releases varietal wines as well as blends based on Cabernet Sauvignon, Merlot, Syrah, Grenache, Mourvedre, Sauvignon Blanc, Chardonnay, Johannisberg Riesling and Muscat of Alexandria, all from the kibbutz's own vineyards, many of those designated as single-vineyard wines. James has succeeded as very few winemakers do to consistently represent a specific Mediterranean *terroir*.

As to the winery's labeling method, it has been confusing in the past, but now, with winemaker Ilan Pik aboard and working together with James, the winery has undergone major updates in equipment and is moving to a more clear system of labeling. The Tzora wines have been kosher since the 2002 vintage.

TZORA, CABERNET SAUVIGNON, SPECIAL RESERVE, 2006: Dark purple towards inky black, intensely tannic, with concentrated black fruits and a tantalizing near-sweetness, the wine shows fine balance and structure. Look as well for Mediterranean herbs, tobacco and licorice. Best from 2009. Tentative Score 89–91. K

TZORA, CABERNET SAUVIGNON, GIVAT HACHALUKIM, 2006: Showing dark garnet in color, highly aromatic, and with generous fruit. Medium to full-bodied, with soft tannins, a moderate hand on the oak, and a rich array of red and black berries, black currants, and an appealing range of spices. Finishes nicely with hints of chocolate and mint. Drink from release. Tentative Score 87–89. K

TZORA, CABERNET SAUVIGNON, NEVE ILAN, 2006: Medium to full-bodied, this deep garnet-towards-royal-purple wine's firm tannins are integrating with wood and fruits. Showing generous raspberry and red currant and a youthful cranberry hint, with the tannins coating the mouth nicely. Opening to reveal earthy minerals, and, on the long finish, gentle hints of spicy wood and freshly picked mushrooms. Drink from release. Tentative Score 87–89. K

TZORA, CABERNET SAUVIGNON, SHORESH, 2006: Dark royal-purple, with appealingly herbal and earthy notes. Medium to full-bodied, showing generous cherry, berry and cassis fruits, those finishing with hints of coffee and tobacco. Drink from release–2010. Tentative Score 88–90. K

TZORA, CABERNET SAUVIGNON, NEVE ILAN, SINGLE VINEYARD, 2005: Oak-aged for 18 months, dark ruby towards royal-purple, this full-bodied wine shows soft, near-sweet tannins integrating nicely and ripe blackberry, currant and raspberry fruits, those supported by appealing hints of tobacco and red licorice. Drink now–2010. Score 89. K

TZROA, CABERNET SAUVIGNON, GIVAT HACHALUKIM, SINGLE VINEYARD, 2005: Dark ruby towards garnet, medium to full-bodied, with soft tannins and generous spicy wood. Opens to show generous red and black fruits, those supported nicely by hints of freshly turned earth and tobacco. Drink now–2010. Score 90. K

TZORA, CABERNET SAUVIGNON, GIVAT HACHALUKIM, 2004: Deep garnet towards purple, medium-bodied, with somewhat chunky tannins giving the wine a country-style. On the nose and palate generous currant and blackberry fruits, those coming together with spicy oak and a light hint of earthiness that has come to typify this wine. Drink now. Score 87. K

TZORA, CABERNET SAUVIGNON, GIVAT HACHALUKIM, 2003: Dark garnet, medium to full-bodied, with appealing aromas and flavors of plums, currants and a light earthiness that come together nicely. Well balanced and long. Drink now–2010. Score 89. K

TZORA, CABERNET SAUVIGNON, NEVE ILAN, SPECIAL SELECTION, 2003: Aged in oak casks for 20 months, this medium to full-bodied blend of 66% Cabernet Sauvignon and 34% Merlot shows almost impenetrable garnet in color.

Firm tannins and spicy wood are well balanced by black currant, wild berry and plum fruits on an earthy, mineral-rich background. Drink now–2010. Score 88. K

TZORA, CABERNET SAUVIGNON, NEVE ILAN, MISTY HILLS, 2003: A blend of 85% Cabernet Sauvignon and 15% Merlot, aged in oak for 20 months. Deep purple towards black in color, with generous tannins and wood, but those in good balance with black currant, purple plum and blackberry fruits. Drink now–2009. Score 89. K

TZORA, CABERNET SAUVIGNON, NEVE ILAN, 2003: Showing richer and more complex than at earlier tastings. Deep garnet, medium to full-bodied, with its once firm tannins now integrating nicely and re-vealing hints of smoky oak and a clean herbal-earthiness that supports generous black currant, blackberry and plum fruits. Drink now–2010. Score 90. K

TZORA, CABERNET SAUVIGNON, GIVAT HACHALUKIM, RESERVE, 2001: Dark garnet in color, the once searing tannins of this oak-aged blend of 90% Cabernet Sauvignon and 10% Merlot have finally receded and now show excellent balance with wood, black fruits and herbaceous-ness, all on a light peppery background. Drink now. Score 89.

TZORA, CABERNET SAUVIGNON, NEVE ILAN, 2001: Almost as if waking from a long sleep, this wine has sprung back to life and is better than ever before. Having matured gracefully, its tannins are now soft and round, the wood showing as a gentle sweet-and-spicy overlay and highlighting a generous mouthful of blackberry, currant and blueberry aromas and flavors. On the long finish look for tempting herbal and tobacco overlays. Drink now. Score 90.

TZORA, CABERNET SAUVIGNON, ILAN, BIN 72, 2001: Dark garnet, medium to full-bodied, this wine is now fully mature, its tannins soft and complementing an array of currant, berry and plum fruits, those with overlays of herbs, espresso coffee and hints of leather. Long and mouth-filling. Drink up. Score 88.

TZORA, CABERNET SAUVIGNON, NEVE ILAN, 2000: Fully mature now, its tannins round and caressing, the generous herbaceousness and wood that once typified this wine are now comfortably in the back-ground and it is showing a tempting array of ripe black fruits. Lingers nicely on the palate. Drink up. Score 88.

TZORA, CABERNET SAUVIGNON, BIN 72, 2000: Aged for 20 months in *barriques*, this intense wine is now fully mature and showing a dark ruby-toward-purple color and a complex interplay on the palate be-tween black currants, blackberries, pepper, sage and spicy cedar aromas and flavors along with hints of dark chocolate, eucalyptus and leather on the long finish. Drink up. Score 90.

TZORA, CABERNET SAUVIGNON, BIN 64, SPECIAL SELECTION, 1999: A blend of 85% Cabernet Sauvignon and 15% Merlot, this complex, concentrated and full-bodied wine spent 20 months in oak. Now fully mature, garnet toward purple, with abundant but well-integrated tannins, and aromas and flavors of currant and blackberry fruits, those nicely matched by vanilla and a tantalizing hint of spicy cedarwood on the finish. Drink up. Score 89.

TZORA, CABERNET SAUVIGNON, BIN 72, SPECIAL SELECTION, 1999: Even though this wine was made from the same grapes and received the same treatment as the wine reviewed from bin 64, the grapes came from different rows in the same vineyard. This wine is darker in color and has more of an earthy-herbal than fruit personality. Tannins still firm enough to hide whatever spices, vanilla and cedarwood are present. Drink up. Score 88.

TZORA, MERLOT, NEVE ILAN, 2006: Garnet-red with orange and purple reflections, this medium to full-bodied wine shows generous but near-sweet soft tannins integrating nicely, and already opening to reveal bountiful red fruits and an appealing spicy overlay. Tannins and steely minerals rise pleasantly on the finish to make this a very fine Merlot. Drink from release. Tentative Score 87–89. K

TZORA, MERLOT, GIVAT HACHALUKIM, 2005: Ruby towards purple, medium-bodied, with soft, perhaps even flabby tannins and an unwanted hint of bitterness that interferes with the currant, berry and plum fruits. Drink from release. Tentative Score 83–85. K

TZORA, MERLOT, SHORESH, SINGLE VINEYARD, 2005: Dark royal-purple, medium to full-bodied, with soft, mouth-coating tannins and spicy wood integrating nicely to show berry, cherry and orange peel aromas and flavors, those leading to a moderately long finish. A bit sharp on the palate now but in time promises to show elegance. Score 90. K

TZORA, MERLOT, SHORESH, 2004: This single-vineyard release is medium to full-bodied, and oak-aged for 24 months. Showing generous wood but soft tannins, and appealing blackberry and black cherry fruits along with tempting spices. Drink now–2009. Score 86. K

TZORA, MERLOT, NEVE ILAN, 2003: Dark garnet in color, with soft tannins integrating nicely, this round and soft wine shows aromas and flavors of raspberries, currants and purple plums supported by light herbal and spicy overlays and just the right hint of oak. Generous if only moderately long. Drink now–2009. Score 87. K

TZORA, MERLOT, NEVE ILAN, 2001: Deep garnet towards royal-purple, this medium to full-bodied blend of 90% Merlot and 10% Cabernet Sauvignon shows soft tannins and gentle wood, both integrated nicely to reveal an array of currant and berry fruits, those on a background of Mediterranean herbs, vanilla and Oriental spices. On the long finish a generous hint of espresso coffee. Drink now. Score 89.

TZORA, SYRAH, 2006: Made from grapes of low-yield vines, this dark, full-bodied and concentrated red shows soft, mouth-coating tannins, spicy wood, and hints of smoked meat and earthiness, those opening to reveal generous red fruits. Intense but gentle and already showing elegance. Drink from release–2010. Tentative Score 88–90. K

TZORA, JUDEAN HILLS, 2004: Dark garnet, this medium-bodied blend of 62% Cabernet Sauvignon and 38% Merlot was aged in French *barriques* for 18 months. Somewhat chunky tannins and spicy oak, which yield slowly in the glass to show blackberry and currant fruits. A pleasant country-style wine. Drink now–2009. Score 85. K

TZORA, CABERNET SAUVIGNON-MERLOT, NEVE ILAN, SPECIAL SELECTION, 2003: Dark royal-purple in color, with soft, already well-integrating tannins, this blend of 50% each Cabernet Sauvignon and Merlot offers generous currant and berry fruits on a long smoky finish. Drink now–2009. Score 87. K

TZORA, MERLOT-CABERNET SAUVIGNON, ILAN, MISTY HILLS, 2003: A blend of 70% Merlot and 30% Cabernet, showing dark ruby towards garnet, with its once chunky tannins now settling down to reveal spicy oak and currant, cassis and plum fruits. Moderately long. Drink now–2009. Score 88. K

TZORA, MERLOT-CABERNET SAUVIGNON, ILAN, MISTY HILLS, 2001: An oak-aged blend of 60% Merlot and 40% Cabernet Sauvignon. Dark garnet in color, showing appealing herbal, plum and cassis aromas and flavors. Marred somewhat by overly-generous acidity. Drink up. Score 86.

TZORA, MERLOT-CABERNET SAUVIGNON, ILAN, MISTY HILLS, 2000: Dark ruby towards garnet, full-bodied, with now soft tannins. Sweet cedar and spices dominate on first attack but those yielding nicely to currant, berry and plum fruits. Long and generous. Drink up. Score 86.

TZORA, CABERNET SAUVIGNON-ZINFANDEL, 2003: Aged in oak casks for eight months, this medium-bodied blend of 67% Cabernet Sauvignon and 33% Zinfandel is a bit stingy on the nose but offers generous flavors of berries, black cherries and spices. Drink up. Score 85. K

TZORA, SHORESH, JERUSALEM HILLS, 2003: A medium-bodied blend of Cabernet Sauvignon and Merlot grapes from a variety of vineyards. Appealing, fairly sharp berry and plum flavors, somewhat coarse tannins and a good deal of heat give the wine a distinct rustic style. Drink now. Score 85. K

TZORA, SAUVIGNON BLANC, 2005:

Light golden-straw in color, light and lively on the palate, with appealing aromas and flavors of citrus and summer fruits. Straightforward and refreshing. Drink up. Score 86. K

TZORA, JOHANNISBERG RIESLING, 2005: Light gold in color, bright and lively, with peach, apple and spicy floral aromas and flavors that linger nicely on the palate. Drink up. Score 87. K

TZORA, GEWURZTRAMINER, DESSERT WINE, 2006: Light, sweet and silky, almost calling to mind an ice wine, with distinct honeyed pineapple and pear fruits and a hint of kumquat marmalade on the finish. A low 8% alcohol content and good balancing acidity to make the wine both lively and tempting. Drink now–2009. Score 88. K

Tzuba ✳✳✳

Founded by Moti Zamir on Kibbutz Tzuba in the Jerusalem Hills, the winery's first releases from the 2005 vintage were of 30,000 bottles. The winery currently issues wines in three series: the top-of-the-line Hametzuda that will be produced only in selected years; Tel Tzuba of varietal and blended wines, and the popularly priced Hama'ayan. The winery also produces a red dessert wine.

Tel Tzuba

TEL TZUBA, CABERNET SAUVIGNON, 2005: A blend of 85% Cabernet Sauvignon, 9% Cabernet Franc and 6% Merlot, aged in French oak for 14 months. Ruby to purple, medium to full-bodied, with soft tannins and gentle wood. Showing clean red fruits on a lightly spicy, moderately long finish. Drink now–2009. Score 86. K

TEL TZUBA, MERLOT, 2005: An oak-aged Merlot with the addition of 6% Pinot Noir. Ruby towards garnet, medium to full-bodied, with gripping tannins and generous wood yielding slowly to reveal blackberry, currant and plum aromas and flavors. Drink now–2009. Score 87. K

TEL TZUBA, SHIRAZ, 2005: Dark ruby towards purple, medium-bodied, with soft tannins integrating nicely and showing appealing plum and berry fruits, those supported by hints of spices and saddle leather. Drink now–2009. Score 87. K

TEL TZUBA, CHARDONNAY, 2006: Light gold in color, medium-bodied, with grapefruit and green apple aromas and flavors and good balancing acidity to keep it lively. Drink now. Score 86. K

TEL TZUBA, VIOGNIER-SAUVIGNON BLANC, 2006: A blend of 63% Viognier and 37% Sauvignon Blanc. Developed in French oak for four months, this light straw-to-golden-colored wine is showing generous acidity and appealing grapefruit, citrus peel and green apple aromas and flavors. Not complex but lively and refreshing. Score 85. K

Hama'ayan

HAMA'AYAN, SANGIOVESE, 2005: Made entirely from Sangiovese grapes, oak-aged for 14 months, this red is showing soft, well integrating tannins, a moderate overlay of spicy wood and appealing berry, cherry and plum fruits. A good quaffer. Drink now. Score 85. K

HAMA'AYAN, SEMILLON, 2006: An unoaked blend of 88% Semillon and 12% Sauvignon Blanc, dominated by grapefruit aromas and flavors. Drink up. Score 79. K

Vanhotzker **

Founded by Eli Vanhotzker in 2003 on Moshav Meron, the winery has its own vineyards with Cabernet Sauvignon and Merlot grapes on the slopes of Mount Meron in the Upper Galilee. Releases, entirely of Cabernet Sauvignon from the 2004 and 2005 vintages, were of 1,500 bottles, and production from the 2006 vintage was 3,000 bottles, that including the winery's first Merlot.

VANHOTZKER, CABERNET SAUVIGNON, 2005: Dark garnet, medium to full-bodied, with firm tannins and ripe and juicy currant, black cherry and kirsch aromas and flavors. On the finish herbal and vanilla notes. Drink now–2009. Score 86. K

VANHOTZKER, CABERNET SAUVIGNON, 2004: Medium to full-bodied, with generous soft tannins and spicy oak already integrating nicely and showing good balance with black currant, plum and blackberry fruits. Generous and moderately long. Drink now. Score 87. K

Villa Wilhelma ∗

Founded in 2003 by Motti Goldman and Amram Surasky and located on Moshav Bnei Atarot not far from Ben Gurion Airport on the central plain, the winery draws its red grapes from the vineyards of Karmei Yosef at the foothills of the Jerusalem Mountains. Wines are released in a Grand Reserve and regular series, and the winery released 3,500 bottles from the 2003 vintage, 14,000 from the 2004 vintage and 17,000 from the 2005 and 2006 vintages.

Grand Reserve

GRAND RESERVE, CABERNET SAUVIGNON, 2004: Deep royal-purple, full-bodied, with generous oak and firm tannins well balanced by fruits and acidity. On the nose and palate traditional Cabernet currant, blackberry and spicy aromas and flavors. Drink now–2009. Score 86.

GRAND RESERVE, CABERNET SAUVIGNON, 2003: Dark garnet, full-bodied and reflecting 18 months in oak with firm, somewhat dominating tannins, yielding slowly to reveal currant, blackberry and tar aromas and flavors along with hints of smoky wood and oriental spices. Drink now. Score 86.

GRAND RESERVE, MERLOT, 2004: Firm and focused, ripe and smooth, with blackberry and currant flavors supported nicely by hints of spices and chocolate, all lingering nicely on the palate. Drink now–2009. Score 86.

GRAND RESERVE, MERLOT, 2003: Medium to full-bodied, garnet towards dark royal-purple in color, with dusty cedarwood, generous acidity and near-sweet tannins. On the nose and palate, wild berries, purple plums and hints of spices. Drink now. Score 85.

GRAND RESERVE, MEDOCABERNET, 2004: Named after Bordeaux's Medoc wines, this medium to full-bodied red shows generous spicy and smoky wood after having spent 20 months in oak, along with aromas and flavors of wild berries, cassis and Mediterranean herbs. Drink now. Score 85.

GRAND RESERVE, GRAND CHARDONNAY, 2004: Developed for only ten months in French oak but somehow extremely oaky, the wine picked up not so much the spices or vanilla of the wood but the sap, and took on a deep, almost maple syrup-like color. Medicinal on the nose, and on the palate only skimpy fruits and an odd bitterness that comes in on the finish. Drink up. Score 70.

Villa Wilhelma

VILLA WILHELMA, CHARDONNAY, 2005: Golden-straw in color, with basic grapefruit, pineapple and citrus flavors along with light mineral notes. Drink now. Score 80.

VILLA WILHELMA, CHARDONNAY, 2004: Darkly golden, almost as if going to brown, dominated by bitter almonds and wood sap that hide the fruit. Score 68.

VILLA WILHELMA, SAUVIGNON BLANC, 2005: Light straw in color, opening with strong sulphur and earthy aromas that linger on and interfere with whatever fruits may be here. Score 72.

VILLA WILHELMA, EMERALD RIESLING, 2005: Categorized as half-dry but lacking acidity and sweetness. Floral and medicinal on the nose, and with a distinct hint of sour pineapple juice on the palate. Score 60.

VILLA WILHELMA, MUSCAT OF ALEXANDRIA, DESSERT WINE, 2003: Made from late-harvested grapes and developed *sur lie*, its fermentation stopped by the addition of grape brandy, the wine has a golden-maple syrup color, is aggressively floral on the nose and lacks acidity. Its cloying sweetness doesn't yield fruits on the palate but rather a distinct caramel flavor. Score 60.

Vitkin ★★★★

ויתקין Vitkin 2002

ויתקין קברנה פרנק

🍇

יין אדום יבש 750 מ"ל 13% אלכוהול

Established by Doron and Sharona Belogolovsky on Moshav Kfar Vitkin on the central Coastal Plain, this winery released its first wines from the 2002 vintage. Winemaker Assaf Paz relies on Cabernet Sauvignon, Merlot, Zinfandel, Carignan, Cabernet Franc, Syrah, Tempranillo, Petit Verdot, Petite Sirah, Viognier, French Colombard, Johannisberg Riesling, Gewürztraminer and Muscat grapes from vintners in the Jerusalem hills as well as several other parts of the country. The winery is currently producing 30,000 bottles annually.

VITKIN, PINOT NOIR, 2005: Made from grapes harvested in the Judean Hills and aged in new and used French oak for 15 months, this medium-bodied wine has soft tannins that integrate well with raspberry, blackberry and cherry fruits, those on a background of persimmons and hazelnuts. Drink now–2009. Score 86.

VITKIN, PINOT NOIR, 2004: Dark cherry-red, medium-bodied, the wine reflects its 14 months in small oak casks with spicy wood and soft tannins, and also shows black cherry, currant and purple plum fruits along with hints of chocolate and light earthiness. Drink now. Score 87.

VITKIN, PINOT NOIR, 2003: A blend of Pinot Noir, Petit Verdot and Cabernet Sauvignon (90%, 6% and 4% respectively) that was aged in used oak for 12 months. This deep cherry-towards-garnet, medium-bodied, very softly tannic wine offers up appealing berry, cherry and currant fruits on a background of vanilla and mocha. Drink now. Score 87.

VITKIN, CARIGNAN, 2005: Made from grapes of 30–40-year-old vines, this full-bodied red offers up generous oak and tannins, those integrating well and showing fine balance with purple plums, blackberries and spices. Light meaty and mineral overlays. Drink now–2011. Score 91.

VITKIN, CARIGNAN, 2004: Deep purple, medium to full-bodied, with firm tannins that are now integrating nicely to reveal spicy wood, earthy minerals and blackberry and plum fruits, those overlaid nicely with a pleasing gamey sweetness that lingers on the long finish. Drink now–2010. Score 90.

VITKIN, CARIGNAN, 2003: Deep garnet, full-bodied, oak-aged and blended with 10% Petit Verdot, the wine shows generous tannins and acidity well balanced by smoky oak and hints of vanilla, all coming together well with plum, wild berry and light hints of tobacco. Long and generous. Drink now. Score 89.

VITKIN, CARIGNAN, 2002: Medium-dark royal-purple and medium-bodied. With its chunky, country-style tannins now receding, the wine shows generous blackberry and black currant fruits, those matched nicely by spices and hints of chocolate and smoked meat that come in on the finish. Drink up. Score 87.

VITKIN, CABERNET FRANC, 2005: Deep garnet towards royal-purple, oak-aged for 16 months and blended with 12% Petit Verdot, the wine offers up generous tannins integrating nicely with the wood. Already showing an abundant array of spicy black cherries and currants, those with overtones of Madagascar green peppercorns, herbs and smoked meat. Long and satisfying. Drink now–2011. Score 90.

VITKIN, CABERNET FRANC, 2004: Deep, almost impenetrable royal-purple in color, this blend of 90% Cabernet Franc and 10% Petit Verdot shows fine balance between wood, moderately firm tannins and vegetal-fruity characteristics. On first attack pepper and spicy wood, that followed by black currants, plum and blackberry fruits, all supported by hints of cloves, Oriental spices and on the long and mouth-filling finish, Mediterranean herbs. Drink now–2011. Score 90.

VITKIN, CABERNET FRANC, 2003: Dark garnet towards royal-purple, medium to full-bodied, this oak-aged blend of 90% Cabernet Franc, 6% Petit Verdot and 4% Cabernet Sauvignon shows generous dark plum, black cherry and spice flavors, all complemented nicely by chocolate notes. On the clean, long finish hints of kirsch liqueur. Drink now. Score 87.

VITKIN, PETITE SIRAH, 2005: Made from old vine grapes and oak-aged for 16 months. Full-bodied, impenetrably dark purple-black, with deep spicy overlays and firm tannins all coming together beautifully. On the nose and palate black and blue berries, sur-ripe currants and a light meaty overlay. An enchanting hint of raspberry jam on the long finish. Drink now–2011. Score 89.

VITKIN, PETITE SIRAH, 2004: Deep, dark and intense, reflecting its 16 months in partly new French oak, with fine balance between firm tannins, sweet cedar and spicy oak. This concentrated wine opens slowly in the glass but when it does open it explodes with blackberry, plum, mineral, meaty and herbal aromas and flavors. Long, tannic and with a gentle hint of bittersweet chocolate on the finish. An elegant wine. Drink now–2010. Score 91.

VITKIN, PETITE SIRAH, 2003: Dark ruby towards garnet, this medium to full-bodied and moderately tannic blend of 90% Petite Sirah and 10% Cabernet Franc developed for 14 months in oak. Aromas and flavors of blackberries and purple plums and a long spicy finish. Drink now. Score 86.

VITKIN, RED, ISRAELI VOYAGE, 2005: Showing spices and vanilla from the *barriques* in which it aged, this blend of Cabernet Sauvignon, Shiraz and Carignan shows a generous near-sweet plummy personality. On the moderately long finish hints of flowers and sweet herbs. Drink now. Score 85.

VITKIN, CLASSIC, 2004: Aged in *barriques* for ten months, this medium-bodied, well-balanced, softly tannic blend of Shiraz, Cabernet Sauvignon and Carignan shows appealing red berries and cherries on first attack, those turning to currants, spring flowers and spices that linger nicely. Drink now. Score 86.

VITKIN, CLASSIC, 2003: An unlikely blend of 40% Cabernet Sauvignon, 35% Syrah and 25% Carignan, each vinified and aged in oak separately for six months before blending, then an additional six months afterwards. Medium-bodied, with soft, somewhat flabby tannins, and with berry-cherry and currant flavors that fail to come together. Drink up. Score 85.

VITKIN, PINK, ISRAELI VOYAGE, 2006: An odd but successful semi-dry blend of Tempranillo, Carignan and several unspecified varieties. Dark pink towards orange in color, light to medium-bodied, with generous raspberry, cranberry and blueberry fruits supported by good acidity to keep it lively. Drink up. Score 86.

VITKIN, PINK, 2005: A crisply dry blend of Syrah, Carignan, Tempranillo and Cabernet Franc, in color somewhere between strawberry-red and shocking pink. Light to medium-bodied, with fresh acidity and aromas and flavors of strawberries and raspberries, those with light peppery overtones, all lingering nicely on the palate. Drink up. Score 87.

VITKIN, RED DESSERT WINE, N.V.: A medium to full-bodied blend of Petite Sirah, Carignan, Cabernet Sauvignon and Petit Verdot, reinforced with white alcohol to 17% strength. On the nose candied fruits, straw-berries, exotic spices, and chocolate, its generous sweetness balanced nicely by good natural acidity. Drink now. Score 87.

VITKIN, JOHANNISBERG RIESLING, 2005: Golden-straw in color, this medium-bodied and deeply aromatic white shows an appealing flowery nose and, on the palate, fine balancing acidity and primarily grapefruit aromas and flavors, those with a hint of the oily aromas that give the wines of Alsace their charm. Drink now. Score 87.

VITKIN, JOHANNISBERG RIESLING, 2004: Perhaps the first Israeli white to show the oily, floral, kerosene-like aromas of fine Alsace or Rhine Rieslings. Gold in color, medium-bodied, with good balancing acidity, refreshingly dry and showing appealing citrus, melon and sum-mer fruits. Drink now. Score 88.

VITKIN, BLANC, ISRAELI VOYAGE, 2006: A medium-bodied, partly oak-aged blend of Viognier, French Colom-bard and Gewurztraminer, categorized as dry but so packed with litchi, pineapple, ripe peach and apricot fruits that you will swear the wine is sweet. Best as an aperitif. Drink now. Score 86.

VITKIN, BLANC, ISRAELI VOYAGE, 2005: Light gold in color, medium-bod-ied, and on the nose and palate rose pet-als, orange blossoms and tropical fruits, those matched by hints of litchis and tapioca. Drink now. Score 87.

VITKIN, RIESLING, LATE HARVEST, 2005: Pale gold, medium-bodied, with lightly honeyed summer and tropical fruits and an appealing floral-citrus finish. Drink now–2009. Score 86.

VITKIN, RIESLING, LATE HARVEST, 2004: With about 20% of the grapes in this wine affected by botrytis, this lightly funky, bronzed-gold-colored wine shows unabashed near-honeyed sweetness, and on the nose and palate dried apricots, tropical fruits and wild spring flowers. Drink now–2009. Score 86.

Yaffo ★★★

מרלו

Founded in Jaffa in 1998 by Moshe and Anne Celniker and today located in the basement of their home in the Tel Aviv suburb of Ramat Hachayal, this small winery is currently producing about 10,000 bottles annually. Grapes, primarily Cabernet Sauvignon and Merlot, come from kibbutz Netiv Halamed Hey in the Jerusalem Hills and from the Golan Heights. The winery also produces a Port-style wine.

YAFFO, CABERNET SAUVIGNON, 2005: Medium-bodied, with supple tannins and spicy plum, wild berry and currant fruits, opening to reveal hints of incense and sage. Tannins rise on the finish along with a generous mineral hint. Drink now–2010. Score 88.

YAFFO, CABERNET SAUVIGNON, 2004: Dark ruby towards garnet, medium-bodied, with chewy tannins integrating nicely with black fruits, spices and an appealing herbal overlay. Drink now. Score 86.

YAFFO, CABERNET SAUVIGNON, 2003: Deep garnet towards royal-purple, this still firmly tannic, medium to full-bodied and generously oaked wine shows good structure along with aromas and flavors of spicy black fruits, freshly picked herbs and an appealing earthy undercurrent that lingers nicely on the palate. Drink now. Score 86.

YAFFO, CABERNET SAUVIGNON, 2002: Dark garnet, this medium to full-bodied oak-aged wine shows soft tannins along with black currant, cherry and berry aromas and flavors. Light spices and herbs come together on a round, moderately long finish. Drink now. Score 87.

YAFFO, MERLOT, 2005: Medium to full-bodied, with rich red currant and black cherry fruits complemented by mocha and vanilla from the oak barrels in which it was aged. Tannins rise on the long finish. Drink now–2010. Score 88.

YAFFO, MERLOT, 2004: Soft and round, deep garnet-red, reflecting its 12 months in *barriques* with hints of spices and vanilla and with soft tannins integrating nicely. On the nose and palate blueberry, blackberry and plum fruits. Moderately long, with a hint of milk chocolate on the finish. Drink now. Score 87.

YAFFO, MERLOT, ORGANIC VINEYARD, 2004: Dark ruby towards garnet, medium to full-bodied, with soft, caressing tannins and ripe berry, black cherry fruits and a hint of spicy wood that runs through the long finish. Drink now. Score 88.

YAFFO, MERLOT, 2003: Medium to full-bodied, with soft tannins integrating nicely and generous plum, cassis and spicy oak aromas and flavors. Drink now. Score 86.

YAFFO, MERLOT, 2002: Medium-bodied, with generous soft tannins and berry, black cherry, and appealing vanilla-spicy hints that come in from mid-palate. Good touches of sweet wood and a light herbaceousness. Drink now. Score 86.

YAFFO, MERLOT, 2001: Medium-bodied, with moderate tannins, plenty of black fruits and hints of vanilla and toasty oak all coming together on a moderately long finish. Drink up. Score 86.

YAFFO, ROUGE, 2005: Dark garnet, with smoky oak and soft tannins, this wine opens to show blackberries and currants on a spicy background. Satisfying and long. Drink now–2009. Score 87.

YAFFO, ROUGE, 2004: A blend of 45% Merlot, 50% Cabernet Sauvignon and 5% Shiraz, with gentle oak influences, silky tannins and generous black fruits and spices leading to a mouth-filling finish. Drink now. Score 86.

YAFFO, ROUGE, 2003: Deep garnet, medium-bodied and with soft tannins, this blend of Cabernet Sauvignon and Merlot shows generous ripe plum, currant and berry aromas and flavors. Moderately long. Drink up. Score 86.

YAFFO, ROUGE, 2002: A blend of 45% each of Cabernet Sauvignon and Merlot and 10% of Shiraz, this soft and round red offers up appealing berry, cherry and currant fruits together with well-integrated tannins and good acidity. Not complex but a pleasant quaffer. Drink up. Score 86.

YAFFO, CHARDONNAY, 2006: Wisely aged in oak for only three months, showing crisp acidity and appealing hints of citrus, melon and minerals. Drink now–2009. Score 87.

YAFFO, CHARDONNAY, 2005: Crisp, lively and refreshing. Medium-bodied, with lime, green apple and tropical fruits along with hints of spices and bitter citrus peel. Drink now. Score 86.

YAFFO, BLANC, CHARDONNAY, 2004: Light golden-straw in color, medium-bodied, with crisp minerality and on the nose and palate grapefruit, citrus peel and green apples. Drink up. Score 86.

YAFFO, BLANC, CHARDONNAY, 2004: Damp straw in color, medium-bodied, and showing appealing aromas and flavors of citrus and melon. Light mineral and flowery overlays. Drink now. Score 86.

Yatir ★★★★★

Set in a state-of-the-art winery near the archaeological digs of Tel Arad at the foot of the Judean Hills, this boutique winery draws its name from the Yatir Forest. Originally a joint venture of Carmel and the vintners of the Yatir region, the winery is now owned solely by Carmel but maintains complete autonomy under the supervision of Australian-trained winemaker Eran Goldwasser. Releases include the age-worthy Yatir Forest and Yatir wines. In 2004 the winery produced the label Forester-Lodge but that was issued only for one year. The winery cultivates its own vineyards with Cabernet Sauvignon, Merlot, Shiraz, Sauvignon Blanc, and Chardonnay grapes. Its first wines were from the 2001 vintage. Current production is about 120,000 bottles annually and growth over the next two to three years is estimated at about 150,000 bottles.

Yatir Forest

YATIR FOREST, 2005: A Bordeaux blend of 77% Cabernet Sauvignon, 13% Petit Verdot and 10% Merlot. A third aged in new and two-thirds aged in old wood *barriques* for 15 months, this deep royal-purple wine casts intense orange and green reflections. Soft tannins integrating beautifully and the intentionally gentle hand with the wood come together nicely to let the wine open with spicy berry and cassis aromas and flavors, those going on to show blackberries and an underlying and fascinating mélange of bitter herbs. Long, generous and destined for elegance. Best 2009–2014. Score 93. K

YATIR FOREST, 2004: Elegant, full-bodied and solid, with soft tannins, smoky wood and vanilla, all in fine balance with ripe blueberry, black currant, and plum flavors. Look as well for an appealing, earthy undercurrent leading to a long and generous finish. Drink now–2014. Score 90. K

YATIR FOREST, 2003: This blend of 85% Cabernet Sauvignon and 15% Merlot reflects its 12 months in *barriques* with gentle spices and lightly dusty wood and is showing fine balance between tannins, wood and acidity. On the palate light herbal and white pepper traits underlying rich blueberry and black currant fruits. Well focused, long and elegant. Drink now–2012. Score 93. K

YATIR FOREST, 2002: Made from 100% Cabernet Sauvignon grapes, this dark garnet-toward-purple, full-bodied wine is now showing still-firm tannins, gentle and well-integrated smoky oak and sweet cedar aromas, those coming together very nicely with aromas and flavors of ripe currant and purple plum fruits as well as generous hints of chocolate and mint. Throwing sediment and worth decanting. Drink now–2009. Score 90. K

YATIR FOREST, 2001: Dark ruby towards garnet, this medium to full-bodied blend of 85% Cabernet Sauvignon and 15% Merlot shows good balance between soft tannins and oak. Rich aromas and flavors of currants, wild berries and cherries integrating nicely with spicy oak and generous minerals. A luxurious and elegant wine. Drink now–2009. Score 91. K

Yatir

YATIR, CABERNET SAUVIGNON, 2006: Rich and deeply extracted, with generous blackberry, currant, black cherry and wild berries that are highlighted by mocha, vanilla and cedarwood overtones. Destined for elegance. Best 2010–2015. Tentative Score 93–95. K

YATIR, CABERNET SAUVIGNON, 2005: Blended with 15% of Shiraz, this dark garnet with purple and orange reflections is showing fine balance between gentle spicy wood and mouth-coating tannins that are integrating nicely. On first attack blackberries and currants, those yielding to raspberries, spices and light overlays of earthiness and leather, all with a hint of what at one moment feels like lead pencil and the next like cigar box. Long, generous and destined for elegance. Best 2009–2014. Score 92. K

YATIR, CABERNET SAUVIGNON, 2002: Well focused, with deep, soft, near-sweet tannins and ripe flavors of cherries, currants, anise and nice touches of earth and minerals. A distinctly Mediterranean wine. Drink now–2009. Score 91. K

YATIR, MERLOT, 2006: Dark and dense but even at this early stage showing admirable depth, length and complexity. On the nose and palate layer after layer of currants, black cherries, chocolate and mocha all backed up by tannins that are simultaneously soft and powerful. Best 2009–2014. Tentative Score 92–94. K

YATIR, MERLOT, 2005: Medium to full-bodied, with generous near-sweet tannins, this seductive wine is already showing delicious blueberry, blackberry, mocha and vanilla flavors. Plush and round, on the way to becoming a delicious, complex and concentrated wine. Drink now–2012. Score 90. K

YATIR, MERLOT, RAMAT ARAD, 2002: Full-bodied, tannic and muscular for a Merlot, but with finely tuned balance between wood, fruits and acidity that gives the wine grace and elegance. Black plums, wild berries and currants here, together with freshly picked Mediterranean herbs and a hint of granite that comes in on the long finish. Drink now–2009. Score 90. K

YATIR, SHIRAZ, 2006: Tasted from two yet unblended barrels, the first an Australian clone that shows medium to full-body, firm but yielding tannins and a distinct hint of peppermint over spicy blackberry and black cherry fruits, all well focused and showing hints of exotic spices and white pepper. The second, a French clone with far softer tannins

Cabernet-Merlot-Shiraz
Judean Hills

but no less depth, unfolding to show blackberry, prune, meaty and dark chocolate. Both show enormous potential. Best 2009–2015. Tentative Score 93–95. K

YATIR, SHIRAZ, 2005: Dark, almost impenetrable garnet in color, intentionally aged in old oak *barriques* in order to highlight the typical characteristics of the variety, the wine opens with meaty and herbal aromas, those yielding nicely to cherry, red currant and berry fruits and finally, creeping in comfortably, an agreeable hint of saddle leather. Long, generous and destined for intense elegance. Best 2009–2014. Score 93. K

YATIR, CABERNET FRANC, 2006: Deep royal-purple, full-bodied, and showing faithful to the variety with complex black cherry, blackberry and cassis fruits accented by spices, cedarwood, coffee and hints of tar and vanilla. Drink from release–2011. Tentative Score 89–91. K

YATIR, PETIT VERDOT, 2006: Deep purple, a powerful wine with intense tannins, concentration and complexity. On the nose and palate layers of plum, blackberry, pomegranate, coffee and earth, those already showing hints of smoky oak. An outstanding example of a variety that is not often bottled on its own. Best from 2009–2013. Tentative Score 92–94. K

YATIR, CABERNET SAUVIGNON-MERLOT, 2001: A blend of 60% Cabernet Sauvignon and 40% Merlot, this medium to full-bodied wine shows a dark royal-purple color, soft, well-integrated tannins and generous black currant, plum, berry, and earthy-mineral aromas and flavors. Look as well for hints of spicy oak that develop from mid-palate. Drink now. Score 89. K

YATIR, BLENDED RED, 2005: A blend of Merlot, Shiraz, Cabernet Franc, and Petit Verdot (35%, 37%, 16% and 12% respectively). Aged in oak for 12 months, this still young wine shows firm tannins nicely balanced with lightly spicy wood. Starts with a rich blackberry nose and then goes on to aromas and flavors of wild berries, currants, and anise, all on a gently herbal background. Best 2009–2012. Score 91. K

YATIR, CABERNET SAUVIGNON-MERLOT-SHIRAZ, 2004: A blend of 40% each Cabernet Sauvignon and Merlot and 20% Shiraz, this full-bodied red shows depth and concentration but never loses sight of elegance. Deep royal-purple in color, with near-sweet tannins and appealing smoky and light vegetable overlays highlighting aromas and flavors of ripe plums, blackberries, cherry, and licorice. On the long finish a tantalizing hint of spicy oak. Drink now–2012. Score 91. K

YATIR, CABERNET SAUVIGNON-MERLOT-SHIRAZ, 2003: A blend of 56% Cabernet Sauvignon, 33% Merlot and 11% Shiraz. Aged in oak for one year, this medium to full-bodied wine shows ripe berry, cherry and currant fruits, those with just a hint of toasted oak, all backed up with vanilla and spicy aromas and flavors. Long and caressing. Drink now–2011. Score 90. K

YATIR, CABERNET SAUVIGNON-MERLOT-SHIRAZ, 2002: A blend of 75% Cabernet Sauvignon and 15% Merlot with 10% of Shiraz, this inky purple-towards-black, medium to full-bodied wine spent one year in new and used oak casks. Showing good balance between smoky wood, generous but soft tannins, plum and currant fruits, black pepper and a very appealing overlay of near-sweet herbaceousness, all leading to a long, satisfying finish. Drink now. Score 89. K

YATIR, ROSÉ, 2005: Made entirely from Syrah grapes that were allowed only one hour of skin contact and then treated to cold fermentation, this stylish wine has surprising depth and complexity for a rosé. With dried cherry, rose petal, spice and mineral flavors, this salmon-colored wine has just a hint of oak and a lightly spicy finish to tantalize. Drink now. Score 88. K

YATIR, SAUVIGNON BLANC, 2006: Fermented in stainless steel and then transferred to used oak for only three months in order to keep the crisp fruitiness of the wine intact, this light golden-straw, medium-bodied wine sits gently on the palate, its fresh acidity highlighting pineapple, citrus and light grassy overtones. Easy to drink yet with a touch of elegance. Drink now. Score 90. K

YATIR, SAUVIGNON BLANC, 2005: Aged in half new, half one-year-old *barriques* for three months, this lightly golden, medium-bodied white shows fresh, concentrated and vibrant aromas and flavors of passion fruit, green apples, hay, honeysuckle and citrus peel. Crisp, elegant and harmonious. Drink now. Score 91. K

YATIR, SAUVIGNON BLANC, 2004: This bright straw-colored wine shows well-enunciated aromas of citrus, tropical fruits and light grassy-herbaceousness. Medium-bodied, with crisp acidity, a tantalizing hint of the oak in which it developed for several months, and a long and complex finish. Drink up. Score 90. K

Forester-Lodge

YATIR, FORESTER-LODGE, 2004: A medium-bodied blend of 75% Merlot and 25% Cabernet Sauvignon, aged for eight months in *barriques*. A lovely, silky-smooth red with red berry, cherry and cassis aromas and flavors, just the right hint of toasty oak, soft tannins and a long-caressing finish. Drink now. Score 89. K

Ye'arim ***

Located in the village of Givat Ye'arim near Jerusalem, this small winery is owned by Sasson Ben-Aharon, who is also the winemaker for Binyamina Wineries. With vineyards in the Judean Mountains, the winery produced 1,000 bottles from the 2000 vintage and is currently releasing about 3,000 bottles annually.

YE'ARIM, CABERNET SAUVIGNON, SASSON'S WINE, 2004: Dark garnet, medium to full-bodied, with silky smooth tannins and a gentle hand with spicy wood, opening to show generous red currant, berry and cherry fruits, those matched nicely by spices and hints of licorice that come in on the long finish. Drink from release–2010. Tentative Score 88–90.

YE'ARIM, CABERNET SAUVIGNON, SASSON'S WINE, 2002: This garnet-red, medium to full-bodied wine is showing spicy cedar from its 18 months in oak along with well-integrated tannins now somewhat more gripping than in the past. Generous aromas and flavors of currants, ripe berries, sweet herbs and vanilla. Drink now. Score 87.

YE'ARIM, CABERNET SAUVIGNON, SASSON'S WINE, 2000: Deep garnet, this medium-bodied unfiltered blend of 95% Cabernet Sauvignon and 5% Merlot was aged in French oak *barriques* for 14 months and shows soft tannins and some spicy oak. Fully mature now and taking on a light herbal overlay while still showing appealing berry, currant and black cherry flavors. Drink up. Score 86.

YE'ARIM, MERLOT, SASSON'S WINE, 2003: Made entirely from Merlot grapes, garnet towards purple in color, well balanced and medium-bodied. With soft tannins, and reflecting 15 months in French oak with a gentle touch of spicy wood, the wine shows aromas and flavors of cherries, wild berries and tobacco as well as an appealing hint of minty-chocolate on the finish. Drink now–2009. Score 87.

Yehuda *

Located on Moshav Shoresh in the Jerusalem Mountains, this winery was founded by Avi Yehuda in 1998. Cabernet Sauvignon, Merlot and Sauvignon Blanc grapes come from the winery's own nearby vineyards as well as from Moshav Shoresh. Current production is 2,000–3,000 bottles annually.

YEHUDA, CABERNET SAUVIGNON, 2004: Rustic and chewy, with modest cherry fruits overlaid by spicy bell pepper, maraschino cherry and leathery notes. Drink up. Score 78.

YEHUDA, CABERNET SAUVIGNON, 2003: A country-style, somewhat coarse, medium-bodied wine with chunky tannins and showing only skimpy black fruits. Drink now. Score 79.

YEHUDA, CABERNET SAUVIGNON, 2002: Dark ruby towards garnet, medium-bodied, with firm tannins that fail to integrate with the wood, both of those holding back whatever fruits may be here. A country-style wine showing too earthy barnyard sensations. Drink now. Score 77.

YEHUDA, CABERNET SAUVIGNON, 2001: Deep cherry-red and medium-bodied, with chunky tannins and generous blackberry and cassis aromas and flavors overlaid by sweet herbs, this is a simple and distinctly country-style wine. Drink up. Score 79.

YEHUDA, MERLOT, 2004: Opens with juicy black cherry and cola aromas and flavors but goes bitter and herbal as it lingers on the palate. Drink up. Score 77.

YEHUDA, MERLOT, 2003: Garnet red, softly tannic and with its berry and plum fruits marred by a lightly muddy sensation. Drink up. Score 72.

YEHUDA, MERLOT, 2002: Light garnet with a bit of browning showing early aging. Soft tannins and stingy with its plum and wild berry fruits. Drink up. Score 77.

YEHUDA, MERLOT-CABERNET SAUVIGNON, 2001: A pleasant, medium-bodied and moderately tannic blend of 40% Merlot and 60% Cabernet Sauvignon. The wine was aged in oak for several months and shows hints of vanilla and anise, on a pleasing core of cherries and wild berries. Drink up. Score 86.

Yiftah'el *

Founded in 1999 in the community of Alon Hagalil in the Upper Galilee, owner-vintners Tzvika Ofir and Avner Sofer rely on Cabernet Sauvignon, Merlot, Petite Sirah and Sangiovese grapes from their own vineyards. Current production is about 10,000 bottles.

YIFTAH'EL, CABERNET SAUVIGNON, 2004: Oak-aged for about 12 months, showing firm tannins and generous spicy wood along with currant and berry fruits. Somewhat coarse on the palate. Drink up. Score 78.

YIFTAH'EL, SHIRAZ, 2005: Dark garnet, medium to full-bodied, with chunky, country-style tannins and appealing plum, herbal and earthy-minerals that linger nicely. Drink now. Score 85.

YIFTAH'EL, SANGIOVESE NOUVEAU, 2006: Light, soft and round with straightforward raspberry and strawberry flavors. Drink up. Score 83.

YIFTAH'EL, SANGIOVESE, 2004: Deep garnet, medium to full-bodied, this rustic red shows rather coarse tannins, excessive acidity and somewhat dusty fruits dominated by marked hints of earthy, tar and herbal notes. Drink up. Score 75.

YIFTAH'EL, SANGIOVESE, 2003: Light cherry-red in color, with only scarce tannins and berry, strawberry and banana aromas and flavors. Drink up. Score 80.

YIFTAH'EL, PETITE SIRAH, RESERVE, 2005: Dark, almost impenetrable purple, full-bodied, with soft, mouth-coating tannins and fine balance between spicy wood and black fruits. Drink now–2009. Score 87.

YIFTAH'EL, PETITE SIRAH, 2005: Aged in oak for only four months, this simple but pleasant country-style wine shows soft tannins and generous red fruits. Drink up. Score 85.

YIFTAH'EL, PETITE SIRAH, RESERVE, 2004: Dark garnet in color, with firm tannins just starting to yield, the wine shows aromas and flavors of plums and berries on an earthy, mushroom overlay. Drink now. Score 85.

YIFTAH'EL, PETITE SIRAH, 2004: Dark cherry-red towards garnet, with chunky, country-style tannins and with primary aromas and flavors of very ripe plums. Starts off near-sweet and turns somewhat bitter on the finish. Drink up. Score 80.

YIFTAH'EL, CABERNET-MERLOT, 2002: A medium-bodied, lightly tannic, oak-aged blend of 60% Cabernet Sauvignon and 40% Merlot. Not complex but pleasant. Drink up. Score 83.

Zauberman ★★★★

Founded in 1999 by Itzik Zauberman and located in the town of Gedera in the Southern Plains, this small winery draws on organically raised grapes from its own vineyards nearby as well as using grapes from Karmei Yosef. Current production is about 3,000 bottles annually.

ZAUBERMAN, CABERNET SAUVIGNON, LIMITED EDITION, 2004: Deep royal-purple, full-bodied, intense and concentrated, with generous soft tannins, moderate spicy oak and showing raspberry, black currant, chocolate and light earthy herbaceousness. Best from 2009. Tentative Score 91–93.

ZAUBERMAN, CABERNET SAUVIGNON, LIMITED EDITION, 2003: Dark garnet, full-bodied, with generous tannins starting to integrate and equally generous spicy wood. Showing blackberry, plum and cassis fruits, all leading to a long, intense finish. Best from 2009. Score 91.

ZAUBERMAN, CABERNET SAUVIGNON, LIMITED EDITION, 2002: Deep garnet-red, full-bodied, with intense tannins and generous, almost powerful wood integrated nicely with plum, raspberry and currant fruits along with spicy and earthy aromas and flavors. On the long finish generous hints of well-roasted nuts. Consider decanting before drinking. Drink now–2012. Score 90.

ZAUBERMAN, CABERNET SAUVIGNON, LIMITED EDITION, 2001: Dark royal-purple toward black, full-bodied, concentrated and tannic, with aromas and flavors of dried plums, cherries, red berries, chocolate, honey and spices. This powerful, near-massive and complex wine, made by drying the grapes before pressing them much in the *ripasso* method, is approachable now if given at least 30 minutes in the glass to open. Drink now–2012. Score 93.

ZAUBERMAN, CABERNET SAUVIGNON, 2000: Well balanced, dark and rich, this concentrated wine shows good currant, plum, vanilla and herbal aromas and flavors well balanced by tannins and wood. Rich bittersweet overtones call to mind wines made in Italy by the *ripasso* method. Long and mouth-filling. Drink now–2009. Score 90.

ZAUBERMAN, MERLOT, 2004: Dark, almost impenetrable garnet, full-bodied, with soft tannins, spicy oak, and plum, currant and berry fruits. Long and generous. Drink now–2009. Score 89.

ZAUBERMAN, MERLOT, 2003: Dark ruby towards garnet, medium to full-bodied, with good balance between generous smoky oak, firm but caressing tannins, black and red berry fruits and hints of coffee and chocolate. Drink now–2009. Score 89.

ZAUBERMAN, MERLOT, 2002: Deep garnet toward royal-purple, this medium to full-bodied unfiltered wine shows good balance between smoky oak, soft tannins and aromas and flavors of berries, currants and anise. A moderately long, earthy finish. Drink up. Score 91.

ZAUBERMAN, MERLOT, 2001: The best Merlot as yet from this winery, and one of the best made in Israel. Remarkably rich and full-bodied, this deep garnet-toward-purple wine shows delicious plum, cherry and currant fruits along with anise, vanilla and spicy oak and a complex and long finish. Well focused and harmonious. Drink up. Score 93.

Zemora ✳✳✳

Set in a facility in Moshav Beit Zayit in the Jerusalem Mountains, winemaker Baruch Yosef released his first wines from the 2000 vintage. Grapes are drawn largely from the Jerusalem Mountain area and include Cabernet Sauvignon, Merlot, Cabernet Franc, Shiraz, Petit Verdot, Sangiovese, Viognier and Chardonnay, some of which are being raised organically. The winery releases wines in two series, the Bordeaux blends Castra, and single-variety wines Zemora. Current production is about 50,000 bottles annually. Starting with the 2004 vintage, the wines have been kosher.

Castra

CASTRA, RED, 2004: Deep inky garnet, this full-bodied blend of Merlot, Cabernet Sauvignon, Cabernet Franc, Shiraz and Petit Verdot (65%, 20%, 10%, 3% and 2% respectively) spent 24 months in new French oak. Generous toasty wood balanced by firm tannins. On the nose and palate purple plums, blackberries and cherries, those leading to a long, spicy finish. Primarily for those who like their wines with an ample overlay of oak. Drink now–2011. Score 88. K

CASTRA, BLACK, 2004: The mirror image of the Castra Red. Here, with the amounts of Merlot and Cabernet reversed, containing 65% Cabernet and 20% Merlot. Full-bodied, with generous wood and firm tannins complemented by blackberries, black cherries, currants and dark chocolate and, on the moderately long finish, a hint of smoked meat. Drink now–2011. Score 88. K

CASTRA, 2003: Almost impenetrably dark garnet, medium to full-bodied, with still-firm tannins integrating nicely. A well-balanced blend of 75% Cabernet Sauvignon, 20% Cabernet Franc and 5% Merlot, showing up-front cherry and blackberry fruits, those complemented by spicy, smoky cedar. Drink now–2009. Score 89.

Zemora

ZEMORA, CABERNET SAUVIGNON, 2006: Royal-purple, medium to full-bodied, with still-firm tannins and spicy oak waiting to integrate and show the currant and berry fruits and light minty overlay that need time to develop. Drink from release–2010. Tentative Score 84–86. K

ZEMORA, CABERNET SAUVIGNON, 2005: Deep royal-purple in color, with soft tannins integrating nicely and reflecting its 14 months in medium and heavy-toasted French oak with a generous, toasted cedar overlay. On the nose and palate opens to reveal blackberries, blueberries, cassis and vanilla. Soft, round and moderately long. Drink from release–2010. Tentative Score 86–88. K

ZEMORA, CABERNET SAUVIGNON, ORGANIC, 2005: Garnet towards purple, medium-bodied, with light tannins and showing berry, black cherry and currant fruits. Not complex but promises to be a good quaffer. Drink from release. Tentative Score 84–86. K

ZEMORA, CABERNET SAUVIGNON, 2004: Blended with 3% of Merlot, this generously oak-aged, medium-bodied and softly tannic wine shows aromas and flavors of raspberries, red currants and red plums, those with just enough spiciness to add complexity. Drink now. Score 85. K

ZEMORA, MERLOT, 2006: Ruby towards garnet, medium to full-bodied, with soft but mouth-coating tannins. On the nose and palate a basic berry and black cherry personality, the fruits overlaid with hints of sweet herbs. Drink from release. Tentative Score 85–87. K

ZEMORA, MERLOT, 2004: Dark-garnet red, reflecting 18 months in oak with generous smoky wood and soft tannins, those opening to reveal aromas and flavors of spicy berry and black cherry fruits. Drink now. Score 85. K

ZEMORA, MERLOT, 2003: Dark ruby towards garnet, medium-bodied, with soft tannins, generous wood and forward berry and cherry fruits. Somewhat one dimensional. Drink up. Score 84.

ZEMORA, SHIRAZ, 2005: Youthful royal-purple, medium-bodied, its soft tannins integrating well with spicy oak and berry-cherry aromas and flavors. Round and soft. Drink from release–2009. Tentative Score 85–87. K

ZEMORA, SHIRAZ, ORGANIC, 2005: Dark royal-purple, medium to full-bodied, with intense, ripe currant, plum and black cherry aromas and flavors, and an appealing light beefy overlay. Somewhat on the acidic side. Drink from release. Tentative Score 85–87. K

ZEMORA, SANGIOVESE, 2004: Ruby-red, medium-bodied, with perhaps too-generous acidity. A few cherry-berry fruits are not enough to save the wine. Drink up. Score 79. K

ZEMORA, SANGIOVESE, 2003: Blended with 15% of Cabernet Sauvignon but still lacking backbone and showing rather flabby tannins. Light to medium-bodied, perhaps even a bit diluted on the palate, with skimpy berry-black cherry fruits. One dimensional and short. Drink up. Score 80.

ZEMORA, CABERNET FRANC, 2005: Deep garnet, full-bodied, with chewy tannins and smoky oak opening to reveal plum and black cherry notes, those supported by leather and cedar all leading to vanilla and spices on a moderately long finish. Drink from release–2010. Tentative Score 86–88. K

ZEMORA, CABERNET FRANC, 2003: Made from grapes harvested in the Meron vineyards, this medium-bodied red shows chunky, country-style tannins and ample oak yielding a good deal of smoke and vanilla, those overshadowing somewhat the plum and berry flavors. Drink now. Score 85.

ZEMORA, CABERNET FRANC, 2002: Medium to full-bodied and dark garnet in color, with a distinct country-style coarseness that is set off by berry, cherry and plum fruits. Ripe and mouth-filling. Drink up. Score 85.

ZEMORA, PETIT VERDOT, 2005: Dark purple, medium-bodied, opening with a floral nose and showing spicy oak and soft tannins in fine balance with a core of plum, blueberry and currant fruits. Makes up for its lack of complexity with a long and harmonious finish. Drink from release–2009. Tentative Score 87–89. K

ZEMORA, PETIT VERDOT, ORGANIC, 2005: Medium-bodied, with soft tannins and toasty oak. Shows berry and currant fruits, those with a light spicy overtone. Not complex but promises to be a good quaffer. Drink from release. Tentative Score 83–85. K

ZEMORA, CABERNET SAUVIGNON-CABERNET FRANC, 2003: A generously oak-aged blend of 60% Cabernet Sauvignon and 40% Cabernet Franc, showing chunky tannins and heavy spices but those balanced nicely by appealing currant, berry and black cherry fruits. Not complex or long but a good quaffer. Drink up. Score 85.

ZEMORA, CHARDONNAY, 2006: Developed in new medium-toasted French *barriques* and thus reflecting a toasty wood personality, that complemented by grapefruit, tropical fruits and citrus peel. Medium-bodied and moderately long. Drink now. Score 85. K

ZEMORA, CHARDONNAY, 2005: Darkly golden, aged in oak for five months, this medium-bodied white offers peach and citrus aromas and flavors along with a light, unwanted bitter streak that runs throughout. Drink up. Score 84. K

ZEMORA, VIOGNIER, 2006: Golden-straw in color, unoaked, floral and sweet on the nose but crisply dry on the palate. Look for aromas and flavors of peaches and golden apples. Picks up a hint of lightly bitter lemon peel on the finish. Drink now. Score 85. K

ZEMORA, VIOGNIER, 2005: Golden-straw in color, medium-bodied, with fresh citrus, guava and pear fruits matched nicely by a silky texture. On the finish hints of honey and figs. Drink up. Score 85. K

Zion **

Founded in the old city of Jerusalem in 1848 by the Shor family, until recently this winery produced primarily wines for sacramental purposes. Managed by the ninth generation of the family, starting three years ago the winery began to release dry wines. Now located in Mishor Adumim, not far from Jerusalem, the winery produces about 1,500,000 bottles annually of which 100,000–150,000 are dry, those in three series, Armon, Tidhar and Erez. The winery currently relies largely on Cabernet Sauvignon, Merlot, Carignan, Petite Sirah and Emerald Riesling grapes and is developing vineyards with Chardonnay, Sauvignon Blanc and Viognier.

Armon

ARMON, CABERNET SAUVIGNON, 2005: Developing now in oak *barriques*, this is a full-bodied, generously tannic and cedar-rich wine, those elements in fine balance with natural acidity and fruits. Dark garnet, opening to show currant, blackberry and plum fruits on a background of spices and earthy minerals. Drink from release–2009. Tentative Score 85–87. K

Tidhar

TIDHAR, CABERNET SAUVIGNON, 2005: A garnet-red, lightly oaked, medium-bodied and softly tannic blend of 85% Cabernet Sauvignon, 10% Merlot and 5% Petite Sirah. Black and red berries, ripe purple plums and light spices that run throughout making this an easy-to-drink quaffer. Drink now. Score 85. K

TIDHAR, CABERNET SAUVIGNON-MERLOT, 2005: Medium-dark cherry in color, medium-bodied, with firm tannins that do not want to yield. Appealing berry and currant fruits but somewhat biting on the finish. Drink now. Score 80. K

TIDHAR, CARIGNAN-MERLOT-CABERNET SAUVIGNON, 2005: Dark ruby-red in color, this lightly oaked, light to medium-bodied wine shows soft tannins and opens with light minty aromas and flavors going on to raspberry and plums. A refreshing quaffer. Drink now. Score 84. K

Erez

EREZ, MERLOT, 2005: Blended with 15% of Cabernet Sauvignon, this medium-bodied dark ruby wine shows soft tannins and straightforward red berry and currant fruits. Not complex but pleasant. Drink now. Score 84. K

EREZ, CABERNET SAUVIGNON-MER-LOT, 2004: Medium to full-bodied, this blend of 52% Cabernet Sauvignon, 44% Merlot and 4% Petite Sirah shows chunky, country-style tannins and a too-heavy dose of wood after spending 14 months in oak. Black fruits now developing an herbal-earthy overtone. Past its peak. Drink up. Score 76. K

EREZ, PETITE SYRAH-MERLOT, 2005: Petite Sirah and Merlot in equal parts. Ruby to garnet, clean and fresh, with soft tannins, a hint of spicy wood and generous red fruits. Not complex but easy to drink. Drink now. Score 83. K

Afterword

Wine Cabinets

Some wines are meant to be consumed in their youth, while others will be at their best starting only three, five or even ten and twenty years from their release. Whether wines will remain drinkable over the years is much a question of how they are stored. Heat, humidity and fluctuations in temperature as well as bright light harm wines and almost guarantee that they will age and deteriorate too rapidly.

With ever-increasing awareness, many wine lovers are becoming justifiably concerned about how to best store and age their wines. In countries such as England or Canada, storage is no problem, for most homes have either a basement or a closet that is cool and dark and can easily double as a wine cellar, especially when the wines are not rare or extremely dear. In many parts of the world, however, where interior temperatures often reach 30°C (86°F), storing wines is considerably more difficult. Since only few people have either the physical space or the means required to build a true wine cellar, the solution to storage is invariably a refrigerated wine cabinet, and those are available now in many shapes and prices.

The very first commercially manufactured wine cabinets appeared in England and the United States in the mid-1930s. The earliest models were custom made and cost a small fortune. Multi-millionaire Cornelius Vanderbilt, for example, had five wine cabinets, one for his New York City town house, one for his winter home on Jeckyll Island, Georgia, one for his summer home on Martha's Vineyard in Massachusetts and two for his yacht (one for the dining room and one for his private cabin). Winston Churchill limited his purchases to two cabinets, only one of which held wine, however, for he used the other to store his cigars.

Fortunately, wine cabinets are no longer as dear as they

once were. Far less expensive than building a wine cellar, easy to maintain, and often physically attractive, they offer an excellent solution both for wine lovers who wish to build a collection of wines, and to restaurateurs and hoteliers, for use either as storage or as display cabinets to encourage the sale of the wines listed on their menus.

Regardless of whether purchased for at-home or commercial use, all well-made wine cabinets should meet certain basic requirements. It is critical, for example, that all such cabinets be odor-free and as close to vibration-free as possible. They also must be well insulated, since in case of power failure it is important to maintain the appropriate temperature for a prolonged period of time.

All of the cabinets available are divided by shelves, so that one can either store or display wine by categories (e.g. whites, reds, rosés, sparkling wines), and some feature sliding shelves that can be pulled out. In many you will find different temperature zones ranging from 7°C (45°F) to 15°C (60°F). However, most cabinets have a steady temperature of 12°C (55°F), because in addition to being appropriate for aging red wines it also has the advantage of leaving the white wines at or nearly at their perfect serving temperature.

Wine cabinets should also maintain a proper level of humidity. Although a humidity level of 50% is acceptable, the ideal is 70%. At higher than that, labels will become moldy and deteriorate, and at lower than 40% the corks will dry out and thus allow air to seep into the bottle.

Finally, cabinets should allow for the bottles to lie in a reclining position so that the corks are covered by the wine and kept moist. New models also have alarms that warn if the temperature fluctuates or if the humidity drops, and a lighting system which is UV free. Some also feature a fan to maintain a flow of fresh air and prevent mold, and the latest boast a remote-control system.

Most wine cabinets are available in sizes that hold 50–600 bottles and several offer storage of up to 1,250 bottles. In finishes they range from stainless steel to hi-tech plastic and high-quality wood (teak and mahogany, among others). The most sophisticated cabinet makers use aluminum for the internal lining, as this is considered the best temperature conductor.

Since the price range of wine cabinets is enormous, ranging from a few hundred to thousands of dollars, depending on size—custom-made cabinets cost even more—a bit of comparison shopping is in order. It is well known that prices for identical cabinets can vary by as much as 40% from store to store, and even more if the purchase is made in online outlets.

A Guide to Tasting Wines

Wine tasting is not a complex or difficult task. All that is required is the use of one's senses of sight, smell and taste. Before setting out to taste wines, try to eliminate as many distractions as possible. During the actual tasting, for example, extraneous aromas (e.g. food, perfume and aftershave lotion) should be avoided as they interfere with the ability to appreciate the aromas and bouquet of the wine. Also, during a tasting, try as hard as possible to ignore the comments by others in order not to be influenced by their opinions. Be sure to use high-quality glasses (ideally of thin crystal) as this enhances the flavors and aromas of wines. A separate glass should be provided for each wine, this allowing the taster to return to earlier tasted wines in order to make comparisons. The glasses should be, of course, perfectly clean, without any aroma of soap or detergent. Glasses should be filled to no more than 20% of their capacity as this will give ample room for swirling the wine, that process serving to aerate and release the more subtle aromas and flavors of the wine being tasted.

Basic Rules for Tasting Wines

- Professionals can sample fifty or more wines at a single sitting, but it is widely agreed that in a private tasting, alone at home or at a friendly gathering, the number of wines for tasting should not exceed eight.
- White wines should be tasted before reds, and within each group wines that are light in body should be tasted

before fuller-bodied wines. When tasting wines of the same variety, such as Cabernet Sauvignon or Merlot, always start with the youngest wines and end with the most mature.

- Wines should be served at their proper temperatures. Young reds should be opened about fifteen or twenty minutes before the tasting, and more mature reds about half an hour before they are poured.

- You can either place the bottles on the table with the labels exposed or place each bottle in a paper bag, each bag identified only by a number, for a blind tasting. I prefer blind tastings, for the power of suggestion is strong and it is difficult to be entirely objective vis à vis a label of a prestigious Chateau.

- Wines should be arranged on the table in the order they are to be tasted. I suggest using a felt-tipped pen to put a number on each bottle and then to mark the corresponding number on the base of each glass in order to avoid any confusion.

- Professional wine tasters spit the wine in order to avoid intoxication, but there is no need to spit at a home tasting where much of the pleasure comes from drinking the wine. For those who choose to spit, prepare adequate receptacles (clay jugs, low vases and Champagne buckets are ideal).

- Allow half a bottle per person. That is to say, for eight people you will need four bottles. When pouring during the tasting, remember that the average sampling should be small enough to allow room for swirling the wine in the glass. Whatever wines are left over after the actual tasting can be served with the meal or snacks afterward.

- Use a tasting form, such as that illustrated in the following section, or record your impressions on a piece of paper. Making notes helps people make up their minds before they commit themselves.

- Food should be served after a wine tasting and never before or during because food changes the taste of wine. If you must have something on the table, use unsalted and sugar-free white bread.

Wine Appreciation

1. VISUAL APPEARANCE

In order to best see the color and clarity of a wine, hold your glass against a white background (a white tablecloth or even a blank sheet of white paper will do) and tilt the glass away from yourself slightly so that the exposed surface is larger. Red wines can be anywhere from bright cherry-red in color to dark and opaque, in fact almost black. Although most white wines will have a light golden-straw color, they can range from almost colorless to deep golden, and rosé or blush wines are only rarely true pink and can vary from purple-pink to orange or even bright ruby-red. Whatever the color, the wine should be perfectly clear. Wines that have thrown a sediment will become clear as the sediment settles.

Consider whether the color is deep or pale and whether it is vivid and youthful or browning and perhaps showing age. While the glass is tilted look as well at the rim (that point where the wine meets the glass), for it is not generally a positive sign if the color at the rim fades to an almost watery consistency. After noting the qualities of the color, swirl the wine in the glass gently and then hold it up to see the legs or tears—these are the threads of wine that appear and linger on the inside of the glass. These are an accurate indicator of the alcohol level in the wine; the broader and more viscous the legs, the greater the alcohol content and, according to many, a good indicator of the wine's ability to age. At the same time, note whether the wine is *frizzante*, that is to say, whether it has tiny little bubbles in it. Although this is acceptable in some white wines (e.g. Muscadet de Sevres et Maine *sur lie*, Vinho Verde, Moscato d'Asti), and occurs in many white wines when they have been overly chilled, such bubbles indicate a fault in nearly all red wines. When evaluating Champagnes or other sparkling wines, the bubbles should be sharp, small and long lasting, rising from a central point in the glass.

A hint: Never taste wines under fluorescent light as this makes all red wines appear brown.

2. SMELL

It surprises many to realize that people with a normal sense of smell can identify more than 1,000 different aromas. That should not be daunting, however, as the process of identifying aromas is a largely automatic one and although we may sometimes "struggle" to distinguish between the aroma of a blackberry or raspberry, our associations with aromas are quite strong. In order to best evaluate and appreciate the aromas of a wine, swirl the glass rapidly for a few seconds, place your nose well into the glass and inhale deeply through your nostrils.

One of the first sensations to be evaluated is the alcohol content of the wine. If the wine appears to be highly alcoholic, ask yourself whether it is a fortified wine (e.g. Sherry, Port, Madeira) or whether the strong alcoholic aromas reflect a fault. After that, consider whether the wine smells as youthful or as mature as it appears to the eye, whether the aromas are smooth and harmonious, whether they are distinctive, bland or reticent and whether they are simple or complex. Consider as well whether there is a creamy, spicy or vanilla note to the aromas as this may give a hint about whether the wine was aged in oak. Also consider whether the wine has any "off" aromas that may indicate a fault. With a bit of practice it becomes possible for many to identify from aroma alone the variety of the grape used and even the region in which the wine was made.

A hint: A slight musky aroma can add great charm, but when exaggerated almost always reveals a fault in the wine.

3. TASTE

When actually setting out to taste the wine, take a good mouthful, close the lips firmly and swirl the wine vigorously in order to coat the entire mouth. This is important because different taste sensations are perceived by different parts of the mouth (sweetness on the tip of the tongue, sourness on the sides, bitterness on the back and the roof of the mouth, saltiness on the fronts and side of the tongue). Some tasters also draw a bit of air into the mouth, believing this will accentuate the flavors.

The first thing to be noted is whether the flavors are in accord with the aromas of the wines. Then, with the wine lingering in the mouth, identify the various taste sensations imparted. Ask yourself: Are the flavors pronounced and easily identifiable or somewhat confused; is the wine clean or muddy; are the tannins, acidity, wood and fruits in balance; are the tannins and wood in good proportion to the fruits; is the level of sweetness appropriate for the wine?

Keep in mind that the major goal of tasting is not only to evaluate a wine but to determine whether it is to your taste. Wine tasting is not a guessing game but with increased practice and repeated tastings, many come to the point where they can identify and discuss the grape variety, area of origin and age and quality of the wines they are tasting.

A hint: A wine dominated by a single flavor is one dimensional and thus lacking excitement.

Among the fruit aromas and flavors to be sought in white wines: citrus (especially lemon, grapefruit, lime and citrus peel), apple, melon, pear, peach, apricot, grapes, figs and, especially in sweet dessert wines, dried fruits. Also in white wines look for hints of grassiness, herbaceousness, honey, and a creamy sensation. Fruits to be found in red wines include, among others, black and red currants (sometimes referred to as cassis), plums and a variety of berries. Other taste sensations that may be imparted by red wines are chocolate, coffee and tobacco. In both reds and whites look for aromas and flavors imparted by oak aging, those including spicy or smoky oak, sweet cedar, asphalt and vanilla. Be aware that some of the aromas and flavors traditionally found in a red may appear in a white and vice versa.

TASTING FORMS

Because few of us have perfect memories, one of the very best aids in tasting wines is to use an organized sheet for keeping notes. Such sheets, used by professional wine tasters as well as amateurs, help to organize our thoughts and to leave a permanent record for future reference with which to compare the same wine or similar wines. The act of writing our reactions down also serves to implant our thoughts in long-term memory.

The tasting form that is illustrated on the opposite page (and is in larger format on the inside of the dust jacket of this book) is meant for those purposes. Readers may feel free to reproduce this form for their own use or for the use of friends, and should the original be lost, a downloadable and printable copy can be found at:

www.tobypress.com/rogov/tasting.pdf

Several Words about Scores

A great many people walk into wine stores and order this or that wine entirely on the basis of its high score. This is a mistake. A score is nothing more than a critic's attempt to sum up in digits the overall quality of a wine. Scores can provide a valid tool, especially when awarded by experienced critics, but they should not be separated from the tasting notes that precede them; for although a score may be a convenient summary, it says nothing about the style, personality or other important traits of the wine in question and therefore cannot give the consumer a valid basis for choice.

There are, however, three major advantages to scores. First of all, scores can serve as initial guides for the overall impression of the wine in question. Second, scores also give an immediate basis for comparison of that wine to others in its category and to the same wine of the same winery from earlier years. Finally, such scores give valuable hints as to whether the wine in question is available at a reasonable value for one's money.

The scores awarded in this book should be taken as merely one part of the overall evaluation of the wine, the most important parts of which are the tasting notes that give details about the body, color, aromas, flavors, length and overall style of the wine. It is also important to keep in mind that scores are not absolute. The score earned by a light and hyper-fruity wine made from Gamay grapes, a wine meant to be consumed in its youth, cannot be compared to that given

ROGOV'S GUIDE TO ISRAELI WINES RATING CHART

Toby

Name of Wine:	Date of Tasting:
Vintage Year:	Date Obtained:
Country of Origin:	Price:
Wine Region:	

	COMMENTS
VISUAL APPEARANCE: (0–5 POINTS)	
Clarity: (*cloudy, dull, clear, brilliant*)	
Depth and Intensity of Color (*watery, pale, medium, deep, dark*)	
Color: White Wines—green tinge, pale yellow, yellow, gold, brown	
Red Wines—purple, garnet, red, brown	
Viscosity: Light sparkle, watery, normal, heavy, oily	
Champagnes Only:	
Length of mousse	
Finesse and Sharpness of bubbles	
Duration of bubbles	Points: _____
AROMAS AND BOUQUET: (0–15 POINTS)	
Attractiveness (*neutral, clean, attractive, outstanding, off*)	
Aroma and Bouquet (*fruits and others*) (*none, light, positive, identifiable*)	
Intensity (*pleasant, complex, powerful, overpowering*)	Points: _____
FLAVORS AND PALATE IMPRESSIONS (0–15 POINTS)	
Sweetness (*bone dry, dry, medium-dry, medium-sweet, very sweet*)	
Acidity (*flat, refreshing, marked, tart*)	
Body (*very light and thin, light, medium, full-bodied, heavy*)	
Tannin—(*Red wines only*) (*astringent, hard, dry, soft*)	
Tactile impression (*slight sparkle, watery, normal, heavy, oily*)	
Flavor (*stingy, medium, generous, exaggerated*)	
Taste Sensations (*fruits, oak, vanilla, spices, herbs, etc*)	
Alcohol (*low, medium, ideal, high*)	
Finish (*Length*) (*short, medium, long, very long*)	
Balance (*unbalanced, well balanced, very well balanced*)	Points: _____
OVERALL IMPRESSION (0–15 POINTS)	
Coarse, poor, acceptable, fine, outstanding	Points: _____
To arrive at a final score, add up the points in each of the boxes and add 50.	Score: _____

to a deep, full-bodied wine made from a blend of Cabernet Sauvignon, Merlot and Cabernet Franc, the peak of drinking for which may come only five, ten or even thirty years later on. Numerical comparisons between the wines of the great Chateaux of Bordeaux and those meant to be consumed within weeks or months of the harvest is akin to comparing, by means of a single number, the qualities of a 1998 Rolls Royce and a 1965 Volkswagen Beetle.

Even if there was a perfect system for rating wines (and I do not believe such a system exists), no two critics, no matter how professional or well intentioned they may be, can be expected to use precisely the same criteria for every facet of every wine they evaluate. Even when similar scoring systems are used by different critics, readers should expect to find a certain variation between them. The trick is not in finding the critics with whom you always agree, but those whose tasting notes and scores give you direction in finding the wines that you most enjoy.

My own scoring system is based on a maximum of 100 points, interpreted as follows:

95–100	Truly great wines
90–94	Exceptional in every way
86–89	Very good to excellent and highly recommended
81–85	Recommended but without enthusiasm
70–79	Average but at least somewhat faulted
Under 70	Not recommended

Glossary of Wine Terminology

ACIDIC: A wine whose level of acidity is so high that it imparts a sharp feel or sour taste in the mouth.

ACIDITY: An important component of wine. A modicum of acidity adds liveliness to wine, too little makes it flat and dull, and too much imparts a sour taste. The acids most often present in wines are tartaric, malic and lactic acids.

AFTERTASTE: The flavors and aromas left in the mouth after the wine has been swallowed.

AGGRESSIVE: Refers to the strong, assertive character of a young and powerful wine. Aggressive wines often lack charm and grace.

ALCOHOL CONTENT: Percent by volume of alcohol in a wine. Table wines usually have between 11.5–13.5% in alcohol content but there is an increasing demand for wines as high as 15–16%.

ALCOHOLIC: A negative term, referring to wines that have too much alcohol and are thus hot and out of balance.

AROMA: Technically, this term applies to the smells that come directly from the grapes, whereas bouquet applies to the smells that come from the winemaking process. In practice, the two terms are used interchangeably.

ASTRINGENT: A puckering sensation imparted to the wine by its tannins. At a moderate level, astringency is a positive trait. When a wine is too astringent it is unpleasant.

ATTACK: The first sensations imparted by a wine.

ATYPICAL: A wine that does not conform to its traditional character or style.

AUSTERE: A wine that lacks fruits or is overly tannic or acidic.

BALANCED: The term used to describe a wine in which the

acids, alcohol, fruits, tannins and influence of the wood in which the wine was aged are in harmony.

BARNYARD: Aromas and flavors that call to mind the barnyard, and when present in excess impart dirty sensations, but when in moderation can be pleasant.

BARREL: The wood containers used to ferment and hold wine. The wood used in such barrels is most often French or American oak but other woods can be used as well.

BARREL AGING: The process in which wines mature in barrels after fermentation.

BARRIQUE: French for "barrel" but specifically referring to oak barrels of 225 liter capacity, in which many wines are fermented and/or aged.

BIG: A term used to describe a wine that is powerful in flavor, body or alcohol.

BLANC DE BLANCS: White wines made entirely from white grapes.

BLANC DE NOIRS: White wines made from grapes usually associated with red wines.

BLEND: A wine made from more than one grape variety or from grapes from different vintages. Some of the best wines in the world, including most of the Bordeaux wines, are blends of different grapes selected to complement each other.

BLUSH WINE: A wine that has a pale pink color imparted by very short contact with the skins of red grapes.

BODY: The impression of weight or fullness on the palate. Results from a combination of fruits and alcohol. Wines range from light to full-bodied.

BOTTLE AGING: The process of allowing wine to mature in its bottle.

BOTRYTIS CINEREA: Sometimes known as "noble rot", this is one of the few fungi that is welcomed by winemakers, for as it attacks the grapes it shrivels them, drains the water and concentrates the sugar, thus allowing for the making of many of the world's greatest sweet wines.

BOUQUET: Technically, the aromas that result from the

winemaking process, but the term is used interchangeably with aroma.

BRUT: Bone dry. A term used almost exclusively to describe sparkling wines.

BUTTERY: A positive term for rich white wines, especially those that have undergone malolactic fermentation.

CARBONIC MACERATION: Method of fermenting red wine without crushing the grapes first. Whole clusters of grapes are put in a closed vat together with carbon dioxide, and the fermentation takes place within the grape berries, which then burst.

CARAMELIZED: A wine that has taken on a brown color, and sweet and sour aromas and flavors, often due to exposure to oxygen as the wine ages.

CHARACTER: Balance, assertiveness, finesse and other positive qualities combine to create character. The term is used only in the positive sense.

CHEWY: Descriptive of the texture, body and intensity of a good red wine. A chewy wine will be mouth-filling and complex.

CLONE: A vine derived by vegetative propagation from cuttings, or buds from a single vine called the mother vine.

CLOYING: A wine that has sticky, heavy or unclean aromas or flavors.

COARSE: A wine that is rough or overly alcoholic. Appropriate in some country-style wines but not in fine wines.

CORKED: A wine that has been tainted by TCA (2, 4, 6-Tricholoraniole), increasingly caused by faulty corks. TCA imparts aromas of damp, moldy and decomposing cardboard to a wine. Sometimes only barely detectable, at other times making a wine unapproachable.

COUNTRY-STYLE: A simple wine that is somewhat coarse but not necessarily unpleasant.

CREAMY: A soft, silky texture.

CRISP: A clean wine with good acidity.

DENSE: Full in flavor and body.

DEPTH: Refers to complexity and intensity of flavor.

DESSERT WINE: A sweet wine. Often served as an accompaniment to goose liver dishes at the start of a meal.

DIRTY: A wine typified by off aromas or flavors resulting from either poor vinification practices or a faulty bottling process.

DRINKING WINDOW: The predicted period during which a wine will be at its best.

DRY: The absence of sugar or sweetness.

EARTHY: Sensations of freshly turned soil, minerals, damp leaves and mushrooms.

ELEGANT: A wine showing finesse or style.

EVERYDAY WINES: Inexpensive, readily available and easy-to-drink wines, lacking sophistication, but at their best pleasant accompaniments to food.

FAT: A full-bodied wine that is high in alcohol or glycerin but in which the flavor overshadows the acidity, giving it a heavy, sweetish sensation. A negative term.

FERMENTATION: A process by which yeast reacts with sugar in the must, resulting in the creation of alcohol.

FILTRATION: Usually done just prior to bottling, the process of filtering of the wine in order to remove large particles of sediment and other impurities. Over-filtration tends to rob wines of their aromas and flavors.

FINESSE: Showing great harmony. Among the best qualities of a good wine.

FINISH: The aromas and flavors that linger on the palate after the wine has been swallowed.

FIRMNESS: The grip of a wine, determined by its tannins and acidity.

FLABBY: The opposite of crisp, often a trait of wines that lack acidity and are thus dull and weak.

FLAT: Synonymous to flabby.

FLINTY: A slightly metallic taste, sometimes found in white wines such as Chardonnays. A positive quality.

FORTIFIED WINE: A wine whose alcoholic strength has been intensified by the addition of spirits.

FRIZZANTE: Lightly sparkling.

GRASSY: A term often used to describe white wines made from Sauvignon Blanc and Gewurztraminer grapes.

GREEN: In the positive sense, wines that are tart and youthful but have the potential to develop. In the negative sense, a wine that is unripe and sour.

HARD: A sense of austerity usually found in young, tannic red wines before they mellow and develop with age.

HARSH: Always a negative term, even more derogatory than "coarse".

HERBACEOUS: Implies aromas and flavors of grass, hay, herbs, leather and tobacco.

HOT: The unpleasant, sometimes burning sensation left on the palate by an overly alcoholic wine.

ICE WINE: A dessert wine made by a special method in which the grapes are left on the vine until frozen and then pressed while still frozen. Only the water in the grape freezes and this can be removed, leaving the must concentrated and very sweet. In warm weather areas the freezing process may be done in the winery.

INTENSE: A strong, concentrated flavor and aroma.

INTERNATIONALIZED WINES: Reds or whites that are blended to please any palate. At their best such wines are pleasant, at their worst simply boring.

LATE HARVEST: In such a harvest, grapes are left on the vines until very late in the harvest season, the purpose being to obtain sweeter grapes that will be used to make dessert wines.

LEES: Sediments that accumulate in the bottom of the barrel or vat as a wine ferments.

LEGS: The "tears" or stream of wine that clings to a glass after the wine has been swirled.

LENGTH: The period of time in which the flavors and aromas of a wine linger after it has been swallowed.

LIGHT: Low in alcohol or body. Also used to describe a wine low in flavor.

LIVELY: Clean and refreshing.

LONG: A wine that offers aromas and flavors that linger for a long time after it has been swallowed.

LONGEVITY: The aging potential of a wine, dependent on balance and structure.

MALOLACTIC FERMENTATION: A second fermentation

that can occur naturally or be induced, the purpose of which is to convert harsh malic acid to softer lactic acid.

MATURE: A wine that has reached its peak after developing in the bottle.

MELLOW: A wine that is at or very close to its peak.

METHODE CHAMPENOISE: The classic method for making Champagne by inducing a second fermentation in the bottle.

MID-PALATE: Those aroma and taste sensations felt after the first attack.

MOUSSE: The foam and bubbles of sparkling wines. A good mousse will show long-lasting foam and sharp, small, concentrated bubbles.

MOUTH-FILLING: A wine that fills the mouth with satisfying flavors.

MUST: The pre-fermentation mixture of grape juice, stem fragments, skins, seeds and pulp, that results from the grape-crushing process.

NOSE: Synonymous with bouquet.

NOUVEAU: Term that originated in Beaujolais to describe very young, fruity and light red wines, often made from Gamay grapes and by the method of carbonic maceration. Such wines are always meant to be consumed very young.

N.V.: A non-vintage wine; a term most often used for sparkling wines or blends of grapes of different vintage years.

OAK: The wood most often used to make the barrels in which wines are fermented or aged. The impact of such barrels is reflected in the level of tannins and in its contribution to flavors of smoke, spices and vanilla to the wines.

OAKED: A wine that has been fermented and/or aged in oak barrels.

OXIDIZED: A wine that has gone off because it has been exposed to oxygen or to high temperatures.

PEAK: The optimal point of maturity of a given wine.

PERSONALITY: The overall impression made by an individual wine.

RESIDUAL SUGAR: The sugar that remains in a wine after fermentation has been completed.

RICH: A wine with full flavors and aromas.

RIPASSO: A second fermentation that is induced on the lees of a wine made earlier.

ROBUST: Assertive, full-bodied and characteristic of good red wines at a young age, or country-style wines that are pleasingly coarse.

ROTTEN EGGS: Describes the smell of hydrogen sulfide (H_2S). Always an undesirable trait.

ROUND: A wine that has become smooth as its tannins, acids and wood have integrated.

RUSTIC: Synonymous with country-style.

SHARP: Overly acidic.

SHORT: A wine whose aromas and flavors fail to linger or to make an impression after the wine has been swallowed.

SIMPLE: A wine that has no nuances or complexity.

SMOKY: A flavor imparted to a wine from oak casks, most often found in unfiltered wines.

SMOOTH: A wine that sits comfortably on the palate.

SPICY: A wine that imparts a light peppery sensation.

STALE: A wine that has lost its freshness, liveliness or fruitiness.

STEWED: The sensation of cooked, overripe or soggy fruit.

STINGY: A wine that holds back on its aromas or flavors.

SULFITES: Usually sulfur dioxide that is added to wine to prevent oxidation.

SUR LIE: French for "on the lees". A term used to describe the process in which a wine is left in contact with its lees during fermentation and barrel aging.

SUR-RIPE: Grapes that have been allowed to develop on the vine to their maximum point of ripeness and sweetness.

TANNIC: A wine still marked by firm tannins. In their youth, many red wines tend to be tannic and need time for the tannins to integrate.

TANNINS: Phenolic substances that exist naturally in wines and extracted from the skins, pips and stalks of the grapes, as well as from development in new oak barrels. Tannins are vital for the longevity of red wines. In young wines, tannins can sometimes be harsh, but if the wine is well balanced they will blend with other substances in the wine over time, making the wine smoother and more approachable as it ages.

TCA: 2, 4, 6-Tricholoraniole. See "corked".

TERROIR: The reflection of a vineyard's soil, altitude, microclimate, prevailing winds, and other natural factors that impact on the quality of the grapes, and consequently on the wines produced from them.

THIN: Lacking in body or fruit.

TOASTING: Searing the inside of barrels with an open flame when making the barrels. Heavy toasting can impart caramel-like flavors to a wine; medium toasting and light toasting can add vanilla, spices or smokiness to the wine, all positive attributes when present in moderation.

VANILLA: Aroma and flavor imparted to wines from the oak barrels in which they age.

VARIETAL WINE: A wine that contains at least 85% of the grape named on the label.

VARIETAL TRAITS: The specific colors, aromas and flavors traditionally imparted by a specific grape variety.

VEGETAL: An often positive term used for a bouquet of rounded wines, in particular those made from Pinot Noir and Chardonnay grapes, whose aromas and flavors often call to mind vegetables rather than fruits.

VINTAGE: (a) Synonymous with harvest; (b) A wine made from grapes of a single harvest. In accordance with EU standards, a vintage wine must contain at least 85% grapes from the noted year.

WATERY: A wine so thin that it feels diluted.

WOOD: Refers either to the wood barrels in which the wine ages or to a specific aroma and flavor imparted by the barrels.

YEAST: A kind of fungus, vital to the process of fermentation.

Contacting the Wineries

Agur Winery
Moshav Agur 99840
Tel: 02 9910483 Fax: 02 9910483
yashuv@netvision.net.il

Alexander Winery
POB 8151
Moshav Beit Yitzhak 42970
Tel: 09 8822956 Fax: 09 8872076
a_wine@netvision.net.il

Aligote Winery
Moshav Gan Yoshiya 38850
Tel: 054 4748893 Fax: 04 6258492
aligote@aviv-flowers.co.il

Alon Wineries
Moshav Alonei Aba 36005
Tel: 054 4237745 Fax: 04 9800727
alonwine@ netvision.net.il

Alona Winery
Moshav Givat Nili 37825
Tel: 052 2425657
ap_azoulay@hotmail.com

Amphorae Vineyard
POB 12672 Herzliya 46733
Tel: 04 9840702 Fax: 04 9704318
gil@amphorae-v.com
www.amphorae-v.com

Amram's Winery
Moshav Ramot Naftali 13830
Tel: 050 5222901 Fax: 04 6940039
amramswin@hotmail.com

Anatot Winery
POB 3390
Givat Ze'ev 90917
Tel: 02 5860187 Fax: 02 5362565
Aharon@anatotwinery.co.il
www.anatotwinery.co.il

Assaf Winery
POB 69
Moshav Kidmat Tzvi 12421
Tel: 04 4779722 Fax: 04 6963014
kedemas@walla.com

Avidan Winery
253 Weizmann St.
Ra'anana 43721
Tel: 09 7719382 Fax: 09 7712679
advianwine@walla.com

Bar Winery
22 Ha'avoda St.
Binyamina 30500
Tel: 04 6388545
alanbar@zahav.net.il

Baram Winery
Kibbutz Baram 13860
Tel: 052 8313208
dror@baram.org.il

Barkai Vineyards
Moshav Roglit 99865
Tel/Fax: 02 9993281
barkaimi@bezeqint.net

Barkan Wine Cellars
POB 146
Kibbutz Hulda 76842
Tel: 08 9355858 Fax: 08 9355859
winery@barkan-winery.co.il
www.barkan-winery.co.il

Bashan Winery
Moshav Avnei Eitan 12925
Golan Heights
Tel: 054 4603213 Fax: 04 6762618
bashanwinery@013.net

Bazelet Hagolan Winery
POB 77
Moshav Kidmat Tsvi 12421
Tel: 04 6827223 Fax: 04 6820084
bazelet@netvision.net.il
www.bazelet-hagolan.co.il

Beit-El Winery
Beit-El 90628
Tel/Fax: 02 9971158
hmanne@netvision.net.il

Ben Barak Winery
Moshav Ramot Naftali 13830
Tel/Fax: 04 6940462

Benhaim Winery
34 Ben-Zvi Ave.
Ramat-Gan 52247
Tel: 03 6762656
benhaim@benhaim.co.il
www.benhaim.co.il

Ben Hanna Winery
Moshav Gefen 99820
Tel: 052 5434253
shlomi@ben-hanna.com
www.ben-hanna.com

Ben-Shoshan Winery
Kibbutz Bror-Hail 79152
Tel: 08 6803321 Fax: 08 6803667
niva_yuval@walla.com

Ben-Zimra Winery
Moshav Kerem Ben Zimra 13815
Tel/Fax: 04 6980056
ashk_y@netvision.net.il

Binyamina Wine Cellars
POB 34
Binyamina 30550
Tel: 04 6388643 Fax: 04 6389021
info@binyaminawines.co.il
www.binyaminawines.com

Birya Winery
Birya 13805
Tel: 052 5405223 Fax: 04 6923815
drporat@zahav.net.il

Bnei Baruch Winery
POB 1552
Ramat Gan 52115
Tel: 054 6696704 Fax: 03 9226741
Boris_beloter@yahoo.com

Bustan Winery
POB 55
Moshav Sharei Tikva 44860
Tel: 054 4892757
bustanwinery@yahoo.com

Bustan Hameshusheem Winery
Moshav Had Ness 12950
Tel: 052 4358407

Carmey Avdat Winery
Midreshet Ben Gurion 84990
Tel: 08 6535177 Fax: 08 6535188
Carmey-avdat@bezeqint.net
www.carmey-avdat.co.il

Carmel Winery
Rishon Letzion, Zichron Ya'akov
Tel: Rishon Letzion 03 9488888
Tel: Zichron Ya'akov 04 6390105
www.carmelwines.co.il

Domaine du Castel:
Moshav Ramat Raziel 90974
Tel: 02 5342249 Fax: 02 5700995
castel@castel.co.il
www.castel.co.il

The Cave
POB 34
Binyamina 30550
Tel: 04 6388643 Fax: 04 6389021
thecave@zahav.net.il

Chateau Golan Winery
Moshav Eliad 12927
Tel: 04 6600026 Fax: 04 6600274
shatoltd@netvision.net.il
www.chateaugolan.com

Chillag Winery
12 Shabazi St.
Yehud 56231
Tel: 054 4562057 Fax: 03 5369996
chillag@netvision.net.il

Clos de Gat
Kibbutz Har'el 99740
Tel: 02 9993505 Fax: 02 9993350
harelca@netvision.net.il
www.closdegat.com/intro.html

Dalton Winery
Dalton Industrial Park, Merom Hagalil 13815
Tel: 04 6987683 Fax: 04 6987684
info@dalton-winery.com
www.dalton-winery.com

Dico's Winery
Moshav Ginaton 73110
Tel: 08 9243135

Ein Teina Winery
Moshav Givat Yoav 12946
Tel: 050 8217554 Fax: 6920414
Yotam76@yahoo.com

Ella Valley Vineyards
Kibbutz Netiv Halamed Hey 99855
Tel: 02 9994885 Fax: 02 9994876
ella@ellavalley.com

Erez Winery
Rechalim 44829
Tel/Fax: 02 9409026
Yekev-erez@barak.net.il

Essence Winery
Ma'aleh Tsvi'a 20129
Tel: 04 6619058 Fax: 04 6619054
essencewines@zvia.org.il

Flam Winery
9 Avshalom St.
Rishon Le Zion 75285
Tel: 02 9929924 Fax: 02 9929926
golan@flamwinery.com

Gad Winery
Moshav Sdot Micha 99810
Tel: 050 5601886

Galai Winery
Moshav Nir Akiva 85365
Tel: 08 9933713 Fax: 08 9931287
galai-winery@bezeqint.net
www. galai-winery.com

Galil Mountain Winery
Kibbutz Yiron 13855
Tel: 04 6868740 Fax: 04 6868506
winery@galilmountain.co.il
 www.galilmountain.co.il

Gat Shomron Winery
Karnei Shomron 44855
Tel: 050 7264855
na_lior@walla.co.il

Gesher Damia Winery
2 Hatavor St.
Pardes Hannah-Karkur 37011
Tel/Fax: 04 6377451
damiya@walla.co.il

Ginaton Winery
Moshav Ginaton 73110
Tel: 050 3932403 Fax: 08 9254841
ginaton1999@walla.co.il

Givon Winery
POB 140
Givon Hachadasha 90901
Tel: 02 5362966
info@givonwine.com
www.givonwine.com

Golan Heights Winery
POB 183
Katzrin 12900
Tel: 04 6968420 Fax: 04 6962220
ghwinery@golanwines.co.il
www.golanwines.co.il

Greenberg Winery
51 Hameginim St.
Herzliya 46686
Tel: 052 3237689
elegant@netvision.net.il

Gush Etzion Winery
POB 1415
Efrat 90435
Tel: 02 9309220 Fax: 02 9309156
winery@actcom.co.il
www.gushetzion-winery.com

Gustavo & Jo Winery
19 Marvah St.
Kfar Vradim 25147
Tel: 04 9972190
boia@netvision.net.il

Gvaot Winery
POB 393
Shiloh 44830
Tel: 09 7921292 Fax: 09 7921086
info@gvaot-winery.com
www.gvaot-winery.com

Hakerem Winery
POB 645
Qiryat Arba 90100
Tel: 050 8526096

Hamasrek Winery
Moshav Beit Meir 90865
Tel: 02 5701759 Fax: 02 5336592
hamasrek@netvision.net.il
www.hamasrek.com

Hans Sternbach Winery
Moshav Giv'at Yeshayahu 99825
Tel: 02 9990162 Fax: 02 9911703
sk-Gadi@zahav.net.il

Hatabor Winery
POB 22
Kfar Tavor 15241
Tel: 04 6767889
ssiecodo@zahav.net.il

Hevron Heights Winery
Moshav Geulim 42820
Tel: 09 8943711 Fax: 09 8943006
mm@churchill.fr

Kadesh Barnea Winery
Moshav Kadesh Barnea 85513
Tel: 08 6555849 Fax: 08 6571323
winerykb@012.net.il
www.kbw.co.il

Kadita Winery
POB 1052
Safed
Tel: 050 6933219
winery@kadita.co.il
www.kadita.co.il/winery/intro.html

Karmei Yosef Winery
Karmei Yosef 99797
Tel: 08 9286098
bravdo@bravdo.co.il
www.bravdo.com

Katlav Winery
Moshav Nes Harim 99885
Tel/Fax: 02 5701404
yosss@bezeqint.net

Katz Winery
Moshav Mesilat Tzion 99770
Tel: 054 4573950 Fax: 02 5855356
jossi@katz-winery.com
www.katz-winery.com

Kfir Winery
POB 4125
Gan Yavne 70800
Tel: 08 8570354 Fax: 08 8673708
meirkfir@gmail.com
www.kfir-winery.co.il

Kleins Winery
19 Tchelet Mordechai St.
Jerusalem 94396
Tel: 02 5022946   Fax: 02 5022947
yomtov@kleins1.com

La Terra Promessa Winery
Moshav Shachar 79335
Tel: 08 6849093   Fax: 151 50684775
laterrapromessa@bezeqint.net

Lachish Winery
Moshav Lachish 79360
Tel: 054 7920151
galiam@bezeqint.net

Domaine de Latroun
Latroun Monastery 99762
Tel: 08 9255180

Lavie Winery
15 Shemen Zeit St.
Ephrata 90435
Tel: 02 9938520

Levron Winery
10 Orbach St.
Haifa 34985
Tel: 04 8344837   Fax: 04 8246724

Maccabim Winery
Maccabim-Re'ut 71908
Tel: 050 8503362
info@maccabimwinery.com

Maor Winery
Moshav Ramot 12948
Tel: 052 8515079
danny@maorwinery.com
www.maorwinery.com

Margalit Winery
POB 4055
Caesarea 38900
Tel: 050 5334433 Fax: 04 6262058
a_m_n_l@netvision.net.il
www.margalit-winery.com

Meishar Winery
Moshav Meishar 76850
Tel: 08 8594759
zosh_s@netvision.net.il
www.meishar.co.il

Meister Winery
33 Schoonat Hashalom,
Rosh Pina 12000
Tel: 054 4976940
meister@bezeqint.net
www.ruth-meister.co.il

Miles Winery
Moshav Kerem Ben Zimra 13815
Tel: 04 6980623
mils013.013.net.il

Miller Winery
114 Ya'alom st.
Sha'arei Tikva 44810
Tel: 050 5211079 Fax: 09 7687761
yekev@gomiller.co.il

Mony Winery
Dir Rafat Monastery
POB 275
Beit Shemesh 99000
Tel: 02 9916629 Fax: 02 9910366
monywines@walla.co.il
www.ymp.co.il/moni/

Na'aman Winery
Moshav Ramot Naftali 13830
Tel: 04 6944463 Fax: 04 6950062
naaman@017.net.il
www.naamanwine.co.il

Nahal Amud
Moshav Kfar Shamai 20125
Tel: 04 6989825

Nachshon Winery
Kibbutz Nachson 99760
Tel: 08 9278641 Fax: 08 9278607
winery@nachshon.co.il
http://winery.nachshon.org.il

Nashashibi Winery
Kfar Eehbelin 30012
Tel: 054 6387191
nash_win@hotmail.com

Natuf Winery
Kfar Truman 73150
Tel: 052 2608199
natuf@012.net.il

Neot Smadar Winery
Kibbutz Neot Smadar 88860
Tel: 08 6358111

Noga Winery
POB 111
Gedera 70700
Tel: 08 8690253
nogawinery@bezeqint.net

Odem Mountain Winery
Moshav Odem 12473
Tel/Fax: 04 6871120
megolan@012.net.il

Pelter Winery
POB 136
Kibbutz Merom Golan 12436
Tel: 052 8666384 Fax: 04 6850343
tal@pelterwinery.co.il
www.pelterwinery.co.il

Psagot Winery
Psagot 90624
Tel/Fax: 02 9978222
info@psagotwines.com
www.psagotwines.com

Ra'anan Winery
Moshav Ganei Yochanan 76922
Tel: 08 9350668
orsss@zahav.net.il

Ramim Winery
Moshav Shachar 79335
Tel: 054 4608080 Fax: 08 6849122
enrade@multinet.net.il

Ramot Naftali Winery
Moshav Ramot Naftali 13830
Tel: 04 6940371 Fax: 04 6902661
Yitzhak3@012.net.il

Recanati Winery
POB 12050
Industrial Zone, Emek Hefer
Tel: 04 6222288 Fax: 04 6222882
info@recanati-winery.com
www.recanati-winery.com

Red Poetry Winery
Havat Tal
Karmei Yosef 99797
Tel: 08 9210352
talfarm@bezeqint.net

Rosh Pina Winery
Rosh Pina 12000
Tel: 04 6827062
bloom_r@walla.com

Rota Winery
Havat Rota 85515
Tel: 054 4968703 Fax: 03 9732278
rotawinery@walla.com

Ruth Winery
Kfar Ruth 73196
Tel: 050 6980098
maortal@012.net.il

Salomon Winery
Moshav Amikam 37830
Tel: 04 6380475

Saslove Winery
POB 10581
Tel Aviv 69085
Tel: 09 7492697 Fax: 03 6492712
winery@saslove.com
www.saslove.com

Sassy Winery
24 Ha'atzmaut Ave.
Bat Yam 59378
Tel: 052 2552012

Savion Winery
41 Bareket St.
Mevaseret Zion 90805
Tel: 02 5336162

Sde Boker Winery
Kibbutz Sde Boker 84993
Tel: 050 7579212 Fax: 08 6560118
winery@sde-boker.org.il
www.sde-boker.org.il/winery

Sea Horse Winery
Moshav Bar Giora 99880
Tel: 050 7283216 Fax: 02 5709834
info@seahorsewines.com
www.seahorsewines.com

Segal Wines
Kibbutz Hulda 76842
Tel: 08 9358860 Fax: 08 9241222
segal@segalwines.co.il

Shdema Winery
Kibbutz Revivim 85515
Tel: 050 5255128 Fax: 08 6562397
motis@revivim.org.il

Sifsaf Winery
Moshav Safsufa 13875
Tel: 06 7498928
eazywine@bezeqint.net

Smadar Winery
31 Hameyasdim St.
Zichron-Ya'akov 30900
Tel: 04 6390777

Snir Winery
Kibbutz Snir 12250
Tel: 04 6952500 Fax: 04 6951765

Somek Winery
16 Herzl St.
Zichron Ya'akov 30900
Tel/Fax: 04 6391194
hillabg@yahoo.com

Soreq Winery
Moshav Tal Shachar 78805
Tel: 08 9450844 Fax: 08 9370385
soreq@barak.net.il

Sraya Winery
Moshav Tomer 90680
Tel: 02 9944704 Fax: 02 9944705
brosho1@netvision.net.il

Srigim Winery
POB 174
Moshav Srigim 99835
Tel: 050 6991398 Fax: 02 9991512
ursr10@netvision.net.il

Tabor Winery
POB 422
Kfar Tavor 15241
Tel: 04 6760444 Fax: 04 6772061
twc@twc.co.il
www.taborwinery.co.il

Tanya Winery
Ofra 90627
Tel: 054 4354034
Yoram5733@walla.co.il

Teperberg
POB 609
Kibbutz Tzora 99803
Tel: 02 9908080 Fax: 02 5340760
office@efratwine.co.il
www.efrat-winery.co.il

Tishbi Estate Winery
33 Hameyasdim St.
Zichron Ya'akov 30900
Tel: 04 6389434 Fax: 04 6280223
tishbi_w@netvision.net.il
http://www.tishbi.com

Tulip Winery
24 Hacarmel St.
Kiryat Tivon 36081
Tel/Fax: 04 9830573
tulip@tulip-winery.co.il

Tzora Vineyards
Kibbutz Tzora 99803
Tel: 02 9908261 Fax: 02 9915479
info@tzorawines.com
www.tzorawines.com

Tzuba Winery
Kibbutz Tzuba 90870
Tel: 02 5347678 Fax: 02 5347999
winery@tzuba.org.il

Vanhotzker Winery
Moshev Meron 13910
Tel/Fax: 04 6989063
Elivan1@bezeqint.net

Villa Wilhelma Winery
Moshav Bnei Atarot 60991
Tel: 054 4564526
Motti_goldman@yahoo.com

Vitkin Winery
POB 267
Kfar Vitkin 40200
Tel: 09 8663505 Fax: 03 7256258
vtknwine@netvision.net.il

Yaffo Winery
15 Rozov St.
Tel Aviv 69716
Tel: 03 6474834
yaffowine@zahav.net.il
www.yaffowinery.com

Yatir Winery
POB 5210
Arad
Tel: 08 9959090 Fax: 08 9959050
y_yatir@zahav.net.il
www.yatir.net

Ye'arim Winery
Moshav Givat Ye'arim 90970
Tel: 052 5791080
sassons_wine@hotmail.co.il

Yehuda Winery
Moshav Shoresh 90860
Tel: 054 4638544 Fax: 02 5348100
yekev_yehuda@neve-ilan.co.il

Yiftah'el Winery
Alon Hagalil 17920
Tel: 04 9865811
hadassr@bezeqint.net

Zauberman Winery
50 Piness St.
Gedera 70700
Tel: 08 8594680
www.zaubermanwines.com

Zemora Winery
POB 451
Mevaseret Tzion 90805
Tel: 052 2636850 Fax: 02 5346166

Zion Winery
Rehov Charuvit 45
Mishor Adumim
Tel: 02 5352540 Fax: 02 5355535
yossi@zionfinewines.co.il
www.zionfinewines.co.il

Index of Wineries

About the Author

Daniel Rogov is Israel's most influential and preeminent wine critic. He writes weekly wine and restaurant columns in the respected newspaper *Haaretz*, and contributes regularly to two prestigious international wine books—Hugh Johnson's *Pocket Wine Book* and Tom Stevenson's *Wine Report*.

The fonts used in the book are from the Chaparral family

The Toby Press publishes fine writing,
available at bookstores everywhere. For more information,
please contact *The* Toby Press at www.tobypress.com